THIS BOOK IS YOUR BEST INVESTMENT!

It exploits the myths about:
- Inflation, the runaway curse that *will* eventually end
- Real estate, the breakneck boom that is destined to die
- Gold, the precious metal that can only go so far

... and delivers the facts about:
- The depression that can come through the back door
- The easy way to open a Swiss bank account
- The magic in smart borrowing

Inflation-proof *your* investments — and prepare for the future without knowing what the future will bring!

Other books by Harry Browne

---

*NEW PROFITS FROM THE MONETARY CRISIS (1978)
COMPLETE GUIDE TO SWISS BANKS (1976)
YOU CAN PROFIT FROM A MONETARY CRISIS (1974)
HOW I FOUND FREEDOM
IN AN UNFREE WORLD (1973)
HOW YOU CAN PROFIT FROM
THE COMING DEVALUATION (1970)

*Published by
WARNER BOOKS

INFLATION-PROOFING YOUR INVESTMENTS

HARRY BROWNE
AND
TERRY COXON

WARNER BOOKS

A Warner Communications Company

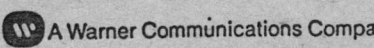

To
Ludwig von Mises
Henry Hazlitt
Murray N. Rothbard
and
Milton Friedman
for helping us to understand
how the world works

CONTENTS

APPENDICES

PROLOGUE

1

COPING
WITH INFLATION

IT'S OBVIOUS BY NOW THAT INFLATION ISN'T A TEMPORARY problem that will soon disappear. There's little hope of America returning shortly to the days when inflation rates of 1% or 2% were the rule. In fact, any politician who might manage to reduce the inflation rate to "only" 8% would be considered a hero.

But although inflation is now accepted as a permanent condition, it is still as hard to live with as ever. It derails every attempt by the stock market to keep up, it hammers away at bond prices, it erodes the value of savings accounts, and it traps businessmen and investors into paying taxes on phantom earnings. Worst of all, inflation adds to the uncertainty your financial plans must deal with.

And just when you think you've found a way of adjusting to the current inflation level, it moves higher—and you have to start all over, trying to figure out what to do.

Is there any way you can cope with inflation? Is it possible to protect your savings—without knowing what next year's inflation rate, political problems, tax laws, and investment fads will be? Obviously, you have to do *something* if you want your savings and capital to maintain their value. If you give up the struggle, what you've earned will be destroyed, steadily and surely.

But what can you do? There are two basic answers to the question—and the right answer to inflation depends upon the type of investor you are.

The first answer is for the active trader—the investor who

13

watches several markets constantly, who is always looking for new opportunities, and who shifts his money when he thinks that better prospects lie elsewhere.

This investor needs to understand how inflation affects investment markets. But he should not think of the current inflation rate as a goal to beat; he shouldn't aim at "keeping up" with inflation or at running ahead of it. Whether the current inflation rate is 2%, 6%, 12%, or 20%, he will profit most with the same broad strategy that would work in a non-inflationary economy. He should pick the investment with the best profit and risk considerations. When his choice is correct, he should "let his profits run" and make the most of being right; when his choice proves to be wrong, he should "cut his losses" as soon as the mistake is apparent.

If he's good at what he does, he'll certainly stay ahead of inflation—whatever the rate may be. But if he's not suited for investment trading, he'll lose very quickly—and he should look for another way of handling his capital.

Unfortunately, most people aren't good at investment trading. For one thing, they don't have the time to do the job properly. They are too involved with their work, their families, and other interests. Even if the time is available, many people simply aren't equipped with the skills and the temperament needed for successful short-term investing. It is a talent, and the talents of most people lie in other areas.

So the second basic answer to the question of what to do about inflation applies to the non-trader. If you are not a good short-term trader, how can you preserve your capital?

PROTECTION

As we see it, you can best protect yourself through a three-step process.

Understanding

The first step is to understand what you're up against. You have to have at least a rough understanding of the workings of inflation—what causes it and how it affects various investments and areas of the economy in different ways—so that you won't base your decisions on ideas that are really just slogans or clichés. This understanding will help you distinguish between the investments that can reduce financial uncertainty and those that would only make your problems worse.

And you need to understand that inflation doesn't shower its affection on any one investment. There is no simple "inflation hedge" that will, year in and year out, show a profit because of inflation. One of inflation's worst consequences is the chaos it creates in the economy and in the investment world. Because of inflation, almost all investments go through extreme cycles of boom and bust.

It is often said that gold is an inflation hedge. But, while gold has been an excellent long-term investment for the past ten years, it has not been an inflation hedge. The relationship between the price of gold and the inflation rate has been vastly overstated—as we'll explain in Chapter 6. It should also be noted that the price of a true inflation hedge wouldn't drop during a period of declining inflation rates; it would simply go up more slowly.

The stock market, the supposed inflation hedge of the 1960s, has already proven that it doesn't fill the bill. And the real estate boom of the late 1970s, which seemed to be providing a "sure-thing" hedge against inflation for many people, suddenly turned sour in late 1979. No one investment will profit from every stage of an inflationary cycle.

In addition, it's important to realize that twenty years of accelerating inflation can't be brought to a painless conclusion. No simple solution—such as wage and price controls or balancing the federal budget—is going to give us a quick and easy transition to a low-inflation economy.

But at the same time, it must be understood that the present inflationary trend *will* end—and possibly within the next ten years or so. For a capital-intensive economy like that of the U.S., inflation creates problems that grow worse as the inflation proceeds. Eventually, unless it turns back, the government exhausts its ability to paper over these problems with still more inflation. Then it faces the stern choice of either halting its own inflation-producing activities or permitting the currency to collapse entirely. Because inflation won't go on

15

forever, a long-term investment program must be prepared for the chaos that may accompany the cure.

So the first step involves understanding how inflation works—so that you can operate with a realistic attitude about the present and the future.

Alternatives

The second step is to become acquainted with the range of investment alternatives and techniques available to you.

You may need to reexamine investments that you've rejected in the past. The "progressive thinker" who disdains the gold standard doesn't have to pledge allegiance to gold in order to assign a proper place to it in his investment portfolio. And the confirmed gold-bug needs to see that such often-rejected investments as annuities, bonds, and mutual funds can serve a definite purpose—even in an inflationary world—if he knows how to use them properly.

Above all, you must be open to all the possibilities available to you.

Balanced Portfolio

And the final step is to construct a portfolio so well balanced that you can forget about your investments. Then you can return to the things in life that interest you more—confident that you're protected and that you should profit no matter how inflation evolves and no matter how and when it comes to an end.

This seems like a tall order, and it is. It will require some time, attention, and patience on your part. Any simple and easy way that might be offered would be too good to be true.

But it will be much easier to get started if you know that you need to do the job only once. Having done it properly, you won't be forced to keep reopening the matter—month after month and year after year—changing course with every change in the news.

Three Steps

The purpose of this book is to lead you through the three-step process:

1. To provide an understanding of inflation that will permit you to make realistic decisions—so that you can not only decide *what* to do, but also know *why* you did it.
2. To provide a menu of techniques and alternatives, so that your investment plan can draw on the best components available.
3. To provide a method by which you can construct a suitable long-term investment portfolio. Your circumstances are unique, and they call for a portfolio that will not be precisely the same as the next person's. But there is a method, a procedure, for creating a portfolio—and anyone can use it.

If you do the job properly, your portfolio should protect you through periods of prosperity, accelerating or decelerating inflation, or even deflation—without any requirement that you do the job over again. In fact, the portfolio should serve you until the day that it's obvious we've returned to a stable, non-inflationary environment.[1]

SHORT & LONG TERMS

In *New Profits from the Monetary Crisis*, Harry Browne (aided by Terry Coxon) suggested that most investors could profit by dividing their investment capital into two portfolios —a Permanent Portfolio and a Variable Portfolio.

A Permanent Portfolio is meant to be left undisturbed for many years. Its principal ingredients are the investments that you expect to perform best during the next five to ten years—even though you may expect them to have temporary ups and downs. In addition, there are hedges that will limit the portfolio's losses if your principal expectations prove to be wrong. The logic of the Permanent Portfolio assumes that

---

[1]At which time we'll write our long-awaited sequel, *How You Can Survive in Good Times.*

you will *not* respond to any changes in short-term investment prospects.

The Variable Portfolio, on the other hand, is subject to change at any time—depending upon changes in the short-term prospects of the investments it contains. You must monitor the Variable Portfolio regularly and alter its investments as your strategy dictates.[2]

The division of capital between the two portfolios is made according to the amount of time and attention you're willing to devote to the job of investing, and according to the extent of your confidence that you can recognize changes in short-term investment trends.

If you believe you can profit from frequent changes in your investments, you might have only 10% to 40% of your capital in the Permanent Portfolio and the rest in the Variable Portfolio. If you're less confident, you might have 75% or more in the Permanent Portfolio. And for many people it makes sense to have 100% in the Permanent Portfolio and a blank sheet of paper as the Variable Portfolio.

This book concentrates on the Permanent Portfolio. Its purpose is to help you construct a collection of investments that can weather the next ten years or more without your having to make new decisions along the way. The portfolio should allow for any special circumstances, such as a large percentage of your capital that's tied up in your pension fund, your company, or your home—as well as any other difficulties that might prevent you from allocating your capital in the way that you would wish.

If you're an active trader, the purpose of this book may be less compelling for you. But you may still find it profitable to be acquainted with the wide assortment of investment alternatives we'll cover. For one thing, some of them can be used in short-term trading. For another, you may be able to profit from some of the tax planning ideas— or you may have some illiquid investments that you're worried

---

[2]*New Profits from the Monetary Crisis* (described in the Suggested Reading on page 515) provides a strategy for a Variable Portfolio.

about and for which you'd like to construct a hedge. And even if you're a top trader, having some funds in a Permanent Portfolio can serve as a safety net that might make you feel a little easier about the risks you take.

BALANCE

Some of the investments we'll describe may seem exotic to you, but we'll do our best to explain them clearly and to show you how to use them.

And some of the investments (such as annuities) may seem outrageous in an inflationary world. But this is true only so long as you consider an investment in isolation—as though you were going to invest *all* your money in it. When combined with other assets, the outrageous investment might serve a useful purpose.

The key consideration will be a proper *balance* among several different investments. It is this balance that makes it possible for you to "walk away" from your portfolio and leave it to do its job—without having to worry whether tomorrow's news will upset your plans.

When the job is done correctly, you'll be hedged against every possibility that investments can hedge against. You can't anticipate every twist and turn the economy (or the politicians who try to manage it) might take, but the right portfolio can eliminate the need to anticipate. However, the portfolio should do more than that. It should grow in purchasing power on its own.

The concept of hedging is often misunderstood. A proper use of hedges should *not* immobilize your portfolio—causing it to break even no matter which way the investment markets move. A good hedge will cut into your profits a little, but it will still allow you to make a sizeable profit if the investment markets move in the way you expect—while preventing a catastrophic loss if the markets move the other way. It is like insurance; you pay a small premium to eliminate the possibility of a large loss.

For example, we'll describe one hedging technique that permits you to use listed put options to protect your company

19

against the effects of a 1929-style crash. Another allows you to offset large fixed-dollar investments that are tied up in a pension fund.

We believe there are many hedges that have been overlooked by investors who could use them to reduce their vulnerabilities. These hedges make it possible to leave your portfolio unattended without anxiety.

CONTENTS

To build the proper portfolio, we must begin with a proper understanding of inflation. So the first part of the book deals with this subject—in a way that we hope will make it easier to understand precisely how inflation affects the investment markets.

Previous books by Harry Browne discussed the causes of inflation and what the process leads to. Now that many of inflation's unwelcome consequences are a part of the present and no longer something to anticipate, we are going to explain the process of inflation in a different way—with special emphasis on the new problems that may lie ahead.

The first part will also discuss the five main possibilities for the next few years—that we'll have (1) a leveling off of the inflation rate; (2) a somewhat painless end to inflation; (3) a 1929-style deflation; (4) a runaway inflation; or (5) an indefinite continuation of the present trend, with rising inflation rates and poor economic conditions.

The second part of the book will offer an approach for dealing with the uncertainty created by these many inflation possibilities. Without an investment philosophy, you can find yourself making decisions in a vacuum—with nothing to help you evaluate the many opinions you'll hear about the economy and about investments, and no way to deal with the uncertainty that the conflicting opinions dramatize.

The third and fourth parts will present a catalog of investment tools—many of which are little-known or poorly understood. The book also will show how to put familiar investments to new uses.

We'll discuss ways to hold a permanent, low-cost position in the stock market in preparation for prosperity; the reasons that gold is an essential portfolio component, but isn't enough for investment safety; and methods to offset overly large holdings in real estate. We'll suggest that fixed-dollar assets are important, even at inflation rates of 15% or more, and offer ways by which you can hold dollars safely and without large losses in purchasing power And, because banks are particularly vulnerable at this stage of inflation, we'll tell you how you can get along without them.

Since taxes are ever-present. the fifth part will offer a number of ways for keeping the Internal Revenue Service out of your portfolio—but without compromising investment safety. Among other matters. we'll discuss ways to defer or even eliminate taxes on investment income: how to turn interest income into capital gains (to be taxed at lower rates); how to create your own pension plan or personal corporation to reduce taxes and improve investment safety; and how to get the tax advantages of being in debt without the risks. We'll cover the reasons why municipal bonds are, at best, a second-choice way of avoiding taxes: and we'll look at an investment technique that makes your children's education tax-deductible.

The sixth part will bring these tools together. providing guidelines for choosing among them It will show you how to design a portfolio that needs only a glance each year: how risky investments can be combined to make a low-risk portfolio: the critical difference between borrowing and being in debt: how to reduce taxes by rearranging the investments you already have; and all the details necessary to get things done.

As we proceed, we'll define any term we think might be misunderstood. If you're not sure what we mean by any key word, check the Glossary on page 497 to see if it's defined there. Also, if you wonder where in the book you've read a description of something, the Index at the back of the book is especially detailed and can help you find what you need.

If we've done our job. you should be only a few days away from eliminating most of your financial anxiety. It will take a few hours to read the book, a few days to consider it and come up with a portfolio that satisfies your requirements, and perhaps a few days more to give the proper instructions and see that they're carried out.

So let's get started.

PART I

THE FUTURE OF INFLATION

2
MONEY & INFLATION

JUST ABOUT EVERY ECONOMIC GROUP OR INSTITUTION HAS BEEN blamed for inflation—labor unions, big business, Arabs, oil companies, welfare recipients, even shoplifters.

But it is a fact of life that each person normally charges as much as he can for his product or his work. To expect people to do otherwise is to look for a world that never was and never will be. Yet there have been many periods of little or no price inflation, so there must be something at the root of inflation other than the desire of individuals or groups to get more for what they sell.

In recent years there has been a growing recognition that the "something else" is the money supply. While it is true that money is the key to inflation, it isn't enough to consider merely the supply of money. The *demand* for money, which we hear little about, is equally important.

Price inflation means that most things require more money to buy than they did before. Or, stated differently, each dollar buys less. It is natural to focus on the things that are costing more, rather than on the money that is buying less, since by habit we think of money as the measure of value. But in fact it is a change in the money that causes a change in prices, rather than the reverse.

The value of money, like the value of anything else, is influenced both by the existing supply of it and by the demand for it. During the early years of price inflation, it is changes in the supply of money that account for the rise in prices and for the accompanying disturbances in the economy. But we are now in a later stage of inflation, when changes in the demand for money can be a greater source of disruption.

This chapter examines the supply of money and the demand for it, attempting to show how the inflationary process works. The two chapters that follow discuss the different avenues that inflation may travel in the near future.

THE DEMAND FOR MONEY

Money is a loose synonym for wealth, but it is really only one form of wealth. In addition to money, your wealth is in many other forms—a car, a house, the food in the cupboard, stocks, bonds, and so on. The list is long; anything you own that is of any value to you or to anyone else is part of your wealth.

Your wealth may seem large or small to you but, in either case, it is limited. Consequently you have to decide how much of your wealth to devote to each possible use—since anything you own is owned at the expense of all the things you could have acquired instead.

What you invest in stocks or bonds, for example, you can't invest in real estate or spend on a new car. The need to budget your wealth is as inescapable as the need to budget your monthly income among different kinds of expenditures.

You decide how much of each kind of asset to hold by comparing the benefits it could bring with the benefits that other things might bring. You do without one thing only because the benefits flowing from other things are more important to you.

You might buy stocks, for example, because of the dividends they pay and because you expect their prices to rise. But you limit the amount invested in stocks because you want to enjoy the benefits of other assets—the steady income from a bond, the comfort of a house, the apparent security of a savings account, or maybe just the pleasure of spending more money now.

26

Benefits of Money

Money is an asset—just like stocks, bonds, or a house. Whatever part of your wealth you devote to holding money can't be used for anything else until you are ready to part with the money. As a general rule, people prefer the things that money can buy over money itself. And yet you always devote some of your wealth to money because holding it offers certain benefits.

One benefit is money's *convenience* as the recognized medium of exchange. You can't easily trade a share of stock, a bond, or the spare tire from your car for groceries. Another benefit is *security;* keeping a quantity of money on hand assures that you'll be able to buy the things you need even if your income is interrupted for a few months. And money also provides *predictability;* although the dollar's value is slowly slipping away, there have been no dramatic drops in its purchasing power from one day to the next, or even from one month to the next. The value of almost any other asset fluctuates, so you can't be sure what you'll be able to trade it for in the near future.

The three benefits of holding money—convenience, security, and predictability—add up to *liquidity,* the assurance of ready purchasing power.

The benefits of holding cash are real, and yet you don't hold all your wealth in the form of money. To do so would mean forgoing too many of the things that money can buy. You compare the benefits of holding money with the benefits of acquiring investments and products to consume, and arrive at a comfortable level of money holding. The amount you decide to hold represents your *demand for money.*

Level of Holdings

You might not be able to define precisely how much money you want to hold, but there is definitely a right amount. When you don't have enough, you begin to feel uneasy, insecure; you tend to reduce spending until you feel comfortable again. When you have more than you need for convenience and security, you find it easy to spend money on things that you otherwise might have forgone, things that you don't consider essential.

The demand for money, the amount each person wants to hold, varies from person to person. One individual will feel comfortable holding only one week's expenses in the form of money; another might feel secure only if he has enough to cover all expenses for a year or more. In either case, a choice is made—a choice that fits the priorities of the individual.

The choice of how much cash to hold may be intuitive, rather than well-defined, but you make the choice nevertheless. It is demonstrated in your actions.

If you discover that your cash balance is too small, compared with your income and the rest of your wealth, you will take steps to increase it. You might do so by working extra hours to increase your income, or by selling an investment or something else you own. Or you might reduce living expenses until your regular income has brought your money balance up to the desired level. Whatever course you take, all possible steps for increasing your cash holdings have one thing in common—they make you, for the time being, more of a seller than a buyer.

If your money holdings are too large, compared with your income and the rest of your wealth, there will be less of a feeling of crisis than if they're too small, and the steps you take to adjust your holdings won't be made under any emotional pressure. Even so, you'll act to change things. You'll spend money more readily, you'll respond less vigorously to opportunities to increase your income, and you might increase your investments. One way or another, you'll be more of a buyer than a seller.

Each person has his own supply of money and his own demand for money—his actual cash balance and the amount of cash he wants to hold.

SOCIETY'S DEMAND FOR MONEY

At any time, there is a definite quantity of money in existence. So any increase in your money holdings must be offset by a decrease in some other person's holdings. You can decrease your money balance only if someone else increases his.

Normally this is no problem. Our world functions as well as it does because each person is different. It is the *differences* among us that provide the harmony of human society. If we all wanted exactly the same things, we would be trapped in a struggle for the limited supply of whatever the· universally desired things were. Cooperation and exchange are possible only because each participant has a somewhat different objective. Each person can offer to exchange something he values less for something he values more, trading with someone whose preferences are opposite.

So if you choose to alter your money balance, either upward or downward, your choice normally will harmonize with the choices of others; and someone else—perhaps unseen by you—will offset your actions. Occasionally, however, something can happen to cause the intentions of most people temporarily to be similar; the usual result is trouble.

Suppose, for example, that your cash balance is $7,000, and you decide that you need only $6,000. You can buy something you've wanted with the extra $1,000. Now suppose that everyone else also intends to reduce his cash balance. Since every dollar has to be held by someone, the general attempt to hold less money can't possibly succeed. Someone, perhaps everyone, will wind up with more money than he plans to.

The failure is certain. It isn't possible, even temporarily, for everyone to spend more than he receives, because one person's expenditure is another person's income. It isn't possible for everyone to buy more than he sells, because one person's purchase is another person's sale. Someone's intention —perhaps everyone's intention—to reduce his cash balance must fail.

Obviously, everyone will find something to spend his money on; the failure won't occur because you or anyone else is unable to *spend* as much money as he sets out to. It will occur because everyone will *take in* more money than he expects to.

If you have a piece of property that's been sitting on the market for nine months, the buyer you were hoping for will

29

finally show up—just when you need him the least. Obviously, you won't turn him away; you'll assume that you can find a good use for the money.

If you're a retailer, you'll find that sales are overwhelming your ability to keep your inventory replenished. You'll have too much cash and not enough inventory to take advantage of the increased demand. But you won't lock your doors; you'll continue selling, and you'll order more merchandise from your wholesaler.

If you're employed by someone else, your employer will be eager to profit from the unexpectedly large volume of business. He'll ask you to work more hours, and he'll be happy to pay you for the extra effort.

Although the general attempt to reduce cash balances can't succeed (short of someone volunteering to burn $100 bills), it won't continue forever. But the attempt, which reflects a decline in the demand for money, will cause a serious disturbance in the economy. As we'll see, part of that disturbance is price inflation. But first, let's look at the other side of the coin—the supply of money.

THE SUPPLY OF MONEY

The money we're discussing is, of course, the supply of U.S. dollars that we use as a medium of exchange. As we've said, money is an asset, a form of wealth. For each of us, it is just as hard to obtain money as it is to acquire anything else; to get it, you must offer a service or a product in exchange.

However, the *creation* of money is a different process from the creation of other assets. Wheat is available because a farmer applies labor and machines to the task of growing it. Dry cleaning is available because someone will spend the time and effort to do the cleaning, and because someone else has spent the time and effort to produce the dry-cleaning machines.

But money isn't produced this way (although it was during the classic gold standard). The money we use is produced by the U.S. government, which merely prints figures on pieces of paper. About two cents worth of labor and

30

capital are needed to print a dollar bill, and it costs no more to print a $100 bill. So the supply of money isn't limited by the availability of real resources (time and energy). The supply is governed by the decisions of the monetary authorities.

Creation of Money

The government might, in principle, use any means to put new money into circulation. It could mail everyone a $50 bill, it could give every congressman a billion dollars to spend on his secretary, or it could even use Air Force helicopters to shower money onto the streets.

Instead, the government puts the money into circulation by buying things. But its shopping list is very short. It includes only bonds and certain other debt instruments.

The government's purchasing agent is the Federal Reserve System, a group of government-controlled banks that has been given the legal authority to create money. The new money is created when the Federal Reserve buys bonds from bond dealers.

Normally, the Fed (the Federal Reserve System) buys U.S. government bonds—the same bonds that you might buy. And they are bought from the same sources from which you might buy them—Merrill Lynch, Bank of America, Chase Manhattan, and so forth.

The only difference between your bond purchase and the Fed's purchase is that the Fed pays for the bond it is buying by creating new money—in effect, printing money to buy back some of the government's IOUs.

The Fed's purchases (and its occasional sales) of bonds alter the nation's money supply. When the Fed buys bonds, it adds new money to what is available to the public. When it sells bonds, it takes in money, which it retires from circulation. This is the mechanism through which the government controls the supply of money in the United States.

At any time, then, the supply of money depends on the actions of the Federal Reserve. And the demand for money results from the cash-holding preferences of all the people in the country.

We said earlier that a general reduction in the demand for money (a decline in the amount of cash people feel they need to hold) would lead to price inflation—a lowering of the value of money. In the same way, an increase in the supply of money, without a corresponding increase in the demand for it, also will lead to price inflation.

To see just how this occurs, we'll trace an injection of newly created money moving through the economy. As we do, we'll see the rise in prices and the other consequences that flow from money creation—consequences we are living with today.

THE INFLATION PROCESS

The Federal Reserve System consists of a Board of Governors and twelve Federal Reserve Banks—in which are held much of the cash reserves that U.S. commercial banks are required by law to keep.

When the Federal Reserve buys a bond from a dealer, it sends a message to the dealer's local bank, instructing the bank to credit the dealer's checking account for the amount of the purchase. The Federal Reserve pays the local bank for doing this by crediting the same amount of money to the bank's account at one of the twelve Federal Reserve Banks.

Providing the credit costs the Fed nothing; the deposit at the Reserve Bank is created out of thin air. If the local bank should ask to withdraw actual currency from its account at the Reserve Bank, the Federal Reserve would honor the request by simply printing more currency—more of the Federal Reserve notes that you carry in your pocket every day.

In normal transactions, a payment means that one person's checking account balance is reduced, while the balance of the person receiving the payment rises. In addition, the cash reserves of the bank receiving the payment are increased, while another bank's cash reserves are reduced. When the Fed buys a bond, however, things are different. The bond dealer's checking account is enlarged and the cash reserves of his local bank increase—but no other person or bank suffers a reduction. Thus the overall supply of money increases.

The Money Flows

When money is deposited in a commercial bank, the bank doesn't leave all of it sitting in the vault or on deposit at the Federal Reserve Bank. The bank is in business to earn money—and it does so by lending out some of the deposits it receives. When it receives a new deposit from a bond dealer, it will put part of the money to work for itself.

Like you, a bank has an idea of how large its money balance should be. It wants to have enough to cover any likely withdrawal requests, to have money available to pay its bills, and to make loans to good customers on short notice.

Beyond those needs, however, any further holdings of idle money would be a waste, since the money could be earning interest. One way for the bank to earn interest on the additional money that the Fed has created is to lend it to its customers.

The demand for loans, like the demand for anything else, is affected by the price—in this case, the interest rate. So if a bank has additional cash to lend, and if it doesn't want to lower its credit standards, it will find new borrowers only by charging a lower interest rate than before. The lower interest rate will attract new customers and induce existing customers to go more deeply into debt.

Capital Investment

But lower interest rates do more than just expand the *quantity* of loans that are made; they change the *character* of the loans.

For example, a businessman might believe he could profit by building a factory for a new product if he could borrow the money to finance it at 10% interest. If the current interest rate is 12%, he'll pass up the project, because he believes the project wouldn't produce enough additional profit to cover the 12% rate. But when the Federal Reserve

33

creates enough new money to cause the interest rate to drop to 10%, the new factory becomes an attractive venture.

And so the businessman borrows the money from the bank and begins his project. He hires workers and pays them out of the new money. He buys building equipment and materials from his suppliers—and his suppliers pass on much of the new money they receive to their own suppliers and to their employees. Wages and business incomes increase.

Spending Patterns

Each person affected has a higher money balance than before. Since nothing has happened to increase his demand for money equivalently, he will tend to spend the additional money, rather than permanently increase his cash holdings. And, of course, the people from whom he buys things will see their cash balances increase too.

The new money flows through the economy, but the result isn't an even, across-the-board increase in all types of purchases. A key element of the process is that the new money is *not* distributed evenly; it is distributed first to a few people in a few industries. And the people who receive it do not simply buy more of the things they had been buying before. Their spending patterns change.

The new money means two things to the recipients. First, it is a sign that their incomes may be permanently higher. Because they feel wealthier, they will spend part of the new money on what are to them luxury goods.

Second, much of the new money will be regarded as a windfall. It will be spent on durable goods (long-lived goods —such as cars, houses, and appliances) and on investments. Both types of purchases are attempts to stretch out consumption of the windfall over an extended period. Thus luxury goods, long-lived goods, and investments tend to receive an extra share when new money is created.

Investment Markets

The investment markets also receive some of the new money by a more direct route.

The Federal Reserve's purchases add to the demand for bonds—causing their prices to be higher than they would be otherwise. And, as in the factory example. the money flows outward The individuals who sell their government bonds (indirectly to the Fed) have more money than before, cash they don't need to keep. Because the money was received for an investment, a good deal of it will be reinvested perhaps now in stocks or corporate bonds—adding further to the demand in the securities markets.

With securities prices higher, corporations are inspired to sell new securities—issuing new shares of stock because the market appears to be receptive, or selling new bonds because interest rates are lower. They don't want the money as an addition to their cash holdings. They plan to spend it to build new factories, buy new equipment, and launch new projects—just as though they had borrowed it from a bank.

Stimulation

Easier credit at banks and higher investment prices are the two main routes along which the newly created money makes its way into the economy.

Along each route the money stimulates investment because capital is available on cheaper terms. Along each route the money stimulates the purchase of luxury and durable goods by making consumers feel wealthier. And along each route the money keeps moving because it is more than people need to hold.

The process seems to be fairly obvious. But if you happen to be one of the recipients of the new money, you'll have no reason to believe that it is money creation that has changed your circumstances. You'll naturally believe your experience is special Your services are more in demand; you are finally being paid what you deserve; the market finally recognizes the value of the investment you've been holding. If you knew what had caused this, and what was coming next, you'd treat all the excess money as a windfall. But you don't know where the money's coming from, so you assume that it will keep coming.

THE NEXT STAGE

As we've seen, the new money means that many people have larger cash balances than they need; the supply of money is greater than the demand for it. And so these people spend more than they would have otherwise.

This causes a fall in the available inventories of the goods these people favor. Retailers find that their stocks of products are too low, so they increase their orders from wholesalers, passing the excess cash along to them. Wholesalers repeat the experience, ordering more from factories.

But when manufacturers see their own inventories drop, the process reaches a critical stage. There is no one from whom the manufacturers can order more inventory; they have to produce it. To accommodate the increased demand, they will have to expand their factories, hire more workers, buy more machines. But there is just so much of these resources available. The wave of excess money has run into the barrier of limited resources.

To meet the increased demand for their goods, manufacturers will turn to older, less efficient factories that have been idle since the last boom. They consider it a temporary expedient until new facilities can be constructed, which might take two to four years. Until then, the older plants will expand production, but their operating costs will be higher.

In the same way, additional raw materials can be produced, but only at higher operating cost. The increased demand causes raw-material producers to use less-efficient, hurry-up production methods and to use sources they normally would pass over.

Wages

The labor market is affected also. To expand production, manufacturers need more manpower—and there are only three ways to get it.

The first source is the unemployed. They are available, but many of them are inexperienced in the work they are asked to do; this increases the cost of each unit produced. The second source is the supply of experienced workers who have jobs elsewhere. To induce them to change jobs, the manufacturer will have to offer more money.

And the third source is the manufacturer's present staff; he can obtain more manpower by offering his present employees a premium to work extra hours. But, of course, this raises the cost of each hour worked. And the longer the overtime continues, the higher the premium will have to be—because the workers' "inventory" of willing overtime hours is only so large, and will be depleted in the same way that inventories of products are being depleted.

All three sources of additional labor are expensive; whichever source or combination of sources the manufacturer taps, the cost of each unit produced will increase.

HIGHER PRICES

Because resources are limited, manufacturers will be able to satisfy only part of the increased demand for their products, resulting in lower inventories at the wholesale and retail levels. And the goods they do ship will cost more to produce. Manufacturers will have to raise their prices in order to cover the increased costs. They'll do so without fear of losing business, since they're being asked for more goods than they can produce anyway.

First there was a wave of new money rolling from consumers toward manufacturers. Now there is a wave of higher prices rolling back toward the consumer. Manufacturers' costs go up, and so they raise prices to wholesalers. Wholesalers pay the higher prices because if they don't, they'll have nothing to sell. They assume that they can pass the increased cost on to the retailers—who are calling them daily, asking for delivery.

The retailer pays the wholesaler more and raises his prices to the consumer. Since the consumer is at the end of the line, there is no price for him to raise (although he may ask for another raise from his employer). He can only complain that the manufacturers, wholesalers, retailers, labor unions, and Arabs are gouging him.

Later, the price increases spread even to the items that haven't experienced any increase in demand. This occurs because the manufacturers of these items must compete for resources (factories, materials, and labor) with the manufacturers for whom there *was* an increase in demand. The higher costs have to be paid or there will be no way to produce.

And so eventually price increases become general, although still uneven.

CASH POOR

The price inflation that results from the new money is the method by which the economy solves the problem of too many people attempting to reduce their cash balances at one time.

In this case, price inflation occurred because the supply of money increased beyond what people needed to hold. It would occur also if the money supply remained constant but, for some reason, most people decided to reduce their money holdings (a drop in the demand for money).

As we've seen, it isn't possible for everyone to reduce his cash balance at once. But how does price inflation resolve the problem?

It is natural for an individual to choose his desired money balance on the basis of his normal income or expenses. For example, someone may feel comfortable holding three months' expenses in a checking account. In this way, he knows that if he loses his income, he'll be able to support himself for three months with the money he has on hand, without having to liquidate other assets that he owns.

If this individual normally spends $2,000 per month, he'll aim at holding around $6,000 in cash. But after the creation of the new money has led to price inflation, his expenses may be $2,200 per month. As a result, his desired cash balance (his demand for money) will rise to $6,600.

The same thing happens to everyone else in the economy. With higher prices, everyone needs a higher money balance than he did before. Eventually, when prices have risen sufficiently, their cash balances will cease to be excessive, and they'll slow down their spending.

This is how price inflation assimilates the new money into the economy and stops the spending competition. However, the price inflation doesn't end promptly when people run out of excess cash.

Some manufacturers' inventories are still too low, and they will raise prices further. Others, who have become accustomed to the consumer's acceptance of higher prices, will expect the trend to continue, and so will continue to raise their prices—hoping to stay ahead of future cost increases. Businesses and unions argue over how high price inflation will be, but they agree that it will continue—and so they negotiate two-year and three-year contracts with built-in raises.

The mere expectation of continued inflation won't keep inflation going indefinitely. But it will keep it going for a while at a gradually slowing pace. Because prices continue rising even after the need for cash has risen to match the supply, inflation eventually turns a cash-rich economy into a cash-poor economy. Before, people had more cash than they wanted to hold. Now they have less cash than they want to hold.

Large Inventories

The buying demands that were overwhelming retailers begin to subside. But neither the retailer nor anyone else attributed his increased sales to an increased money supply; he assumed that his own business was finally being appreciated. And he expects his success to continue. So when his sales fall off a little, he assumes that it's merely a temporary lull, and he doesn't stop ordering new merchandise from wholesalers. And, at first, wholesalers and manufacturers respond to reductions in sales with similar optimism.

The merchandise keeps pouring through the pipeline to the retail level. But, eventually, it becomes apparent that the falloff in sales isn't temporary. Retailers realize that they now have too much inventory, not too little.

And at higher prices, each business requires a larger holding of money to provide the same convenience and security that a smaller balance provided earlier. It becomes increasingly obvious to the businessman that he has too much inventory and not enough cash. And, of course, it is the businesses that profited most in the early stages of the money creation that feel this pinch the worst. They geared up to a new level of demand that they assumed would be permanent; now they are geared too high.

As a result, the previous sequence of events is played back in reverse. Not only does overtime end, but workers who are no longer needed are laid off. Orders for raw materials fall off. The flow of spending slows. Everyone who had been feeling richer now feels poorer.

People made decisions that were based on higher incomes, higher cash balances, and stable prices. When prices rose, the higher incomes and higher cash balances were insufficient to support the grand plans. Consequently, most people reach a point where they feel they don't have enough money.

Just as excess cash stimulated spending, a cash shortage subdues it. With cash holdings short of the desired levels, consumers cut back on purchases—especially purchases of luxury items and long-lived goods. The boom in durable goods turns into a recession.

Higher Interest Rates

The cash shortage also causes interest rates to rise. Banks and other lenders are no longer looking for borrowers to take money off their hands. The rise is reinforced by inflation-shy lenders who want to be compensated if price inflation continues.

The pressure on interest rates is aggravated further by the cutback in consumer spending. With inventories unexpectedly large, businessmen require financing for longer periods than expected—causing the demand for credit to increase.

In fact, the combination of price inflation and the need to finance swollen inventories pushes interest rates to levels higher than those that prevailed before the inflation.

Abandoned Projects

At the beginning of the process, we cited the businessman who decided to build a new factory because the interest rate dropped to 10% from 12%. By now, it's time for him to refinance the loan, but the rate is up to 15%. His warehouses are already overflowing with goods, and he has no need for a new factory or a new product. The project is canceled in midstream, workers are laid off, and some suppliers and subcontractors go bankrupt.

Even the businesses that manage to survive the cash shortage face losses, as they've incurred higher costs that can't be passed along to customers who now are cutting spending.

Investments

Meanwhile, individuals sell investments in an effort to replenish their cash balances. Stock, bond, and other investment prices decline. And the falling investment prices reinforce the deflationary atmosphere. Investors see the values of their assets decline and so, as consumers, they cut back further on personal spending.

In the first stage of the process, most people were trying to buy more than they were selling. At this point, everyone is trying to sell more than he buys—hoping to augment a cash balance that has become too small.

CONTINUING PROCESS

We have told the story of money creation as a one-shot affair—a single bundle of money dropped into the economy, causing a cycle of boom and bust. After such an episode, the price inflation rate would eventually retreat to around 0%, and spending and investment habits would gravitate back toward the pattern that prevailed before the inflation. It would take a while to restore a sense of "normality," but in time confidence would return.

We have limited the story to a one-time inflation because, in economics, it is useful to imagine events occurring in isolation—in order to determine how they unfold. But in reality money creation is seldom a one-shot affair. The Federal Reserve continually alters the supply of money, and the economy never really gets back on an even keel.

Because inflation is continuous, many problems have developed that wouldn't occur with a one-time-only increase in the money supply. In the next chapter we'll examine those problems, including some that have already occurred and others that are yet to come.

WHAT CAUSES INFLATION?

We began this chapter by acknowledging that everyone would like to receive a higher price for his product or service. By now it should be clear that there's a natural rein on anyone's ability to get a higher price. Just asking for it isn't enough.

If there's no change in the quantity of money available, society will spend more freely only if the overall demand for money has declined. Barring such a reduction in the demand to hold money, people can spend more for one thing only by reducing their spending on something else. In fact, this happens all the time as tastes and resources change. The price of one thing goes up, and the price of something else goes down.

These price changes are a vital part of a functioning economy. Without freely changing prices, there's no way for producers to know what consumers want. This is one of the reasons that wage and price controls speed the deterioration of an inflated economy; they make it illegal for buyers and sellers to communicate.

Anyone can choose to raise his asking price. But if the supply of money hasn't increased, there are only two possible outcomes. The first occurs if the raise will overprice his service. He'll not only sell fewer units of the service, but his overall profit will be reduced, even at the higher asking price. The price increase won't last for long.

The second possible outcome is that consumers will pay the higher price (buying less of something else), and he'll continue to sell almost as much as he did at the lower price —resulting in a higher overall profit. If this happens, it is evidence that his service had been underpriced all along. There may even be room for a further price increase. But once he reaches the right price, he'll find that any additional rise will discourage buyers and hurt his profits.

Oil Prices

The oil price increases of recent years have had two causes. First, the rapid expansion of the U.S. money supply has caused the dollar prices of all things to rise. Second, foreign producers of oil succeeded where producers of various goods usually have failed; they organized a profitable cartel.

A cartel is an agreement among sellers to raise asking prices and to reduce production. The agreement to limit production is essential, since consumers are certain to respond to higher prices by buying less. The cartel's chance for success hinges on the amount by which production must be cut back; if only a small cut is needed, it will be easier for the cartel members to agree on how much less each will produce.

Would-be cartels generally fail because members find it profitable to cheat on one another, and because any temporary success invites new suppliers and alternative products into the field. Cheating occurs when members fail to cut production as much as agreed on—or even increase production to take advantage of higher prices. If the agreed-upon cut in production doesn't occur, it becomes impossible to make the cartel's official price stick for very long.

The oil-producer's cartel (OPEC, the Organization of Petroleum Exporting Countries) has succeeded where others have failed (for example, in sugar, silver, and coffee) partly because the required cutbacks were small and partly because it takes so long to find new oil reserves and put them into production.

A further advantage enjoyed by OPEC has been the co-operation of the U.S. government. The way for OPEC was prepared by the government's long-standing controls on the price of natural gas. Price controls on natural gas, which is an easy substitute for oil in many uses, discouraged exploration for gas and for its geological cousin, oil. So, when OPEC opened for business, the U.S. was less able to expand its production of oil and gas.

43

After OPEC became active, the U.S. government compounded the problem by extending price controls to domestically produced oil, thereby further discouraging exploration by the thousands of U.S. companies that could have threatened the cartel with increased supplies. These later price controls, together with the "windfall" profits tax enacted in 1980, have added years to OPEC's life expectancy.

The formation of the oil cartel made consumers in the U.S. slightly less well-off than they would have been without it. Having to spend more for oil, they have less to spend on other things. But that isn't inflation. Inflation existed before OPEC, and it has continued, sometimes at peak rates, during periods when OPEC prices were stable.

A comparison of inflation rates in other countries is helpful. One member of the cartel is Venezuela—which doesn't worry about higher oil prices because oil is what the country produces. Price inflation there was 24.2% as of July 1980.[1]

At the opposite end of the world is Switzerland. The only oil produced in Switzerland is what someone can squeeze out of a piece of cheese. If high oil prices were an important cause of inflation, Switzerland should have about the highest rate in the world. But the inflation rate was only 3.8% as of September 1980.[2]

OPEC has little effect on price inflation because it influences neither the demand for money nor the supply of it. OPEC's main contribution is to provide the politicians with one more scapegoat to blame for the damage they are doing. If OPEC fell apart tomorrow, and its former members cut prices to compete for business, inflation would continue as before. The only change would be a political shift to a new scapegoat. Someday maybe they'll pick on you.

Balanced Budget

We should also note that balancing the federal budget won't bring an end to price inflation. The Federal Reserve's

---

[1]*International Financial Statistics*, International Monetary Fund, October 1980.
[2]*Schweizerisches Handelsamtsblatt*, Bern; October 10, 1980.

principal objective when it increases the money supply is to stimulate the economy. It will continue to try—regardless of the state of the federal budget.

It is true that federal deficits add to the pressure to inflate the money supply. A federal deficit increases the amount of debt that must be financed in the marketplace—causing upward pressure on interest rates. Since the Fed doesn't want high interest rates to interfere with prosperity, it is obliged to increase its bond purchases when federal deficits are large. But inflation would exist (and has existed) without the deficits.

We suggest that you pay no attention if you hear that inflation is about to yield to some easy solution. Wage and price controls, balanced budgets, and cheaper oil are only three of the possible panaceas you might hear of. We couldn't begin to think of all the others that will be offered.

SUPPLY & DEMAND

While individual prices constantly adjust, upward and downward, only a change in the supply of money or in the demand for it can cause the general price level to change.

The usual cause of price inflation is an increase in the supply of money without a corresponding increase in the demand for it. But inflation can be caused simply by a decrease in the demand for money. The usual cause of deflation (a falling general price level) is a decrease in the supply of money without a corresponding decrease in the demand for it. But a deflation might be caused simply by an increase in the demand for money.[3]

The idea that both supply and demand are involved in money's influence on the economy is vital to an understanding of inflation and where it may lead in the future. In the past, it was the supply side that had the most influence. But we are now at a stage where changes in the demand for money may dominate our future.

---

[3]To the best of our knowledge, this relationship was first defined in 1912 by Ludwig von Mises in *The Theory of Money & Credit* (listed in the Suggested Reading on page 518).

3

AN END TO INFLATION

OUR DESCRIPTION OF THE INFLATIONARY PROCESS HAD A BE-
ginning and an end. That alone might make you wonder how
accurate it is. Inflation has been with us so long that it seems
permanent, almost normal. Talking about an end to inflation
sounds like one of those familiar political promises that is routinely made and routinely disregarded.

And yet it won't go on forever. To understand why inflation's demise is inevitable, and the ways in which the end
might come, we first need to look at the political sources of
inflation and at the problems that accumulate in an inflated
economy.

POLITICAL CONTROL

Money creation is politically convenient. The apparent
prosperity it generates helps those in power to stay in power.
The demand for labor increases, investment markets rise, people believe they are better off, and there is plenty of activity
that appears to be productive. If anyone is hurt by the new
money, he's somewhere in the background where his distress
isn't noticed—and he certainly doesn't know what is causing
the distress. Money creation seems to confer visible benefits
while it hides the problems it causes.

The political gains accrue mostly to the President and
Congress, but it is the Federal Reserve that actually manages
the job. The elected politicians don't have day-to-day control
over the Federal Reserve's actions, yet they generally find the

47

Fed cooperative. It is a creature of Congress—and Congress could, at any time, pass a law that would alter the Fed's powers.

The Federal Reserve System is run by a board of seven governors, who are themselves politicians—otherwise they probably wouldn't have sought or accepted jobs that give them enormous authority over the lives of others. They understand the getting and using of power, and the commerce in favors that is the business of politics. And they appreciate the importance of not making powerful enemies.

Each governor is appointed by the President; a full term is fourteen years. Unlike cabinet officers or ambassadors, a governor—once appointed—can't be dismissed at the President's pleasure. This "job security" and the length of a full term would seem to insulate a governor from political pressure, but the insulation is far from absolute.

Every two years one of the seven terms expires. So, if a President serves for eight years, he will be able to appoint four governors—a majority of the board. And in practice the reappointment rate is greater than one every two years. If a governor resigns before his term is over, a successor is appointed—but only for the remainder of the term, not for fourteen years. So a President may appoint several board members during even a four-year administration.

A President naturally will want to appoint only people he finds it easy to get along with and who will help him realize his political objectives. And even the governors he hasn't appointed know that opposition to his policies is somewhat futile—since it won't be long until the President appoints enough of his own people to create a friendly majority.

This doesn't mean that the Federal Reserve is run by ward heelers and congressional in-laws. The governors by and large are people of considerable knowledge and experience who would be well qualified for positions outside government. But, for some reason, all of them choose to work in Washington.

It would be incorrect to imagine them dangling on a string held by the President or Congress. In fact, there have been times when the Fed has said no to both of them. But the governors understand that their power comes from the President and Congress; when the politicians ask for something, the Fed wants to find a way to say yes. And what the politicians usually ask for is more money.

TIMING

As we saw in the last chapter, money creation causes problems. But the problems don't surface immediately; it takes time for the new money to produce all its effects. The delay is what makes it possible for the government to inflate without being blamed for the consequences.

On average, changes in the money supply affect the stock market one to three months later. Maximum effects on business activity (employment and other economic indicators) come about one year after the injection of new money. The strongest effect on price inflation comes with a delay of 18 to 24 months.

The time lags mask the relationship between new money and price inflation. The inflation comes later, perhaps at the very time the Federal Reserve is holding back on money creation. This convinces many people that there's no correspondence between the Fed's activities and the inflation rate, and leads a few others to believe that tight money and high interest rates cause inflation.

Even if the politicians realize what they're asking the Fed to do, the apparently pleasant effects of money creation come first; the obviously painful effects come later—perhaps after the next election.

CONTINUOUS INFLATION

In the last chapter we traced the effects of a single injection of new money. But in practice inflation is continuous. The Federal Reserve is always in the money markets, trading bonds and altering the nation's money supply. It is there partly to try to offset the damage done by past money creation.

When we worked our way through one inflationary cycle, we could see that resources were squandered on long-term projects that were never finished. And goods were produced out of proportion to the needs of the population; too much of some things were produced, too little of others.

This is why some people attribute recessions and depressions to previous periods of "overproduction," and why, when a new recession is under way, analysts often say that the consumer has become saturated with goods and is going to cut back his spending.

Both observations miss the mark. The problem can never be too much production, because human desires are insatiable, while resources for production are always limited. We will never be able to produce enough to satisfy every want.

The problem is not that *too much* has been produced, but that things have been produced in the wrong proportions. The false signals given by monetary inflation have diverted production into luxuries and durable goods—things that people would gladly buy if they were as wealthy as the money temporarily made them feel. When reality reasserts itself, further production of these goods can't be sustained by consumer demand.

Businessmen often make mistakes about what can be produced profitably—and about what next year's tastes, available supplies, and interest rates will be. But in an economy that isn't molested by inflation, the mistaken forecasts of different businessmen cancel out, or they are offset by the shrewdness of a few who recognize, ahead of all the others, what will be wanted or needed next year.

Only a one-sided, widespread miscalculation by most businessmen can cause what we think of as a recession or a depression. That occurs when the signals that businessmen rely on have been distorted—when the creation of new money lowers interest rates (a key signal) and places unusually large amounts of cash in the hands of one part of the public. The spending of this segment encourages overproduction of certain things and diverts resources away from the production of everything else.

As we've seen, a recession is the inevitable reaction. And then, when the economy is cash-poor, the President and Congress pressure the Fed to make more credit available—

to do something to reduce interest rates. The Fed can do this only by creating more money, and so it does.

As a result, the distortions caused by the previous money creation are never completely resolved. New problems are created—even as the economy is still trying to recover from the old problems.

During the continuing inflation, each cycle of money creation takes its toll on the economy. Resources are wasted and can't be recovered. And since the economy never gets back to normal, many industries continue to produce the goods that were inspired by money creation—continuing to divert resources from the uses consumers want most.

LONG-TERM INFLATION

In the early stages of a long-term inflation, the overall demand for money may actually increase a little. People see prices rising slightly and assume that they'll fall back to normal next year. So they postpone large purchases, accumulating cash while they wait for prices to drop.

But when it becomes obvious that the inflation isn't temporary, the demand for money declines. Then people purchase sooner instead of later, wanting to buy before prices go higher yet.

The declining demand for money is of itself inflationary. So once the long-term inflation is well under way, there frequently are periods when the rate of price inflation is greater than the rate of money creation.

Pressure for Acceleration

And, as we've seen, the aftermath of each injection of new money is a recession. From the day the economy starts to slide into a recession, political pressure builds for the Fed to "do something." What it is asked to do may be called easier credit, lower interest rates, moderation, flexibility, or just "living up to its responsibilities." But the code words all mean the same thing: the Fed should put an end to the recession by stepping up its printing of money.

The job can require quite a lot of stepping up. In the first place, each recession creates an intermission in the long-term decline in the demand for money, since the general feeling of uncertainty that accompanies a recession adds to the desire for the security that cash provides.

In the second place, the inflation rate itself increases the "normal" cash balance to a larger number of dollars. If wages and prices are rising at a rate of 10%, for example, people will want to adjust their cash balances upward by about that much—just to be holding the same number of months' expenses in the form of money.

And third, the Fed can't "stimulate" the economy just by accommodating the temporary increase in the demand for money and the upward adjustment caused by the inflation rate. A surprise is needed every time. The original stimulation worked *not* because people received more money than they had before, but because people received more money than they expected.

To stimulate the country out of a recession, the injection of new money must be large enough to overcome all three elements of resistance.

And because inflation causes resources to be wasted, it weakens—and may even overwhelm—the economy's natural capacity for growth. Thus each recession tends to be a little more painful, and each recovery a little less satisfying—which increases the demand for the Fed to do more.[1]

Even though the inflationary process is continuous, there still is a rather well-defined four-or-five-year business cycle, with a boom stage and a bust stage. But inflation doesn't disappear during the downturns, nor does unemployment disappear during the recoveries. Instead, during each recessionary period, inflation retreats a bit, but it stops retreating at a point higher than where it bottomed the last time. And during each recovery, unemployment doesn't really go away, nor is there a business and stock market boom that makes up for the purchasing power lost since the last boom.

---

[1]Government taxing and regulatory policies also discourage growth and contribute to stagnation, of course; some of their consequences are discussed in Chapter 12.

Through it all, the economic miscalculations grow, which means that the eventual readjustment to a normal economy will be more difficult the longer it is postponed.

The Fed has a tiger by the tail, and its name is inflation. If the Fed lets go, the tiger will run wild—causing depression in all the industries that have been supported by money creation. But if the Fed holds on, the tiger will just get madder and run faster—causing the inflation rate to rise still higher.

POSSIBILITIES

There are five possible courses the future may take:

1. Inflation could level off at some steady rate.

2. The rate could continue to rise as it has been—in periodic waves, but not dramatically.

3. The rate could accelerate and culminate in a runaway inflation in which prices rise so fast that the money eventually is rejected entirely.

4. We could have an end to inflation through a soft landing, with the economy easing down to normalcy and avoiding the trauma of a depression.

5. We could have a deflationary depression that would purge all the mistakes of the past thirty years.

The first possibility is a stabilization at the present rate. The second and third involve increases in the rate—one slow, the other dramatic. The last two possibilities are for a dropping in the rate—either painless or violent.

The rest of this chapter will discuss four of these possibilities, and the fifth, deflation, will be the subject of the next chapter.

STABILIZATION

The first possibility is that the government might reach some level of monetary expansion—the current rate, for example—and just stay there. Price inflation would be high but somewhat stable.

The chance of this occurring is virtually nil. As the inflationary cycle progresses, the money supply must increase at a faster rate just to keep the economy going and to keep the

53

misinvestments of the past from failing. So, once inflation is well under way, a constant rate of expansion can be no more stimulative than a reduction in the rate would have been earlier. In other words, once we've come this far, we can't stand still. We either go faster or go slower, since trying to stand still results in falling over.

In addition, it's unlikely that a government that would tolerate 10% inflation would stay at any one rate for very long. As problems develop, the temptation to solve them with "just a little more" money creation would be too great.

This possibility is the least likely of the five. In fact, we include it only to cover all the possibilities conceivable, and because investment clients have raised the question from time to time.

CONTINUATION OF THE PRESENT TREND

The second possibility is that the present trend will continue for a long time. That is, the inflation rate would continue to rise in little spurts every few years; and ten years from today we might be facing inflation of 25% or 35% yearly.

This is a very real possibility. As we hope to show in this and the next chapter, there are built-in factors in an inflation that tend to make it erupt ultimately into a runaway inflation or a deflationary depression. But we don't believe it's possible to know how much time must pass or how high the rate must go before the eruption occurs. Therefore we have to acknowledge that the present conditions of rising inflation could continue for many years.

Since gradually rising inflation is what you're used to, there's no need for a description from us; you already know what it's like. Later parts of this book will offer a number of suggestions for dealing with it.

RUNAWAY INFLATION

One reason the inflationary cycle can't continue indefinitely is that each restarting requires the creation of new money at a faster clip than before. In 1959 the economy was rescued from a recession by increasing the money supply at an annual rate of 2%. By 1968 it took a rate of 8%.

To speed up the end of a recession, it isn't sufficient merely for people to receive more money than they had before. They must receive more than they feel they need for convenience and security, so that the supply of money outruns the demand for it. Only in this way will some of the new money be excess cash, the hot potato that stimulates the economy. Because of this, each boom-bust cycle produces a higher rate of price inflation.

United States inflation peaked for the latest cycle at 14.7% in March 1980. The monetary expansion required to end the 1980–1981 recession may result in an inflation peak of 16% to 25% a few years later. And the cycle following that one might take inflation well over 30%.[2]

Accelerating Inflation

Once inflation has become somewhat permanent, it is self-accelerating. This is because of a constant repetition of four themes:

1. Higher inflation causes the recurring recessions to become more painful, calling for larger doses of new money.

2. The larger doses of new money increase price inflation.

3. Increased price inflation causes the demand for money to drop.

4. The lower demand for money increases price inflation.

The repetition of these four themes pushes price inflation to higher and higher levels. At first, the process moves slowly —slight increases in the inflation rate from year to year. But the higher the rate goes, the more people reduce cash balances whenever possible. Noticeable changes in prices begin to occur more frequently; increases are visible from month to month, and then from week to week.

Eventually the acceleration can reach a point at which

---

[2]Throughout the book, any inflation rate cited is the change in the U.S. government's Consumer Price Index over the previous twelve months—not the annualized one-month rate of change.

prices are rising visibly every day—and that is runaway inflation. With prices rising so rapidly, no one wants to hold more cash than is needed for a day or two. And once that point is reached, the currency is only a step away from complete destruction.

If the government doesn't throw in the towel then, but instead continues to a still higher rate of money creation, the money will cease to have value—because it will cease to be useful. It will no longer be a convenience, since you would have to spend it very quickly to avoid having its purchasing power evaporate in your hands. It would no longer provide security or predictability. It would no longer serve the function of money, and the dollar would be suitable only for framing as a nostalgia piece.

It is difficult to imagine America without a usable money system. We can assume that some business would continue—with pre-1965 silver coins used for small transactions, gold coins for larger transactions, some use of foreign currencies, some barter, and so on. But it wouldn't be the kind of economy we know. There would be no way to pay employees of large companies, no way to pay phone bills, no way to run the kind of economy we are used to. The country would have to start all over again to develop the civilized mechanisms we take for granted.

Cash-Reduction Systems

In addition to the forces for acceleration that feed any chronic inflation, there is an additional force working toward runaway inflation in a modern economy that wasn't present in the past. This is the development of systems that reduce the need to hold cash.

Inflation is, in effect, a tax on cash holdings. If inflation is running at 10%, it costs you 10% in purchasing power each year to hold whatever level of cash balance you're accustomed to. The higher inflation goes, the higher this tax rate.

As with any other tax, you'll rearrange your affairs to lessen its impact. In general, you'll use less of the thing that's being taxed. In this case, you'll hold less cash; your demand for money will drop. If you held six months' expenses in cash when inflation was 10%, you'll hold only four or five months' expenses when the inflation rate is 15%.

You don't just give up using money once inflation reaches 15% or 20%, because you still need the convenience and security that money provides. Today, however, there are devices that permit you to live conveniently with very little cash. There are credit cards, electronic money transfers, zero-balance checking accounts (with overdraft facilities), and computer-based planning systems that enable businesses to co-ordinate income with expenditures. All these devices permit one to reduce cash holdings without giving up the convenience or security of money.

Except for credit cards, these devices are not yet in wide use. But at inflation rates of 30%, 40%, or more, their use might increase rapidly—facilitating a drop in the demand for money and pushing the inflation rate higher. Thus the threshold of runaway inflation, the point at which people would abandon money in earnest, may be much lower today than it was in the past.

Inevitable?

With the inflation rate already going to higher and higher levels with each four-to-five-year boom-bust cycle, what is to prevent the process from escalating eventually into a runaway inflation? Basically, there are two reasons that it may not happen.

The first reason is the possibility that economic events will run ahead of the government's inflationary activities and cause a deflationary depression. This will be the subject of the next chapter.

The second reason rests on economic history. Every instance of runaway inflation we know of occurred because the government was unable to finance its expenditures by taxing and borrowing. The government turned to the printing press as the only way to pay its bills. In such a case, the government *has* to print faster and faster in order to pay the higher and higher prices caused by its previous printing.

In America, money creation is used as a means of stimulating the economy. So long as the tax-collecting mechanisms and the bond markets survive, the government won't have to print money in desperation over its finances. As we've seen, the desire to stimulate the economy is the political force behind inflation; stopping inflation wouldn't cause the government to go broke.[3]

Historical Reversals

Still, after twenty years of rising inflation rates, there's a feeling of inevitability about it—a feeling that inflation must continue getting worse and worse. It's hard to believe it can be reversed once it has gone as far as it has. But it has been reversed before—many times.

In 1922, inflation had reached 3,453% in Germany and 2,496% in Austria. In Germany, the rate climbed to 437,956,104% in 1923—resulting in the total destruction of the Reichsmark and its replacement by a new currency, the Rentenmark. But the same year, Austria's inflation rate declined to 16.4%, and its financial system survived.[4]

The U.S. inflation rate was 30% in 1864. The Civil War ended the following year, but the government announced that it wouldn't resume the convertibility of dollars into gold (suspended in 1862) for many years, an announcement that tended to keep inflationary expectations alive. Still the inflation was halted, and prices *dropped* by 38% between 1864 and 1879—the year that gold convertibility was resumed.[5]

In September 1975, the British inflation rate reached

---

[3]In February 1980, as interest rates soared to their cyclical peak and bond prices plunged, there was public speculation over whether the bond markets were dead. But the markets revived, as they had after the 1974 inflation peak. The bond markets may indeed die someday, but you can expect to hear a number of obituaries before they do.

[4]*The Economics of Inflation* by Constantino Bresciani-Turroni (listed in the Suggested Reading on page 519), 1937 edition, pages 161–162.

[5]Bureau of Labor Statistics, reported in *Long-Term Economic Growth, 1860–1970*, U.S. Department of Commerce.

27.7% (about twice the rate reached so far in the U.S.). By June 1978, a policy of tight money had lowered it to 7.4%. The economic chaos caused by the money shortage induced the British authorities to oil up the money-printing machine again, so the country didn't escape inflation for good. But a drop to 7% from 27% means that the point of no return is much higher than the U.S. has reached so far.[6]

While these examples don't prove that runaway inflation will be avoided in the U.S., they at least demonstrate that there's nothing inevitable about it.

Will we have a runaway inflation? We don't know. Don't bet everything you have on it, but don't depend on its not happening. It is one (and only one) of the possibilities your investment plans should allow for.

SOFT LANDING

The fourth possibility is that the economy may accomplish a soft landing, coming down gently from high rates of inflation and avoiding a spectacular crash.

The theory of the soft landing says that the creation of new money could be slowed a little each year. The money supply might grow by 9% this year, 8% next year, then 7% and so on. Eventually, the growth rate would be only around 4% or 5%, whatever is considered necessary to supply a growing economy. Then it would remain steady at that fixed rate.

The slowing of the growth rate, it is said, would eventually bring price inflation to an end and would be accompanied by nothing worse than a period of sluggish growth, or perhaps a long, shallow recession—but not a depression. If the policy were widely publicized and if the Federal Reserve stuck to it for a year or more, inflationary expectations would lessen and the decline in the demand for money would be halted.

The optimists believe the economy would suffer from a

---

[6]The inflation rates are taken from *Economic Trends*, United Kingdom Central Statistical Office, January 1976 and January 1979.

low-grade fever, but nothing more serious. Unemployment might run 7% or 8%, and business profits would be low. But there would be no breadlines and no wave of bank failures, as in the Great Depression.

Problems

If the policy were continued long enough, inflation would indeed end, but there's no way to know how painful the end would be. All the remaining misinvestments of the past thirty years would come to light and could drag the economy into a depression. Just how many skeletons are in the closet to come out is something that no one knows.

We do know that inflation doesn't shower its benefits on all markets equally, so the withdrawal pains from inflation wouldn't be felt evenly throughout the economy. In general, the industries that had been most stimulated by money creation would be the most threatened by an attempt at a soft landing. The danger is that the problems of a few industries would be so severe that they might turn an intended soft landing into a crash.

Real estate provides a good example. As we'll see in Chapters 11 and 12, one result of the way U.S. tax laws are written is that inflation tends to divert capital away from operating businesses and toward real estate. This is why real estate has done well during the inflation, while the stock market has been falling behind. There may be no graceful way for this distortion to be undone.

Two years or so into an attempt at a soft landing, price inflation rates would be falling noticeably. Even skeptics would be taking the government's pledge of an end to inflation seriously. The decline in inflationary expectations, coupled with the higher interest rates (relative to inflation) that would accompany slower money growth, would be deadly for the real estate market. Prices would not simply stop rising, they would fall—precipitously.

The fall in real estate prices during a soft landing would affect more than real estate investors; it would affect their creditors as well—the banks and savings institutions that had provided 80% and 90% of the capital for many purchases.

Defaults would be widespread as property values fell below mortgage debts.

The losses to banks and savings institutions would force some of them into insolvency. If the number were great enough, the failures could overwhelm the resources of the FDIC and the FSLIC (the federal agencies that insure deposits) and lead to a banking panic. The landing wouldn't be very soft.

Even if a banking panic didn't develop, there are industries that have stayed alive only because of a continually expanding money supply. A flurry of large bankruptcies in these areas could so alarm the public that the desire to hold cash as protection against bad times would escalate. The result, despite only a mild reduction in money growth, would be a large shortage of money. This would lead to further bankruptcies, and the process could snowball into a deflationary depression.

Not Likely

Just what would come of a soft landing attempt is impossible to know for sure. In fact, one thing to keep in mind is that nobody knows. America has had brief episodes of inflation before, but never a period of inflation as lengthy as the one we're in now. There are no precedents to fall back on.

We believe that a soft landing is an unlikely outcome. It would succeed only if everything went right, and very little has gone right up to now. It would take enormous political support to stick to the program long enough for inflation to end. And if the program were adhered to, the landing could turn out to be far bumpier than expected.

Thus we're not betting on the soft landing, but we will suggest steps to take to protect against the possibility.

DEFLATION

This leaves us with one last possibility—that of a 1929-style deflationary depression. We are going to devote a whole chapter to it because it is the possibility least respected today —even by people who know there's trouble afoot.

We don't believe that any of the five possibilities is a certainty, but we think the chance of a deflationary depression has been understated. So we are going to describe in detail one way it can come about.

4

DEFLATION

Among those who have written about the trouble that lies ahead, a large majority feel that runaway inflation is inevitable. They believe that, in order to avoid a deflationary depression, the politicians will continue the acceleration of inflation until it results in a runaway inflation.

This is understandable when inflation is viewed solely as a political issue. The Federal Reserve is always in the position of having either to dish out the new money or to hold back. It is assumed that politicians are more afraid of unemployment than they are of inflation, and so the Fed always will err on the side of more inflation.

POLITICAL POSSIBILITIES

Even if inflation were driven solely by political forces, there still would be some flaws in the argument that runaway inflation is inevitable.

The argument assumes that unemployment is a greater political liability than inflation. It's true that until 1979–1980 inflation wasn't really a public scandal. Despite the damage that inflation had done to the economy, most people still believed that only pensioners were hurt very badly. And while they sympathized with the widows and orphans, they weren't going to kick anyone out of office for failing to get inflation back to 2%.

That may be changing now. Inflation was one of the biggest issues of the 1980 election—causing even the former

President to be born again as an anti-inflationist. With price inflation reaching 14% in February 1980, we're in a different political atmosphere.

Most people know they're affected, and from here on the political pressure to err on the side of unemployment may be greater than we've seen before. After all, at the worst of the 1930s depression, only 25% of the labor force was unemployed. In 1980 almost everyone is hurting from inflation. Which problem has the largest constituency demanding a solution?

The belief that the government will always err on the side of inflation is behind the times. Not only are political pressures changing, but the Fed no longer has the room to maneuver that it had when inflation rates were lower. We can't protect ourselves by repeating the clichés of the 1960s and 1970s, or by counting on the Fed to repeat the mistakes of those years.

Political Maneuvering

Also, one can think of several circumstances that might prompt a politician to take deliberate steps to end the inflation—even if he knew the havoc an end to inflation might cause.

A President who understood the process might end the expansion of the money supply as soon as he was inaugurated. If he allowed the economy to adjust freely, without interference from the government, the worst might be over within two or three years. By the time he ran for reelection, the economy would be humming, and he could present himself as the man who brought the 20-year inflation to an end.

Or, for another possibility, a President might clamp down on monetary expansion without understanding what he was provoking. By the time he realized the consequences, he might have lost his bid for reelection. His successor would be free to let the depression run its course, explaining that it wasn't of his making. He could be as popular as Franklin Roosevelt.

Or there's a third possibility. Suppose that midway

through an election year, the President realized he had absolutely no chance of being reelected because his brilliance wasn't appreciated. In order to prove to the country that it should have retained him, and to pave the way for a comeback, he might take steps, six months before his successor was to be inaugurated, to get the depression underway. The bad news would start flowing after he left office, and his successor would take the blame.

There's nothing that a politician wouldn't try if he thought it would further his career. If you give the matter a little thought, you probably can add to the list of inflation-ending scenarios.

EXPERTISE

The belief that the Federal Reserve or the President wouldn't let a depression occur assumes that the government is so skilled and powerful that it can accomplish whatever it wants—short of restoring the economy to a permanently healthy condition.

This just isn't so. If nothing else, we need only remember that many people believed there would always be a boom during an election year, in order to help the President's reelection or the election of his personal favorite. What happened to the boom in 1980? Confidence in the Fed's ability is misplaced.

The 1974–1975 "recession" (which, incidentally, was far more painful than the 1921 "depression") went far beyond what any incumbent politician would want. It didn't escalate into a full-scale deflationary depression, but it brought down the Franklin National Bank, caused a record number of business bankruptcies, and produced an unemployment rate of 9.2%.[1]

Why did the Federal Reserve let it go so far? If the Fed has the power to avoid what it doesn't like, why didn't it stop the recession before it went so far? One reason is that the

---

[1]The unemployment rate is from the *Federal Reserve Bulletin*, December 1975, page A52.

"government" isn't a single, omniscient person with one mind and one set of objectives. It is literally millions of people—each with his own knowledge and goals.

Personnel

More specifically, it is the twelve members of the Federal Reserve Open Market Committee, the organ of the Federal Reserve that decides how much new money will be spent in the bond market each week.

Who are these people? The committee is composed of the seven governors of the Fed (whom we discussed in the last chapter), the president of the New York Federal Reserve Bank, and four of the eleven other Reserve Bank presidents (among whom four memberships rotate annually).

The committee's membership changes frequently. The four Reserve Bank presidents serve for only one year at a time. The New York president serves for five years. A Fed governor might serve for as long as fourteen years, but seldom does. As of December 1, 1979, seven of the twelve members had served less than one year, and the average time of service was twenty-four months.[2]

These are the people entrusted with the job of preventing the next depression. It is they, not some automatic mechanism, who will respond to any deflationary conditions that develop. All decisions will be made by majority rule. To assume that these twelve people have the same objectives, know precisely what they're doing, and will interpret all future events wisely is asking a lot.

You might as well appoint a committee of your town's leading citizens to supervise brain surgery at the local hospital.

Methods

The Open Market Committee's record so far is not very good. It has never, for example, shown any understanding of

---

[2]Various issues of the *Federal Reserve Bulletin.*

the long and unpredictable time lag between changes in monetary policy and the results for the economy.

The Fed typically responds to high inflation rates with policies that are mildly restrictive. But it is impatient. Without allowing sufficient time for its policies to work, it becomes more and more restrictive until it throws the country into a worse recession than intended. Then it stimulates the money supply rapidly, trying to undo the damage it has caused.

One day the Fed may move too slowly in fighting a recession. It takes time for stimulative policies to work, just as it takes time for restrictive policies to take effect. Caution, divided opinion, or divided purpose could keep the Fed from moving fast enough.

The tools used by the Open Market Committee are clumsy ones. They are so clumsy that no one even talks about "fine-tuning" the economy anymore. National income figures are only rough approximations. The money supply is estimated weekly by reports from some of the nation's banks. The estimates are crude and have to be revised when reports from a broader segment of banks arrive later.

And the Fed isn't able to control the money supply directly. It must act indirectly—through its attempts to peg interest rates or to change the size of bank reserves. Because of the nature of fractional reserve banking, the Fed never knows exactly how much new money its bond purchases will lead to.

The expectation that government *fiscal* policy would rescue the country is just as out of touch with reality. Federal aid programs are mostly public relations projects; the money is very slow to reach anyone beyond the bureaucrats involved.

SUPPLY & DEMAND

Discussions of inflation that acknowledge the importance of money usually focus on the money supply alone, even though no other economic issue is examined by looking only at supply. Both supply and demand must be considered.

We suspect that the demand for money has been ignored mostly because of the vagueness of the concept. The supply of money is a clear and simple idea, and the Fed issues weekly estimates of its size. But the demand for money is a psychological factor—lodged in the minds of human beings. No economic indicator can measure it directly.

As we said earlier, changes in the money supply have dominated the inflation picture for the past thirty years. But if there's a runaway inflation, it will be brought on by a rapid decline in the demand for money. And if there's a deflation, it probably won't be caused by the Federal Reserve swearing off the printing of money. Instead, it would be triggered by a sudden change upward in the demand for money —making the economy feel cash-poor and creating deflationary pressure as great as though the supply of money had suddenly fallen.

Demand Reversal

When the erosion of money's value becomes chronic, the demand for money naturally lessens. Individuals find ways of getting by with a smaller reserve of purchasing power.

The demand for money has been dropping slowly over the past thirty years, as shown in the graph on page 69. Is it possible that this long-term trend could suddenly be reversed —even during a period of high inflation? We believe so.

During the past five years, haven't you at some time increased your cash reserve—even though you knew the cash would be less valuable a year later? Individuals here and there do so all the time. Usually what one person does is offset by someone else. But it's possible that a series of events could cause considerations of convenience and security to outweigh inflationary expectations—causing a widespread and unexpected shift upward in the demand for money. A deflation would follow.

WHAT IS MONEY?

For purposes of this discussion, we'll define money as *any instrument that is immediately acceptable as a medium of exchange*—that is, anything that is immediately spendable.

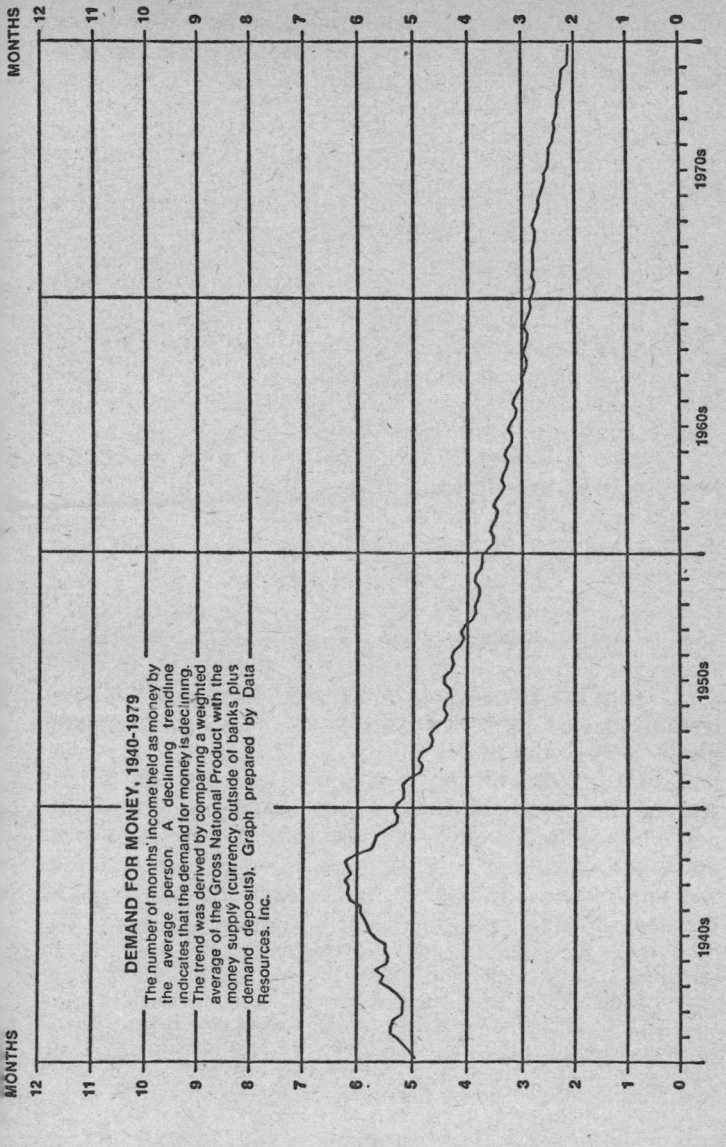

DEMAND FOR MONEY, 1940-1979

The number of months' income held as money by the average person. A declining trendline indicates that the demand for money is declining. The trend was derived by comparing a weighted average of the Gross National Product with the money supply (currency outside of banks plus demand deposits). Graph prepared by Data Resources. Inc.

By this definition, money in the U.S. consists of:

1. Dollar bills and higher denominations;
2. U.S. coins;
3. Checking accounts; and
4. Savings accounts that can be withdrawn on demand.

This definition rules out a number of financial instruments that are close to money (such as Treasury bills, commercial paper, money market funds, etc.), but which are not immediately spendable. The key is that, in each case, these "near moneys" are never spent directly for goods and services, but are exchanged only for money itself. They are held *in place of* money as another means to satisfy one's desire for liquidity. Since they are held instead of money, we'll refer to them as *cash substitutes*.

In the same way, commodities—gold, silver, and others —are not U.S. money today because they are not widely accepted as purchasing media. And we exclude bank time deposits, certificates of deposit, and some savings accounts because they are not immediately spendable.[3]

CASH SUBSTITUTES

There has been an enormous growth in the use of cash substitutes over the past twenty years, reflecting the general decline in the demand for money.

When price inflation is no more than 1% to 2% per year, an individual will hold as much money as he needs for convenience and to satisfy his desire for a secure reserve of liquid purchasing power.

---

[3]No definition of money is the "best" definition. The usefulness of any definition depends upon the discussion in which it will be used. Different definitions of the money supply are created to measure different things—such as purchasing power, liquidity, or a link to price inflation. We have chosen our definition because it will make our meaning more precise in the scenario that follows. Also, the definition isn't meant to be ideological; it doesn't identify what would be the "best" money for the economy.

But as price inflation grows, the cost of holding money (the amount by which it depreciates in purchasing power yearly) becomes an important factor for many people. They may not think of the problem in terms of declining purchasing power; more likely, they'll think of all the interest they're losing, since inflation means high interest rates. Either way, they'll act. They'll look for a cash substitute—something with the liquidity of money, but which pays interest.

The four principal cash substitutes today are:

1. *U.S. Treasury bills*—short-term (one year or less) readily marketable IOUs of the U.S. government issued in denominations of $10,000 or more. They are the safest cash substitutes.

2. *Commercial paper*—short-term IOUs, usually for $100,000 or more, of well-known corporations; they can be resold in the open market at any time.

3. *Bankers' acceptances*—short-term business debts, usually for $50,000 or more, that have been "accepted" (guaranteed) by a bank; they can be resold at any time.

4. *Negotiable certificates of deposit*—deposits of at least $100,000 at banks and thrift institutions; they can be resold at any time.

The volume of these instruments has grown dramatically over the last twenty years (see the table on page 73), keeping pace with the dramatic rise in interest rates. They pay interest approximately equal to the current twelve-month inflation rate. They allow banks, governments, and companies to raise cash—and individuals and businesses to earn interest.

Unlike bonds, all four instruments are short-term, maturing in no more than a year, and so their prices fluctuate very little. Even when interest rates rise abruptly, the resale value of a large CD or a bankers' acceptance will deteriorate only slightly.

Money market funds (explained in Chapter 17) serve to upgrade cash substitutes, making them closer to money itself. The funds buy various cash substitutes and sell shares in their holdings to the public. The fund shares are more liquid than the large-denomination cash substitutes because the shares can be bought and sold in small and fractional amounts. For many people, it is the money market funds that make it practical to shift out of cash.

As cash substitutes have expanded, they have cut into the demand for money itself, since they are an alternative source of liquidity. By using cash substitutes instead of cash itself, people have chosen to emphasize income at the expense of a small reduction in convenience and what they assume to be a negligible reduction in security. The demand for money has been reduced, but not the demand for liquidity.

One of the services of money is its reliability in short-term planning. Except in a runaway inflation, you know what a dollar will be worth tomorrow, next week, and even (approximately) next month. A financial instrument can serve as a cash substitute only if it has the same reliability.

So long as the cash substitutes retain their reliability, the demand for money will continue to drop during an inflation. But if that reliability were lost, if people began to doubt whether the commercial paper, CDs, bankers' acceptances, and money market funds they had been counting on for liquidity would really pay off, there would be a mass attempt to acquire cash itself.

Of course, this attempt would be doomed to failure, since there would be no additional cash to be acquired. But the result of the attempt would be a deflationary convulsion, as people dumped inventories, investments, and other assets onto the market in a vain effort to sell more than they were buying.

We will now offer a scenario, a series of events, that could trigger such a rush to acquire money. Please understand that we are not *predicting* the future. We're only constructing a conceivable scenario in order to show that such a thing is possible—so that you won't ignore it when making investment decisions. Since the story is hypothetical, we give no dates; it might happen this year, ten years from now, or not at all.

ONCE UPON A TIME

As our story begins, price inflation has been rising for three years in its latest cycle, and has reached a level of 12%. The Federal Reserve's Open Market Committee is highly con-

CASH SUBSTITUTES OUTSTANDING
(in billions of dollars)

	Oct 1966	June 1980	% Change
Treasury bills	$ 62.3	$ 184.7	196.5%
Commercial Paper	13.0	123.9	850.1%
Bankers' Acceptances	3.4	54.4	1,518.7%
Large CDs	15.9	160.2[1]	908.3%
Totals	94.6	523.2	453.1%
Money Supply (M1b)	172.7	389.7	125.7%
Money Supply (M2)	474.9	1,587.0	234.2%

[1]September 1978 (latest date for which data is available for all banks).
Sources: *Federal Reserve Bulletins*, December 1966, pages 1792, 1803, 1807, 1812; August 1980, pages A13, A19, A25, A32.

cerned; it votes (9 to 3) to lower the growth rate of the money supply to 5% from 7%.

Three months later interest rates have risen sharply, and the stock market is in the doldrums. But the price inflation rate has continued to rise to 13½%, apparently immune to the money-tightening. The Fed votes (8 to 4) to lower the growth rate further, to 4% from 5%.

Three more months pass. Although price inflation continues to rise, the economy is feeling the pinch. Construction falls off, business inventories rise as products go unsold, there are large layoffs in the auto and steel industries, and other economic indicators flash recessionary signals. Interest rates continue to rise, and the stock market takes a sharp drop.

Members of the Fed's committee are concerned about a potential recession, but price inflation is now up to 15%. With great trepidation, the Open Market Committee votes (7 to 5) to lower the money growth rate to 3½% from 4%.

Over the next six months, the usual recessionary pattern unfolds—declining sales, rising inventories, more business failures, rising unemployment. The prime rate reaches 22%—no longer reflecting the demands of increasing business activity, but instead reflecting the need of many businesses to finance the inventories they are stuck with. The stock market is in a long, slow downward slide—reaching a level of 746 for the Dow Jones Industrial Average.

Then a large steelmaker reveals that it will go under if it doesn't receive help from the federal government—and it asks both for money and for protection against imports of foreign steel. The company pleads urgency, but the government is slow to make up its mind. With a large issue of commercial paper due for repayment, the company finally borrows enough from banks to make the repayment. But the company's credit rating has suffered too much to allow it to issue new paper.

The 12-month price inflation rate reaches 17% and then drops the next month to 16½%. Although the one-month decline isn't confirmation of a change in trend, the Fed takes it as a good sign and loosens its monetary restraint a little. But by this time, conditions have deteriorated badly. Economists say that the recession may be more severe than anticipated.

In Santa Barbara, a bank is bombed by a protest group

that blames a "banking conspiracy" for the high interest rates that are causing unemployment.

ROTORS

One day it is reported that American Rotor Co. has refused to take delivery of $20 million worth of rotor parts it had ordered from National Foundry Corp. Foundry insists that it has a firm, non-cancellable order from Rotor, and it wants its money.[4]

Each company's stock price takes a sharp drop. There is speculation over the reason for Rotor's refusal and its effect upon both companies. Pretty soon a rumor circulates that American Rotor won't accept the parts because its sales are down too far; it can't use the parts and it doesn't have the money to pay for them.

True or false, the rumor seems to make sense (since many manufacturers have large inventories they can't sell). The story is especially important because Rotor plans to issue $45 million in commercial paper the following week. The proceeds of the issue are to be used to pay off an older issue that matures the same week.

The rumors refuse to go away, and the new issue goes unsold. With doubts about Rotor's future, no one wants to take a chance on its commercial paper. Commercial paper is a cash substitute, not a speculation.

American Rotor finally arranges a bank loan that permits it to pay off the old commercial paper, and the financial markets breathe a sigh of relief.

Just days later, however, more bad news is reported. A consortium of Middle Eastern banks announces that it is pulling out of a deal to buy Western Lumber Company's timberland in Brazil. Western has to pay off $125 million in commercial paper next month, and the company had planned to do so with the down payment from the timber sale.

Coming on the heels of American Rotor's close call, there's a great deal of concern among bankers, corporate

---

[4]In this story, all company names are fictional, and all place names are purely for example.

treasurers, financial analysts, and individual investors. Will Western Lumber be able to pay off? In the resale market, its commercial paper begins trading at a 10% discount from face value.

Again at the eleventh hour, Western receives a loan from a group of New York banks—arranged with the help of the Federal Reserve. Again, a sigh of relief. The market has been spared a messy default, and some speculators have earned a quick 10% profit on the commercial paper.

From this point onward, every company finds it difficult to sell its commercial paper. The reputation of commercial paper as a safe cash substitute has been badly tarnished.

By now the stock market has slid to a Dow Jones of 710. But financial analysts forecast a new bull market just ahead. They point out that dividend rates are at all-time highs, price-earnings ratio are at record lows, stocks are selling at record discounts to book value, and the market has already assimilated and discounted all the bad news to come. There's nowhere to go but up. And, in fact, the Dow rallies to 745.

However, two more medium-sized companies get into trouble—finally defaulting on their commercial paper. Interest rates in general are now falling, but commercial paper is an exception. Rates on it are rising, reflecting a shift in demand away from riskier paper and toward cash substitutes that are still considered to be safe.

The general fall in interest rates seems to confirm the view that the bear market in stocks is over, and that the pressure for recession is easing. The unemployment rate is 9½%, but it is expected to begin falling soon.

But after two months of falling interest rates, the trend is reversed. Another cluster of defaults on commercial paper, combined with worsening economic news, has put new demands on the money markets.

Lower-grade companies have to offer higher interest rates to sell their commercial paper, but some issues go unsold even at the high rates. Disappointed issuers add to the demand for credit at banks. The prime rate, after falling to 18½% from its peak of 22%, moves back up to 20%.

Economists say that their recent estimates may have understated the severity of the recession.

There is no panic, no general dumping of commercial paper. But new issues are increasingly difficult to sell. And a lot of companies maneuver to arrange backup protection from banks—while some banks maneuver to renege on past promises of backup protection.

Other companies, unable to pay the high interest rates, try to raise cash by unloading inventories, laying off employees, and canceling orders for new equipment.

FED RESPONSE

The Federal Reserve watches all this with growing concern. The recession threatens to go beyond all other postwar recessions in severity. But the price inflation rate is still at 14½ % (down from its peak of 17%). There are arguments among members of the Open Market Committee—some believing that strong stimulative measures are needed, others worried that price inflation is still the greater danger.

Finally the Committee votes (7 to 5) to abandon its money growth targets completely. It steps up its purchases of government bonds in the open market—feeding new reserves into the banking system. In one step, it lowers the discount rate to 12% from 15%—to provide a public show of confidence, and to encourage commercial banks to borrow more from the Fed and make loans to their customers. With the discount rate now 5% below the prime rate, the Fed expects banks to borrow heavily. The Fed also lowers bank reserve requirements and repeals a number of anti-inflation measures it had imposed the previous year.

The announcement receives a mixed reaction. Some people feel reassured that the Fed won't let the situation get out of hand. Others suspect the Fed's unprecedented moves mean that the situation is unprecedentedly bad.

Whether or not the measures are appropriate, they still will require considerable time to affect the situation.

ESCALATION OF DEMAND

The following week the government of Nigeria and Iraq, citing the recent sharp fall in oil exports to the U.S., announce that they are suspending payments of principal and interest on debts to Western banks and governments. An emergency meeting is held at the World Bank to determine whether it will take over the suspended loans. The Bank agrees to do so.

A month later three large companies default on their commercial paper in the same week. The resale market for commercial paper becomes a shambles. Discounts of 15% from face value are offered by people wanting to unload—creating annual yields of over 40%. Many investors who had relied on commercial paper as a cash substitute sell out to speculators who hope to make money from the deep discounts.

The demand for money escalates, with two forces propelling it. As cash substitutes become unreliable, investors and businesses turn to money itself for liquidity. And for others, the turmoil in the economy creates a desire for the security that money alone provides. The money may have less purchasing power next year, but covering this year's needs is all that matters.

Throughout the country, businesses, banks, and individuals try to cut expenses, collect bills, reduce inventories, and build cash positions. The unemployment rate rises to 11% (a postwar high), the prime rate is back at 22%, defaults on commercial paper grow.

END OF A MARKET

Within two months no commercial paper is marketable. A $100 billion pool of cash substitutes no longer exists.

Banks holding commercial paper have to wipe much of it off the books. They attempt to call in loans in order to replenish their liquidity. Cuts are made in lines of credit, "ready reserve" overdraft facilities, and credit card limits. Loans "repayable on demand" are called; but, of course, no one borrows money in order to keep it handy for repayment on demand, and so there are defaults on bank loans.

Commercial paper had been created in response to a demand for liquidity. That demand hasn't disappeared. In fact, the atmosphere of uncertainty has heightened it. Investors fleeing the commercial-paper market are now more concerned about security than about earning high interest, and their choices are narrowed to Treasury bills and money itself.

TOO MANY SELLERS

Thousands of large businesses, which owned much of the commercial paper directly, and millions of individuals and small businesses, which owned the paper indirectly through money market funds, begin trying to adjust to the cash shortage. But their attempts are tragically similar—they all are trying to sell more than they buy.

Many businesses cancel orders they had placed with suppliers—and rush to ship orders to customers before the customers cancel. Some firms drag their feet in paying invoices, and press their customers for speedier payment—while the customers are dragging their own feet. Investment projects are suddenly scrapped and work forces are cut.

Most retailers launch aggressive advertising campaigns to reduce their swollen inventories. But shoppers, many of whom are out of work or afraid they soon will be, are reluctant to buy.

Individuals who had invested in money market funds tied to commercial paper dry their tears and cut back on unnecessary purchases, planning to accumulate enough cash to replace the liquidity that's been lost. They believe it will take no more than a few months of belt-tightening—provided nothing interferes with their regular income.

The number of houses for sale rises to two and then three times the normal level. Listings accumulate, prices drop, but no one buys.

MONEY SUPPLY INCREASE

The demand for money is growing, and the supply is growing too.

Over the past three months, the Fed has increased bank reserves at an annual rate of 25%, but is this fast enough? There's no way for the Fed to know. Because commercial paper was not a perfect substitute for cash, its disappearance hasn't raised the demand for money dollar-for-dollar. But how much has it raised the demand? 75 cents on the dollar? 50 cents on the dollar? Some other amount?

The Fed isn't free simply to double the U.S. supply of money overnight; to do so would cause tremendous price inflation. At the same time, a 5% increase obviously would be too little. But where in between the two extremes of 5% and 100% is the right rate? The persons in control will be held responsible publicly for the rest of their lives if they cause a disaster by going overboard in either direction. Arguments rage among the members of the Open Market Committee.

Lacking any clear measure of the increase in the demand for money, the Fed, as it turns out, makes an estimate that's too low, and the supply of money increases less than the demand for it. The economy is pointed into a deflation.

The following month, the Consumer Price Index actually falls by 1½%—the first absolute fall in the index since 1965—lowering the twelve-month inflation rate to 13%. The Commerce Department cites aggressive price-cutting by retailers as the cause.

The last of the government-guaranteed loans to the large steelmaker are paid out, and the company is assured of survival for at least another two years. Two other leading steelmakers appeal to the government as an alternative to bankruptcy. The President promises that any company with 50,000 or more employees will be protected.

The World Bank takes over more suspended loans of Third World countries—buying the loans from commercial banks, many of them in the U.S.

The stock market, its rally long since over, is down to 665—but it gets a lift. The feeling is growing that the governments of the world have drawn the line and won't let things get worse.

But a new rash of loan defaults—led by the governments of Brazil, Kenya, and Indonesia—are announced. These governments blame their troubles on the high interest rates they've had to pay to U.S. banks during the period of tight money. The World Bank appeals to member governments for more funds, but only the U.S. and German governments (whose commercial banks are the hardest hit) respond to the plea.

BANKS

The number of bank failures reaches a postwar high. But the failing banks are mostly smaller institutions, and the Federal Deposit Insurance Corporation (the government agency that insures bank deposits) has arranged orderly liquidations, with no losses to depositors.

Then a $7 billion bank with 120 branches goes under—after borrowing $3.5 billion from the Federal Reserve in the past year. Although the FDIC's financial resources seem adequate to the task, its administrative facilities are overwhelmed by the sheer size of the case. There are delays in sorting out the bank's liabilities and getting money to depositors.

The Federal Reserve governors, after working for a year to save the bank, are stunned by the defeat. At a Saturday meeting the governors decide that unlimited aid must be given to all banks. They instruct the twelve Federal Reserve Banks to inform all commercial bank managers by telephone that the "discount window" is wide open—meaning that the Fed will approve all requests by commercial banks for loans. The Fed also cuts reserve requirements.

The Federal Reserve Banks' staffs report on Sunday for the telephoning. Unfortunately, it is an inopportune time in some parts of the country. In Minnesota, for example, telephone lines have been knocked out by a blizzard—and go unrepaired because of a strike by telephone workers. They are protesting the layoff of 17% of the telephone company's employees.

For one reason or another, many bankers aren't reached on Sunday. That evening the Fed governors meet again to decide whether the instructions should be released to the press so that all bankers will be aware of them. The board decides (by a vote of 4 to 3) not to release the news—for fear of increasing public anxiety.

The next day three banks in Arizona have to close their doors because they can't satisfy public requests for currency.

The banks aren't insolvent, nor even illiquid by official standards, just short of the banknotes requested by depositors. One reason for the shortage is a truckers' strike that has delayed cash shipments from the Federal Reserve Bank branch in Los Angeles. Banknotes are flown in overnight, and the three banks open again the following day.

But news reports of the one-day closing cause the demand for banknotes to spread throughout the Southwest. Planes bring fresh banknotes from the Bureau of Engraving. But the governor of one state in the area declares a one-day banking holiday while awaiting the currency shipments.

The Treasury Department orders twenty-four-hour shifts at the engraving plant, and military planes are placed on alert to make sure the currency can be transported.

At a joint news conference, the chairman of the Federal Reserve System mentions over and over that there is absolutely no shortage of cash, nor are any banks unable to meet their commitments. And the FDIC's chairman, a little nervous his first time on television, reminds the nation that all insured deposits are safe.

For some reason this heightens anxiety rather than alleviating it. The demand for currency spreads, and lines form at banks everywhere. Most banks begin enforcing the requirement for 30-day notice for withdrawals from savings accounts.

PRICES & ECONOMIC INDICATORS

During this period, the price of gold—which had recently suffered a three-month drop—moves up quickly, reaching $525. It appears that gold is the third most desired asset—after banknotes and Treasury bills. The anxiety level in the world has risen considerably, and gold—the world's anxiety hedge and the only investment salable worldwide—has responded accordingly.

Unemployment is now at 15%—and bankruptcies, bank failures, and business failures are at all-time records.

The inflation rate, which had fallen last month to 13%, isn't reported this month. The employees of the U.S. Bureau of Labor Statistics have walked off their jobs—demanding their wages in cash. The Secretary of Commerce had refused, believing it would set a bad example and a bad precedent, and insisting that the Department's computer system couldn't handle a cash payroll.

The Dow Jones is at 560. Many economists estimate that the recession may be worse than had been reestimated.

FIGHTING BACK

Over the next few weeks, the currency shipments catch up with the demand, and the crisis blows over. The Dow Jones rallies to 590. Some of the security analysts still employed urge their clients to buy stocks now—near the bottom.

The government employees return to work, and new inflation figures are released. They show that the Consumer Price Index dropped by 4½% over the previous six weeks. Government economists say that the large drop is misleading and shouldn't be considered deflationary—since most of the drop came from falling oil and real estate prices. The twelve-month inflation rate is down to 9% from 13%.

Companies everywhere are slashing prices, trying to liquidate inventories and raise cash. It is reported that some union workers, in desperation, have secretly rebated part of their wages to their employers—so as not to be priced into unemployment. Others who have been laid off agree to work for less than the minimum wage.

The Justice Department vows to prosecute all companies that slash prices "unfairly" or that employ workers at less than the minimum wage. The tendency toward deflation is now obvious—and the government wants to stop it by propping up prices and wages. Congress cooperates by raising the minimum wage.

Despite official attempts to decree higher prices, bargains abound in all areas of the economy. Merchandise of all kinds is pressed on consumers at prices far below the wholesale prices of six months ago. Art works and precious stones that previously rated full-page photos in auction catalogs are offered at giveaway prices in personal and business bankruptcy sales. Recently minted silver commemoratives and other instant collectibles are sold in job lots for pennies on the dollar.

Bank financing disappears from the real estate market,

and distress sales become common as owners find they can no longer hold out for last year's prices. Seeing no reason to carry a property that is worth less than its mortgage, many investors simply walk away from their commitments. Lenders are stuck with hundreds of thousands of repossessions, and one Florida bank announces a half-price sale.

MORE BANKING PROBLEMS

A California bank, one of the state's largest, uses up the last of its liquid resources. It always has shown large amounts of Treasury bills and other liquid assets on its balance sheet, but most of those assets had been pledged to secure deposits by trust accounts. Now all the liquid assets that weren't tied up have been sold.

Various Federal banking agencies have been working with the bank for over a year to save it from failing. The Fed already has lent the bank over $4 billion. The Fed governors meet in all-night session to decide what to do. The bank's remaining assets are illiquid—consumer loans, mortgages, participations in companies, loans to Third World governments, etc.—and a majority of them are of doubtful value.

The Fed decides to keep the bank afloat—afraid of the shock its failure would cause. The problem is kept secret.

But two days later the story is leaked to the press by an officer of the bank who is bitter because his company stock option has become worthless. The bank is hit by a wave of deposit withdrawals.

Up to this time, the President hasn't addressed the nation on the crisis for fear of raising further doubts, although he has made reassuring remarks at press conferences and through spokesmen. But he finally gives in and delivers a fireside chat on television—hoping to repeat the success of last year's heart-to-heart talk about inflation.

He says there is no shortage of cash and no chance that bank depositors could lose money. He reminds them that the Federal Deposit Insurance Corporation will make good on all bank deposits. And he advises people to put their cash back into the banks where it can help to get America moving again.

He also reveals that he will ask Congress for an emergency package of $200 billion in various kinds of projects to supply the jobs that are needed—since the unemployment rate is now at 18%.

The stock market rallies 17 points the next morning. Commodity prices are unchanged for the day, after two months of steady decline.

NEW TROUBLE

A week later two Federal Reserve computers—in different parts of the country—are destroyed by bombs. The Fed has employed every security device available to prevent such a thing, but still it happens. An investigation is promised. Credit for the bombing is claimed by the People's Anti-Bank League and Union of Militants (PABLUM)—a Trotskyite splinter group.

Operations in two Federal Reserve districts are brought to a halt while backup systems are activated. Meanwhile, there are no records of the Reserve Banks' dealings with commercial banks. The Fed governors order the Reserve Banks to give the commercial banks whatever they need and sort out the problems later.

With the computer explosions, the Dow Jones falls through the 500 level. Commodity prices tumble; some are down 60% from last year. Trading on the futures exchanges is halted because price limits are days behind the cash prices. A number of large commodity investors fail to meet margin calls, the contracts can't be sold, and three brokerage houses go under. Gold is at $725.

The Bureau of Labor Statistics, unable to keep up with the volatile situation, issues a preliminary estimate—showing a one-month fall in the Consumer Price Index of 9%, bringing the twelve-month inflation rate down to 3%. It also estimates an unemployment rate of 24%.

Economists say there is no way to foresee how deep the recession will be. "We're not prophets, and we've never claimed to be," insists a spokesman for the Charles River Institute. "All we do is delimit the parameters."

85

Congress finally approves the President's emergency fiscal package. But of course it will be months before any of the money reaches the public.

At a meeting with auditors from the Fed, the large California bank reveals that it will need at least $4 billion more over the next month to meet withdrawal demands. In addition, the Fed estimates that the nation's largest banks will require, collectively, about $40 billion in the same period.

The California bank, with 235 branches, is forced to close its doors. There's no way it can be rescued. The demand for banknotes intensifies, and the panic spreads throughout the U.S. Riots occur in bank lobbies and in streets in front of banks.

In three days, the Dow Jones plunges 74 points, dropping to 416. The price of gold reaches $925.

THE RESCUE

The President spends the weekend at Camp David, consulting with a parade of public figures—among whom are the Fed chairman, the Secretary of the Treasury, Ralph Nader, Coretta King, Sheikh Yussaf (now the largest landowner in the U.S.), Robert Redford, the Supreme Leader of PABLUM, Harold Stassen, and Richard Nixon.

On Monday evening the President addresses the nation on television again. He says that an unreasoning fear, completely unfounded, has taken over the country. But he announces that the worst is soon to be over—because of what he is about to do.

He announces that federal troops will enforce martial law in every large city. He is also closing all banks, stock exchanges, and commodity markets in the U.S. for one week, to neutralize the panic.

And he says that emergency plans are being activated to distribute food and vouchers so that life and commerce can go on during the week.

At the close of his address, he acknowledges that this recession has been quite severe—due to drops in the oil price, an unusually warm winter, and the boycotting of the Cape Town Olympics. But he reminds us how fortunate we are that the government is equipped to prevent a depression such as that which struck the country in the 1930s.

The next day the Bureau of Labor Statistics announces that the Consumer Price Index fell by another 8% last month. The twelve-month change is now minus 4% and dropping.

As it turns out, it is three weeks (rather than one) before the banks reopen. And then only about half the nation's banks remain. The rest are hopelessly insolvent, partly because of overwhelming debts to the Federal Reserve System.

When the stock exchanges reopen, the Dow Jones is at 275.

FDIC

Among the failed banks are seven of the nation's fifteen largest. Three of them each have net liabilities that are greater than the total resources of the Federal Deposit Insurance Corporation.

Congress votes a loan to the FDIC of $140 billion (15 times its total assets) to meet its obligations at failed banks. But this, a compromise measure, is $93 billion short of what the FDIC needs.

Congress also authorizes the FDIC to give preference to claims from depositors who are economically disadvantaged, and to determine what percentage of claims will be paid to "unneedy" depositors. There is another provision that depositors who don't receive cash will receive special, unmarketable, 25-year government bonds for what is due them.

The stock market begins to rise, the price of gold falls by 50% over the next two months, commodity prices move up cautiously, and the long-term cycle begins anew.

And, three months later, the Federal food stamps and vouchers arrive in the cities.

WHAT WILL HAPPEN?

Is this what will happen? Perhaps not.

The scenario is not an attempt to predict the future. If any event we've included should occur, it isn't a signal that the rest will follow. Some of the things we've described may happen (and, in fact, have already happened) without the house of cards tumbling. There is no signal that will tell you the train of events is irreversibly in motion.

If the Great Deflation does occur, it might be triggered by a different set of circumstances from those in our story. And the deflation would differ in many ways from what we've described—so it would be a mistake to try to use our scenario as a roadmap. Many of the events we've mentioned—political, economic, and social—are included merely to point out that they are possible.

The important point is that it *can* happen. We can't tell you the way it will occur—or even that it's inevitable. But we'd like you to realize that the slogan "the politicians won't let it happen" is no protection. We've tried to show that economic events can sweep away inflationary expectations and political intentions.

Economists and investment advisors arc often asked to predict the future. Supposedly, the one who predicts most accurately will be the most profitable for his clients. In fact, no one can predict the future.

What a good investment advisor can do is point out possibilities that his clients have overlooked, or show that some widely expected event has little or no chance of occurring. This information can help his clients prepare more realistically —not for a certain future, but for potential events that could hurt or help them. Our scenario is an attempt to show what can happen, to caution you not to take inflation for granted.

You can't protect yourself with the belief that you know the future or that you'll recognize what's happening before it's too late. You can protect yourself only with a balanced portfolio that allows for what can't be foreseen.

PART II

INVESTMENT PRINCIPLES

5

DEALING WITH UNCERTAINTY

IT'S EASY TO THINK THAT YOU KNOW WHAT THE FUTURE holds—whether inflation will rise or fall, which investments will do well and which poorly, what the political shape of America will be in five years.

But the future invariably contradicts our expectations in some way. Often you can be right in your general expectations, but wrong about the specifics—so that the investments you bet on don't work out.

Over and over again we are proven wrong when we bet too much on our expectations, and yet each time we're tempted to believe we've found a sure thing. But sure things don't exist in the real world. Every economic event results from the motivations and actions of literally billions of people. To assume that you can predict what all those people will do is not only presumptuous, it is dangerous.

There is no way you can eliminate uncertainty or obtain a private line to the future. You have to let the future unfold as it will. Uncertainty is a fact of life.

However, you do have expectations; you believe that some things are more likely to happen than others. It would be foolish to treat those expectations as certainties, but it would be equally foolish to ignore them—since disregarding them would leave you exposed to the dangers you see and unable to profit from what you believe will happen.

Uncertainty doesn't mean that you know nothing at all, that your opinions have no merit, or that you are helpless to prepare for the future. It does mean that you should allow for surprises—never taking anything for granted and never treating an investment as a sure thing.

INVESTMENT ADVISORS

If you recognize your own inability to predict the future, you may be tempted to put your financial affairs in the hands of someone who seems to know more. This can cause problems of its own.

Every investor's situation is different in some way, and no advisor can understand yours completely. To some degree or other, he will suggest that you take too many risks—or too few—and place you in a position you don't find comfortable. You also may find that the advisor whom you chose for his perfect record will lose his touch as soon as you begin following his advice.

And the investment advisor has objectives of his own that can get in the way of yours. Because his goals are different from yours, he may be under too much pressure to produce quick results or under no pressure to succeed at all.

At one end of the spectrum is the advisor who is in a hurry to achieve spectacular profits. Most newsletter writers feel this way because so many of their readers are short-term trial subscribers who need to be convinced that they've found someone special. The writer wants to come up with something big—and right now, before the current batch of trial subscriptions expire.

Because the only way to achieve quick, visible results is to take big risks, a good share of the investments he recommends won't work out. But the advisor assumes that if he's right only part of the time, he'll keep enough subscribers to make his publication profitable. Unfortunately, the mistaken investments may be so costly that being right part of the time won't make up for the losses.

At the other end of the spectrum is the advisor whose only standard is to avoid doing anything unconventional. A bank trust officer is often in this position. A man dies, and the bank is asked to manage his estate for his widow, who knows little about investing. It is important, to reassure the widow, that the trust officer not do anything that *appears* risky—which in practice means he must put everything into high-grade bonds and blue-chip stocks.

The advisor won't be faulted if he loses money on these "first class" investments. Those losses can be blamed on poor economic conditions, Russians in Afghanistan, or some other excuse. But he could be fired (and the bank sued) if he loses money fooling around with gold or anything else unusual. So he plays it safe—but safe for his job, not for the portfolio.

Not all investment advisors are hampered by conflicts of interest. You may find an advisor whose efforts to help you are genuine. But you won't find anyone who can be responsible for your future—someone who understands exactly what you need and can provide precisely for your circumstances, and who has no objectives of his own to consider.

Advisor's Role

Still, you can't be an expert in everything. And there are many matters in which you rely on the experience and intelligence of others. So why can't you get outside help with your investments? You can, if you know what to expect from an advisor and what to demand of yourself.

Once you define the circumstances of your own life—by identifying your objectives and expectations, and by deciding on the risks you're willing to take—an investment advisor can be a big help. His experience should help him identify risks you've overlooked and alternatives you weren't aware of.

He can help you create a plan that aims at your objectives without taking avoidable risks. The eventual result may not be the 10,000% gain you originally imagined, but you'll probably sleep more easily—especially when some of the risks he identified turn into realities.

Even with his help, the main burden still falls on you—to be truthful with yourself about your abilities and your attitudes, and to be realistic about your objectives in view of the time and energy you can devote to investments. The job of investing your money is yours alone; there's no way to get rid of it.

RESPONSIBILITIES

Basically, your job is twofold:

1. You need to understand the general forces at work in the world. With this understanding, you are less likely to be surprised by what happens. And you'll have a sense of the probable, which can help you ignore fashionable opinion when it is wise to do so. As long as you distinguish between expecting and predicting, your understanding will save you from many costly mistakes.

2. You need to arrange your economic affairs in a way that reflects your expectations but, at the same time, allows for the possibility you're wrong. In other words, you should hedge against your main investments—so that the inevitable surprises won't be catastrophic.

To make money on your investments, it isn't necessary to know the future. It *is* necessary to base your opinions upon understanding—not upon hope or wishful thinking. And it is necessary to have an investment program that is realistic, that relies only on what you're actually able to do—not on what might be profitable if we were all as clever as we wish we were.

HEDGES

The next two parts of the book will discuss specific investments. We'll explain how each one works, the uses to which it can be put, and how it might perform in various circumstances.

We know that some of the investments are unattractive when viewed in isolation, and we're not going to suggest later that all of them belong in your portfolio.

But an investment shouldn't be evaluated as though you were going to put all your money into it. An investment that is unattractive by itself might be just right for a small part of your portfolio—as the counterpoint to a risky situation you're in now, or as part of a low-risk strategy for reducing taxes.

It is easy to discard an investment possibility because of its obvious problems. For example, a security that promises to pay you a fixed number of dollars in the future seems ill-suited for a world of rising inflation. And yet the security may have its uses. It might be the most appropriate hedge against deflation or the perfect balance to investments you own that are weighted too much in the other direction.

In addition, if the interest from a dollar investment can be protected from taxes, the investment will have a good chance to maintain most of its purchasing power—even when inflation is running at a high rate. Thus, while inflation continues, the dollar investment provides low-cost protection against deflation. Part Five will offer several ways that investment income can be sheltered from taxes, so we don't believe that dollar investments should be rejected out of hand.

No investment is good or bad by itself. It must be placed in the context of who you are, the circumstances of your life, and what you want to accomplish. And it must be evaluated as a companion to the other things you own. As we'll mention many times, it is the result for the *portfolio* that matters, not the result for any single investment it contains.

DIVERSITY

After we have surveyed the investments, we'll offer tools with which you can build a portfolio that matches your opinions about the future and your attitude toward risk. One of the tools is diversity.

We are going to try to dissuade you from betting everything you have on the one investment you think will do best. We'll encourage you to add the second best and the third best. Not only that, we'll encourage you to put a little money into things you expect to do poorly. This isn't because we want you to lose the money, but because we want you to respect uncertainty.

If the portfolio is properly constructed, you'll probably do quite well over the next decade. If your "best" investment proves out, you'll profit—although by a smaller amount than if you had bet everything on it.

If your favorite turns out to have been ill-chosen, the right portfolio should allow you to hang on to what you started with—perhaps a little more, perhaps a little less—so you won't have to begin your financial life all over again.

RISK & OPPORTUNITY

It is impossible to avoid risk completely. But you can decide how much risk you're willing to tolerate for how much opportunity.

Each person's motivation is different. The 60-year-old man with $12,000,000 who wants to protect his fortune for his children needs one kind of plan; the 28-year-old man with $12,000 and the desire to retire at age forty needs another. For these two people to adopt the same investment stance would be a mistake for at least one of them.

The extent to which you balance your portfolio against risk is a personal choice. You might make safety your only goal, so that whatever comes won't hurt you—even though you know you won't make much of a profit. Or you might ignore safety and try for the greatest profit possible.

There is a wide range between these two extremes. It's up to you to decide where to position yourself within that range

If you choose a portfolio that's too risky for you, you'll worry about it constantly. But you'll be just as uncomfortable if you choose a portfolio that's too safe for your taste; then you'll accuse yourself of letting timidity stand between you and riches.

An even more common mistake is not choosing at all—simply drifting with what you have or accepting whatever is offered to you, because you don't have a clear idea of the alternatives. This mistake is the most wasteful of all, because the neglected alternatives may include ways to reduce risk without lessening your opportunity for profit, or ways to increase your opportunity for profit without taking on more risk.

As we'll discuss in Part Six, there's a method for finding the right balance—the right place on the risk-opportunity spectrum. But be aware now that the choice is solely yours. No decision, no single portfolio, is "right" for everyone.

INFLATION'S FUTURE

We tried to make it clear in the last part that we don't know how the inflationary era will end.

Our understanding of economics provides little hope that inflation will disappear magically with the coming of wage and price controls, a balanced budget, lower oil prices, changes in human nature, WIN buttons, slogans, or the tooth fairy. The other possible endings we've discussed are harder to rule out —but none of them is a certainty.

We want you to be prepared for all the possibilities because we believe that neither you nor we can know for sure how all this will end. Even if your opinion about how inflation will end is generally correct, it could be wrong about many critical details.

For example, inflation might fool us by flirting with one alternative for a while before settling on another. We could go through a bone-crushing deflation, during which the Fed printed so much money as an antidote that it led to runaway inflation. The man who bet all he had on runaway inflation would be proven correct, but he'd be wiped out before he had a chance to crow.

So as we examine each investment, we'll be concerned about all five possibilities—that inflation:

1. will level off at some rate and stay there;
2. will continue to rise slowly, just as it has for the past twenty years;
3. will speed up and culminate in runaway inflation;
4. will ease down gently in an unpleasant but not violent conclusion; or
5. will fall violently toward a deflationary depression.

We're not completely agnostic about the future. We think possibility #1 is very remote. And we feel that possibilities #2, #3, and #5 are the most likely for the next ten years— and are also the possibilities that need the most creative portfolio planning.

Now we're ready to examine the menu of investments. We hope you choose a balanced diet.

PART III

EQUITY
INVESTMENTS

6
GOLD

By 1970 it was clear to many investors that the U.S. economy was in trouble. They saw little hope for such traditional investments as stocks, bonds, and savings accounts— and they felt a need for something out of the ordinary to get them through the years ahead.

Three investments seemed especially suited to the times. They were the "hard-money" investments, as they are commonly called—gold, silver, and the Swiss franc. Each one seemed capable of profiting from deteriorating economic conditions. And in case the economy revived, each one offered a special reason to expect dramatic profits—a long history of government price suppression that appeared to be close to an end.

During the 1970s, the price suppression did come to an end, and all three investments paid off for those who bet on them. Gold rose by 1,389%—from $35.20 to $524 per ounce. Silver appreciated by 1,699%—from $1.79 to $32.20 per ounce. And the Swiss franc rose by 172%—from $.2320 to $.6305 per franc.[1]

Investors who bought these assets early had a good thing. But many people discover a good thing only after it has run its course. Because they don't understand the reasons for the past, they mistakenly expect the future to replay it.

---

[1]The increases are from December 31, 1969, to December 31, 1979. The gold and silver prices are the London afternoon fixings, and the Swiss franc prices are the Swiss National Bank's daily quotes. Gold and silver moved higher in 1980 before dropping.

The 1970s were turbulent years, and most investors assume that the hard-money investments rose only because of that turbulence. Because the 1980s seem to be no calmer, they expect the hard-money investments to repeat their spectacular performances.

PRICE CONTROLS

It's obvious that the economic worries of the 1970s contributed to the demand for hard assets. But the primary cause of the spectacular price increases was the collapse of the government's efforts to control the prices of precious metals and foreign currencies.

By 1970 each of the three investments had been the object of many years of government price control. Gold's price had been fixed at $35.00 per ounce since 1934; the Swiss franc had been fixed at $.2320 since 1940; and the U.S. government had been fixing the price of silver one way or another since 1878—as recently as 1967 at $1.29 per ounce.

When any long-standing effort to control a price ends, the price can be expected to move rapidly to make up for lost time. The prices of the hard-money investments had been suppressed for so many years that they were ready to explode. And they did. Ironically, the government's intervention had created enormous profits in the very investments it had tried to suppress.

Because of their special circumstances, the three investments—gold, silver, and the Swiss franc—served investors very well. We only wish we had something as simple and high-powered to offer today. But, unfortunately, we can't count on the hard-money investments to be as profitable as they were in the 1970s. The explosive consequences of price control are over, and so we have to look at each investment anew—to see what purpose it might serve now.

We believe that each of the three still has something to offer—even if it's not the once-in-a-generation opportunity of ten years ago. Gold is the premier hedge against uncertainty and chaos. Silver, at $10 to $20 per ounce, may not yet be at its ultimate price goal. And the Swiss franc offers a special role in a safe portfolio for as long as Switzerland perseveres in its policy of monetary restraint.

But we have to look at each of the investments individually; they are not simply three forms of the same thing. This chapter and the next two examine the three investments, beginning with gold.

GOLD & EMOTIONS

Gold has evoked a great deal of emotion during the past decade. To some people, gold is almost a religion. And, perhaps in reaction to that religious fervor, other people find gold somehow to be odious; they wouldn't buy it if it were recommended by a burning bush.

Some of the strong feeling is caused by a confusion of two issues concerning gold, issues that should be considered separately: (1) Should gold be the basis of the nation's monetary system? and (2) Is gold a good investment?

Whether the nation needs a gold standard to save its currency is an important economic question, but the answer doesn't tell you whether you should own gold personally. How best to assure your own financial survival is a different question entirely. You are likely to come up with the wrong answers if you fail to distinguish between the two questions.[2]

If you overload your portfolio with gold as an act of faith, you may jeopardize your financial security without advancing the "cause" of gold one step. Or if you adamantly refuse to consider gold as an investment, you will forego a valuable balancing element for your portfolio—without proving a thing about gold and the monetary system.

In either case, the investment slogans and clichés will provide neither wisdom nor profit. A goldbug slogan such as "Only hard money will survive the hard times" tells you noth-

---

[2]In fact, the authors of this book differ on the gold-standard question; but each of us believes that gold is an essential element in a balanced portfolio.

ing about how much gold you should have or how to plan for the bear markets gold buyers must endure. (Was gold the investment to have during the hard times of 1935 to 1945?) The insight that "gold pays no dividends or interest" is equally useless (many stock and insurance policies pay no dividends). And the cliché "you can't eat gold" is persuasive only to the gourmet investor who has mastered the art of sautéing stock and bond certificates.

Whatever your ideological attitude, you should consider gold in the same way you would consider any other investment. Think about your own welfare, not about the "great issues" of the day. If gold makes sense as an investment, you should buy the amount that's necessary for proper portfolio balance—no more, no less.

PROMISES & GOLD

The key to gold's role as an investment has to do with the promises by which we live.

Most of what people think of as investments are pieces of paper with promises written on them. Such things as stocks, bonds, bank deposits, and insurance policies are merely claims on someone else—claims that may or may not be honored.

Paper claims can be good investments in a society where promises are kept. But the claims lose value if the breaking of promises becomes routine—either because of an inability to pay or a desire to cheat.

Unless you've been hurt personally, it may be hard to realize that paper claims are no longer as secure as they were twenty years ago. The chance of a large corporation being regulated out of business, the possibility that a famous-name company will repudiate its debts, the idea that the money you deposited in a bank has already been lost—all these disappointments are much more likely now than they were a generation ago.

Today paper claims are not enough for financial security; something impersonal and independent is needed. The virtue of gold is that its value doesn't depend on anyone's promise. It is the security of last resort.

104

Portfolio Purposes

In a time of uncertainty, this security provides two reasons for having gold in your portfolio.

The first reason is your own immediate protection. If the conditions around you become chaotic, gold's self-sufficiency will be directly and immediately important to you. Gold is portable, divisible, and easily recognized—so you can take it anywhere and spend it anywhere. It is the one form of money that's accepted worldwide.

Because of this, gold tends to appreciate when most other investments are turning sour—which is the second reason for including it in your portfolio. When paper currencies seem threatened by inflation, when an economy is heading into a depression, when governments are confiscating property or threatening war, people look to gold.

Even if the turmoil doesn't touch you, the gold price will be pushed upward by people who *are* affected or who fear that they might be. Because gold is the security of last resort, the demand for gold increases when economic, political, or social conditions deteriorate.

Thus gold in a portfolio is a balance to assets that depend on stable conditions—as well as a profit-making opportunity in a world of growing uncertainty.[3]

GOLD'S FUTURE

Gold responded to the turmoil of the 1970s, and it will respond to the turmoil of the 1980s. However, the long-term bull market in gold got off to an especially fast start because of the preceding years of price control. Gold's appreciation probably won't be as rapid during the 1980s, although there will be plenty of excitement.

We need to remember that the effects of price control are over; gold no longer offers the luxury of an investment on

---

[3]A more detailed explanation of why gold behaves this way is given in chapter 15 of *New Profits from the Monetary Crisis*, described in the Suggested Reading on page 515.

which the government has rigged the odds in the buyer's favor. From here on, gold will rise or fall in response to the turmoil of the day.

And it is turmoil itself that matters for gold, not inflation. Gold's response to inflation is particularly strong because inflation imperils the other haven from uncertainty—cash. But gold responds also to political upheaval, bad economic conditions, social chaos, war—almost any type of ugly headline.

The gold market is worldwide. The U.S. economy and investment markets are the world's largest, but they aren't the only ones. It would be a mistake to assume that every gold buyer in the world makes his decisions with one eye on the U.S. inflation rate. Gold has already appreciated by many times the amount of U.S. inflation—a phenomenon that seems strange only if you think of gold as purely an inflation hedge.

The long-term path of gold is pointed upward because there will be no shortage of disorder in the years ahead. The chance of an orderly retreat from the world's economic and political problems is small.

Possibilities

U.S. inflation is only one factor affecting gold, but we can examine the effect that each of the five inflation possibilities would have on gold—as long as we realize that other events also will influence the gold price.

1. *Constant inflation:* If inflation levels off and remains at a somewhat constant rate, gold will continue to run ahead of inflation for a while, as more inflation victims become buyers. But then gold should slow down and rise only along with prices in general.

2. *Rising inflation:* A continuation of the present gradual long-term rise in inflation would be symptomatic of the worsening economic problems that feed the demand for gold. The gold price should continue as it has been—rising in dramatic waves and then falling partway back.

3. *Runaway inflation:* If inflation speeds up and culminates in runaway inflation, holding gold will be even more profitable and important than it has been. The chaos alone

would increase the demand for gold. In addition, gold might become society's primary money, adding still further to the demand.

4. *Soft landing:* A soft landing from inflation (not just an attempt, but a success) would be the worst possibility for gold. The price would recover briefly whenever the landing got a little bumpy. But once the soft landing seemed headed for success, the prosperity visible ahead would undercut the demand for a hedge against bad times. Unless the world were faced with severe non-economic problems, the price of gold should fall drastically—perhaps by 60% or 80% from its high.

5. *Deflation:* A sudden deflation is more than just falling prices; it introduces uncertainty, social upheaval, the possibility that rapid inflation will be imposed as a cure, the prospect of war as a politician's device for distracting the country, and a number of other reasons for wanting a portable form of wealth. Gold would profit from these fears. But once the disorder began to wane, the price of gold would chase other prices down.

Gold and the rest of your portfolio might offset each other, in terms of purchasing power, through both stages of the deflation. But Treasury bills are a more efficient deflation hedge; they would profit from a fall in consumer prices, but would not decline after fear had reached its peak.

GOLD CYCLES

Gold is no longer responding to the past—trying to overcome the effects of 34 years of price control. From here on, the price of gold will be reacting to the events of the present. And one feature of the present is the extreme swings between optimism and pessimism that chronic inflation induces.

In 1974 it was difficult for many people to see how the U.S. would survive the bank failures, bankruptcies, high interest rates, unemployment, unending inflation, and falling stock prices. But by 1976 many of those same people were wondering what all the worry had been about. Then came 1979 and 1980 and a renewal of pessimism.

Someday the bottom may actually fall out—and we can't

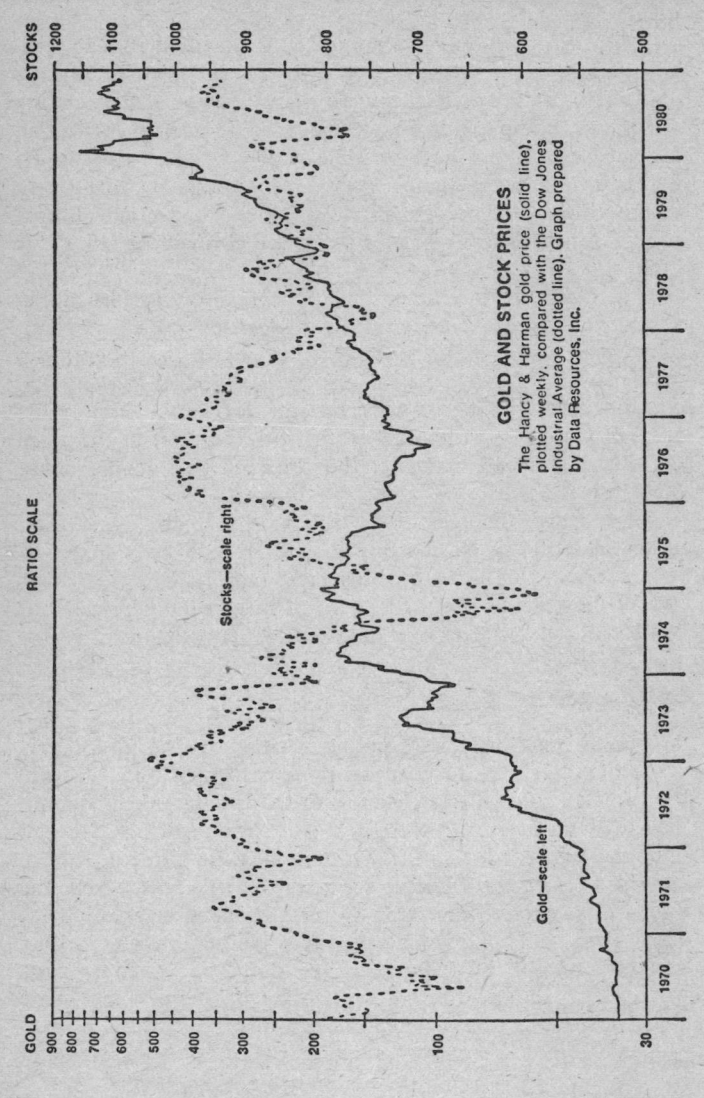

GOLD AND STOCK PRICES

The Hancy & Harman gold price (solid line),
plotted weekly, compared with the Dow Jones
Industrial Average (dotted line). Graph prepared
by Data Resources, Inc.

STOCKS

1200
1100
1000
900
800
700
600
500

RATIO SCALE

Stocks—scale right

Gold—scale left

GOLD

900
800
700
600
500
400
300
200
100
30

1970 1971 1972 1973 1974 1975 1976 1977 1978 1979 1980

tell you when that might be. But unless and until it happens, the swings will continue. By 1982 a new boom may be on, with the stock market humming and the country apparently prosperous once again. If so, gold again will be thought of as yesterday's mania. But then the boom will pass, pessimism will return, and gold will revive and go to still higher levels.

The boom-bust cycles are illustrated in the graph on page 108. It compares the price of gold with the U.S. stock market (measured by the Dow Jones Industrial Average) since 1970.

From day to day, or even week to week, the two investments have no set relationship. But over longer periods, the two paths move in opposite directions. The stock market rises when confidence reigns; it falls when bad news prevails. And because the world looks to the U.S. for economic leadership, gold moves in the opposite direction; it thrives when confidence deteriorates, and falls when conditions appear to be improving.

These cycles are one reason not to put all your wealth into gold. You can never be sure you're not buying at a temporary top—or that you won't need to sell some gold at a temporary bottom. The difference between a top and a bottom can be dramatic; the price of gold dropped from $850 on January 21, 1980, to $474 on March 18, 1980—a decline of 44% in 63 days.

Even if you intend to hold the gold for ten years, the swings can produce a great deal of worry—making it impossible for you to relax and ignore your investments. Security isn't achieved with a portfolio that rises and falls by 50% within a year; that's more excitement than most people want.

On the other hand, a portfolio without gold is vulnerable; it has no anchor in a sea of uncertainty. It is a portfolio of promises.

Properly used, gold provides stability for a portfolio, because the swings in gold usually are counterparts to opposing swings in other investments. During periods of bad news, the appreciation in gold offsets the depreciation of conventional investments. This allows you to ignore the economy's problems and concentrate on your own life.

But your portfolio doesn't have to be neutral. Our suggestions in Part Six will help you tilt your portfolio in favor of gold (if that's how you want it to tilt) without being hurt badly if you're wrong.[4]

GOLD INVESTMENTS

There are a number of ways by which people take positions in gold. In our view, however, the purpose of gold in your portfolio narrows the good choices to just two possibilities—gold coins and gold bullion.

Gold Coins

There are a number of coins, known as bullion coins, that sell for little more than the value of the gold they contain. The coin is simply a convenient way of packaging gold. For one thing, it makes the gold immediately recognizable, so that it doesn't have to be assayed.

The excess of a coin's price over the current value of the gold in the coin is called the *premium,* and it reflects the value of the packaging. The premium varies from day to day, and it could go down after you buy the coin, just as the price of gold itself could go down. But the premium is not a commission or brokerage cost. When you sell the coin, the packaging will be intact, and you'll collect whatever the market thinks it is worth—perhaps more than you paid, perhaps less.

Because premiums fluctuate, it is wise to buy only the low-premium bullion coins—so that your investment is in gold and not in the premium. The table on page 112 lists the names and characteristics of a number of bullion coins. The Krugerrand is currently the best known and the most widely traded gold coin in the world.

Bullion coins can be purchased from a coin dealer. Four dealers that sell through the mail are listed on page 474.

---

[4]And on page 192, we will show how you can make a smaller investment in stocks than you do in gold, but still profit enough from a rise in stocks to offset most of any loss in your gold investment. On the other hand, if gold rises, you'll make more on the gold than you lose on the stocks.

There are many other dealers, probably some listed in the Yellow Pages of your city.

Prices vary widely from dealer to dealer and from day to day. So when you're ready to buy, we suggest that you spend a little time on the telephone to get prices from more than one dealer.

Control of Coins

We think it's important that you buy and hold the coins in a way that fits their purpose in your portfolio. They are meant to be a buffer against almost anything that might happen, since they will appreciate in the same conditions of social and economic disorder that might destroy the value of other things you own. And if the usual channels of commerce break down, the coins might be the only marketable asset you own.

In such conditions, no one's promise would be worth much. And we would expect the government to abandon whatever is left of its self-restraint—confiscating anything and everything in sight. So it's important that at least some of the coins be where they can't be taken from you—and, if possible, that their existence not be known to anyone but you.

This means, first of all, buying them with cash, over the counter. Coin dealers are used to receiving large amounts of currency without asking questions. They are not legally required to obtain your name or report the transaction.[5]

No one has to know that you own the coins. You're breaking no laws by doing this, since there are no taxes for you to report or pay until you sell the coins. To further your privacy, you can obtain several receipts when you buy the coins, each receipt covering a few of the coins purchased. Whenever you sell a few coins, you can report the transaction on your income tax return—with a supporting receipt that doesn't point to the other coins you own.

---

[5]However, some dealers have interpreted the Bank Secrecy Act as requiring them to report cash transactions of over $10,000, so you may want to ask each dealer what his policy is.

BULLION COINS
(Gold coins priced close to the value of the gold they contain)

Coin	Ounces of Fine Gold	Price Oct. 22 1980	Price per Gold Ounce	Premium
South African Krugerrand— 1 ounce	1.00000	$680.00	$680.00	3.0%
South African Krugerrand— 1/2 ounce	.50000	352.16	704.32	6.7%
South African Krugerrand— 1/4 ounce	.25000	179.07	716.28	8.5%
South African Krugerrand— 1/10 ounce	.10000	73.22	732.20	10.9%
South African 2 Rand	.23541	165.87	704.59	6.8%
Canadian Maple Leaf	1.00000	678.00	678.00	2.7%
Austrian 100 Kronen "Corona"	.98018	646.00	659.06	-0.1%
Mexican 50 Pesos "Centenario"	1.20565	823.00	682.62	3.4%
British Sovereign (new)	.23541	167.50	711.52	7.8%
Netherlands 10 Guilders	.19445	135.00	694.27	5.2%
German 20 Marks	.23046	158.00	685.59	3.9%
Gold Bullion			**$660.00 per ounce**	

"Ounces of fine gold" is the weight of pure gold in the coin, and (except for the Canadian Maple Leaf) is less than the gross weight. The "Premium" is the amount by which the coin's retail price on October 22, 1980, exceeded the value of the gold contained in the coin. Premiums fluctuate from day to day, but the premiums for these coins are likely to remain in the general range shown. "Price Oct. 22, 1980" is the price on October 22, 1980, at Bank Leu, Zurich—except for the fractional South African coins, which are prices for the same day from Monex International, Newport Beach, Calif., and have been adjusted slightly to conform to the bullion price prevailing at Bank Leu. Figures may not agree because of rounding.

NUMISMATIC COINS

The following coins are valued for their rarity, and should not be purchased as gold investments because the premiums can rise or fall dramatically. The premium is shown in parentheses.

United States Double Eagle (20.7%)
Soviet Union Chervonetz (15.9%)
British Sovereign (old) (21.6%)
Swiss 20 Francs "Vreneli" (16.8%)

Belgian 20 Francs "Lator" (13.4%)
French 20 Francs "Napoleon" (37.7%)
Italian 20 Lira "Lator" (25.0%)
Swiss 10 Francs "Vreneli" (78.1%)

Second, store the coins yourself—in or near your home, or in a safe-deposit box. Coins stored with a dealer or in a bank vault would be an easy mark for government confiscation during a war or, perhaps, following the Economic Stabilization Act of 1982 or the Anti-Inflation Program of 1984.

For at least some of your gold coins, it is important that you not be dependent on anyone's goodwill. Acting privately and retaining control over the coins may turn out to be as important as your decision to buy them at all.

Gold Bullion or More Coins

However, there's more to owning gold than just protection against the worst possibilities. Gold also offers balance and profit potential to a portfolio. You don't have to keep close at hand anything beyond the coins you might need for an extreme emergency. And there's a limit to how many coins you can keep yourself without worrying about theft.

So if your portfolio calls for more gold than a small coin budget, the additional amount should be kept at a Swiss bank (to be discussed in Chapter 9) where it, too, will be safe from private theft and government confiscation.

This additional gold can be either bullion (bars of gold) or more coins. Bullion doesn't have to be assayed to be resold if it is left in storage with the bank. However, coins have the advantage of coming in small units—which allows you to buy or sell exactly the amount you want. The smallest bar of gold that carries no premium is one kilogram (32.15 ounces).

PAPER GOLD

There are other investments that are related to gold but which are not gold itself. They include gold mining stocks, futures contracts, and call options on gold. Each one is a paper claim, and thus is a poor substitute for gold itself.

Gold Stocks

Gold mining stocks are stocks first—and only secondly an interest in gold.

113

A gold mine's value is affected by the price of gold. But it also depends on the talents of the mine's managers, on operating costs, on accidents of nature, and on political conditions in the country where the mine is located. So it's possible for the price of gold to rise and the price of a gold mining stock to fall at the same time.

South Africa is a good example. Because of its location at one of the critical points of ocean transport, South Africa's political complexion is important to the economies of Europe and North America. Invasion or revolution in South Africa would drive the price of gold skyward. But the same problems would drive the prices of South African gold mining stocks to very low levels.

A gold stock can be a good investment if you choose the right mine and if you correctly forecast the political future of the surrounding area. We have nothing against gold stocks; but in planning a portfolio, don't count them as a form of gold.

Gold Futures

Futures contracts for gold are closer to gold itself than are mining stocks. But they are still a paper investment. A futures contract depends on the honesty of dozens of people in the brokerage firm, most of whom you will never meet, and on the financial integrity of the clearinghouse associated with the futures exchange.

Normally this is no problem. But the purpose of gold is to help you survive the abnormal; a rapid rise in the price of gold would weaken the ability of normally reliable people, including some who had sold short, to keep their promises.

And the rules at the futures exchanges can change suddenly to your disadvantage—as shown by the government's closing of the grain markets in January 1980, and by the restrictive new rules the exchanges wrote for silver trading that same month.

Gold futures are a short-term speculative medium, suitable for use only in normal times.

Gold Options

Call options on gold are a means of obtaining an interest in a large amount of gold with a small cash outlay. When viewed in isolation from the other assets you might own, a call option is a speculative instrument. But in some circumstances, options can be useful for balancing a portfolio.

A call option is a contract that allows its owner to purchase an investment at a fixed price (known as the striking price) no matter how high the price of the investment goes on the open market. Normally, the option is valid only until a stated expiration date.

A call option on gold costs far less than gold itself. For example, when gold is selling for $400 per ounce, a call option that's good for six months and has a striking price of $400 might cost $25 per ounce.

If, six months later, gold has risen to $600 per ounce, the option will be worth $200—the $600 per ounce at which gold can be sold minus the $400 at which the option holder can buy it. On the other hand, if gold closes out the six-month period at any price below $400, the entire $25 investment will be lost—since the right to purchase gold at $400 will have no value. But $25 is the maximum loss possible.

Options can be useful in balancing a portfolio that's dominated by assets that can't be sold. Suppose that an investor's portfolio is worth $200,000 and that $160,000 of it is tied up in a business or pension plan, or is for some other reason inaccessible. This leaves him with only $40,000 to deploy to balance his portfolio. He would like to have $40,000 (20% of the total) in gold. But after allowing for the other investments he wants, he has only $10,000 left to work with.

If he used the $10,000 to buy gold coins, his gold holdings would amount to only 5% of his portfolio—far short of the goal. However, if he purchased just $2,500 worth of call options on gold, they would give him an interest in $40,000 worth of gold for six months.

If the price of gold failed to rise during the six-month period, the entire $2,500 (but no more) would be lost. With

$10,000 in his gold budget, he could repeat the investment for at least two years, even if none of the options paid off. If some of the options did pay off, the profits would allow him to renew the position for an even longer period.

If the price of gold rose sharply while he was holding an option, he would profit almost as much as if he had purchased $40,000 worth of gold outright. And if the price of gold fell, no matter how far, his loss would be limited to the cost of the option.

Gold options can help someone whose illiquid assets have put him in a financial corner, and they are a useful tool for short-term speculation. But they involve extra work, as well as the separate, non-recoverable cost of the option. If the gold price neither rises nor falls by much, you may have the feeling you're not getting anything for your money.

What's more, options are paper promises. So it's important to look behind the paper promise to see what you might receive if things get so bad that the price of gold doubles overnight.[6]

GOLD & PORTFOLIOS

We expect the 1980s to be difficult and full of surprises. If your portfolio doesn't contain an investment that will appreciate from turmoil, you can expect the portfolio to depreciate. To our knowledge, no investment will profit more from adversity than gold.

Although the impetus provided by the price suppression of gold is over, we believe that gold continues to occupy a special place in a long-term portfolio. If we could make only one investment that couldn't be touched for the next ten years, it would be gold.

Fortunately, those aren't the rules of the game; we don't have to depend on any one investment. But gold is the cornerstone of a portfolio designed to protect against uncertainty.

---

[6]Any Swiss bank can purchase Valuers White Weld gold options for you, and many U.S. stockbrokers can handle orders for them or for Mocatta Metals options.

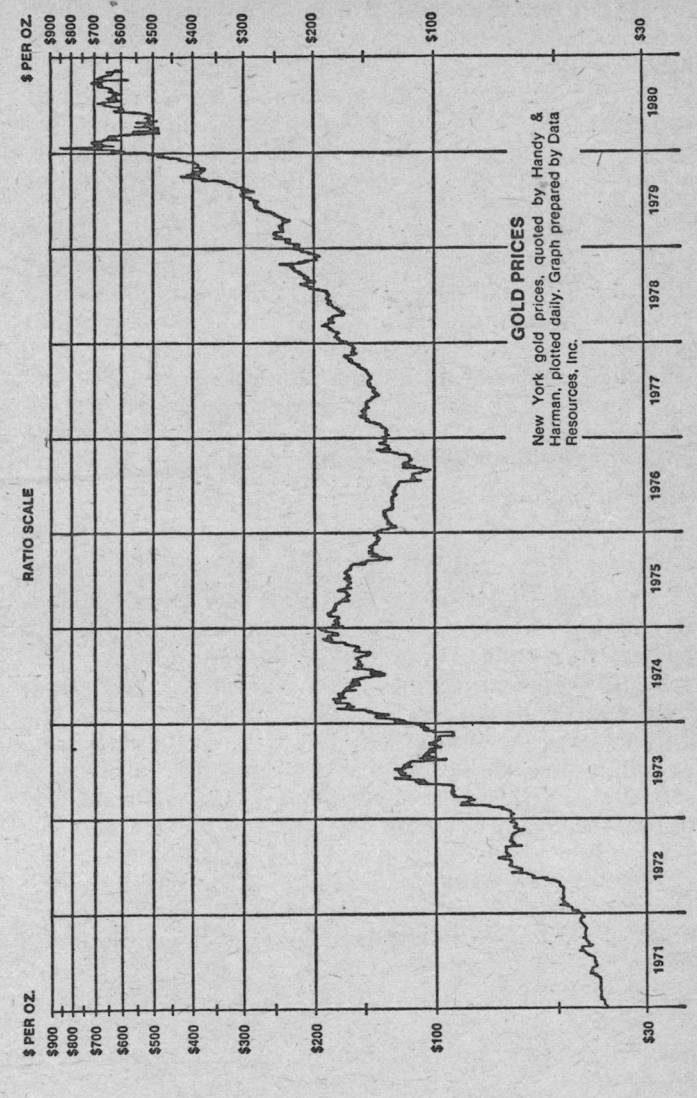

RATIO SCALE

$ PER OZ.

GOLD PRICES

New York gold prices, quoted by Handy & Harman, plotted daily. Graph prepared by Data Resources, Inc.

7

SILVER

SILVER IS THE SECOND OF THE HARD-MONEY INVESTMENTS that did so well during the 1970s.

As we said in the introduction to the previous chapter, it would be a mistake to assume that the hard-money investments will repeat their advances even if the 1980s prove to be as unsettled as the last decade. This is especially true for silver —because silver is primarily an industrial metal, not a monetary hedge. Its dramatic rise during the 1970s was mostly the aftermath of price controls, and only to a lesser degree a response to the turmoil of the decade.

To understand where silver might go in the future, we need to review where it's been.

PRICE CONTROLS ON SILVER

From 1878 to 1971, the U.S. government tried to fix the price of silver.

During most of the time until 1958, the government offered to buy silver at artificially high prices—keeping the price high to please voters in silver mining states. Not surprisingly, production was over-stimulated, a lot of people sold to the government at the high prices, and the U.S. government accumulated a two-billion-ounce stockpile of unneeded silver.

In the twentieth century, silver became an important industrial metal—and by the end of World War II, more silver was being consumed than produced. The government filled the gap by selling the silver it had acquired over the previous 70 years—now trying to keep the price down. Its purpose was to keep the price from rising above $1.29—the level at which the silver in a silver dollar is worth exactly $1.00.

By 1967 most of the stockpile was gone, and the government gave up and began withdrawing from the silver business. By 1971 the government was out completely, and the price of silver was free to move upward.

The upward movement was inevitable. Just as the government's artificially high price had stimulated overproduction, the low price had stimulated overconsumption. Industrial users had become dependent on cheap silver, and were using twice as much as was being produced.

The disparity would end only when the silver price was high enough to motivate industrial users to consume less and miners to produce more. There was no way to know what price would accomplish this, but the economics of silver production and consumption seemed to make a spectacular rise inevitable.

The production of silver responds only mildly to price increases, because most new silver is a minor by-product of copper, gold, lead, and zinc mining. A moderate price increase would inspire only a few silver mines to step up their output noticeably.

And the level of silver consumption is less affected by the price than is the case for most commodities. Silver is consumed in photographic film and other products for which the metal is a minor element of the product's total cost. So even a doubling of the silver price would have little effect on the demand for the products in which silver is used.[1]

It seemed obvious that the eventual price would be several times the $1.29 that prevailed in 1967 and 1971, the $3.30 that prevailed in 1974, and even the $5.00 that prevailed in 1978.

---

[1]The main exception is sterling silver, which accounts for about 15% of silver consumption.

1978–1980 SILVER MARKET

As you're probably aware, the price exploded between 1978 and 1980—rising from $5 to $50 and then dropping back to $10. The bull market was commonly attributed to speculators trying to corner the market, but we think it was just another chapter in the attempt to end the production-consumption imbalance.

As with any bull market, the price advance attracted speculators who eventually bid the price beyond its fundamental level—causing industrial demand to fall and the bull market to end. But speculators didn't start the price rise. When the bull market ended, the price retreated only to $10.50—still double the $5 price at which the rise began—evidence that the advance was the result of production and consumption considerations.

There may be more bull markets before the consumption gap is closed for good.

MONETARY DEMAND FOR SILVER

Silver and gold have many things in common, including a history of usage as money.

Like gold, silver is portable, divisible, and easy to store —and it can be independent of anyone's promise. So it is common for people to think of the two metals as twins. But silver is not just a different form of gold; it is a different investment.

Industrial consumption is the principal factor affecting the price of silver, while gold is in demand mainly for protection against adverse conditions. Although there's also a monetary demand for silver, that demand is not the prime mover in the silver market—just as the industrial demand for gold is dwarfed by the monetary demand. As a result, industrial demand affects the two metals differently.

The amount of gold mined each year is very small compared with the already-existing supply (the gold held by governments and investors). Normally, industrial consumers use up almost as much as is produced. But even if they failed to take what was produced, the total available supply of gold would be little changed—and the effect on the price would be modest.[2]

For silver, however, each year's new production equals a significant fraction of the already existing supply. If industrial consumption fell, as it probably would during any period of disorder, the unused new silver would add greatly to the existing supply and would tend to depress the price. This would be true even if production fell by the same degree, since a matched decline would reduce the speed at which the silver stockpile is being used up.[3]

If the monetary demand (or anything else) pushes the price of silver upward, industrial demand is reduced—tending to pull the price back downward eventually. Because industrial demand dominates the silver market, we think it is unwise to count on silver as a hedge against hard times.

SILVER'S FUTURE

It is doubtful that the $15–$20 price prevailing in late 1980 has completely closed the production-consumption gap. Still, silver is much closer to that goal than it was two years before. The probability of even a doubling from $15 is not nearly as great as a tripling from $5 appeared to be in 1978.

This doesn't mean that silver can't rise further, or that no one can make money betting on a rise. Any price is possible. But money will be made also in soybeans, penny stocks, food franchises, inventions, and a variety of other investments.

---

[2]Yearly gold production is generally between 40 and 50 million ounces. Industrial consumption is usually between 35 and 45 million ounces. The existing supply is estimated to be around 2 billion ounces. Sources: *Gold 1980*, Consolidated Gold Fields Ltd. and *International Financial Statistics*, International Monetary Fund.

[3]Yearly silver production is 250–270 million ounces; industrial consumption is 400–420 million ounces. The existing supply is estimated to be around 1.2 billion ounces. Source: *The Silver Market 1979*, Handy & Harman, New York.

Silver was special a few years back because there were strong reasons for expecting a large price increase. Now, at $15, silver has risen by 1,063% from its old controlled price, and it is no longer the nearly sure thing it once was. But it still can have a place in a balanced portfolio, because it has some features that complement gold.

First, no government possesses a large enough stockpile of silver to threaten the price. Gold, on the other hand, always faces the threat that the governments of the world may dump some of their 1.2 billion ounces on the market. While that wouldn't stop gold in the long run, it could stall the rise for many years.

Second, because industrial uses are so important for silver, a soft landing from inflation would be beneficial for silver, while it would be disastrous for gold.

And third, at a price under $15, there probably still is a considerable gap between production and consumption. So long as this gap persists, there is strong pressure for the price to rise.[4]

Inflation Possibilities

We can't write a script that silver (or any other investment) must follow. No matter how logical the story, the investment would surely flub some of its lines. But for each of the five inflation possibilities, there is one response for silver that is most likely.

1. *Constant inflation:* If inflation were to level off at a constant rate, silver would continue to rise faster than other prices (from the range of $10 to $20) until the production-consumption gap was closed. The price would continue to be volatile, but not so volatile as it has been up to now.

2. *Rising inflation:* If inflation continues its present ris-

---

[4]The rise above $10 didn't occur until the closing months of 1979, so it had little effect on the silver consumption statistics for 1979. Worldwide figures for 1980 won't be released until early 1981, so until then we can't know how greatly industrial consumption has been reduced at current price levels.

ing pattern, silver will continue to rise faster than inflation until the production-consumption gap is closed. And it should continue to be volatile even after the gap is closed.

3. *Runaway inflation:* The price of silver would of course rise during a runaway inflation, but at what speed is questionable. The disorder would cause industrial consumption to fall off sharply, but we don't know the degree to which that would be offset by an increase in monetary demand. So we can't say whether silver would rise faster or slower than other prices, but we wouldn't count on silver bullion as a hedge. However, silver coins (discussed below) would be especially valuable during a runaway inflation.

4. *Soft landing:* A successful soft landing might be the best background for silver, although not at first. Once the bumpy parts were past, a non-inflationary prosperity would widen the production-consumption gap.

5. *Deflation:* A deflation would be the worst possibility for silver. Both production and consumption would drop—which would reduce the gap between them, adding to the number of years it will take to use up the existing supply.

SILVER INVESTMENTS

How much silver you should hold depends on the price. As prices rise, the production-consumption gap narrows, and there is less profit potential left. Whatever budget you decide on for silver, some of your holdings should be sold as the price rises.

The portfolio suggestions in Part Six will treat silver a little differently from other investments. There will be a maximum budget for silver if you can buy at $10 per ounce or less—with smaller amounts suggested at higher prices.

There are two ways to invest in silver—silver coins and silver bullion.

Silver Coins

American dimes, quarters, and half-dollars dated 1964 or earlier are 90% silver. Kennedy half-dollars dated between

1965 and 1970 are 40% silver. All other U.S. coinage is minted from copper or nickel.[5]

Silver coins are no longer in circulation, since the silver they contain is worth far more than their face value. The silver in a dime, for example, is worth $.72 when the price of silver is $10 per ounce. Most silver coins have either been melted down for industrial use or are held by investors.

A silver coin, like a gold coin, is a convenient way of packaging the metal. If a runaway inflation led to a total breakdown of the currency, silver coins might provide a medium of exchange for small transactions. If you believe a runaway inflation is possible, it makes sense to have some silver coins in your portfolio.

The trading unit for silver coins is called a *bag;* it contains coins with a total face value of $1,000—that is, 2,000 half-dollars, 4,000 quarters, or 10,000 dimes. A bag of 90% coins contains approximately 720 ounces of silver; a bag of 40% coins contains approximately 295 ounces.

As with gold coins, it is best to keep a small amount of silver coins (perhaps one bag) under your direct control by purchasing them from a coin dealer for cash and storing them privately. If stored with the dealer, they could be an easy mark for confiscation or could be lost in some disorder—just when you'd need them the most.

Because there's a dwindling supply of silver coins, coin prices are not tied so strictly to the value of the metal content as are gold coins. Normally, silver coins sell for around 2% to 5% *below* the value of the silver. However, when silver smelters have a large backlog of coins for melting, the discount can be considerably larger—and was as much as 25% during February 1980. At other times, particularly when the silver price drops, the coins sell at a large premium over their metal content.

Silver Bullion

The volatility of the premium or discount adds a restriction to the coins as an investment. Beyond a bag or two for

---

[5]A 40%-silver dollar has been minted since 1971, but it is a numismatic item. Early silver dollars also sell at collector prices.

protection against runaway inflation, we suggest buying coins only if they are available at a discount. Otherwise, bars of silver bullion are more practical.

And we think the bullion is best purchased through a Swiss bank—for the reasons given for gold purchases on page 113. The smallest bar is one kilogram (32.15 ounces), which is about $480 at $15 per ounce. There is no market in Switzerland for U.S. silver coins.

Paper Silver

Paper investments in silver—stocks and futures—would be inappropriate for a long-term portfolio, for the same reasons given for gold on page 113.

Silver options are available, but we can't think of any situation in which they would be useful for balancing a portfolio.

SILVER IN A PORTFOLIO

Silver is no longer as attractive as it was a few years back. It is a mistake to think of it as a hedge against hard times that will appreciate as monetary turmoil increases. It is primarily an industrial metal whose price has soared in response to the price suppression of the past. As the price rises, silver's profit potential diminishes.

The price explosion was a long time coming, causing silver to become a permanent fixture in many portfolios. We realize that there are investors who have held silver for many years, and who have never thought about selling. It may be hard for them to realize that what they've waited for may already have happened.

We must admit it was difficult for us when we suggested in our newsletter that long-term holdings of silver be sold as the market price reached $40. But we sold, not because we had soured on silver, but because it had done everything expected of it—and more.[6]

Now, at prices around $15, silver offers another oppor-

_____

[6]*Harry Browne's Special Reports*, January 23, 1980.

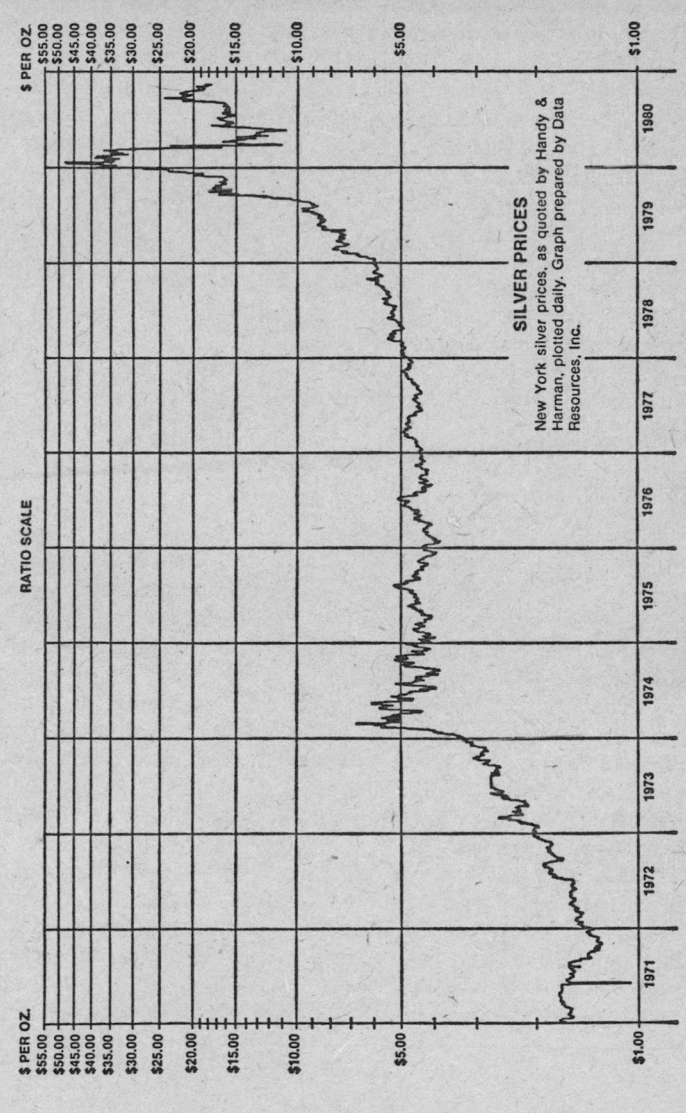

RATIO SCALE

SILVER PRICES

New York silver prices, as quoted by Handy & Harman, plotted daily. Graph prepared by Data Resources, Inc.

tunity, although not of the magnitude it offered before. But in an uncertain era, when the variety of long-term investments is so limited, silver represents a welcome avenue of diversification.

8

FOREIGN CURRENCIES

THE SWISS FRANC (THE CURRENCY OF SWITZERLAND) IS THE third investment that provided protection for investors who saw trouble ahead in the early 1970s. Like gold and silver, the franc rose dramatically because it had long been suppressed by price controls.

Since World War II, the international fixed-exchange-rate system had prevented currency prices from moving freely, even though the fundamental values of currencies were changing. Because the values of many currencies (including the franc) were rising, the fixed-exchange-rate system caused them to become grossly *under*priced against the dollar. Or, from the point of view of foreigners, the dollar became *over*priced against many currencies.

The franc's price was kept at $.23 until 1971. It was adjusted to $.26 in 1971 by the Swiss government, and was held there until the price-control system collapsed in 1973. During the five years following the collapse, it rose to $.70, and then retreated to a range of $.55 to $.65—where it has remained through 1980.

Many investors, attributing the franc's rise to problems in the U.S., assumed that the franc would continue upward at the pace established during 1973 to 1978. As a result, they find it hard to understand why the currency markets have been so quiet since 1978.

However, the dollar's recent strength isn't surprising if we examine the forces that move currency prices. If we look at the fundamental values of currencies, we can understand what has happened already and what is likely to happen in the future. Then it will be easy to see the purpose a foreign currency can serve in an investment portfolio.

FUNDAMENTAL VALUES

The principal demand for a currency is the demand to buy things that are produced in the country where the currency is used.

Currencies are also purchased for investment, but investment demand cannot exist in a vacuum. No investment can rise in price indefinitely on the hope that other investors will bid the price up further. An investment must have a fundamental value, apart from its investment status, that underpins the investment demand. For a currency, the fundamental value is the amount of goods and services a unit of the currency can buy.

Prices & Exchange Rates

When you buy a foreign product, the two ingredients of the price you pay are (1) the foreign producer's price, as stated in his own currency, and (2) the exchange rate (the dollar price of a unit of the foreign currency) that translates the foreign producer's price into a dollar price. And when you sell a product to someone in a foreign country, the ingredients of the buyer's cost are your selling price (in dollars) and the exchange rate for the currency used by your customer.

U.S. inflation increases the prices of products made in America. Swiss inflation raises the prices of Swiss goods, but usually at a slower rate. So U.S. products become comparatively more expensive and Swiss products comparatively less expensive.

So long as U.S. products are more expensive, the demand for Swiss francs (in order to buy Swiss products) is increased, and the demand for dollars (to buy U.S. products) is reduced. The heavier demand for the franc pushes its price upward until it reaches a level at which the prices of Swiss products (when translated into dollars at the new exchange rate) are about the same as U.S. prices.

At these new prices, there is no longer an excess demand for Swiss products and for the Swiss franc, so the franc's advance should stop. But if the franc were to rise higher from there, the demand for Swiss products would be further reduced—creating pressure for the franc to retreat.

Thus, if prices rise by 13% in the U.S. one year, while Swiss prices rise by only 3%, the fundamental value of the Swiss franc will rise by about 10%—the difference between the two inflation rates. With the franc 10% more expensive, the prices of Swiss products (to non-Swiss buyers) become 10% more expensive—and are once again comparable to U.S. prices.

The fundamental values of currencies change constantly, because inflation proceeds at its own rate in each country. And on any day, a currency's actual exchange rate might be above or below its fundamental value; but the fundamental value acts as a magnet, continually drawing the exchange rate back toward it.

The difference between the actual price and the value can be caused by many factors—government intervention in the currency market, exchange controls, money flowing into a country to earn higher interest rates or to find safer conditions, and so on. But when these factors push a currency price above the fundamental value determined by the currency's purchasing power, there is less demand for the country's products, and pressure develops for the exchange rate to move back down.

FIXED-EXCHANGE-RATE SYSTEM

From 1944 to 1973, the currency prices of the world were governed by the fixed-exchange-rate system—a system of price controls by which governments agreed to hold currency prices steady. They accomplished this by buying or selling currencies in the free market, as necessary, to keep currency prices from moving.

During this period, the higher rates of inflation in the

U.S. caused the prices of American goods to become more and more expensive—compared to many foreign products—and it became harder and harder to sell U.S. goods internationally. Consequently, the demand for dollars fell and the demand for Swiss francs (for purchases of Swiss goods) rose.

If the currency markets had been left alone, the price of the Swiss franc and many other currencies would have risen —probably starting in the mid-1960s. The changes would have been relatively undramatic—slow, gradual increases that would have continually adjusted currency prices to levels at which American goods could compete in foreign markets.

But the currency markets weren't left alone. Whenever the demand for dollars was low, foreign governments would buy dollars in the marketplace—offsetting the missing demand and preventing the dollar from falling. Over a period of many years, exchange rates and fundamental values moved further apart.

Finally, in January 1973, the Swiss government withdrew from the price-fixing arrangement, and other governments quickly followed suit. Exchange rates were finally free to move toward fundamental values.

Since the Swiss franc was the most underpriced of the currencies (because of Switzerland's low inflation rate), it achieved the largest gain during the five years that followed. Not too far behind it were the German mark, the Austrian schilling, the Dutch guilder, and the Belgian franc.

The progress of the Swiss franc is shown in the graph on page 133. The dotted line traces the franc's fundamental value—changing from year to year in accordance with the cumulative difference in inflation between the U.S. and Switzerland. The solid line shows the actual exchange rate. Until 1973, large purchases of dollars by the Swiss government (indicated by the vertical lines at the top of the graph) kept the actual price below the fundamental value.

When the fixed-exchange-rate system collapsed in January 1973, the Swiss government reduced its intervention; so there are fewer vertical lines after January 1973. By mid-1973, the franc had arrived at its fundamental value. From

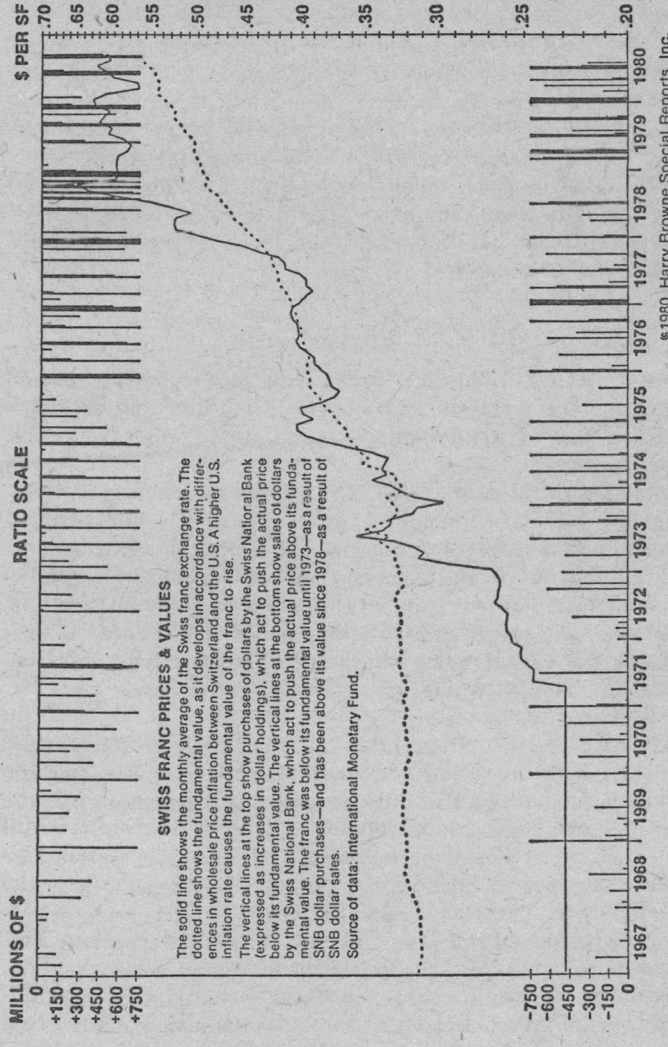

MILLIONS OF $

RATIO SCALE

$ PER SF

SWISS FRANC PRICES & VALUES

The solid line shows the monthly average of the Swiss franc exchange rate. The dotted line shows the fundamental value, as it develops in accordance with differences in wholesale price inflation between Switzerland and the U.S. A higher U.S. inflation rate causes the fundamental value of the franc to rise.

The vertical lines at the top show purchases of dollars by the Swiss National Bank (expressed as increases in dollar holdings), which act to push the actual price below its fundamental value. The vertical lines at the bottom show sales of dollars by the Swiss National Bank, which act to push the actual price above its fundamental value. The franc was below its fundamental value until 1973—as a result of SNB dollar purchases—and has been above its value since 1978—as a result of SNB dollar sales.

Source of data: International Monetary Fund.

©1980, Harry Browne Special Reports, Inc.

then until 1978, the currency price weaved around the fundamental value in a manner consistent with a relatively free market.

In 1978, however, a number of economic problems in the U.S. caused a run out of dollars and into the strong currencies. This pushed the franc *above* its fundamental value, and the franc has been under pressure to retreat ever since. The vertical lines at the bottom of the graph show that since 1978 the Swiss government has been *selling* dollars and buying francs to keep the franc's exchange rate from dropping. By doing so, it has kept the franc from falling back to its fundamental value.

WAITING FOR THE FALL

The 1973–1978 rise in the franc and other currencies attracted the attention of many investors and speculators— another case of people noticing a good thing only after it has run its course.

They attributed the fall of the dollar to the current problems of the U.S. economy. They concluded that if America's troubles were going to continue, the dollar should continue to fall and the stronger currencies should continue to rise.

In fact, however, much of the currency changes in the 1970s simply made up for the inflation that had accumulated during the era of price suppression. Further high inflation rates in the U.S. would cause foreign currencies to rise, but only gradually.

A failure to understand this has left some investors waiting anxiously since 1978 for the dollar to resume its plunge. They have assumed that only government intervention has delayed a further fall in the dollar.

The truth is just the opposite. The speculative interest in the major foreign currencies in 1978 pushed their prices too high. For the first time in decades, the dollar was *under*priced against many currencies—and government intervention was now aimed at keeping the dollar from *rising*.

This intervention kept the foreign currencies from falling against the dollar. But meanwhile, the fundamental values of

134

those currencies have continued to rise—closing the gap between value and actual price. When this was written in 1980, the exchange rates of most major currencies (against the dollar) were quite close to what we believe are their fundamental values.

In our opinion, the days of spectacular movements in currency prices are over.

Investment Demand

Switzerland has a special status as a haven for frightened money. But this doesn't enable the Swiss franc to resist the pull of its fundamental value. If the franc is pushed upward by money fleeing to Switzerland, the demand for Swiss merchandise will be reduced—causing the franc to retreat to its fundamental level again.

DOLLAR COMPARED TO OTHER CURRENCIES

As Americans, we're continually aware of U.S. economic problems. We can see the damage done by inflation and other government programs—and we may conclude that the U.S. is headed for hell in a red, white, and blue handbasket.

It's easy to believe that conditions must be better in other countries. The Germans, the Japanese, the Swiss, and others seem to be harder working, more sensible about inflation, less willing to let their governments intrude. And if this is true, the U.S. and its dollar should sink while the more self-disciplined nations and their currencies survive and prosper.

This image is largely a fiction. We are too involved with problems in the U.S. to be aware that similar problems afflict almost every country in the world. It is only a matter of degree—and, in many cases, the sickness is worse outside the U.S.

The table on page 137 compares the U.S. with other major countries in terms of money supply growth and price inflation. The figures vary from country to country, but they are all bad.

If any country is operating with realistic economic policies, it must be on a different planet.

FOREIGN CURRENCY IN A PORTFOLIO

The spectacular profits of 1973 to 1978 are gone, but foreign currencies still have an investment value. Because there are different degrees of inflation, and because each government presents investors with different risks, currencies can play an important part in a long-term portfolio.

A currency's price (in dollars) will move in accordance with differences in inflation in its country and inflation in the U.S. Thus the price of a currency with very low inflation will tend to rise at a rate almost equal to U.S. inflation—maintaining nearly constant purchasing power. This provides a somewhat stable investment for an inflation-proof portfolio.

Your choice of a specific currency for a long-term portfolio will depend upon your expectations about inflation rates. And predicting inflation rates is a very chancy business.

The past isn't an infallible guide to the future. But Switzerland has the best record of monetary restrain so far—as shown in the table on page 137. And the differences between Switzerland and the U.S. have grown over the past few years. The average Swiss inflation rate during the 1970s was 5.2%, while the U.S. average was 7.4%. And during the last five years of the decade, the Swiss rate dropped to 2.8% while the U.S. rate rose to 8.1%.[1]

We believe the political and economic character of Switzerland makes the Swiss franc the safest bet for the next ten years. That doesn't mean we believe that the Swiss government is completely dependable, that the Swiss will resist inflation at any price, nor that Switzerland is a free-market paradise. It means that, in a world of government intervention and inflation, the Swiss are likely to continue to lag

---

[1]Inflation rates are yearly averages from December 1969 (for the 1970s decade) and from December 1974 (for the last five years) through December 1979. Sources: Swiss National Bank *Monatsbericht* and the Federal Reserve *Bulletin,* various issues.

SELECTED DATA FOR 25 COUNTRIES
(Yearly Average, 1972-1980)

Country	Price Inflation	Monetary Inflation	Exchange Rate Change
Australia	11.6%	11.7%	-0.2%
Austria	6.5%	7.1%	+7.7%
Belgium	7.9%	8.4%	+5.4%
Canada.......................	9.0%	7.2%	-1.9%
Denmark	10.7%	11.0%	+2.9%
England	15.2%	11.4%	-0.4%
Finland	12.3%	15.6%	+1.6%
France	10.5%	10.4%	+2.5%
Germany	5.1%	8.1%	+7.4%
Greece	17.0%	19.7%	-5.3%
Hong Kong	9.3%	11.8%	+1.7%
Ireland	15.0%	14.8%	-2.0%
Italy	15.9%	18.1%	-4.5%
Japan	10.1%	11.3%	+4.2%
Mexico	19.4%	22.4%	-7.2%
Netherlands	7.2%	7.3%	+6.4%
New Zealand	13.2%	11.6%	-2.3%
Norway.......................	8.9%	9.8%	+3.9%
Portugal	20.3%	17.6%	-7.2%
Singapore	8.4%	15.4%	+3.5%
South Africa	11.5%	11.8%	+0.3%
Spain	16.4%	17.4%	-1.5%
Sweden	9.6%	16.5%	+1.7%
Switzerland	4.6%	3.5%	+10.9%
United States	8.9%	5.2%	---
Average	**11.4%**	**12.2%**	**+1.9%**

Price Inflation is the average yearly change in the Consumer Price Index from the 1972 average to mid-1980.

Monetary Inflation is the average yearly growth in M1 (currency outside of banks plus demand deposits in banks) from end-1971 to early 1980

Exchange Rate Change is the average yearly change in the currency price from the 1972 average to September 3, 1980

Sources: 1980 exchange rate from Bank of America, London. All other Hong Kong data from Hong Kong Monthly Digest of Statistics, January 1975 and April 1980. All other data from International Monetary Fund International Financial Statistics, 1979 Yearbook and August 1980

Figures may not agree because of rounding

behind other countries in the money-printing and government-power sweepstakes.

Inflation rates, like everything else, will fluctuate in both Switzerland and the U.S. But we expect the difference in inflation between the two countries during the next few years to be in the range of 5% to 10% per year. And if Switzerland manages to keep its inflation rate under 5%, the difference will grow if the U.S. moves to higher and higher levels.

This isn't a prediction, only a reasonable expectation. The franc is only one component of a balanced portfolio. And one doesn't have to bet his future on the expectation.

Checking on the Swiss inflation rate only every year or two would be sufficient to verify that the franc remains a good bet. Until such time as the Swiss rate rises above the U.S. rate for a year or more, there's no reason to abandon the franc.[2]

INFLATION POSSIBILITIES

Our five inflation possibilities concern the U.S., but the value of the Swiss franc ten years from now will result from events in both the U.S. and Switzerland. We can make our analysis first on the assumption that conditions in Switzerland remain stable, and then add a provision for changes in Swiss inflation.

If Swiss price inflation remains under 5%, the franc should respond to U.S. inflation as follows:

1. *Stable U.S. inflation:* A leveling off of the U.S. inflation rate at, say, 12%, would cause the franc to continue to appreciate against the dollar by 5% to 10% per year.

2. *Rising U.S. inflation:* If U.S. inflation continues as it has been, rising to higher and higher levels, the average yearly increase in the fundamental value of the franc will rise accordingly.

3. *Runaway U.S. inflation:* A runaway inflation in the U.S. would, of course, cause the franc to go sky-high. But the franc would be rising only at about the rate that U.S.

---

[2]If a second foreign currency is necessary for a portfolio, our choice is the German mark.

prices were rising. It would merely be preserving the purchasing power of your investment.

4. *Soft Landing in the U.S.:* A soft landing would narrow or eliminate the difference in inflation rates between the two countries. The result would be a fairly constant Swiss franc price—resulting in no large gain or loss in the value of Swiss franc holdings over a period of time.

5. *Deflation in the U.S.:* A deflationary depression would mean a *negative* rate of inflation in the U.S. So the U.S. dollar would *rise* against any currency whose country wasn't also undergoing a deflation. However, the franc's drop would be roughly equivalent to the gain in the dollar's purchasing power, so Swiss franc holdings wouldn't lose purchasing power drastically.

Currency prices move in accordance with comparative inflation rates, and Switzerland's inflation rate is very low. The franc's attraction is that its purchasing power will hold steady in each of the five possible circumstances. In addition, you can earn a small amount of interest that might put you a little ahead.

If Swiss inflation should move permanently into a range over 5%, franc holdings would continue to appreciate, but not as rapidly as the dollar is losing purchasing power.

SWISS FRANC INVESTMENTS

There are five methods by which you can invest in the Swiss franc: (1) bank deposits, (2) cash, (3) futures, (4) bonds, and (5) annuities. We'll discuss each of these.[3]

Bank Accounts

As we'll show in the next chapter, it is a fairly simple matter to open an account at a Swiss bank. In fact, this is the easiest method for investing in the Swiss franc.

---

[3]We don't consider stocks of Swiss companies to be a Swiss franc investment; their success will depend less on the future of the Swiss franc than on the Swiss stock market's performance and your ability to pick the right issues.

Everything can be handled by mail—just as though you were banking by mail in the U.S. It is particularly simple if your intention is to purchase francs to be held, untraded, as a long-term investment. The specific choices available to you at a Swiss bank will be discussed in the next chapter.

It is possible also to trade dollars for Swiss franc deposits at banks outside of Switzerland—either by contacting the non-Swiss bank directly or by having a Swiss bank place the money for you. These deposits are part of what is called the Eurocurrency market (although some Eurocurrency deposits are placed outside of Europe).

Eurocurrency deposits have two attractions. First, you avoid the Swiss withholding taxes (discussed in page 150). Second, interest rates are usually a little higher than for deposits at a Swiss bank—reflecting a higher degree of risk. But, as with interest-paying investments in the U.S., we believe the risk has been underestimated; the small extra interest offered isn't comparable. We believe it is safer to hold the francs in a Swiss bank.

Banknotes

You can buy Swiss banknotes (cash) at a foreign exchange counter in the U.S. and store them yourself. However, the difference between buying and selling prices (bid and ask) is about 5%—considerably more than the 1% or 2% involved in exchanging dollars for a deposit at a Swiss bank.

Despite the large price spread, you might buy banknotes for either of two reasons: (1) the amount of your investment in Swiss francs isn't large enough to warrant opening an account at a Swiss bank; or (2) you wouldn't feel comfortable sending money to a place several thousand miles from home.

If neither of these reasons applies, we see no point in acquiring Swiss banknotes. It's possible that Swiss cash could be used for purchases during a runaway inflation, but we wouldn't count on it. Gold and silver coins would serve better.

Futures

The International Monetary Market in Chicago offers futures contracts in Swiss francs. As these contracts generally run for no longer than 18 months, a long-term investment in francs would have to be renewed continually. Consequently, the futures market is useful primarily as a tool for short-term speculation—and that's outside the scope of this book.[4]

Bonds

The fourth investment medium is bonds that are denominated in Swiss francs.

The bonds of the Swiss central government (Swiss confederation bonds or *Eidgenossichen Obligationen*) are as safe from default as U.S. Treasury bonds. We wouldn't suggest corporate bonds (Swiss or foreign) unless you're willing to spend the time needed to select issues you regard as safe, and to monitor their performance.

Swiss confederation bonds offer two advantages over bank accounts: (1) you will be almost completely independent of the Swiss banking system; and (2) the interest on the bonds will give you a profit in addition to maintaining your original purchasing power. In recent years, Swiss government bonds have been yielding between 4% and 5%—which is 1% to 2% above bank savings accounts.

However, the bonds have a tax disadvantage when compared with bank accounts. When you sell Swiss francs (or trade them for something else), you'll have a capital gain or loss—based on the franc's rise or fall. Since a bank account has no maturity date, you can hold the francs in an account indefinitely without incurring a capital gain or loss. But a bond has a maturity date. When it matures, you have a transaction to report—even if you replace the bond with a new one.

We believe you should stick with bonds that mature

---

[4]See also our comments on pag 114 regarding the use of futures markets.

within three or four years—so you won't have to be concerned with changes in Swiss interest rates. If the franc continues upward, you'll have a capital gain to report, and taxes to pay, every three or four years.

In addition, a bond pays semi-annual interest that must be reported every year on your tax return. With a non-interest-bearing bank account, there is no income to report until you sell the francs—so the holdings can be completely private without committing tax evasion.

Swiss confederation bonds can be purchased through a Swiss bank. The face value of a bond is 1,000 francs (about $600 in 1980).

Swiss Annuities

You can also invest in the Swiss franc through a Swiss annuity. Like an old-fashioned U.S. annuity, the contract promises to pay you a fixed amount yearly for a specified length of time or for the rest of your life. However, the money you are promised is stated in Swiss francs, not in dollars. So if the franc appreciates, the dollar value of what you receive will increase.

Swiss insurance companies offer a number of variations on the basic annuity contract. For example, you can purchase a contract that guarantees payments only during your lifetime, or you can have a guaranteed minimum amount left for your estate. And you can have the annual payments start now or at some time in the future (accumulating interest in the interim). The costs and returns depend on the choices you make.

A swiss annuity has three advantages over a Swiss bank account. First, there is no Swiss withholding on the interest accumulated in an annuity contract or on the payments to you.[5]

Second, the interest that accumulates in an annuity isn't taxable in the U.S. until you actually start receiving payments. With a bank account, the interest is taxable the moment it's credited to your account—even if you don't withdraw it.

---

[5]The Swiss withholding tax is explained on page 150.

Third, foreign annuities aren't covered in the U.S. law (explained on page 151) requiring you to report foreign holdings. So until you actually start receiving payments (part of which will then be taxable income), the annuity can lawfully be kept completely private.

The disadvantage of a Swiss annuity is that it is costly or impossible to liquidate if you decide to reduce your holdings of Swiss francs. You can get a lump-sum settlement on an annuity that hasn't started paying out, but you'll probably end up with less than if you had left the francs on deposit at a bank. And once the payments start flowing, a liquidation is impossible.

So a Swiss annuity is attractive only for the absolute minimum number of francs you want to hold for many years. Amounts above this minimum should be in bank deposits or Swiss confederation bonds.[6]

Investment Choices

For most people, the most practical method of holding Swiss francs will be a Swiss bank account or Swiss Confederation bonds purchased through a Swiss bank. For capital that can be kept in francs for many years, a Swiss annuity may be appropriate.

THE SWISS FRANC

In our opinion, most major currencies of the world were priced fairly close to their fundamental values in 1980. The days of the great upheavals and the dramatic runs into and out of major currencies are over for the foreseeable future. Money will continue to be made and lost in short-term currency investments, but short-term investing isn't the subject of this book.

We don't believe you should look for another doubling or tripling in the prices of major currencies—except over very long periods or unless U.S. inflation rises permanently above 20%.

---

[6]Two Swiss firms that sell annuities are listed on page. 480.

However, there should be a long, steady appreciation in the currency of a low-inflation country. Such a currency offers relatively stable purchasing power and modest profits; it is a way to diversify internationally, reducing your dependence on the good sense of the U.S. government.

A long-term portfolio shouldn't need to be redesigned for five to ten years. So you should start with the currency that's most likely to remain stable during the years ahead. We choose the Swiss franc.

We don't have absolute faith in the Swiss government, but we would rather depend on it for good monetary sense than on any other government.

9

SWISS BANKS

DIVERSIFICATION IS A PRINCIPAL THEME OF THIS BOOK. AND this chapter suggests that you diversify by keeping some of your portfolio outside the United States.

Aside from the special strengths of Switzerland and Swiss banks, it makes sense to store part of your wealth outside the country where you live. It's simply a matter of spreading risk. There is no country where wealth is completely safe from molestation by the government or immune to local misfortunes. Recognizing this, some Swiss investors routinely keep money in the U.S., and wisely so.

This principle is especially important today. Worsening economic conditions cause governments to become more desperate, reaching ever deeper into the economy—closing markets, raising taxes, restricting the use of private property. You can face these intrusions more calmly when you know that at least some of your assets are beyond your government's reach.

The idea of spreading risk across borders makes sense. But having accepted the idea, it's important to find the country with the best record of financial safety and government restraint.

We think Switzerland is that country. This chapter will provide our reasons for thinking so, along with the details you'll need to open a Swiss bank account.

FINANCIAL CONSERVATISM

The first reason is that Swiss banks, in general, are more conservative financially than banks in most parts of the world.

Deposits in Swiss banks aren't covered by a government insurance program, such as the Federal Deposit Insurance Corp. Although a Swiss bank must abide by various regulations in conducting its affairs, responsibility for financial survival rests with the bank itself.

The banks know this, and the depositors know it too. Because there is no welfare agency for banks and their depositors, many banks compete for customers on the basis of safety. Banks routinely send their financial statements to customers, and many customers examine them carefully.

In addition, a Swiss bank's financial statement displays the bank's assets and liabilities in a way that makes it possible for someone who understands banking to determine how liquid the bank is—that is, what percentage of a bank's depositors could be satisfied if they all wanted to withdraw their money at one time. So it's possible to pick a bank that would be secure even in a banking panic. We haven't found this kind of information to be readily available for banks in most parts of the world.

Six very liquid Swiss banks are listed in the table on page 152.

PRIVACY

Privacy is highly respected in Switzerland. No Swiss banker would answer a telephone inquiry about your account unless he were confident it was you he was speaking with. Nor would a teller shout your balance to you from across the room.

Swiss law reflects this tradition. A court order would be needed to pry information from a bank about your account—or even to find out that you have an account. And a court order is granted only if there is sufficient evidence that a crime has been committed.

This principle applies as well when a foreign government asks the Swiss government to obtain information from banks. A court order must be obtained, and to do that, evidence must be presented that a crime has been committed.

Only acts prohibited by Swiss law are recognized as crimes for the purpose of breaching bank secrecy. And protecting your assets is not a crime in Switzerland. There are no Swiss laws against owning gold, importing or exporting currency, speculating, or any of the many economic activities that are, or have been, regulated in the U.S.

And tax evasion is not a crime in Switzerland (although falsifying receipts or other documents in order to cheat on taxes is considered to be criminal fraud). Simple tax evasion (such as failing to report income) is a civil, rather than criminal, matter between the government and the citizen, and the government has no power to subpoena bank records in such a case.

Occasionally it is announced that Switzerland has passed a new law restricting bank secrecy, has concluded a new treaty to cooperate with foreign governments in tax cases, or is about to do either of these things. Such announcements have been made with some regularity for the past fifteen years —and yet the rules and practices concerning bank privacy today are almost identical to what they were fifteen years ago.

Swiss privacy laws reflect very old Swiss traditions; they aren't public relations gestures designed to lure banking business from overseas. Consequently, whatever the Swiss government's wishes, the laws are not likely to change significantly in the next few years.

Privacy may not seem important to you today—especially if you've paid your taxes faithfully and obeyed the laws of your country. But we still think it's worth your consideration —for at least three reasons.

First, you haven't yet seen the Tax Reform Act of 1983 or the Currency Control Act of 1984 or the Declaration of National Emergency of 1986. Who knows what someone calling himself the U.S. government will decide to do in the future? Breaking his newest law might be the only way you'll avoid losing what you've earned.

It helps to have money out of bureaucratic reach ahead of time so that you don't have to decide how to respond to future laws until they materialize. If you leave your affairs entirely in the open, you'll have no choice but to obey future laws—no matter how destructive you may think they are.

Second, even if your Swiss account isn't kept secret, it still will give you some independence from the government. For example, if the U.S. government should decide to again prohibit the ownership of gold, it would automatically confiscate all gold held at banks or with gold dealers in the U.S.

But if your gold is outside the U.S., you would be able to take your time complying with the law. No one would show up at your door the next morning to confirm that you've sold your gold. Because the gold would be under your control, you would be able to stall, sell when the price is right, or perhaps not sell at all.

And third, the Swiss attitude toward privacy and private property is symbolic of the respect you'll receive at a Swiss bank. This respect for your affairs may be demonstrated someday in an important way that you can't now foresee.

CONVENIENCE

The idea of sending your money across the Atlantic ocean can be a little unsettling at first. But once your account is open, you'll probably become comfortable with it very quickly.

You can open an account by sending an American cashier's check or money order to the Swiss bank, together with typewritten instructions covering the way you want the money to be used.[1]

When the bank receives your money, it will invest it as you request, even as it mails you an application card and other forms. You'll receive confirmations of all transactions, as well as quarterly or semi-annual statements of your account. You can add to your account by sending additional cashier's checks or money orders. When you withdraw money, the bank will transfer funds anywhere you choose or will send you a cashier's check drawn on a U.S. bank.

---

[1]Our suggestions in previous books regarding "typewritten" letters have provoked a few charges that we belabor the obvious. But several Swiss bankers have told us of the many illegible hand-written letters they've received from Americans. The bankers' normal response to such letters is to throw them away, unread, if the writer isn't a client, or to request new instructions, if the writer is already a customer.

Investment instructions can also be given over the telephone. But a bank won't usually accept a telephone instruction to send money anywhere but to the account holder at his home address—since it can't be sure that a phone instruction is genuine.

In addition to providing the services you'd expect from a bank in the U.S., Swiss banks serve as stock, bond, and commodity brokers. And there is an almost endless variety of other ways in which you can use a Swiss bank. But here we'll confine our attention to the things that will help you create an easy-maintenance, long-term portfolio.

TYPES OF ACCOUNTS

There are three types of Swiss bank accounts you're likely to find useful.

Current Account

A current account is the European equivalent of a checking account. The entire balance can be withdrawn at any time, and the account usually pays no interest. Most banks offer current accounts in a choice of several currencies, but we're suggesting only Swiss franc accounts.

Deposit Account

A deposit account is like a savings account. Interest is paid, but the stability of the Swiss franc means that the interest rate is low by American standards. As of May 1980, the interest rate on most Swiss franc deposit accounts was 2½%. However, the main purpose of such an account is the appreciation in dollar value of the Swiss francs themselves, not the interest they'll earn.

Custodial Account

A custodial or safekeeping account is a depository for investments you own—such as stocks, bonds, gold, and so forth. The bank buys the investments in its name and registers them in your custodial account—sending you a statement of your holdings once or twice each year. You're charged for storage and insurance, but these charges normally amount to only a fraction of 1%.

You can also use a Swiss bank to buy investments in other countries—such as U.S. stocks or bonds, Treasury bills, and so on. In these cases, commission charges are usually 50% higher than if you had bought the investment directly.

U.S. TAXES

The U.S. government taxes income earned by its citizens and residents anywhere in the world. Interest earned in Switzerland is taxable for the year in which it is credited to your account—just as if it had been earned at a U.S. bank.

When you sell an investment in Switzerland, any profit is taxable by the U.S. as a capital gain. This includes profits made from appreciation in the price of the Swiss franc itself. Whenever the francs are exchanged back into dollars—or used to purchase another investment—the difference between the dollar value when you bought the francs and the dollar value of the francs on the day you exchange them is a capital gain or loss.

SWISS TAXES

The Swiss government requires the banks to withhold, as tax, 35% of all interest earned on Swiss franc accounts. The bank will provide a form with which you can apply to the Swiss government for a refund of 6/7 of the tax withheld —just by showing that you're not a Swiss taxpayer. The remaining 1/7 can be used as a tax credit on your U.S. tax return—reducing your net U.S. tax by the same amount.

Or you can skip the 6/7 refund and take a U.S. tax credit for the full amount. Either way, the total paid to both governments will be no more than the U.S. tax would have been by itself.

There is no Swiss withholding on investment profits, since there is no capital gains tax in Switzerland.

Negative Interest Tax

In October 1974 the Swiss government—to discourage a growing flow of money into Switzerland—imposed a prohibitive tax, called a negative interest tax, on new bank deposits in excess of 100,000 Swiss francs. And it placed limits on the number of francs that could earn interest for any one individual. The tax and the limits were removed on November 29, 1979. There are no limits now on the size of accounts or the amount of money that can draw interest.

However, the negative interest tax has been imposed three times in the last ten years—and could be imposed again. In each instance, the limits have applied primarily to new accounts and to additions made after the day the limits were announced; existing balances of less than several million francs were unaffected.

U.S. REPORTING REQUIREMENTS

The U.S. government attempts to monitor foreign holdings in two ways.

First, if you have foreign accounts with banks, or with securities or commodity dealers, with a total value of $1,000 or more, you're required to report the fact when you file your yearly income tax return. There are no special taxes, limits, or regulations to meet; the government just wants to be your confidential buddy.

Second, if you carry or mail $5,000 or more in *cash* or other bearer instruments across the U.S. border, you are required to report this to the U.S. government. You are *not* required to report the transporting or mailing of registered securities, or of checks payable to a specific bank, company, or person. You don't have to report the mailing of a cashier's check or money order to a Swiss bank.

CHOOSING A BANK

A bank's liquidity is its ability to turn its assets into cash as quickly as might be needed to satisfy the claims of de-

6 LIQUID SWISS BANKS

Bank Julius Bär & Co. Ltd.
Bahnhofstrasse 36
CH-8022 Zurich, Switzerland
Telephone: (01) 228-5111
Minimum to open account: SF 160,000 (approx. $100,000)
Assets: SF 817 million; Liquidity: 89.4%

Bankinstitut Zurich
Grossmünsterplatz 9
CH-8021 Zurich, Switzerland
Telephone: (01) 47-6063
Minimum to open account: $30,000
Assets: SF 44 million; Liquidity: 102.2%
Contact: Renzo L. Selna, Joe T. Eberhard, Hugo Räber

Banque Indiana (Suisse) SA
50 Avenue de la Gare
CH-1001 Lausanne, Switzerland
Telephone: (021) 20-4741
Minimum to open account: SF 1,000 (approx. $600)
Assets: SF 33 million; Liquidity: 155.6%
Contact: Mrs. Francine Misrahi, William Strub

Cambio + Valorenbank
Utoquai 55
CH-8008 Zurich, Switzerland
Telephone: (01) 47-5400
Minimum to open account: $50,000
Assets: SF 94 million; Liquidity: 130.5%
Contact: Werner W. Schwarz, Hugo Erne, Benny Weiss

Foreign Commerce Bank
Bellariastrasse 82
CH-8038 Zurich, Switzerland
Telephone: (01) 45-6688
Minimum to open account: $10,000
Assets: SF 508 million; Liquidity: 167.4%
Contact: Eduard F. Frauenfelder, Jiri Kucian, Rudolf Hospenthal,
   Bruno Brodbeck, Frank Bachmann, Roger Badet, André Rufer

Ueberseebank AG Zurich
Limmatquai 2
CH-8024 Zurich, Switzerland
Telephone: (01) 252-0304
Minimum to open account: None
Assets: SF 50 million; Liquidity: 119.0%
Contact: Siegfried Herzog, Kurt Kamber, Eginhard Stein, Tomas
   Matejowsky, Bruno Mattle

See explanation on facing page.

"BIG FIVE" SWISS BANKS

Bank Leu Ltd
Bahnhofstrasse 32
CH-8022 Zurich, Switzerland
Telephone: (01) 219-1111
Minimum to open account: $10.000
Assets: SF 5,680 million; Liquidity: 41.8%
Contact: Joseph V. Buschor, Andreas Fleuckiger

Credit Suisse (Swiss Credit Bank)
Paradeplatz 8
CH-8021 Zurich, Switzerland
Telephone: (01) 215-1111
Minimum to open account: No accounts opened by mail
Assets: SF 60,370 million; Liquidity: 34.1%

Swiss Bank Corporation
Aeschenvorstadt 1
CH-4002 Basel, Switzerland
Telephone: (061) 20-2020
Assets: SF 79,985 million; Liquidity: 29.8%

Swiss Volksbank
Bundesgasse 26
CH-3001 Bern, Switzerland
Telephone: (031) 66-6111
Assets: SF 16,517 million; Liquidity: 50.9%

Union Bank of Switzerland
Bahnhofstrasse 45
CH-8021 Zurich, Switzerland
Telephone: (01) 234-1111
Minimum to open account: SF 500 (approx. $300)
Assets: SF 74,148 million; Liquidity: 35.1%
Contact: Eugen Perino

Asset figures and liquidity ratings are for March 1980—except for Bankinstitut, Banque Indiana, and Cambio + Valorenbank, which are for December 1979.

Asset figures do not include accounts under discretionary management.

The liquidity rating shows the percentage of the bank's current liabilities that are covered by liquid assets. Current liabilities are amounts owed to banks and depositors on demand; time deposits due within 90 days; 15% of savings and deposit accounts; acceptances and promissory notes; and unclassified liabilities. Liquid assets are cash on hand; demand deposits at other banks; bills of exchange; money market paper; current secured (non-mortgage) loans; and 50% of securities' holdings.

Accounts may be opened with any convertible currency if the value is equivalent to the minimum shown.

Source of data: Supplied by banks, as well as balance sheets published in *Schweizerisches Handelsamtblatt*.

positors and other creditors. A bank that is 100% liquid could meet every demand that might be made on it today.

Since 1974 we have been monitoring the liquidity of almost half the 485 Swiss banks. In addition, we have dealt with, or been in touch with, a number of Swiss banks. The table on page 152 provides details for six banks with high liquidity ratings, and that specialize in the principal investments covered in this book, have officers who are sufficiently fluent in English to deal with American customers, and welcome mail accounts from outside Switzerland.

Four of the six banks are relatively small, so the table on page 153 lists the better-known "Big Five" Swiss banks as well.

SWISS BANKS

At first it may seem a little adventurous to deal with a bank several thousand miles from home.

If so, you might start by getting your feet wet—sending only enough money to meet the minimum a bank requires to open an account. Once you have the account, you may feel a certain comfort in the fact that at least a small part of your assets are where they can't be destroyed by the politicians' plans.

This may encourage you to add to your overseas holdings —until you've diversified enough to look at the future in a more relaxed way. Tranquility may be the biggest profit you earn at a Swiss bank.[2]

---

[2]The information given in this chapter should be sufficient for using a Swiss bank account for the investments covered in this book. If you're interested in additional Swiss bank services, or have special problems, our book *The Complete Guide to Swiss Banks* (described on page 516) covers the subject in a great deal more detail.

10

COLLECTIBLES

ALONGSIDE THE RISE IN GOLD PRICES OVER THE PAST FEW years, there has been a boom in collectibles—paintings, stamps, diamonds and other precious stones, numismatic coins, rare books, and so forth.

Since the boom in collectibles appears to have resulted from inflation, many investors think of collectibles as a way to protect against inflation or as a more esthetic replacement for gold. They are neither of these things.

There are three reasons that you might buy collectibles. The first is that you want the beauty of a painting, a sculpture, or other collectible in your home. If so, no investment analysis is called for; you know what the pleasure of owing the item is worth.

The second reason for buying a collectible is that you understand its background and market, and believe you can make money with your knowledge. If so, there is nothing we can do to assist you; you're entering a business that we know nothing about.[1]

The third reason is that you've heard that collectibles are a good inflation hedge and you want to get in on the action. Because we believe this widely held idea is dangerous, we'll discuss it here.

GOLD & COLLECTIBLES

At first sight, collectibles seem to be a substitute for gold

---

[1]The only thing we collect is string.

in a balanced portfolio. A collectible is portable, it stores value in a concentrated form, it doesn't depend on anyone's promises and it can't be printed by any government.[2]

But collectibles aren't a good substitute for gold—primarily because they aren't interchangeable in the way that ounces of gold or gold coins are.

Each ounce of gold is identical to every other ounce, making gold easily and universally recognizable. In times of disorder, the market for gold can continue to operate in thousands of small shops and among millions of individuals —since it requires no special expertise to recognize a Krugerrand or other bullion coin.

With collectibles, however, every specimen is unique. And even with a run of prints, multiple castings, or other multi-copy collectibles, the value of a particular specimen will depend on its condition. Opinions on the authenticity, quality, and value of any item will differ from expert to expert. And non-experts who try to judge values will find themselves in over their heads.

In the event of chaos, gold coins, being uniform, can be traded privately and relatively easily almost anywhere. But a diamond or a Ming vase has to be sold to a dealer or through an auction house. If social conditions are disorderly, a dealer will offer a poor price because he must consider the risk of carrying inventory at such a time. And auction houses might not even be operating.

Of course, you don't buy an oriental rug with the intention of trading it for a basket of groceries someday during a riot. But gold and collectibles trade in worldwide markets. The demand for gold increases whenever there's a new disorder anywhere in the world. But since collectibles rely on an orderly market, the same disorder that's bullish for gold can be very bearish for collectibles—even if the disorder is far away. A war in Asia, for example, might flush out hoards of Oriental art objects, depressing the prices of similar items worldwide.

---

[2]Governments can print new stamps, but they can't print old ones—or at least they're not supposed to.

Gold and collectibles are not two varieties of the same kind of investment—not even if the collectibles are numismatic gold coins. The differences are greater than the similarities.

SPECIALIZATION

To make money with collectibles, your knowledge must be more specialized than is necessary with other investments because you have to cope with individual items.

This individuality is overlooked when people talk about the collectibles "boom" of recent years. A bull market in stocks means that the great majority of stocks are moving upward, creating profits for a diversified portfolio of stocks. But reading of record prices paid for paintings at auctions isn't the same as checking the Dow Jones averages in the morning paper.

The fact that one painting or stamp has fetched a record price tells you nothing about the value of the paintings or stamps you own. Every item or series is different, and their prices move differently. Your copy of Lionel Modart's "Snow on a White Background" may be approaching zero value while a Picasso is bringing $3 million at a New York auction.

The individuality leads to extremely high spreads between the price at which you buy from a dealer and the price at which you could sell the item on the same day. Since each item is different, a dealer must do some work to estimate its value, he knows that his estimate is imprecise, and he doesn't know how long his money will be tied up in owning the item.

Once you have bought a diamond, a rare stamp, or an antique car, the market value may have to rise by 30%, 40%, or 50% or more for you just to break even on your investment. So you have to be sure the price will rise, and you have to be willing to wait a long time; you can't change your mind the next day without taking a large loss.

With a stock, a bond, or a gold coin, bid-ask spreads are low—usually less than 2%. So you could buy something and resell it immediately, and suffer a loss of only 2% of your investment. Or if the price were to rise 50% before you sold, your net profit would be 48%.

The high markups in collectibles are an indication of the one thing that most investors overlook—that collectibles are the stock-in-trade of a *business*, like any other merchandise carried in a store. They aren't an investment—like stocks, bonds, or gold. You wouldn't expect to make money investing in aspirins or television sets unless you opened a drugstore or an appliance store. And if you did enter such a business, you wouldn't buy your inventory from other shops.

It must be the mania for beating inflation that has led investors to believe they could profit safely by trading in store merchandise.

COLLECTIBLES

It isn't our purpose to tell you not to buy collectibles, aspirins, or television sets.

We want only to warn you that collectibles are not just another form of investment—similar to, but prettier than, stocks or bonds or gold. Making money in collectibles is a full-time job, not an investment.

Your prospects with collectibles are bad enough during a period of polite inflation—with rates of 5% to 15% per year. But during higher rates of inflation or during a deflation, the market for collectibles could fall apart—as uncertainty and disorder disrupt its operations.

Even during the recent years of polite inflation, we suspect that many people have lost a great deal of money buying items that have fallen in price. And others are pleased with their holdings only because they've never tried to sell.

As with real estate, inflation has sponsored the collectibles boom by providing an incentive to own things that don't produce current taxable income. And the illiquid nature of collectibles has allowed investors' imaginations to run wild; when you can't see a daily quote for your investment, every big-money auction story is taken as proof that what you own is rising too.

Even if you're confident that inflation will continue, the specialized nature of collectibles argues against investing in

158

them. You'll be told that this isn't a problem if you buy from a "reputable" dealer or if you can buy at "wholesale prices." But we've never met a dealer who couldn't convince us he was reputable, and we've never met an investor who paid "retail."[3]

---

[3]We hope we've made it clear that we have nothing against buying a collectible for the enjoyment it offers.

11

REAL ESTATE

FAR MORE AMERICANS HAVE PROFITED FROM REAL ESTATE than from gold or silver. And many of them feel that the boom is sure to continue so long as inflation continues.

During a mild inflation, real estate prices usually rise along with everything else. But since 1965, real estate has risen at a faster rate than prices in general, so inflation alone doesn't explain the rise. The other factor in the rise is the U.S. tax system.

In this chapter, we'll examine the way the real estate market is stimulated by the combination of inflation and taxes. And we'll try to see if the future looks as rosy as the past.

TAX INCENTIVE

During a period of inflation, the interest you pay on a mortgage or other debt is offset by a decline in the purchasing power of what you owe. So the interest payment is equivalent to a repayment of principal. Thus, while inflation makes the nominal cost of borrowing high, it makes the true expense in purchasing power low.

Despite this, a U.S. taxpayer can deduct interest payments from his taxable income every year. If a loan finances an investment that appreciates but produces little or no income, the investor's tax liabilities are pushed into the future—where they can be paid with depreciated dollars.

Real estate is ideal for this kind of tax strategy. You

can deduct the interest yearly from ordinary income, but you pay no tax on the appreciating value of the property until it's sold. Even then, you're taxed at low capital gain rates.

With a real estate investment, you can borrow an especially large part of the purchase price. Since "everyone knows" that inflation pushes up real estate prices, lenders feel comfortable providing 80% or even 90% of the price of a house. Thus $1 of investable cash can be matched by up to $9 of mortgage money.

With this tax mechanism working for real estate, you might expect the authors to own as many apartment houses as they can afford. And yet we can think of many reasons for not investing in real estate now. We will concentrate on six of them here.

END TO INFLATION

The first reason is our old refrain that inflation won't necessarily continue its present pattern.

The boom in real estate depends on inflation—because of the tax incentives we've described and because much of the investment demand for real estate is based on the assumption that inflation will continue to rise. If the inflation rate should level off, real estate prices would most likely drop. And if inflation should end completely or, worse yet, there's a deflation, property values would plunge.

ACCELERATING INFLATION

The second reason for caution is almost the opposite— accelerating inflation. Real estate is threatened as much by an inflation rate of 30%, 40%, or more as it is by an end to inflation.

Real estate benefits only from polite inflation. When inflation is bad enough to cause social or political disorder, real estate can become one of inflation's victims. Property could be destroyed physically in civil disturbances, or financially by "excess profits" taxes and rent controls. Governments would respect and protect property rights even less than they do now, and you could find it difficult to evict delinquent tenants or even squatters.

AT WHAT PRICE?

The third reason to be wary concerns the present high level of real estate prices. The apparent benefits of an investment are only half the story; the other half is the price you must pay for those benefits.

For example, we see many disadvantages to diamonds as an investment, but we'll buy all the 2-carat stones you're willing to sell at $1. In the same way, we pointed out in Chapter 7 that silver has attractive prospects—but not nearly as attractive at $15 as at $5 per ounce. It's all a matter of price.

With real estate, the benefits seem obvious. But how much should you pay for those benefits? They aren't deep dark secrets; any real estate agent will be glad to explain them to you. Today's prices may already reflect those benefits—and a lot more.

If the price of something is expected to be higher next year, investors will purchase it now—pushing the price higher and thereby bringing the anticipated future into the present. The tax and inflation motives for buying real estate have already pushed prices to levels that can't be justified by anything but the possibility that prices will be higher next year. But it appears that next year's prices are already here—as well as 1983 prices and maybe even 1986 prices.

Fundamental Value

A look at the fundamental value of real estate can show us how far real estate prices have run ahead of themselves.

The fundamental worth of any asset depends on the income it generates. The income may be a flow of money, such as the stream of dividends from a share of stock; or it may be the security provided each day by an insurance policy or a gold coin; or it can be the intangible enjoyment received from owning a painting.

In the case of real estate, the fundamental value is the rental income it can bring. The rental value is the one tangible expression of what someone is willing to give up in order to use a piece of real estate. Even undeveloped property has a potential rental value; if it doesn't, it's worthless.

The principle applies even to your own home. A rental price high enough would induce you to rent your home to someone else—and a rental price low enough elsewhere might induce you to sell your present home and move. If you haven't considered these possibilities, it's only because no one has made a tempting offer.

During the past twenty years of inflation, rental rates have risen, but not by nearly as much as real estate prices. In 1963 the average house sold for approximately 170 times its monthly rental. By 1980 the ratio had more than doubled to 370 times rental income. This trend is shown in the graph on page 166.

As rental returns diminish, the character of the real estate market changes. Investors seeking income find that the return on other types of investments (stocks, bonds, mortgages, etc.) is greater, and they begin buying less real estate and more of other investments.

Their place in the real estate market is taken by people who buy only for the tax advantages, or who buy only because they believe the price will be higher next year. In short, the investors disappear and the speculators take their place.

SPECULATION

This brings us to our fourth reason to be cautious about real estate. We certainly have nothing against speculation. But if real estate is being transformed from a conservative, income-producing investment into a speculation, we must look at it as such.

All speculative booms end sooner or later, and the end is often preceded by certain warnings. The evidence is circumstantial, but we see a few danger signs already.

1. *Fundamental values:* We've already cited the rise in the price-rental ratio. Like the high price-earnings ratio at

the end of a bull market in stocks, the present ratio in real estate seems already to reflect all present and future benefits from the investment—and then some.

2. *Extensive use of credit:* Credit allows investors to magnify their opportunities and risks. The end to a speculative market usually comes when the optimists run out of money—since they seldom run out of optimism first. Since so many real estate purchases involve mortgages, it's a question of when the market will run out of credit.

Mortgage lenders look to a loan applicant's income in evaluating his ability to repay the loan. If real estate prices rise faster than incomes and prices in general, more and more would-be buyers must be denied credit—no matter how confident the buyers may be that the real estate boom will continue.

How much longer can credit finance the boom?

3. *Cash-flow problems:* It has been pointed out often that a credit boom in real estate is not the same as a margin boom in stocks. When stock prices drop, margin calls are issued, many investors can't meet the margin calls, and they have to sell their stocks—accelerating the decline in prices. But falling real estate prices don't prompt a "margin call" (or foreclosure) so long as the owner keeps up his mortgage payments. Mortgage debt isn't the same thing as margin debt.

But the difference is as much a threat to real estate as a benefit. Because the property owner must make payments every month (unlike the investor who buys stocks on margin), the debt load alone can force him to sell; mortgage debt can *cause* a decline in prices, rather than just accelerate it.

Today, many mortgages are so large that, even after collecting rents, the property owner must draw from other investments or even from his working income to meet the mortgage payments, property taxes, and maintenance. Even if real estate prices are rising, more cash goes into the property than comes out.

The need to make mortgage payments every month causes real estate to be vulnerable to financial problems outside the real estate market. A property owner might be unable to meet his mortgage payments and be forced to sell

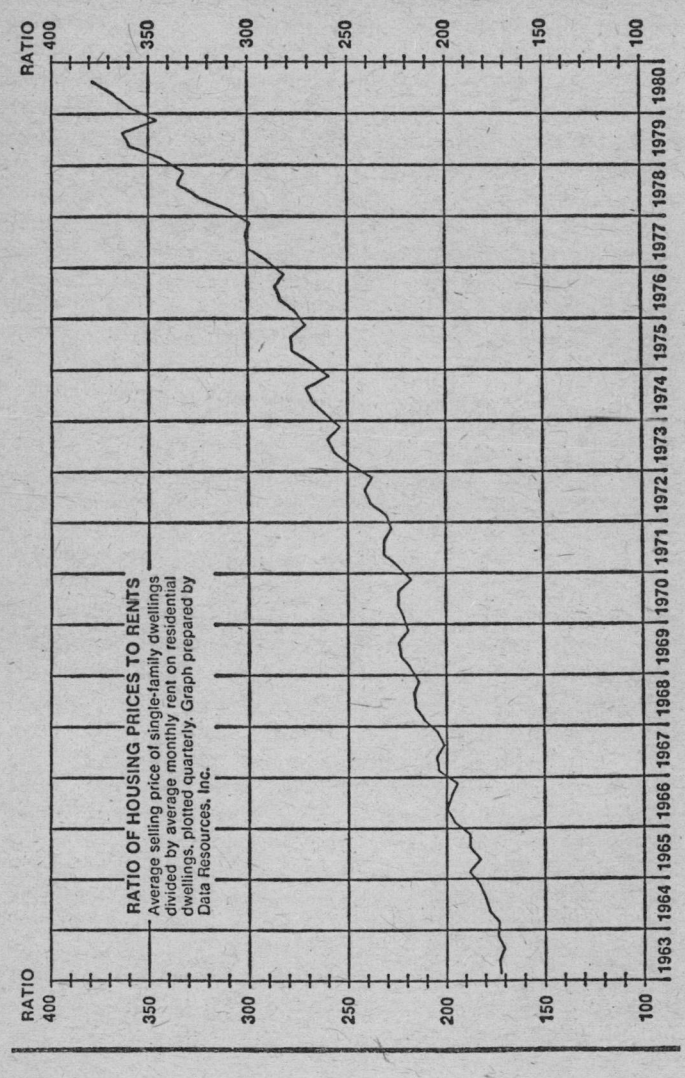

RATIO OF HOUSING PRICES TO RENTS

Average selling price of single-family dwellings divided by average monthly rent on residential dwellings, plotted quarterly. Graph prepared by Data Resources, Inc.

because of a fall in the value of his other investments, a drop in his working income or outright unemployment, or a recession that reduces his rental income.

This possibility is always present, but it's a particular danger today with mortgage debt so high. Because housing prices have been rising faster than prices in general and faster than personal incomes, mortgage costs have outpaced the ability to pay for them.

Rising interest rates add to the danger. If property is appreciating by 10% yearly, it may seem that a 10% interest rate is no greater burden than a 5% interest rate would be with the property appreciating at 5% yearly. But that isn't the case. No matter how much the property appreciates, the owner still must make the payments every month. Higher interest rates mean higher payments—and that discourages a potential buyer.

Bigger mortgages and higher interest rates have made the cash-flow problem a pressing one today. The graph on page 168 shows how the situation has changed over the past twenty years. In 1972 it took only 19% of an average individual's monthly income to meet the payments on a mortgage covering an average house. By 1980 the percentage had risen to 30% of monthly income.

4. *Certainty:* It is difficult to find anyone who has any doubts about the value of real estate as an investment. To many investors, a rising real estate market is the physical law that Newton and Einstein overlooked. It seems impossible that the boom will end.

This attitude of certainty is a sign that investors have already purchased all the real estate they can afford. Only new converts, bringing in new money, can push prices higher, but there may be no one left to convert.

Real estate has been a splendid investment to have been in. There have been few losers and many big winners. There hasn't been a visible decline in real estate prices since 1930—which adds to the feeling of certainty. The adage "Once burned, twice shy" has its corollary: "Never burned, never shy." And that is the attitude of many real estate investors—no one seems to be cautious.

There's no simple way to measure the attitude of certainty

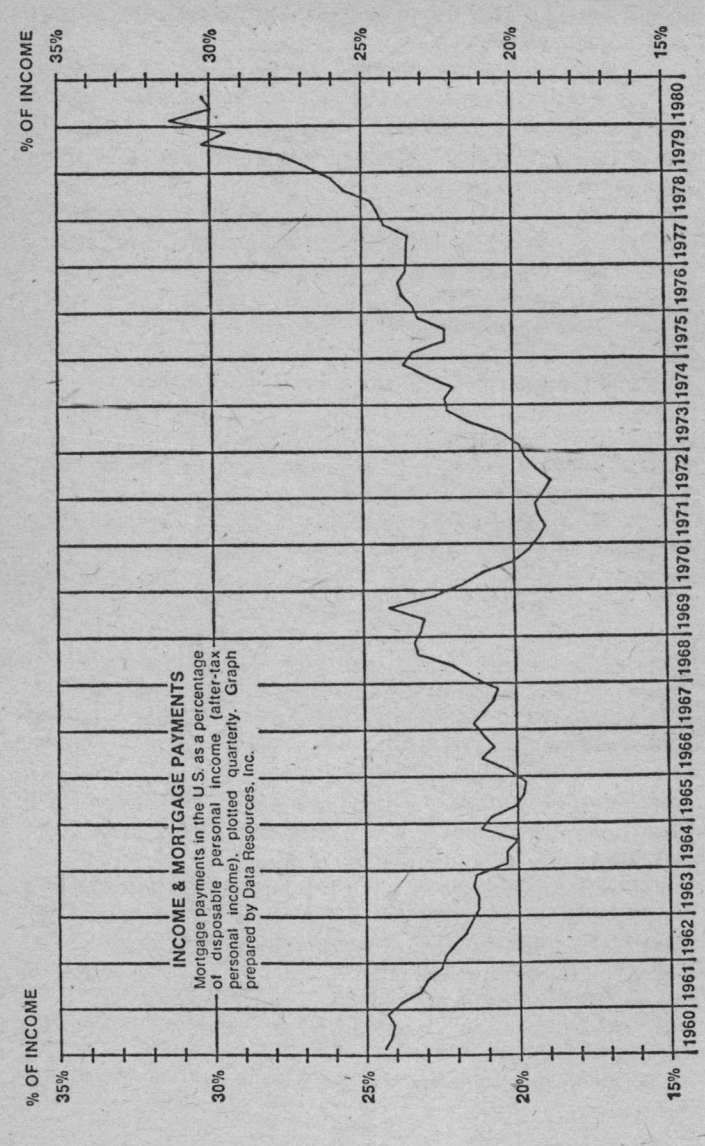

% OF INCOME

INCOME & MORTGAGE PAYMENTS
Mortgage payments in the U.S. as a percentage of disposable personal income (after-tax personal income), plotted quarterly. Graph prepared by Data Resources, Inc.

35% — 30% — 25% — 20% — 15%

1960 | 1961 | 1962 | 1963 | 1964 | 1965 | 1966 | 1967 | 1968 | 1969 | 1970 | 1971 | 1972 | 1973 | 1974 | 1975 | 1976 | 1977 | 1978 | 1979 | 1980

or the availability of new buying power, but when enough people tell you real estate is a sure-thing investment, you begin to get suspicious.

The certainty, the low rental return, the high mortgage debt, and the cash-flow problems are all warnings of the end of a speculative bull market. They don't tell us *when* it will end, but they do suggest that this is a risky time to be over-invested in real estate.

CHANGE IN TAX RULES

If the real estate market today is dominated by speculators and tax avoiders, our fifth reason for caution is that the tax rules can change at any time. Right now, the tax rules are weighted in favor of real estate. If the next wave of tax reform sweeps away its privileged status, real estate will be in trouble.

In addition to the advantages we've mentioned, real estate enjoys four special privileges.

First, for loans taken to finance most investments, net interest deductions (in excess of investment income) cannot exceed $10,000 per year. But mortgage interest is exempt from the ceiling—a considerable advantage for high-income investors.

Second, the deductions you can claim from most tax shelters are limited to your cash investment plus the indebtedness for which you assume personal responsibility—in other words, the amount you have at risk. But the "at risk" limitation doesn't apply to real estate.

Third, exchanges of "like kind" assets are exempt from capital gain taxes. The rule is applied very narrowly to most investments, but it's applied very loosely to real estate. For example, if you trade one numismatic gold coin for another, you're taxed immediately on the profit from the first coin. With real estate, however, an exchange of any property for any other property is tax free.

A fourth special advantage concerns installment sales. An installment sale allows an owner to accept payment over several years when he sells—deferring the capital gain for many years and possibly keeping himself out of higher tax brackets. Any investment may be sold on an installment basis, but the practice is most appropriate for real estate.

The rules favoring real estate result in a great deal of lost revenue for the government, giving it an incentive to close the loopholes. If real estate loses its privileged status, many investors will move on to something else—and real estate prices will fall back to the levels justified by rental values.

Real estate also would be hurt if the tax rules were changed to treat other investments as generously as real estate.

ILLIQUIDITY

Our sixth reason for caution is real estate's illiquidity.

With gold, other commodities, stocks, bonds, and currencies, it's possible to find a firm price for your investment in the morning paper. That firm price exists because someone, a dealer or market-maker, is always available to make an offer to buy your investment from you. If you accept the offer, you'll have the proceeds within a week at the most.

With real estate, your property can be on the market for several weeks or months before anyone shows an interest —even during a bull market in real estate. Until someone makes an offer in writing, you have only a vague idea of the property's value. And when a deal is finally made, you have to wait several more weeks to collect the proceeds.

Real estate's illiquidity means that, even in the best of times, property investments should be accompanied by other assets that are more liquid. And after twenty years of inflation and rising real estate prices, this rule is even more important.

If the market turns against you, there's no way to get your money out in a hurry. And since no one is making a daily offer for your property, you may not even notice when the market turns.

AN END TO A BOOM

We are not opposed to real estate in principle. In fact, real estate might be the appropriate balance to other invest-

170

ments. But we're unable to share the enthusiasm that many investors have for real estate—the idea that the boom is blessed with eternal life and that no amount is too much to invest in property.

The boom will end. We don't know when nor even what the circumstances will be. But it's obvious that the market is vulnerable.

The end may come when interest rates reach heights that put mortgage payments out of the reach of many part-time speculators. Or it might occur when a deep recession cuts into the salary income that many part-time speculators rely on to make mortgage payments. Or it might result from a slowdown in inflation that weakens real estate's efficiency as a tax shelter. Or perhaps it will be changes in the tax rules that close the loopholes favoring real estate—or changes that open up new loopholes for other investments. Or it might even be a reduction in tax rates that lessens the importance of tax avoidance. Or it might be an unexpected deflation that overwhelms real estate along with everything else.

We can't tell you how or when the end will come, but we hope we've given you more reason to think that an end is possible.

INFLATION POSSIBILITIES

Because real estate prices have already outrun rental values by a large margin, none of the inflation possibilities is very favorable for real estate.

1. *Constant inflation:* If inflation levels off at some steady rate, real estate prices would probably resume their climb after a slight dip. But the climb would be slower, allowing rental values to move closer to real estate prices, and causing interest rates to run ahead of property appreciation. After taxes, real estate might be profitable only for high-bracket investors, and only modestly so.

2. *Rising inflation:* A continuation of gradually rising inflation would be the best possibility—but only for awhile. Real estate prices would continue to run ahead of inflation, but would become more and more vulnerable to recessions and credit crunches. And at higher inflation rates, the threat of

social disorder and government interference would grow.

3. *Runaway inflation:* In this case, social disorder and skyrocketing property taxes would prevent real estate prices from rising as fast as prices in general. However, real estate that's heavily mortgaged with a fixed interest rate would be profitable—at least on paper.

4. *Soft landing:* If the money supply were decreased gradually and persistently, causing inflation to decline for more than two years, real estate prices would slump badly. Many investors who had bought property with small down payments would be forced out. However, the real estate problems would threaten the solvency of banks that held the mortgages, encouraging the government to abandon the soft landing or to provide special aid to banks or property owners.

5. *Deflation:* We probably don't need to convince you that a deflation would cause property values to drop by 50% or more.

THE GOOD EARTH

Real estate may seem to be the opposite of a paper investment. You can stand on the land, scoop up the soil, and live in the house. You aren't concerned with a board of directors a thousand miles away, and the property doesn't seem to depend on anyone's promise.

But this apparent substance is an illusion. Real estate is as much a paper investment as a bond or a share of stock. The piece of paper is your government-issued deed. Its value depends on the government's willingness to protect your property, and on its forbearance in not stealing it from you through rent controls, taxes, or eminent domain.

Property taxes are nothing more than rent paid to the true, if not rightful, owner—the government. But the lease is month-to-month; the landlord (the government) changes the terms whenever he feels like it, and he seems to escape all the consequences that afflict others who try to charge too much.

This rent may seem to be a small price to pay during normal times—and may even seem cheap while polite inflation is pushing property values upward. But when inflation gets

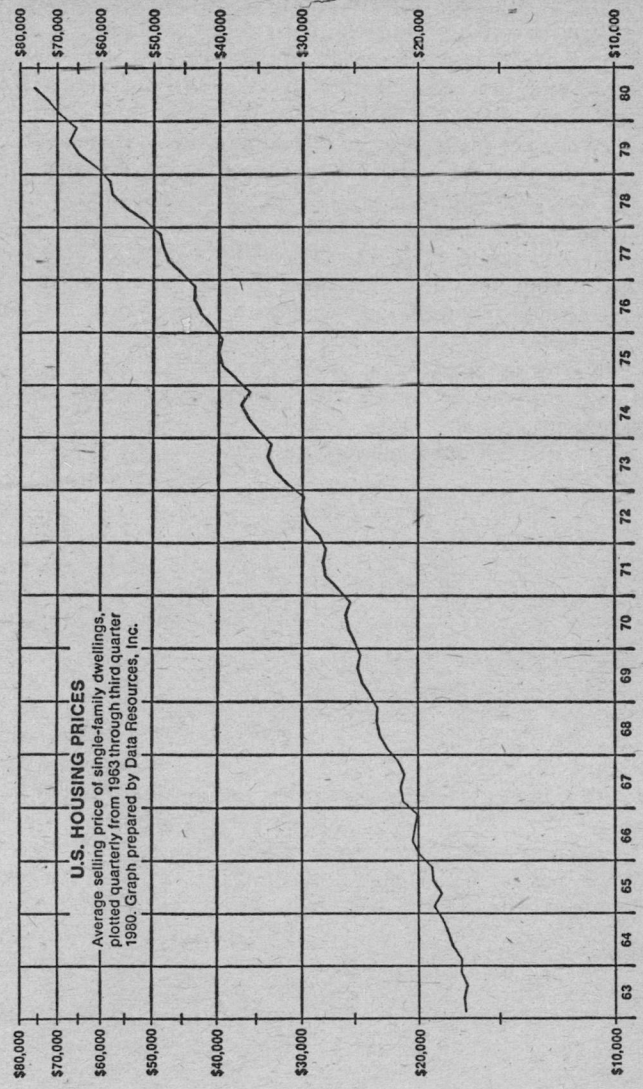

U.S. HOUSING PRICES

Average selling price of single-family dwellings, plotted quarterly from 1963 through third quarter 1980. Graph prepared by Data Resources, Inc.

nasty and the rate reaches 20%, 30%, or more, the cost of holding the property may seem outrageous. On the one hand, the government's willingness and ability to protect your property (the supposed reason for property taxes) will diminish, and the same government will want a larger and larger share of the assessed value.

We're not saying that no one should own real estate. We *are* saying that the boom has to end. And we're saying that you shouldn't think of real estate as a simple substitute for a non-paper, private, portable investment such as gold.

If your real estate holdings constitute no more than, say, 20% of your net worth (perhaps just the home you live in), don't concern yourself too much with what we've said. But if you have 75% or more of your net worth tied up in real estate, or if the gross value of your properties runs to two or three times your net worth, we think you have some serious rearranging to do.

You could lose it all very quickly.

12

STOCKS

THE U.S. STOCK MARKET IS LIVING EVIDENCE THAT INFLATION doesn't push all prices up together.

From January 1966 to September 1980, while the Consumer Price Index rose by 163%, the Dow Jones Industrial Average declined by 4%. The graph on page 176 shows the 63% loss in purchasing power suffered by stocks during this period.

The stock market's failure to keep up has inspired two different attitudes. Some investors feel there's no hope for stocks, even if they can't tell you why this is so. Others feel that stocks are the only bargains left, that sooner or later stocks are going to "catch up" with everything else—which means the Dow Jones must go to 2,000 or more.

We think the truth lies somewhere in between. There are specific problems that have held stocks back. So long as those problems remain, stocks will continue to be a poor investment—no matter how far behind they get. But if the problems are eliminated, there could indeed be an explosive bull market on Wall Street.

This chapter will examine the "catching up" argument, provide our explanation for the poor performance of stocks, evaluate the future for stocks, and show how we think they can add to a portfolio's safety.

CATCHING UP

The price of anything is a reflection of the demand for it and the available supply. Because knowledge, habits, and

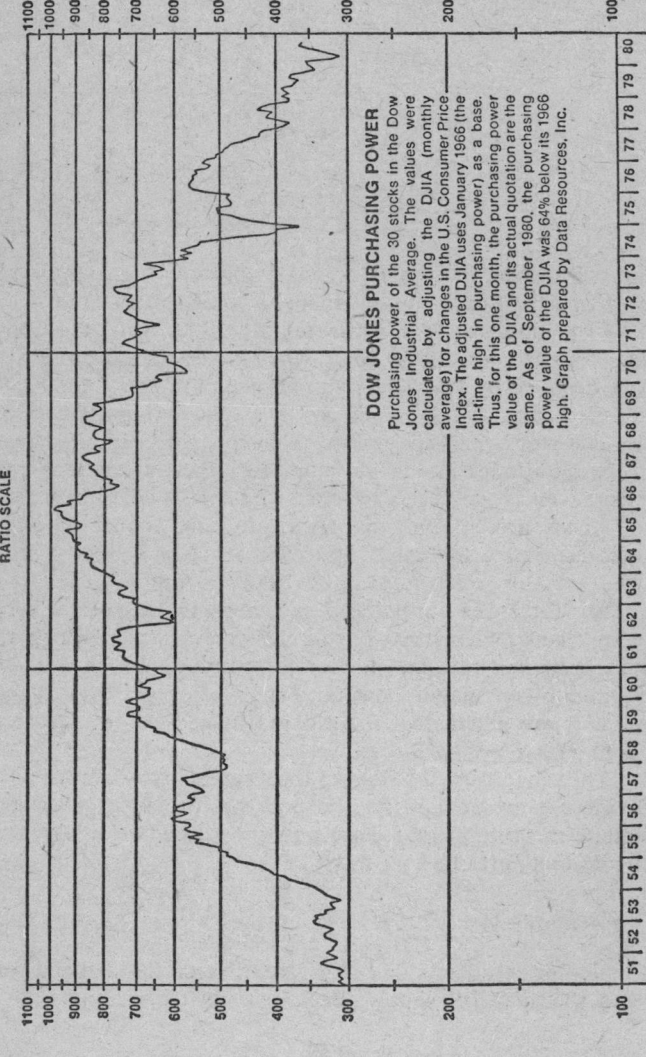

RATIO SCALE

DOW JONES PURCHASING POWER

Purchasing power of the 30 stocks in the Dow Jones Industrial Average. The values were calculated by adjusting the DJIA (monthly average) for changes in the U.S. Consumer Price Index. The adjusted DJIA uses January 1966 (the all-time high in purchasing power) as a base. Thus, for this one month, the purchasing power value of the DJIA and its actual quotation are the same. As of September 1980, the purchasing power value of the DJIA was 64% below its 1966 high. Graph prepared by Data Resources, Inc.

tastes constantly change, the forces of supply and demand are always changing. As a result, prices—and the relationships among prices—never rest.

There is nothing abnormal about price changes, so there's no general reason to expect any two prices to revert back to an earlier relationship. The historical relationships are interesting and sometimes instructive, but they don't tell us what prices must be in the future.

Prices and price relationships change because the world changes. The ratio of land prices in Los Angeles to land prices in London is hundreds of times higher today than it was 300 years ago. Yet London properties probably never will rise enough to restore the "historic" ratio between London real estate and Los Angeles real estate.

Stock prices have fallen behind the prices of other things because of problems that have been worsening since 1960. If stock prices go up dramatically in the next few years, it won't be because some irresistible force is pushing them to catch up with other things; they will rise only if the problems have eased.

CHANGE IN TREND

The graph on page 178 shows that the stock market was in a long-term uptrend until 1966. There were bull markets and bear markets, but each bull market reached a higher peak, and no bear market undid the gains that preceded it.

The situation changed in 1966. Since then, stocks have been in a long-term downtrend. The last 14 years aren't a reverse image of the preceding 23 years, but the downtrend is apparent. Each bear market has gone lower, and while each bull market has reached the 1,000 area, none has been able to move into a higher range.

Obviously something changed in the 1960s. Stocks are no longer the same investment. It is common to say that inflation is bad for stocks, but the market's problems haven't been caused by inflation alone.

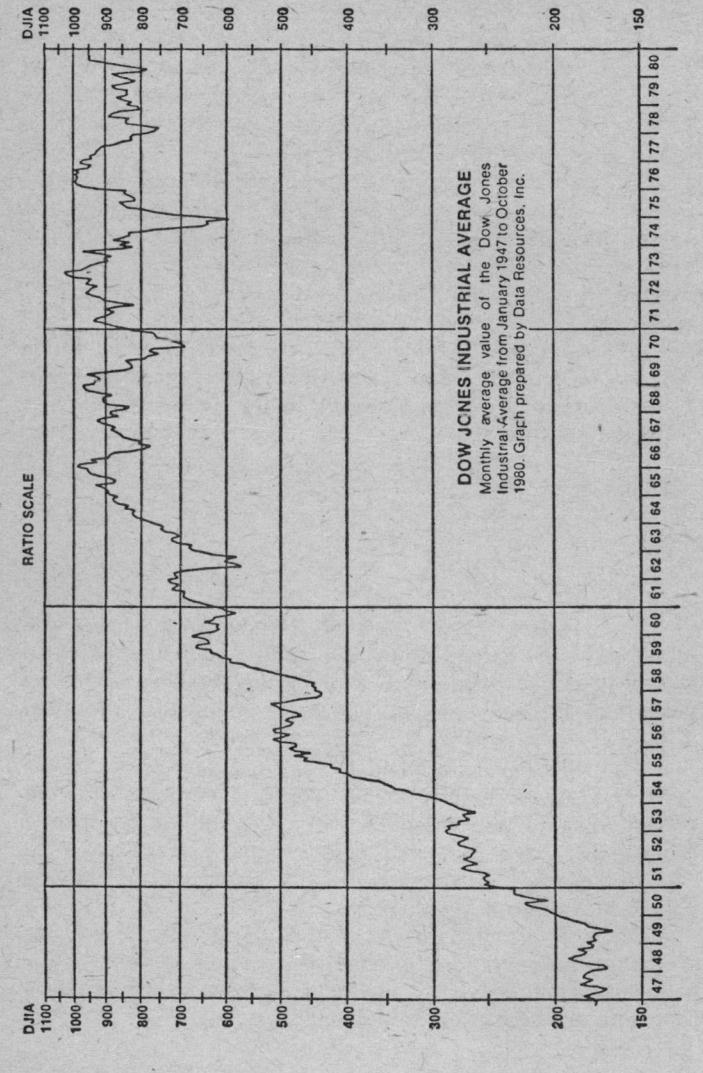

DOW JONES INDUSTRIAL AVERAGE
Monthly average value of the Dow Jones
Industrial Average from January 1947 to October
1980. Graph prepared by Data Resources, Inc.

Government Intervention

The source of the trouble has been the growth of government intervention in the economy. By taxing away business and investment profits, and by telling companies how to run their affairs, government has made it less attractive to own a share in American business.

When auto safety became a popular (or at least publicized) concern, government wasn't satisfied just to hold manufacturers legally liable for injuries suffered by their customers. It wanted to tell the manufacturers how to build cars—even if the designed-in-Washington autos bore little resemblance to the cars people wanted to buy.

When technology's critics discovered that smoke and sewage are dirty, it wasn't enough to set rules to limit the overall emission of waste products. Government wanted to tell each and every firm how much waste it could produce and how it could produce it.

And when government decided to eliminate poverty, it didn't consider encouraging or even tolerating the natural desire to earn and save. Instead, it offered rewards for people to earn less and save nothing. And many people who did want to work were priced out of the market by higher and higher minimum wage laws.

These activities, and hundreds like them, were expensive. Investors could see that the intervention would reduce or eliminate profits. And they could see that even if a business were profitable, much of its earnings would be taxed away—if not today, then later—to finance the government's growing activities and growing debt.

Buying stock looked less like owning a share in American business and more like working on the government's plantation.

DEPRECIATION RULES

The effect of the government's activities on the productivity and profitability of business, and hence on the value of stocks, is a big subject—one that would require a book as large as this one to explore.

But it requires little knowledge of economics to know that a company that must satisfy the government instead of its customers won't be profitable. So long as government intervention grows, American business will continue to deteriorate.

However, there are specific aspects of the intervention that have been especially damaging to business and account for much of the stock market's poor performance. And there's reason to believe that some of these problems might be relieved, even if there's little hope for a fundamental improvement in government's attitude toward business.

The worst problem for the stock market has come from the way the tax rules ignore the effect of inflation on the cost of replacing worn-out equipment.

Suppose you own a company that makes widgets. You produce the widgets with a machine that cost $500,000. You know the machine will wear out in five years, so you must plan for the time when it will need to be replaced.

You do this by setting aside $100,000 each year from the company's income. At the end of five years, you'll have $500,000 in a depreciation fund—money with which to purchase a replacement for the worn-out machine. The tax collector recognizes this need and allows you to deduct the $100,000 from your yearly income before computing your taxes.

So far, there's no problem—because our example has ignored inflation. Suppose, however, that inflation is causing the price of a new machine to increase by about 5% per year. The machine that costs $500,000 today will cost $625,000 five years from now.

So you need to contribute $125,000—not $100,000—to the depreciation fund each year. Unfortunately, the tax collector doesn't care about inflation, so he'll allow you to deduct only $100,000 from your taxable income. As a result, you must pay tax on $25,000 more net income than you really earn. You're being taxed on fictitious profits.

The distortion in profits can be devastating. Suppose that your true profit, after allowing for the full $125,000 in depreciation, is $50,000. The tax collector will insist that the profit is $75,000—because he'll allow only $100,000 for depreciation. If your combined federal and state income tax rate is 50%, you'll pay a tax of $37,500 on the supposed profit of $75,000—which is an effective tax rate of 75% on your true profit of $50,000.

You have plenty to complain about, but you won't do it publicly; you don't want your stockholders to sell their stock and depress the price. You'll accept the government's calculation of your before tax profit as $75,000, subtract the $37,500 in taxes paid, and publish your after-tax earnings as $37,500 —even though you really have only $12,500 after taxes.

And you'll hope that inflation doesn't increase, because at higher rates the problem gets worse. In this example, an inflation rate of 10% would raise the effective tax rate to 150%; above 10% inflation, you'd be paying tax on losses. The table on page 182 shows how various rates of inflation alter the effective tax rates in this hypothetical example.

The tax code's treatment of depreciation is a good deal more complicated than the example we've given. But the example is faithful to the basic problem—which is that during inflation a business must pay more to replace a machine than the tax rules allowed it to deduct as the machine wore out.

The depreciation rules affect future productivity, as well; they discourage additions to productive capacity and the replacement of obsolete machinery. There is no incentive to buy new equipment if the purchase will lead to taxes on imaginary profits. As a result, business investments aren't made when economic logic would call for them, and companies become less productive.

There are other ways in which inflation and the tax laws have hurt company earnings and productivity. But the depreciation rules are the heart of the problem. So long as inflation continues to rise, the problem will continue to get worse. True business profits, after taxes, will get smaller and smaller, even if reported profits continue to grow.

EARNINGS & STOCK PRICES

The price-earnings ratio of a stock is computed by dividing the stock's current price by the company's per-share earnings for the current year.

TAX CONSEQUENCES OF EQUIPMENT DEPRECIATION & INFLATION
(Hypothetical Example)

	Inflation Rates			
	5%	10%	15%	20%
1. Cost of equipment today	$500,000	500,000	500,000	500,000
2. Replacement cost in 5 years	625,000	750,000	875,000	1,000,000
Apparent Situation				
3. Company profit before depreciation	175,000	175,000	175,000	175,000
4. Allowable depreciation	100,000	100,000	100,000	100,000
5. Apparent profit before tax	75,000	75,000	75,000	75,000
6. Tax @ 50%	37,500	37,500	37,500	37,500
7. Apparent profit after tax	37,500	37,500	37,500	37,500
True Situation				
8. Company profit before depreciation	175,000	175,000	175,000	175,000
9. True depreciation	125,000	150,000	175,000	200,000
10. True net profit/(loss) before tax	50,000	25,000	0	(25,000)
11. Tax (from line 6)	37,500	37,500	37,500	37,500
12. True profit/(loss) after tax	12,500	(12,500)	(37,500)•	(62,500)•
13. Effective tax rate	75%	150%		

Line 1: Cost of purchasing equipment today.
Line 2: Cost of replacing equipment five years later, assuming the rate of inflation shown.
Line 3: Company's profit before consideration for depreciation of equipment.
Line 4: Annual depreciation allowance permitted by tax rules—20% of equipment cost.
Line 5: Taxable profit after subtracting allowable depreciation.
Line 6: Tax @ 50% (federal, state, & city).
Line 7: Apparent after-tax profit.
Line 8: Same as line 3.

Line 9. Depreciation allowance needed to replace equipment five years later, assuming the inflation rate shown.
Line 10. True net profit—after calculation of necessary depreciation.
Line 11: Tax computed with allowable depreciation (same as line 6).
Line 12: True profit after taxes (the last three columns show losses).
Line 13: Tax as % of line 10. Last two columns can't be calculated because tax has been levied on a loss.

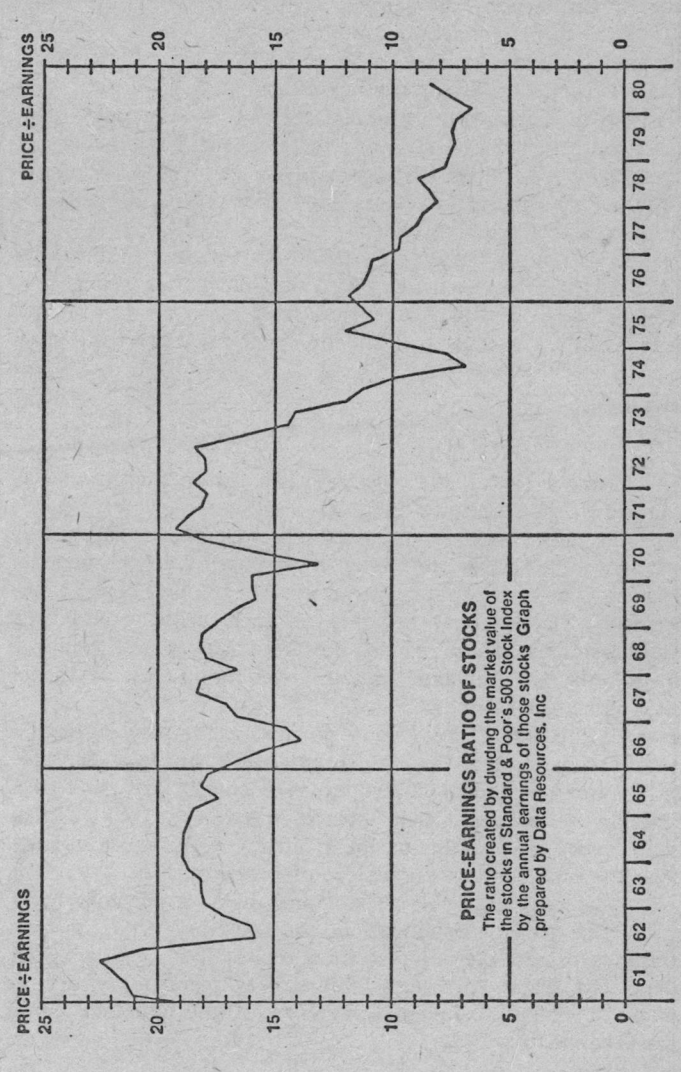

PRICE ÷ EARNINGS

PRICE-EARNINGS RATIO OF STOCKS

The ratio created by dividing the market value of the stocks in Standard & Poor's 500 Stock Index by the annual earnings of those stocks. Graph prepared by Data Resources, Inc

As shown in the graph on page 183, the average share of stock in the Standard & Poor's index sold for 16 times its current earnings in 1966 (it was 22 times in 1961). But while published earnings have continued to rise, investors paid only 8 times current earnings for a stock in 1980. Stock prices haven't risen with the reported earnings.

On the surface, the problem seems to be that something is discouraging investors from paying as much for a share in a company's earnings as they used to. But the depreciation problem is no secret; investors know that the published earnings aren't the true earnings.

In judging what a stock is worth, investors adjust the published earnings to what they think the true earnings are. Thus it is the ratio of stock prices to *published* earnings that is especially low, not the ratio of stock prices to true earnings.

EQUITY & DEBT

Another factor affecting past and future stock prices is the growth in corporate debt.

On page 161, we discussed the way that inflation has supported the real estate market by increasing the tax benefits of borrowing money. Corporations have exploited debt financing, too. The interest they pay on their debts is largely a fiction, since inflation reduces the purchasing power value of the debt by an equivalent amount—yet the interest payments are still tax-deductible.

To the extent that it can borrow, a company is helped by inflation. But there are safety limits on how far this strategy can be followed. A company can't finance as large a fraction of its assets with borrowed money as can a real estate investor, because business income is far more volatile than the rental return on a piece of property.

As a corporation takes on more debt, it becomes more vulnerable to any downturn in the economy or in its own fortunes—since the interest must be paid no matter what happens to sales volume. A company with too much debt is like a speculator using margin; even a little bad luck could cause bankruptcy.

The graph on page 186 shows that corporate debt as a percentage of corporate assets is 1.6 times what it was in 1953. The margin is getting thinner, and investors are finding even blue-chip stocks to be a little dangerous.

The use of debt financing has helped to offset some of the fictitious profits created by inflation, but it also has added to the risk of corporate bankruptcies.

THE BIG BULL MARKET

The main problem for American business has been the combination of inflation and the tax laws.

So long as that combination persists, the stock market will continue to fall behind—and the doubling or tripling of stock prices that many people have been awaiting will not occur. On the other hand, either a sustained reduction in inflation or a change to more realistic tax rules would probably trigger an explosive rise in stocks.

How much hope is there for either change?

Our examination of inflation in Part One left little room for hoping that inflation will fade away and allow the stock market to prosper. Only a soft landing would be good for stocks; the other possibilities either would leave things about as they are or hurt the stock market even more. A deflation, for example, would create a wonderful opportunity to buy stocks at the bottom—but it might be a long way down from here to there.

There is greater reason to hope that the tax laws will be changed. We're not saying the politicians will suddenly see the light, but even they know that there's little incentive left for business to expand.

The politicians aren't oblivious to the problem. Over the past fifteen years, they've included tax credits for investment and other minor incentives in their periodic tax reforms. Although the reforms have been small, they have acknowledged the problem.

And the longer the problem goes unsolved, the worse it will become. As inflation rises, the effective tax rate on business profits won't just rise to 70% or 80% or 90%. It will keep going to 100% and beyond. Then the economy will

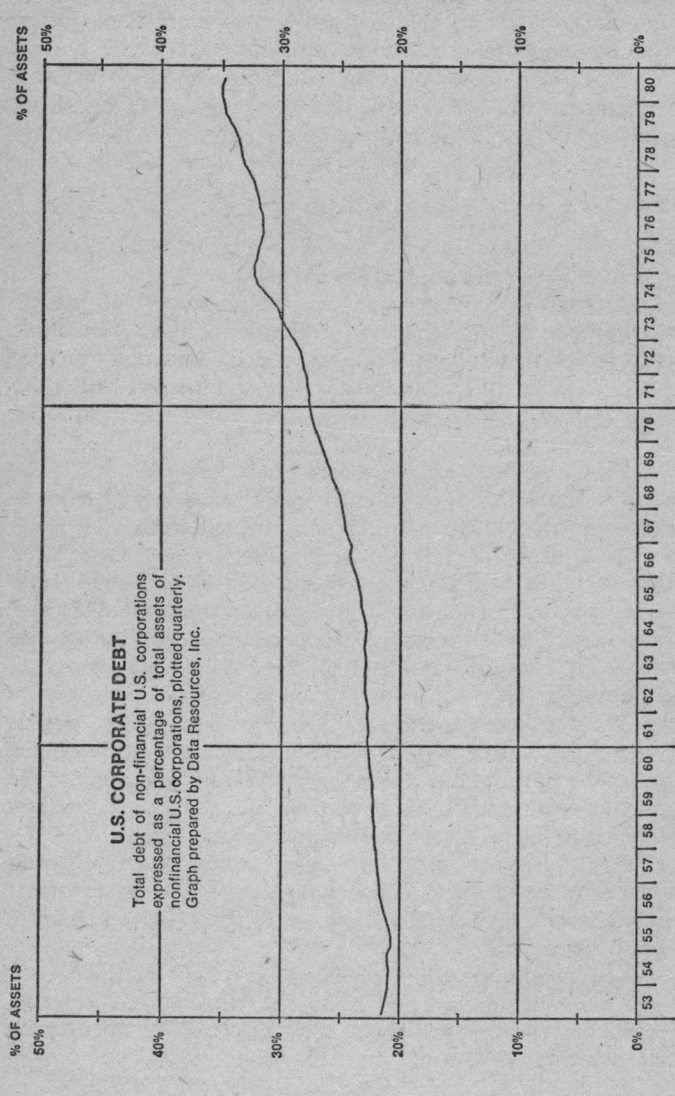

U.S. CORPORATE DEBT

Total debt of non-financial U.S. corporations expressed as a percentage of total assets of nonfinancial U.S. corporations, plotted quarterly. Graph prepared by Data Resources, Inc.

shrivel at such a rate that the problem will be impossible to ignore.

The political climate tomorrow may be quite different from that of today. The political attitude toward inflation has already changed—casting doubt on the common belief that politicians will always inflate in order to avoid unemployment. We may be near the point at which the hypertaxation of business turns into an emergency and forces the government to rewrite the rules.

We think the possibility is great enough to be worth betting on—as long as the risk can be kept within proper bounds.

In the absence of a change in the tax laws, we would expect stocks to do very well in a soft landing, continue to do poorly in level or rising inflation, and to be a disaster in a runaway inflation or a deflation.

STOCKS IN A PORTFOLIO

However, even with those expectations, and even if the tax laws aren't changed, stocks can serve a purpose in an inflation-proof portfolio.

Over the past ten years, stocks and gold have been moving in alternating bull markets. The bull markets in gold have been much more impressive, but the stock market's best performance has been during gold's bear markets—as can be seen in the graph on page 108.

A portfolio with nothing but gold should appreciate over the next ten years. But its owner will be pretty nervous during gold's temporary downturns. If stocks are included, the portfolio might not appreciate as much, but the swings in the portfolio's value won't be as extreme. Such a portfolio might be easier to live with than one containing only gold.

So stocks can provide a little comfort during gold's downturns, and offer the opportunity for a dramatic profit if the tax laws are changed.

LEVERAGED INVESTMENTS

There are two considerations underlying the selection of stock market investments.

First, the best hope for a big rise in stock prices is a hope for changes in the tax laws. While we believe there's a good chance those changes will come, they are not a sure thing.

Second, the stock market remains an area of extreme risk; you could easily lose most of what you invest. Since we expect gold to do better than stocks, the stock investments shouldn't be so large that a stock market crash would offset all the profits from gold.

These conditions suggest that you should invest only a small percentage—perhaps 15%—of your portfolio in the stock market. Fortunately, there are ways to do this without giving up the chance for large profits. Two investments, dual-purpose investment funds and warrants, are highly leveraged. You need to risk only a small amount on them to be able to profit if a new bull market gets underway.

We will explain both these investments, and then look at more traditional ways of investing in the stock market.

Dual-Purpose Funds

A dual-purpose investment fund is similar to a mutual fund—in that it holds a pool of investments, chiefly stocks, that it has purchased with money provided by its shareholders. However, it does not continually offer new shares for sale or buy back existing shares. The number of shares is fixed, and they are traded on an exchange or over the counter.

When it was organized, each dual-purpose investment fund issued two classes of shares—called income shares and capital shares. The owners of the income shares receive all interest and dividends earned by a fund on its investments.

Each fund has promised to buy back its income shares at a fixed price on a specified date in the future. Then the fund's remaining assets will become the sole property of the capital shareholders. The fund may liquidate completely, paying all the assets to the capital shareholders, or it may continue in business as a normal mutual fund.

The amount owed to the income shareholders is fixed—and yet their money will be invested in stocks until the income shares are paid off. If the stocks go up in price, the

LEVERAGE IN DUAL-PURPOSE INVESTMENT FUNDS

	(1)	(2)	(3)	(4)	(5)	(6)
	Income Shares			Example from October 10, 1980		
Fund	Redemption Date	Redemption Value	Net Assets per Capital Share	Gross Assets per Capital Share	Price	Maximum Leverage
Gemini Fund	12-31-84	$11.00	$35.89	$46.89	$31.00	1.5
Hemisphere Fund	6-30-85	11.44	2.82	14.26	4.25	3.4
Income & Capital Shares	3-31-82	10.00	12.25	22.25	10.50	2.1
Leverage Fund of Boston	1-4-82	13.73	30.34	44.07	26.50	1.7
Putnam Duofund	1-3-83	19.75	19.22	38.97	17.50	2.2
Scudder Duo-Vest	4-1-82	9.15	16.04	25.19	13.875	1.8

Column #1 shows the date on which the holders of the income shares are promised the redemption amount shown in column #2. After that date, the fund's capital shares will have no leverage. To determine the maximum leverage in a capital share:

1. Find the table "Dual-Purpose Funds" in Barron's or in the Monday Wall Street Journal.

2. From that table, add the "N.A. Va. Cap. Shs." (net asset value per capital share) to the figure shown in column #2 here.

3. Divide that total by the item "Cap. Shs. Price" (price per capital share) shown in the same table in Barron's or the Journal.

The result is the maximum leverage in a capital share—the value of the stock market assets in which you have an interest for each dollar you spend on capital shares, if the fund is fully invested in the stock market.

The table above shows an example of this calculation for October 10, 1980. The Redemption Value (column #2) is added to the Net Asset Value (column #3), and provides the gross assets (per capital share) in column #4. This is divided by the current price (column #5). The result is the maximum leverage available to a capital share (column #6).

Sources: Columns #1 and #2 are from Mutual Funds Almanac, 1979 Edition; columns #3 and #5 are from Barron's, October 13, 1980.

capital shareholders will reap all the benefit. Thus capital shares contain built-in leverage, because they have the chance to profit with money owed to someone else (the income shareholders).

As it stands now, more than half the typical fund's assets are owed to the income shareholders—due to the poor performance of stocks in recent years. So a big bull market would cause the capital shares to increase in value much faster than the prices of the individual stocks held by the fund. If you own a capital share in a dual-purpose fund, you can lose only the price you paid for the share, but you'll benefit on a leveraged basis from an increase in stock prices.

Seven dual-purpose funds were created in the mid-1960s. One of them has already bought back its income shares. The six remaining funds are shown in the table on page 189. Three of them are due to repurchase their income shares in 1982, while the other three will operate until 1983 to 1985 as dual-purpose funds.

A dual-purpose fund loses its value as a leveraged hedge once the income shares are repurchased, so only the three longer-lived funds are appropriate for a portfolio meant to be left untouched for a few years.[1]

Warrants

Warrants are the second leveraged investment. A warrant is like a stock option—in that it gives you the right to buy a share of stock at a specified price until a specified date. However, unlike an option you might buy from a dealer or through a stock exchange, a warrant is issued by the company whose stock is involved. And while an option usually has a life of only a few months, a warrant may be good for many years.

When a warrant is about to expire, if the price of the stock it covers is higher than the fixed price named in the warrant, the warrant will be worth the difference between those two prices. On the other hand, if the stock's price is

---

[1]Putnam Duofund is traded over the counter; the other five funds are traded on the New York Stock Exchange.

below the fixed price named in the warrant, the warrant will expire without value, and everything its owner paid for it will be lost.

Because a warrant earns no dividends, because it has a limited lifetime, and because it may expire valueless, a warrant costs less than a share of stock—usually much less. So when you buy a warrant, you buy a stake in the future value of the stock it covers, but your investment and risk are less than if you had bought the stock itself.

If the stock rises, the warrant will rise by a somewhat smaller dollar amount. But because the warrant's starting price is lower than the stock's, the warrant will show a greater percentage increase than the stock. If the stock rises 10%, for example, the warrant might rise 20%, 30%, 40%, or more. But if the stock falls, less money will be lost on the warrant than on the stock—because its purchase price will have been smaller.

There is more involved in warrants than we've described here, but this is the essence. The table on page 192 lists (to the best of our knowledge) every warrant that expires in 1984 or later. If your warrant budget is large enough, it should be spread over all 26 companies for proper diversification. Although some of the companies may seem to have better prospects than others, the current price of each warrant will reflect what is commonly known about the company—and will have the potential for leveraged appreciation during a new bull market in stocks.

Even if you purchase all 26 companies, don't rely on warrants alone as your stake in the stock market—since most of the warrants represent small companies. You'll need to devote some of your budget to the dual-purpose funds or to leveraged stocks (covered on page 193).[2]

Leveraged Hedges

Dual-purpose funds and warrants both are leveraged investments.

---

[2]*Using Warrants,* described on page 481, provides additional information about warrants and dual-purpose funds.

26 LONG-LIFE WARRANTS
(with expiration dates)

APL Corporation (12-31-88)
Alleghany Corp. (Perpetual)
American Airlines (4-1-84)
Applied Solar Energy (8-6-85)
Atlas Corp. (Perpetual)

Bio-Response Inc. (10-16-84)
Braniff International Corp. (12-1-86)
Builders Investment Group (12-7-86)

Capital Energy Corp. (12-24-84)
Charter Co. (9-1-88)
Chrysler Corp. (6-15-85)
Commonwealth Edison (Perpetual)
Covington Bros. Tech. (8-15-84)

Eastern Air Lines (6-1-87)

Frontier Airlines (3-1-87)

Goldfield Corp. (12-31-84)
Greyhound Corp. 1984 (5-15-84)

Mattel Inc. (4-5-86)
Modern Controls Inc. (11-13-84)

Rapid American Corp. (5-15-94)*
Reliance Corp. (7-1-87)
Resorts International Inc. (8-1-84)

Textron Inc. (5-1-84)
Trans World Corp. 1986 (10-1-86)

U.S. Air 1987 (4-1-87)

White Motor 1989 (12-31-89)

Source of data: *Value Line Options & Convertibles*, September 22, 1980.

To see how a leveraged investment works, suppose that you decide to invest 10% of your portfolio in stock market investments. Let's assume first that you buy common stocks —and the stock market doubles. The doubling of stock prices would increase the value of your overall portfolio by only the same 10% you have invested.

Instead, suppose that you have invested 10% of your portfolio in warrants or dual-purpose funds. A doubling in stock prices is likely to increase their value three or four times over. Applied to the 10% investment, the rise in the stock market will cause your overall portfolio to appreciate by 30% or 40%. But if the market fails to rise, the most you can lose is the 10% you invested.

However, there's no precise rule governing the response of either the funds or warrants to a given rise in the level of stock prices.

A dual-purpose fund, for example, might fail to take full advantage of a bull market. The fund may not believe the bull market is for real until too late—and fail to invest as much in stocks as it could. Or the management may buy stocks that don't do as well as the market in general.

As for warrants, only about 150 companies have issued them—and most of them are medium-size and small companies. Those companies may do better or worse than the market averages, but they won't do the same.

Because an individual fund or warrant may not move with the direction of the general market, it is safest to use all three dual-purpose funds that expire after 1982 *and* a group of at least 15 to 20 warrants.

These features and the unfamiliarity of the investments may discourage you from using them. So we'll offer alternatives that are a little more familiar.

LEVERAGED STOCKS

There are three general groups of stocks that would be most likely to profit if a change in the tax rules triggered a new stock market boom.

By buying a stock from these groups, your profits could be larger than for the market as a whole, while the most you could lose still would be only the price of the stock. These stocks qualify as leveraged hedges, although the leverage isn't as great as for warrants or dual-purpose funds.

The first group includes those companies that have been hurt most by the present depreciation rules. These are companies that manufacture capital equipment.

They would be prime beneficiaries of a change for the better in the depreciation rules. In addition, their stocks tend to lead the market upward or downward during the current cyclical swings.

The second group of leveraged stocks are the growth stocks. These are the stocks of companies developing or exploiting new products and services. They often work in areas of high technology such as electronics or pharmaceuticals.

Before the stock market developed its present problems, the stocks of growth companies were the market's star performers. But many of these stocks have spent the last fourteen years growing into the ground. If the economic situation should improve, however, these stocks should respond especially well.

A third group includes the stocks of brokerage companies. They tend to do especially well during a bull market because rising prices encourage trading volume and thus add to commission income. In addition, many brokers act as dealers, carrying large inventories of stocks—sometimes on margin—which rise or fall in value as the market moves.

The table on page 195 lists some of the stocks in these categories. If you decide to use them, we suggest that you take at least four or five from each category. The diversification will insure against the possibility that one of the stocks fails to keep up with any boom that develops.

THE FUTURE FOR STOCKS

The stock market has not turned out to be the inflation hedge it was labeled in the 1960s, and we hope you'll remember that the next time you see the label applied to any investment.

The stock market has been the worst casualty of inflation because of the special features of the tax code. If the code

HIGH-LEVERAGE STOCKS
(with Betas)

Capital Goods

Combustion Engineering, Inc. (1.20)
Cooper Industries (1.15)
Emhart Corp. (1.10)
FMC Corp. (1.00)

Huyck Corp. (1.05)
Signode Corp. (1.00)
Warner & Swasey (1.10)
Wheelabrator-Frye (1.10)

Growth Stocks - Electronics

AMP Inc. (1.15)
CTS Corp. (1.15)
Motorola (1.25)
Northern Telecom (1.05)

Plantronics (1.35)
Tektronix, Inc. (1.30)
Texas Instruments (1.30)

Growth Stocks - Pharmaceuticals

Lilly (Eli) & Co. (1.00)
Merck & Co. (1.00)
Pfizer Inc. (1.05)
Robins (A.H.) Co. (1.20)

Schering-Plough (1.15)
Squibb Corp. (1.20)
Syntex Corp. (1.30)
Upjohn Co. (1.10)

Brokerage Firms

Bache Group Inc. (1.60)
Donaldson, Lufkin (1.60)
Edwards (A.G.) & Sons (1.45)
First Boston, Inc. (1.10)
Hutton (E.F.) Group (1.85)

Merrill Lynch (1.60)
Paine Webber Inc. (1.90)
Shearson Loeb Rhoades (1.95)
Witter (D.) Reynolds (1.55)

For an explanation of the beta ratings, see *Beta* in the Glossary on page 499.

All stocks listed are traded on the New York Stock Exchange with the exception of Syntex Corp. (American Stock Exchange) and First Boston, Inc. (over the counter).

Source of data: Harley Hill, Oakland, Calif.

should change, the stock market might have one of the most impressive booms in its history. But without the tax changes (or a non-messy end to inflation), we can wait forever for the stock market to catch up with other investments.

We think the chances for revisions in the tax laws are fairly good. We're not counting on the politicians to change their spots, but a change in the tax laws would be an easy way for them to lessen the harm that inflation is doing to the economy.

So if the risk can be kept within reasonable limits, such as through warrants or dual-purpose funds, we're willing to bet some money on the stock market coming back.

13

DEPRESSION-PROOFING YOUR BUSINESS

UNLIKE THE OTHER CHAPTERS IN THIS PART, THIS ONE DOESN'T focus on an investment market. Instead, it shows how to use a particular kind of investment to achieve a special purpose. The purpose is to insure a business against the losses it probably would incur during a depression, and the investment involved is put options on stocks.

If you own a business, the method described may be just what you need; only you can decide that. If you don't own a business, the method may still be appropriate if a large part of your net worth is tied up in illiquid investments that are vulnerable to a deflationary depression. If neither of these conditions applies, you may want to skip this chapter—although the technique involved demonstrates how careful planning can help you to deal with difficult situations.

PROTECTION

The most difficult investment to handle in a balanced portfolio is a functioning business. Often the size of the business will overwhelm an investor's other assets. If the business itself is not able to withstand the troubles that we believe lie ahead for the U.S. economy, then only the most imaginative planning can make the overall portfolio safe.

If you own a business, the risks you face today are greater than at any time since the last depression. Because so many of your customers depend on inflation to keep the economy going, you do too. If inflation ends, you'll be affected by their troubles. What can you do to protect yourself?

One approach is to assume that you'll be quicker than others—that you'll see the next depression coming in time to jump out of the way. Maybe you will. We'd like to think that the ideas in this book will give you a bit of an edge in seeing what's coming. But having an edge isn't the same as being sure you'll succeed.

Another approach is to keep your business in constant readiness for a depression—stay out of debt, make no investments in new equipment, hire no additional employees, hold plenty of cash. But this kind of preparation means running your business from a financial bomb shelter. The next full-scale depression may be years away, and a business that prepares for it too soon many wither away before the depression arrives.

A more practical approach is to run your business as usual, but insure it against a depression. If the depression occurs, the insurance will pay you an amount roughly equal to the losses your business will suffer. With insurance, you don't have to know when the mishap is going to occur, nor do you need to alter the way you operate your business.

You obtain insurance coverage by making a small payment each month. So long as no depression occurs, much of each month's payment will be lost—as with a fire insurance premium on a building that doesn't burn down. But when a depression occurs, the insurance program will provide a pay-off that offsets the troubles facing your business.

Unfortunately, you can't simply buy this kind of insurance from an insurance agent. You have to construct your own depression insurance program.

The simplest form of insurance would be for someone to agree, in exchange for a monthly fee, to buy your business at a fixed price any time you wished to sell—regardless of the eventual value of the business. This would give you depression insurance; if a depression occurred, you would collect on the insurance by exercising your right to sell the business at a predepression price.

No one is going to make such an offer, but similar agreements do exist for the stock of publicly held corporations. The agreements are called *put options*. And put options on large corporations can be an effective substitute for an insurance policy against a depression.

PUT OPTIONS

A put option is the opposite of the more familiar call option.

While a call option gives you the right to *buy* a stock, a put option gives you the right to *sell* a company's stock at a fixed price, called the *striking price*. The right is good until an agreed-upon *expiration date*. Until that date, you can sell the stock at the fixed price no matter how low the market price of the stock may go.

For example, you might buy a put option on General Motors with a striking price of $50 and an expiration date six months from today. This would give you the right to sell GM stock at $50 per share—regardless of the market price.

If GM stock dropped to $45 per share in the open market before the option expired, your put option would be worth at least $5—the difference between the price at which anyone can buy GM and the price at which you can sell GM. If GM declined to $40 within the next six months, your option would be worth at least $10.

If the put expires with GM selling above $50, the put will be worthless. You'll have lost the entire price of the put, but that's the most you can lose.

Because a put option profits when stock prices go down, a portfolio of puts on the stocks of large corporations can insure your business against a depression. A depression is usually preceded, and then accompanied, by a decline in the general level of stock prices—as large corporations experience the same kinds of problems that would be hurting your business. So the put options would tend to generate large profits at the same time your business is facing depression losses.

And although designed to insure against a full-scale depression, the put option program can generate profits during a bad recession. This will help to offset business losses if the recession catches you by surprise.

The program works like insurance because a put option

is leveraged. A small decline in the price of a stock will produce a rise of a much larger percentage in the price of a put.

Depending on the speed of the decline, a fall of 1% in the stock market can increase the put portfolio's value by 5% to 6% or so. Because of compounding, a 50% drop in the stock market (which would be mild for a depression) could cause a 40- to 50-fold increase in the value of the put portfolio. Without this leverage, the depression insurance would be prohibitively expensive.

HOW THE MARKET WORKS

Put options are traded on the Chicago Board Options Exchange, as well as the Pacific, American, and Philadelphia stock exchanges. Puts are available on the stocks of 147 different companies. Many of the names (listed on pages 202–203) will probably be familiar to you, since they are all large, well-known companies. And there may be puts available for more companies by the time you read this.

The unit of trading is a contract covering 100 shares. Owning five put contracts would give you the right to sell 500 shares.

There usually are a variety of options available on the stock of each company. The various options have different striking prices and different expiration dates. But the desire for standardization keeps the number small.

Exercise prices are limited to round numbers near the current price of the stock. For a stock priced under $50, the round numbers usually are in $5 increments; so a stock selling for $33 might have options available with striking prices of $30 and $35. For stocks priced above $50, the options are usually available in $10 increments—$60, $70, and so forth.

An option expires on the third Saturday of the month named in the option. For any given company, there will be four expiration months spaced evenly through the year—such as February, May, August, and November. However, because the longest-lived option is for nine months, there are never more than three expiration months available at any time. Trading in an option continues until the day before it expires; you can sell it at any time until then.

Option Prices

As with any liquid investment, prices for put options change from minute to minute and are determined by the actions of competing buyers and competing sellers. Conceptually, the price for a put option can be divided into two parts—the *exercise value* and the *premium.*

If a put's striking price is higher than the stock's current price, the option can be *exercised* by buying the stock in the marketplace and selling it at the (higher) striking price. The difference between the stock's price and the option's striking price is the put's *exercise value*—the return that can be obtained right now by exercising the option. If a put option has a striking price *below* the stock's current price, the exercise value is zero.

A put option normally is priced somewhat above its exercise value. This excess is called the option's *premium.* Investors pay this premium because the put offers a large potential profit with a small, limited risk.[1]

An option's premium is greatest when the option is young, because there are several months left in which to produce a profit. As the put approaches its expiration date, the premium will gradually decline to zero. On the expiration date, there's no more potential, so the put will be worth only its exercise value—if it has any.

It isn't necessary to exercise a put in order to collect its exercise value. There are plenty of option traders whose activities keep a put's price in line with its exercise value. So you need only to sell a put just before it expires to get virtually the same proceeds you would collect by buying the stock itself and selling it at the striking price.

CHOOSING THE PUTS

To construct an insurance program for your business, you'll have to decide which stocks you're going to use. As of August 1980, there were 147 companies for which listed put options were available.

---

[1]The word *premium* is sometimes used to mean the entire price of an option, including its exercise value.

COMPANIES WITH LISTED PUT OPTIONS
Names & Principal Businesses

ASA Ltd., gold investment company
Abbott Labs, health & hospital supplies
Aetna Life & Casualty, insurance
Air Products & Chemicals, gas & welding supplies
Allied Chemical, chemicals
Allis-Chalmers, agricultural equipment
Amax Inc., mining
Amerada-Hess, petroleum
American Broadcasting Corp., broadcasting
American Cyanamid, chemicals & agricultural products
Anheuser-Busch, brewing
Archer-Daniels-Midland, food processing
Asarco Inc., metals & mining
Ashland Oil, petroleum
Atlantic Richfield, petroleum
Avco Corp., conglomerate
Avnet Inc., electronics
Avon Products, toiletries & cosmetics

Baker International, oilfield services
Bally Manufacturing, recreation
Bausch & Lomb, precision instruments
Becton Dickinson & Co., health & hospital supplies
Boeing, aircraft manufacturer
Bristol-Meyers, proprietary drugs & household products
Burroughs Corp., computers

Caesars World, hotels & casinos
Charter Co., petroleum
Chase Manhattan Corp., banking
Cities Service, petroleum
City Investing Co., conglomerate
Coastal Corp., natural gas
Communications Satellite Corp., telecommunications
Conoco Inc., petroleum
Control Data, computers
Corning Glass Works, glass products
Diamond Shamrock, chemicals & petroleum

Digital Equipment, computers
Dow Chemical, chemicals
Dresser Industries, oilfield services
DuPont, chemicals

EG&G Inc., nuclear testing & electronics
Eastern Gas & Fuel, coal mining & petroleum
Eastman Kodak, photographic equipment
El Paso Co., natural gas
Engelhard Minerals & Chemicals, metal fabrication & trading
Esmark Inc., food processing
Exxon Corp., petroleum

Federal Express, air freight
Fluor Corp., oilfield & mining services
Freeport Minerals Co., minerals production
Fuqua Industries, conglomerate

General Dynamics, aerospace
General Electric, electrical equipment
General Instrument Corp., electronics
General Motors, autos & trucks
Georgia-Pacific, lumber
Getty Oil, petroleum
Gulf Oil, petroleum

Halliburton Co., oilfield services
Heublein Inc., alcoholic beverages
Hewlett-Packard, computers & instruments
Hilton Hotels, hotels
Holiday Inns, hotels
Homestake Mining, gold mining
Honeywell Inc., computers & automation systems
Houston Oil & Minerals, petroleum
Hughes Tool, oilfield services

Inexco Oil, petroleum
IBM, computers
International Harvester, farm & building equipment
Joy Manufacturing, construction & mining equipment

Kennecott Corp., copper & other metals
Kerr-McGee Corp., petroleum

Lear Siegler Inc., electrical products
Levi Strauss & Co., apparel
Litton Industries, conglomerate
Lockheed Corp., aircraft & aerospace
Louisiana Land & Exploration, petroleum

MAPCO Inc., petroleum & coal
Marathon Oil, petroleum
Marriott Corp., hotels & food outlets
Martin Marietta Corp., aerospace
McDonnell Douglas, aircraft & aerospace
McDermott & Co., oilfield services
Merrill Lynch, securities brokerage
Mesa Petroleum, petroleum
Mobil Corp., petroleum
Motorola, electronics & communications equipment

NCR Corp., business machines
NL Industries, chemicals
National Semiconductor, electronics
Natomas Co., petroleum
Newmont Mining, mining
Northwest Industries, conglomerate

Occidental Petroleum, petroleum
Owens-Corning, glass fiber & products
Owens-Illinois Inc., packaging & containers

Perkin-Elmer Corp., precision instruments
Pfizer Inc., ethical drugs
Philip Morris, tobacco
Phillips Petroleum, petroleum
Pittston, coal mining
Polaroid Corp., photographic equipment
Prime Computer, computers
Proctor & Gamble, household products

Ralston Purina, food processing & animal feeds
Resorts International, hotels & casinos
Revlon Inc., toiletries & cosmetics
Reynolds Metals, aluminum
Rockwell International, aerospace & electronics

St. Joe Minerals, mining
Santa Fe Industries, railroads
Santa Fe International, oilfield services
Schering-Plough, ethical drugs
Schlumberger Ltd., oilfield services
Seaboard Coast Line, railroads
Searle (G.D.) & Co., ethical drugs
Signal Companies, trucks
Smithkline Corp., ethical drugs
Standard Oil (Calif.), petroleum
Standard Oil (Ohio), petroleum
Storage Technology, computers
Sun Company, petroleum
Superior Oil, petroleum
Syntex, ethical drugs

Tandy Corp., retail hobby & electronics stores
Tektronix Inc., electronics
Teledyne Inc., electronics
Teleprompter Corp., broadcasting
Tenneco Inc., natural gas
Texaco Inc., petroleum
Texas Oil & Gas, natural gas
Tiger International, air freight
Time Inc., publishing
Tosco Corp., petroleum
Travelers Corp., insurance

Union Carbide, chemicals
Union Oil Co. of California, petroleum
Union Pacific, railroads
U.S. Steel, steel

Valero Energy Corp., natural gas

Warner Communications, entertainment
Warner-Lambert, ethical drugs
Westinghouse Electric, electrical equipment
Williams Cos., gas & fertilizers

Xerox, office equipment

Zapata Corp., fishing & mining

Source: *The Value Line Investment Survey,* August 15, 1980.

Only two companies need to be excluded from consideration—Homestake Mining and ASA, both of which are tied to the gold mining industry. At the start of a depression, gold stocks may go up in price while other stocks are dropping, so put options on gold stocks serve no purpose in a depression insurance program.

That leaves 145 companies. Any of the 145 companies in a line of business similar to your own should have extra weight in your program. But you should also include companies from other industries, so that your put program will respond to the fortunes of the whole economy.

To get the highest leverage, the highest coverage per dollar spent, buy only options that are "out of the money"—puts that have *no* exercise value because their striking prices are *below* the current prices of their stocks. These puts will have the largest percentage increases if the market drops.

At any time, there will be puts on several companies expiring in each of the subsequent eight months. The put portfolio should include options covering most, if not all, of the eight expiration months. Spreading your holdings across the calendar might prevent a large number of puts from expiring just when you need them most.

Hold each option until its last trading day, and then sell it if it has any exercise value. Replace it immediately with a new option that has eight months to expiration. All options that expire in a given month expire on the same day, so you'll be trading only one day each month.

FIXING THE AMOUNT

With a normal insurance policy, you choose the amount of coverage you need. It's not that simple with this insurance program, because we can't know what payoff the put program will produce if a depression occurs.

In a stock market collapse, the profitability of puts will depend as much on the speed of the collapse as on its depth. The speed of the decline is important because time works against a put.

An option normally trades for more than its exercise

value, but this premium gradually evaporates as the option nears its expiration date. Since you pay a premium for each put you buy, a slow market decline causes the profits from falling stocks to be offset by the evaporation of option premiums. In fact, in a very slow decline, an option's exercise value at expiration day could be less than its original purchase price—even though the underlying stock has fallen.

Because we can't know precisely what downward path the market will take on its way to the next depression, it's impossible to know just how profitable a put portfolio will turn out to be.

Adding to the uncertainty is a lack of experience. Using put options as insurance is a new idea. We know of no one other than a few of our clients who have tried it. But based on that limited experience, we suggest the following guidelines:

1. Determine, in dollars, how much the value of your business would decline in the event of a depression.[2]

2. Deduct whatever amount of this loss you would be willing to bear yourself. As with any insurance, the bigger the "deductible," the smaller the insurance premium.

3. Multiply the net amount to be insured by .0017 (1/6 of 1%). This is the amount to invest monthly in put options. The net cost of the program may be less, however, since some of the options should show a profit even if there's no depression. In that sense, this is a "participating" insurance policy.

Payoffs

Another question to answer is what to do with the profits that are made along the way. Should you withdraw all profits, or hold them in a cash reserve, or reinvest everything?

Again, the difficulty stems from not knowing how the depression will unfold. If profits are reinvested, they can compound into larger profits. But reinvested profits can also

---

[2]This is the decline in the net worth of the company, not the decline in sales volume.

be lost entirely if the decline is interrupted by a long pause—causing the puts you bought with profits to expire worthless.

THE SYSTEM

To try to balance all the possibilities, we've constructed a set of mechanical rules for running the insurance program.

The rules are a bit involved, but a stockbroker will do most of the work for you. It will be a chore for him to handle, but most stockbrokers should welcome the commissions.

To make it easier for both of you, the instructions shown on pages 210–213 tell the broker what he has to do. Your part of the job is limited to three things:

1. Determine the monthly insurance payment that fits your situation—in accordance with the guidelines discussed on the previous page. For our explanation, we'll assume the amount to be insured is $600, so that the monthly payment is exactly $1. You can then multiply the figures we'll use by whatever monthly amount you decide on.

2. Begin by depositing $8 with the broker. He'll invest $4 immediately—$1 each in put options that expire in four, five, six, and seven months. The other $4 will be the start of a cash reserve.

3. On the first day of each month, send the broker an additional payment of $1. He'll use this to buy puts that expire eight months later.

Once the program is four months old, some puts will expire every month. The broker will sell them (for whatever he can get) one day prior to expiration. Half the proceeds of the sale will go into the cash reserve. The other half will be added to your $1 monthly payment, in order to buy new puts that expire eight months later.

A sliding scale in the broker's instructions determines whether he should draw funds from the cash reserve to buy extra puts. The lower the market is, the less he uses the cash reserve to buy extra puts.

The result of the system is:

1. You'll make regular monthly payments of $1 each. A cash reserve will accumulate—since some puts will earn prof-

its, even if there's no economic disaster. Part of the cash reserve will be reinvested each month, but never all of it.

2. If there's a steep stock-market drop, your profits will be divided between additions to the cash reserve and investments in new puts.

3. If the Dow Jones Industrial Average drops to 500, none of the cash reserve will be reinvested; only the $1 monthly payment will be used for new purchases. By that time, the cash reserve should be quite large.

4. At a Dow Jones of 600 or less, the broker will send you a monthly check for 10% of the total value of the account. You can use this money to offset business losses caused by the depression.[3]

5. If there's never a severe market drop, you'll have a continuing expense of $1 per month that should (like fire insurance) be considered a cost of doing business. After 50 years (600 payments), you'll have paid out as much in premiums as you're trying to insure your business for. However, by that time, the cash reserve should have accumulated funds from the profits on some of the puts.

IN TIME OF NEED

When a depression comes, you'll have large profits before your business starts to suffer, because the stock market normally moves before the economy does. The large profits will be telling you there are problems ahead.

That's why the instructions call for withdrawing profits when the market drops to a level that indicates that, at best, a severe recession is on the way. We chose a 600 level for the Dow Jones because we believe that would tell us the economy is in serious trouble. A few years from now, if the market has risen significantly in the interim, you might prefer some other number for the storm warning. If so, you can change the broker's instructions.

---

[3]Note that a constant withdrawal of any given percentage never reduces the account to zero, because a percentage is always only a portion of the remaining amount.

Even when you're withdrawing profits, the monthly payments should continue—just as you'd continue paying insurance premiums after a fire caused a claim to be paid. The program should continue so long as you remain in business.

CASH RESERVE

The cash reserve should be held in the safest form practical. Don't leave it as a simple cash deposit with your broker. If you do, he'll invest the money in commercial paper, bank deposits, or something else that may seem conservative now, but could turn sour at the very time the depression insurance is supposed to pay off. It's important that the cash reserve withstand whatever happens.

Chapters 16 and 17 will discuss Treasury securities and money market funds. We will explain there why we think the safest place for the cash reserve is in either Treasury bills or a money market fund that invests only in Treasury securities. Because the put program requires monthly purchases and sales, a money market fund will be a convenient medium for at least part of the cash reserve. Treasury bills won't be practical unless the reserve exceeds $50,000, because the smallest Treasury bill is $10,000, and fractions of the reserve will be flowing back and forth.

Most stockbrokers have their own money market funds. But only Merrill Lynch's Government Fund invests in Treasury securities; the other brokerage funds invest in such things as commercial paper and certificates of deposit.

Unless you use the Merrill Lynch Government Fund, you have two choices. You can open an account with a money market fund elsewhere, and give the broker power of attorney to deposit and withdraw funds. Or you can deal with the fund yourself—transmitting money back and forth between the fund and the broker.

Handling the money yourself will be a little more work, but not much more. Most money market funds allow you to write a check on the fund (explained on page 268). So when money is to be withdrawn from the cash reserve, you can write a check on the fund at the same time you write a business check for the regular monthly payment. You'll most likely feel safer handling the money yourself.

The instructions on pages 210–211 are to be used if you are going to handle the cash reserve yourself. If the broker is going to handle it, use the instructions on pages 212–213.

Building your own depression insurance policy involves work. But once you establish the program, the broker will handle 99% of the work. You'll need only to write checks or make deposits with the money market fund once each month.

ALTERATIONS

There is a problem of scale in that commissions on options are larger (as a percentage of the value of a purchase) than for stocks. Also, the minimum commission for a transaction might overwhelm an option purchase.

The commissions won't be a problem if the amount you're attempting to insure is $1 million or more. If it's less than that, discuss the situation with the broker who will handle the program. Find out how much of the monthly investment will go into commissions. If it will be more than 15%, consider alternatives such as making purchases only every other month (instead of monthly) with twice the amount per purchase.

TO BEGIN

To get started:

1. Determine the amount of the monthly payment in accordance with the formula we gave on page 205. Once you've done that, multiply every dollar figure we used on pages 206 and 207 by the number of dollars you've picked for the monthly payment.

2. Pick the appropriate letter of instruction from the two on pages 210–213, depending on whether you're going to leave the cash reserve with the broker.

3. Type two copies (or make photocopies) of the instructions, filling in the blank spaces. If possible, make a photocopy of this chapter.

INSTRUCTIONS FOR BROKER

(To be used if a money market fund keeps the cash reserve)

This letter provides instructions for managing my portfolio of put options.

1. *Purpose:* My intention is to hold a diversified portfolio of put options that, in the event of a severe economic recession, will provide a large profit to offset losses that may occur in my business.

2. *To begin:*
   a. Attached is my check for $_____
   b. Purchase an assortment of put options worth that amount. Select the options in accordance with item #5 below, but divide the funds among puts expiring four, five, six, and seven months from now.
   c. I am also placing $_____ in a cash reserve with _____.

3. *Payments:* On the first day of each month, I will send you a check for $_____.

4. *Maintenance:* Each month, on the last trading day for options that expire that month:
   a. Sell any put options that expire that month.
   b. Purchase new put options (selected in accordance with item #5 below) with expiration dates eight months away. For this purchase, use the following amounts of money:
      (i) The monthly payment from me (item #3) above; plus
      (ii) One-half the proceeds of the puts you are selling; plus
      (iii) An additional payment I will send from the cash reserve, which will be a percentage of the cash reserve, based on the level of the Dow Jones Industrial Average, as follows:

      20% of the cash reserve when DJIA = 800 or more   5% of the cash reserve when DJIA = 500 to 599
      15% of the cash reserve when DJIA = 700 to 799   0% of the cash reserve when DJIA = under 500
      10% of the cash reserve when DJIA = 600 to 699

   c. Keep track of the amount in my cash reserve, including the initial deposit I am making (item 2c above), amounts you will transfer to it (item 4d below), and amounts you instruct me to withdraw from it (item 4e below).
   d. Each month, determine the amount that should be withdrawn from, or deposited to, the cash reserve. Subtract one-half the proceeds of the puts just sold (item ii above) from the computation in (iii) above. If the result is positive, telephone me and I will transfer that amount to you from my cash reserve. If the result is a negative figure, please transfer that amount to:

   _____

   _____ : to be credited to my account # _____

e. If the DJIA is below 600, inform me of the total value of my holdings (cash reserve + value of puts). I will then withdraw 10% of that amount from my cash reserves, removing the money from the put program. Note this withdrawal in your record of my cash reserve.

5. Put Selection:

a. Do not purchase options on ASA, Homestake Mining, or any other company that has a major interest in gold mining.

b. Purchase the options of a broadly diversified group of companies. However, 25% to 35% of the funds invested at any time should be in puts for the following companies.

_____

_____

c. Whenever possible, purchase puts that are out of the money (no exercise value), but subject to the following restrictions:

(i) Purchase no put option whose price is less than 1% of the price of its underlying stock.

(ii) No individual purchase of a given company should be for less than $250.

d. Diversify as widely as possible, subject only to the qualifications above.

6. Timing: All purchases and sales should be made at the opening of the market.

If you are ever in doubt, please call me.

Signature _____   Received and understood:

Name _____   _____ Broker's signature

Address _____   _____ Company

City, State _____

Telephone _____

Blanks to be filled in: Item 2a: Four times the monthly payment. Item 2c: Four times the monthly payment, and the name of the money market fund. Item 3: The monthly payment. Item 4d: Name and address of the money market fund, and your account number with the fund. Item 5b: Companies in industries related to your business.

INSTRUCTIONS FOR BROKER
(To be used if the broker keeps the cash reserve)

This letter provides instructions for managing my portfolio of put options.

1. *Purpose:* My intention is to hold a diversified portfolio of put options that, in the event of a severe economic recession, will provide a large profit to offset losses that may occur in my business.

2. *To begin:*

    a. Attached is my check for $ _____

    b. Purchase an assortment of put options worth one-half the amount of my check. Select the options in accordance with item #5 below, but divide the funds among puts expiring four, five, six, and seven months from now.

    c. The rest of the enclosed amount is to be placed in a cash reserve.

3. *Payments:* On the first day of each month, I will send you a check for $ _____

4. *Maintenance:* Each month, on the last trading day for options that expire that month:

    a. Sell any put options that expire that month.

    b. Purchase new put options (selected in accordance with item #5 below) with expiration dates eight months away. For this purchase, use the following amounts of money:

        (i) The monthly payment from me (item #3 above); plus

        (ii) One-half the proceeds of the puts you are selling; plus

        (iii) A percentage of the cash reserve, based on the level of the Dow Jones Industrial Average, as follows:

        20% of the cash reserve when DJIA = 800 or more
        15% of the cash reserve when DJIA = 700 to 799
        10% of the cash reserve when DJIA = 600 to 699
        5% of the cash reserve when DJIA = 500 to 599
        0% of the cash reserve when DJIA = under 500

    c. If the DJIA is 600 or less, send me a check for 10% of the total value of the account (market value of puts + cash reserve)

5. *Put Selection:*

a. Do not purchase options on ASA, Homestake Mining, or any other company that has a major interest in gold mining.

b. Purchase the options of a broadly diversified group of companies. However, 25% to 35% of the funds invested at any time should be in puts for the following companies.

_____   _____

_____   _____

_____   _____

c. Whenever possible, purchase puts that are out of the money (no exercise value), but subject to the following restrictions:

(i) Purchase no put option whose price is less than 1% of the price of its underlying stock.
(ii) No individual purchase of a given company should be for less than $250.

d. Diversify as widely as possible, subject only to the qualifications above.

6. *Timing:* All purchases and sales should be made at the opening of the market.

If you are ever in doubt, please call me.

Signature _____   Received and understood:

Name _____   _____ Broker's signature

Address _____   _____ Company

City, State _____

Telephone _____

Blanks to be filled in:

Item 2a: Eight times the monthly payment.
Item 3: The monthly payment.
Item 5b: Companies in industries related to your business.

4. Ask a stockbroker to read the instructions and this chapter, and tell you if he'll carry out the program for you. If he won't, try another stockbroker.

5. Have the broker sign one copy of the instructions, to confirm that he understands what he is to do. Sign one copy yourself and leave it with him, so that he'll know exactly what he's agreed to do.

6. Give him a check equivalent to eight months' payments.

7. Sleep easier that night.

From there on, the program is self-executing. You'll send the broker a check once each month, and he'll let you know whenever you're to withdraw money from the cash reserve.

WHEN TO START

We can't know where the stock market will be when you read this. Whether the market is high or low, you might feel there's some reason not to start the program at this time. If the market is very low, it may seem that it's already too late for the program to be of any benefit. And if the market is rising, you might think you should wait until it peaks.

If you decide the program makes sense for your business, we think you should start it now. No matter where the market is, you have no way of knowing whether it's headed higher or lower. Even if the market seems to be at an historically low level, it could drop another 25% or more from that point. Stocks were cheap in 1930, but they were a lot cheaper in 1932.

With other investments, if you buy just before the market begins a movement in the opposite direction, it can be a long time before it returns to the level at which you bought. But that's immaterial with options, because every option has a fresh start. The striking price of your first option will be replaced eight months later with a striking price close to where the stock is then. No matter where the market was when you started, anytime the market turns downward substantially, profits start flowing.

214

INSURANCE

No one can testify today that he saved his business with put options. The idea is new and untested, and if you use it, you won't have much company.

The idea also is not completely mature. After the next depression, we'll all know more than we do now about running such an insurance program.

Nevertheless, we believe the idea is sound. Enough is known about the stock market's behavior in a depression to make the idea practical. The program may not only help your business survive, it may enable you to take advantage of the opportunities a depression presents to a businessman with ready cash.

PART IV

DOLLAR
INVESTMENTS

14

INTEREST RATES

THE CHAPTERS IN THIS PART DEAL WITH BONDS, MORTGAGES, money market investments, and other promises to pay a fixed number of dollars. Inflation has given these fixed-dollar investments a bad name, but we hope to show how they still can perform a valuable function in a balanced portfolio.

Because all fixed-dollar investments involve the payment of interest, we will begin by looking at how interest rates are set and at how interest-rate changes affect investment values.

STRIKING A BARGAIN

A loan is a contract to trade present dollars for future dollars. The loan's interest rate is a way of expressing the price at which the trade is being made; it indicates today's price for future dollars.

If I ask you to lend me $100 for a year at an interest rate of 10%, I am offering you 110 future dollars (dated one year from today) in exchange for 100 present dollars. On these terms, today's price for a (one year) future dollar is $.9091 ($100/110 = .9091$). That is, for every $.9091 you give me now, you'll get back $1.00.

Purchasing Power

As with any other exchange, the price must satisfy both parties. And although a loan is quoted in dollars, it is the purchasing power of the dollars that both the borrower and the lender care about.

On the day a loan is made (or a bond issued), the purchasing power of the money is known by both parties, since they know the current prices of the various things they might want to buy. Future purchasing power is another matter. Neither the borrower nor the lender knows precisely how much inflation will occur during the term of the loan, so each party can only estimate what the money is going to be worth.

The borrower uses his inflation estimate in deciding how much interest he's willing to pay. If he has a use for the money that he believes will be profitable (after allowing for inflation), he'll be willing to pay an interest rate that may seem to be very high.

The lender uses his inflation estimate in deciding what interest rates he'll accept. He'll be reluctant to accept an interest rate that's lower than inflation, even if the interest he's offered is unusually high.

In both cases, it is the change in purchasing power that people *expect,* not the change that will actually occur, that affects interest rates. Because a person's expectations are based on his experience, past inflation affects interest rates indirectly —by influencing people's expectations of future inflation.

The graph on page 222 compares the interest rate on 12-month Treasury bills with the change in the Consumer Price Index over the preceding 12 months. The graph on page 223 compares the interest rate on 10-year Treasury bonds with the inflation rate over the preceding 10 years. To no great surprise, interest rates do rise and fall with inflation.

Risk

The risk associated with a loan also affects the interest rate. A loan, after all, is a promise—and sometimes promises are broken. Lenders know this and must be offered an incentive to accept the possibility that they won't be repaid. The greater the chance of default, the higher the interest rate the lender will demand.

As with inflation, it is the risk that people anticipate that influences the interest rate on a loan, not the risk that actually

220

will unfold (or be discovered never to have existed) during the term of the loan.

Investment markets operate because of differences of opinion, and your opinion (about risk or anything else) might be different from that of other investors. If so, you can act on your opinion by buying what others seem to be selling too cheaply, or selling what others are willing to pay too much for, or simply standing aside when the terms are unattractive.

We indicated in Part One that we believe the coming decade will be particularly hazardous. Our feeling is that to-day's markets underestimate the risks of default, and that the normal 2% difference in interest rates between Treasury bills and negotiable CDs, or between Treasury bonds and middle-grade corporate bonds, is too small. In other words, we don't believe the extra 2% is at all comparable to the added risk.

Even if you think the 2% bonus is worth the added risk, you can't take advantage of it unless your portfolio is large enough to spread the risk. Someone with $1 million to invest in bonds could put $10,000 into the bonds of each of 100 companies. If only 1% of the companies defaulted, the additional 2% interest earned from the others would more than offset the loss.

But with a smaller portfolio, you would be able to invest in, perhaps, only four companies. If one of the four were among the 1% that defaulted, you'd lose 25% of your investment—in pursuit of an extra 2% yield.

INTEREST RATES & LOAN VALUES

Interest rates are constantly changing. As they change, they affect the market value of all existing fixed-dollar investments. Bonds are the most visible example.

A bond has three dimensions—its face value, its maturity date, and its coupon rate. The face value is the amount the bond's issuer has promised to repay. The maturity date is the date on which repayment is due. The coupon rate is the dollar interest the bond pays each year—expressed as a percentage of the face value.

For example, you might buy a new 12% bond with a face value of $1,000 and a maturity date of January 2, 1995.

221

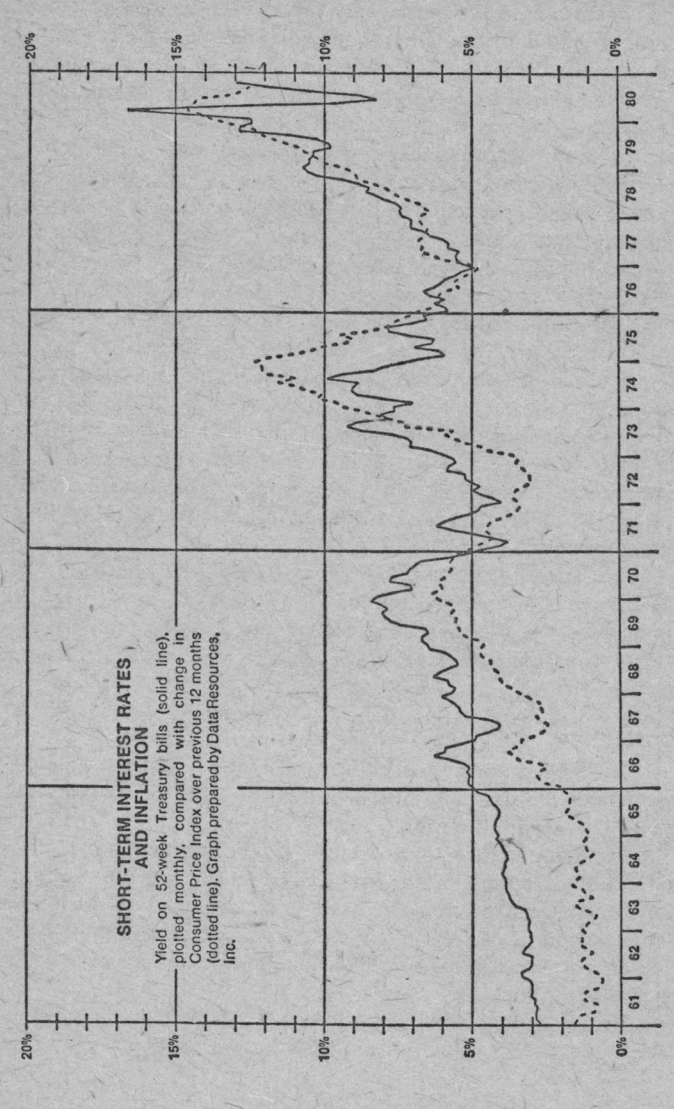

**SHORT-TERM INTEREST RATES
AND INFLATION**

Yield on 52-week Treasury bills (solid line),
plotted monthly, compared with change in
Consumer Price Index over previous 12 months
(dotted line). Graph prepared by Data Resources,
Inc.

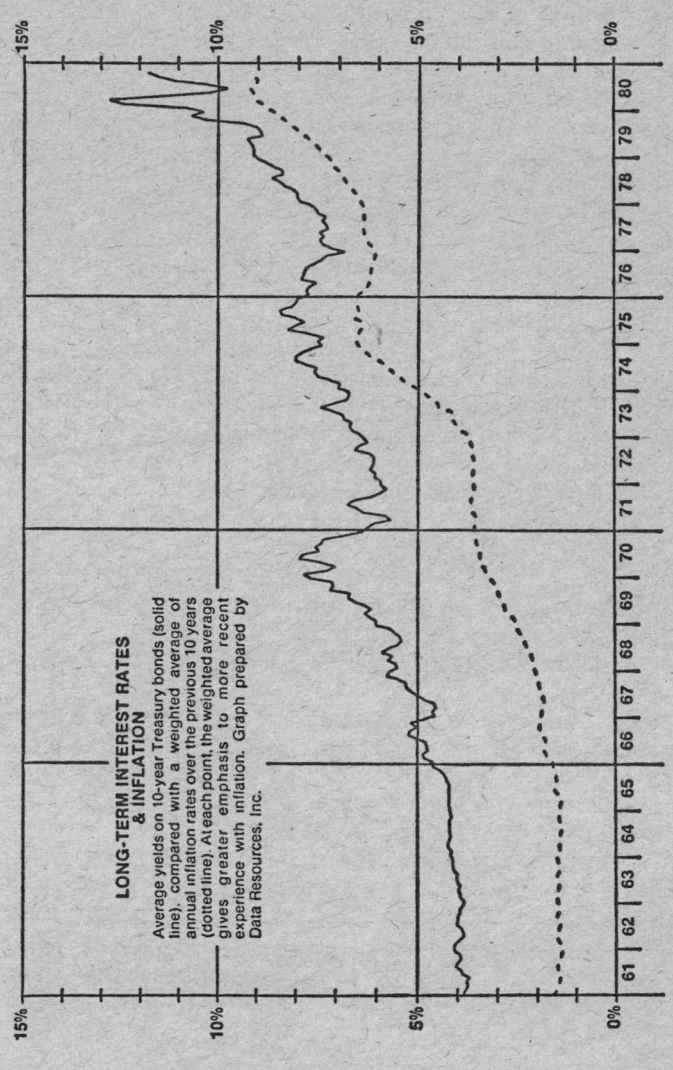

LONG-TERM INTEREST RATES & INFLATION

Average yields on 10-year Treasury bonds (solid line), compared with a weighted average of annual inflation rates over the previous 10 years (dotted line). At each point, the weighted average gives greater emphasis to more recent experience with inflation. Graph prepared by Data Resources, Inc.

This means the borrower promises to pay you (or anyone you sell the bond to) $1,000 on January 2, 1995. The coupon rate of 12% means that the borrower will pay you yearly interest equal to 12% of the $1,000—or $120 per year.

Suppose that interest rates rise after you buy the bond, and similar bonds are being issued with a coupon rate of 14%. If you decide to sell, no one will offer $1,000 for your bond—since it pays interest of only $120 per year, while new bonds are paying $140. You'll be able to attract a buyer only by accepting a price below your bond's face value.

How low must the price be? Computing the exact price is a little complicated, but there's a minimum that's easy to identify. At a price of $860, the buyer would collect the same annual interest rate from your bond ($120/$860 = 14%) as he could get from a new bond.

The $860 price is a minimum because the buyer has a good reason to pay more. When the bond matures, he'll collect the bond's full face value of $1,000—even though he paid less than that. So he might be willing to pay $900 for the bond, accept current interest of a little less than 14%, and collect a profit of $100 when the bond matures.[1]

Long & Short Terms

The prices of all bonds tend to fall when interest rates rise. The reduced prices make it profitable for bond buyers to accept a lower current yield on old bonds than they can get on new bonds.

In deciding how much profit is needed to offset a lower current yield, a bond buyer naturally will consider the number of years he must hold the bond to earn the profit. The more years to maturity, the longer the buyer must wait for his profit, and the larger the profit he'll want.

Consequently, when interest rates rise, long-term bonds fall more in price than short-term bonds. And when interest

---

[1]Corporate and Treasury bonds are usually issued with face values in multiples of $1,000. Their prices are quoted as a percentage of the face value. Thus a $1,000 bond selling for $860 would be quoted as "86."

rates fall, bond prices rise—but the prices of long-term bonds rise more than those of short-term bonds. Up or down, long-term bonds go through bigger price movements than short-term bonds.

Interest rates have been rising since 1941, and the last 27 years of the rise are shown in the graphs on pages 226 and 228. The first graph traces the interest yield for 20-year Treasury bonds; the second shows the market price of a Treasury bond with 20 years to maturity.

Note that the two trends are not straight lines. As the Federal Reserve attempts to spend its way out of each recession, it increases the money supply by buying bonds—temporarily pushing bond prices up and interest rates down. But once the new money has run through the economy, inflation increases and interest rates go to higher levels than before.

FLOATING RATES

The prices of short-term dollar investments are very stable. Even when interest rates are changing rapidly, the prices of one- and two-year bonds move only a little. And the price movements of very short term investments, such as 90-day Treasury bills, are almost unnoticeable.

Some long-term bonds achieve the stability of short-term bonds by paying an interest rate that floats. Each semiannual payment is tied to a formula—such as 3% over the current Treasury bill rate or 2% over the current prime rate.

The formula assures investors that they will always receive an interest payment comparable to what they could get on new bonds. Because of this assurance, the price of a floating-rate bond is nearly constant (provided the issuer maintains his credit standing) no matter how interest rates change—even though the bond may not mature for 20 or 30 years.

INVISIBLE VALUES

The reaction of bond prices to changes in interest rates is visible because bonds are traded publicly and their prices are quoted daily.

For assets that aren't traded in public markets, the re-

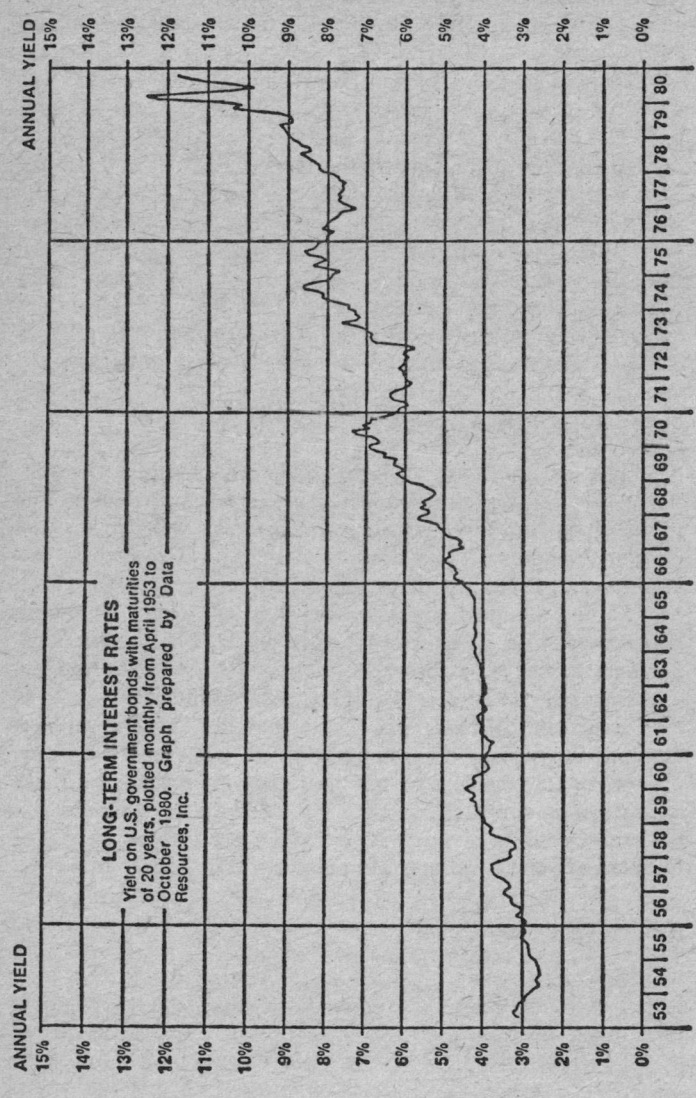

ANNUAL YIELD

LONG-TERM INTEREST RATES

Yield on U.S. government bonds with maturities of 20 years, plotted monthly from April 1953 to October 1980. Graph prepared by Data Resources, Inc.

sponse isn't as easy to see. The newspaper doesn't publish the current market price of your 5-year, 6% certificate of deposit or the value of the 8% mortgage on your house. Nevertheless, all fixed-dollar investments are governed by the principles we've discussed.

Mortgage Values

A mortgage is a good example of an asset whose value can change without being noticed. Suppose that ten years ago you bought a house with a 30-year, 8% mortgage of $50,000. After ten years of monthly payments, you still owe $44,000— with 20 years left to go. In the meantime, the interest rate on new mortgages has risen to 12%.

The mortgage you owe is an asset of the bank that lent you the money. If, instead of lending you the money, the bank had invested $50,000 in 8%, 30-year bonds, rising interest rates would have reduced the bonds' value. Has the bank suffered a similar loss on your mortgage?

The bank won't mention a loss in its annual report, the bank examiners won't notice a loss, and the regulatory agencies won't discuss the subject—but there is a loss. There are at least five different ways to identify it.

1. *Lost income:* If the bank actually had the $44,000 you still owe, it could lend the money out on a 12% mortgage and earn half-again as much as the 8% interest you're paying.

2. *Alternative investment:* At 12%, the bank needs to lend only $33,000 to produce the same monthly payments your mortgage provides. The bank would be $11,000 richer if it weren't locked into your loan; it could invest the extra $11,000 somewhere else.

3. *Resale value:* If the bank offered to sell your mortgage to another bank, it would receive only $33,000 or so—whatever price would give the second bank a 12% return on its money. Just as with bonds, no one will pay face value to acquire an 8% investment when he can get a new investment that earns 12%.

4. *Bond comparison:* We can see how changes in interest rates affect bonds because their prices are published daily. If a bond were no longer traded publicly, or if the newspaper

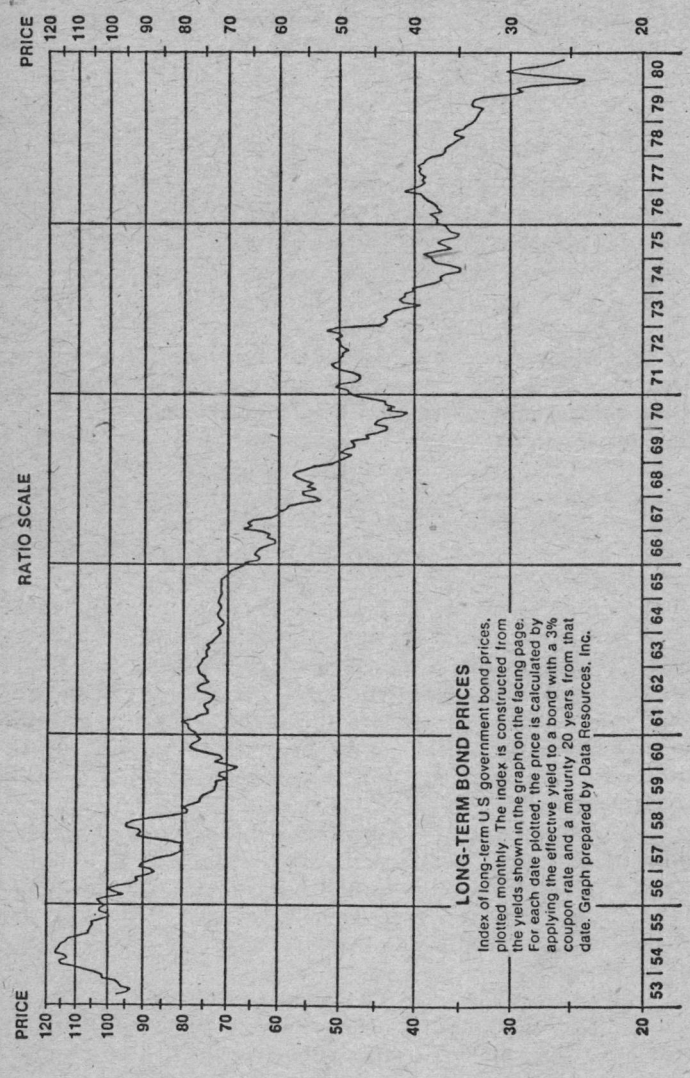

LONG-TERM BOND PRICES

Index of long-term U S government bond prices, plotted monthly. The index is constructed from the yields shown in the graph on the facing page. For each date plotted, the price is calculated by applying the effective yield to a bond with a 3% coupon rate and a maturity 20 years from that date. Graph prepared by Data Resources, Inc.

merely stopped publishing its price, the silence wouldn't insulate the bond's value from interest rate changes. A mortgage is no different; it is simply a custom-made bond that never appears in public.

5. *Prepayment:* If the mortgage were actually worth the $44,000 you still owe, the bank would be indifferent to an early repayment. But if you have any doubts that the 8% mortgage is worth less than $44,000, call your banker and say that you'd like to give him $44,000 to pay it off early. He'll send a limousine to pick you up. He may even drive it himself.

Mortgage Profit

If the bank has sustained a loss, have you made a profit? Definitely. You have the use of 8% money during a time of 12% mortgages, a valuable privilege. And if you wanted to pay off the mortgage, there's even a way to collect the $11,000 profit.

Instead of paying $44,000 to retire your present mortgage, you could invest $33,000 by purchasing a 20-year mortgage on someone else's house—an investment that would return 12% interest. The payments you receive would be equal to the payments you must make on the mortgage you owe. In effect, you'd be relieved of the payments you were making—but at a cost of only $33,000, not $44,000.

If you look at the matter in terms of owning one mortgage and owing another, the payments match—making it easy to see how rising interest rates have reduced the value of your debt. In practice, however, we wouldn't feel safe depending on someone's promise to repay a mortgage on schedule.

Even if the mortgage were only a modest fraction of the property's present value, the borrower might have trouble making payments on time—possibly when you were counting most on receiving them. Rather than purchase a mortgage, it would be more practical to ask the bank for a discount for repayment, or to invest the payoff money in long-term Treasury bonds.

And whether to pay off the mortgage at all is a question that can't be considered in isolation from the rest of your affairs. It is only one of many ways to reduce your *net* dollar indebtedness or to increase your *net* dollar holdings. As we'll see in Part Six, the first step is to decide what your net dollar position should be. Only then can you decide how to get to that position.

Our point here is that the values of all long-term debts and dollar assets are affected by interest rates. As interest rates rise, such things as long-term bank deposits, fixed-rate annuity contracts, and fixed-dollar pension plans all lose value. The loss is unpublicized, but it is very real. If you doubt it, just examine an investment from any of the five viewpoints we described on pages 227 and 229.

The tables on pages 530–533 can help determine the present value of any fixed-dollar investment you own or owe.

INTEREST RATE INVESTMENTS

In an era of rising inflation, fixed-dollar investments have a particularly bad reputation.

The dollars lose purchasing power through the years, but the government taxes the interest as if it were true profit. Dollars would seem to be a particularly bad choice for an inflation-proof portfolio. U.S. government bonds have even been called "certificates of guaranteed confiscation."[2]

But slogans and clichés are not a sound basis for investment decisions. We must always consider the various possibilities for the future of inflation, how different investments would react to those possibilities, and how the investments can be held. When you do this, you often arrive at conclusions different from those suggested by the slogans.

So before you dismiss fixed-dollar investments, consider three points:

1. After 20 years of rising prices, it may be difficult to believe that inflation will end someday. But it must end, and it might end in a violent deflation. If so, dollars may be the only investment that saves your portfolio from great losses. Since you can't know if or when this will occur, you can

---

[2]By Franz Pick many times. For example, the *International Herald Tribune*, June 28, 1980, page 12.

prepare only by holding some dollars during the inflation.

2. Even if a deflation never occurs, there will be wide swings back and forth in investment prices before inflation reaches its conclusion. If you hold some dollars, you'll always have buying power available when investment prices are low. And even if you don't want to exploit these swings, the dollars will contribute to your peace of mind during the intermittent periods when investment prices are falling.

3. If you hold short-term dollar investments, the interest you receive will rise as interest rates rise—staying pretty close to changing inflation rates. If you can protect the interest from taxes so that it can compound fully, the purchasing power of the dollars will stay fairly constant.

In Part Five, we'll offer some safe and relatively simple ways to shelter interest income from current income taxes. With a shelter, and with the tendency for interest rates to rise with inflation. it is still possible to use dollars as a stable reserve of purchasing power.

15

U. S. BANKS

THE BANKING SYSTEM PROVIDES THE PAYMENTS MECHANISM that the economy and every investment in it depend upon. So we will devote special attention to banks—before moving on to individual dollar investments.

Our deflation scenario in Chapter 4 implied that money in the bank may not be entirely safe and secure. Our purpose wasn't to scare you; for most people the daily newspaper takes care of that. Our concern is to help you understand the risks that exist and to show you ways to protect yourself from the ones you prefer to avoid.

We believe that U.S. banks in general are in very poor financial condition, and that they are risky places to keep savings—or even too much spending money.

We aren't predicting that all banks will go under, nor that depositors at banks that do go under will lose all their money. But we're concerned enough that neither of the authors keeps more than one month's expenses in a U.S. bank at any time. Fortunately, there are a number of convenient and profitable alternatives available for many of the functions for which you might normally use a bank.

This chapter will explain why we are doubtful about banks. The two chapters that follow will explore the alternatives.

INFLATION & BANKS

A bank is a dealer in credit. It obtains credit from one group of customers, called depositors, and provides credit to another group of customers, called borrowers.

A bank is profitable only so long as the interest it receives from borrowers is greater than the interest it pays to depositors. And it can repay its depositors only so long as its borrowers live up to their promises to repay their loans on schedule. If either requirement isn't met, the bank is in trouble.

We need to see how inflation has affected both the profitability of banks and the caution they exercise in evaluating would-be borrowers.

Profits

A bank won't deliberately pay more on deposits than it can earn on loans. But inflation can trick a bank into doing so.

Interest rates on long-term loans and deposits are usually higher than on short-term loans and deposits. This relationship reverses temporarily when money is tight, but it holds true most of the time. Consequently a bank usually is motivated to borrow money through short-term deposits and lend it at a higher interest rate on long-term loans.

As an extreme but not uncommon example, a bank might borrow money through 90-day certificates of deposit and lend it out as a 30-day mortgage. This is "borrowing short and lending long"—the bank commits itself to repay on short notice money that it may not get back for many years. So long as interest rates don't rise, the practice can be highly profitable; the bank will collect the difference between what it earns on mortgages and what it pays to attract and hold deposits.

But as inflation moves higher, interest rates also rise— and the bank must pay more and more to renew the short-term deposits, even while its income from the 30-year mortgage is fixed. At some point, the bank will be paying more on the deposits than it is earning on the loan. The loss must be covered by digging into the bank's own reserves. The longer this process continues (and the faster it goes), the weaker the bank becomes. Its ability to survive loan defaults is gradually eroded.

In 1980 most banks are already suffering from high interest rates. The 7%, 8%, and 9% mortgages made years ago are still on the books—and are losing money for banks that must pay 10%, 11%, and 12% on many certificates of deposit. If inflation reaches new highs, the losses will be even worse.

Defaults

Banks face other inflationary problems. Monetary inflation doesn't rise in a steady path; it rises in waves. Each dose of extra money, bigger than the last, is injected when the government fears the economy is sliding too deep into a recession.

The new money rescues many borrowers who had been pushed toward bankruptcy—and also rescues their lenders. As the process is repeated—cycle after cycle—some lenders acquire an overly rosy view of the world and begin to underestimate the risks they're taking.

The government has been buying off recessions for so long that most lenders have never seen what happens when inflation comes to a halt—or what happens when the government merely holds monetary inflation steady for an extended period. Because rising inflation has rescued so many bad loans, banks are willing to make loans they wouldn't have considered thirty years ago.

Trap

The losses from long-term loans and the accumulation of potentially bad loans are both products of inflation. And, together, they have the banking system in a trap.

When the economy enters a recession, the government must decide whether to inflate further. If it does, there will be higher inflation and higher interest rates a year or two later—causing a profit squeeze for banks. If it doesn't, the banks will be swamped by a wave of defaults. Either way, the banks lose.

BALANCE SHEET

A bank's assets (what it owns) include cash, deposits it keeps at other banks, loans to customers, securities such as

235

bonds and Treasury bills, buildings, furniture and equipment, and so forth. Its liabilities (what it owes) include the deposits made by customers and other banks, and various other types of borrowings.

Every year the Federal Reserve publishes a consolidated balance sheet for all insured commercial banks in the U.S.—showing the total holdings of all banks in each of the asset and liability categories. The tables on pages 237–238, 240 (which are condensed from the Federal Reserve balance sheet) compare what banks own (their assets) with what they owe (their liabilities) in three different formats—giving us a look at the health of the banking system.

Spot Liquidity

The first indication of a bank's safety is spot liquidity. It measures a bank's ability to come up with enough cash to meet all possible withdrawal requests and other claims that are payable on demand. It is stated as a percentage; 100% means the bank could cover every claim without outside help.

As the table on page 237 shows, spot liquidity for the average bank is 65%. This means the average bank could raise quickly from its own resources only a little more than 65 cents for each dollar it could be asked to repay on the spot.

Maturity Balance

A second indication of a bank's strength is its maturity balance. This compares the average maturity of the bank's assets with the average maturity of its liabilities.

If the two are close, the bank won't be hurt by the rising interest rates that accompany rising inflation. But if the average time until the bank's loans and investments are due to be repaid is longer than the average time until deposits and other claims on the bank fall due, the bank will lose money with every step up in inflation.

The table on page 238 shows that the average maturity of bank assets is 19 months, while the average maturity of liabilities is only 4 months. This imbalance means that each time inflation moves to a higher level, the interest rates banks

SPOT LIQUIDITY OF U.S. BANKS
(billions of dollars)

Liquid Assets

Cash items		$114.1
Cash	$12.1	
Reserves with Federal Reserve	28.0	
Deposits with non-system banks[1]	4.8	
Cash items in collection	69.2	
Securities		262.2
U.S. Treasury	95.1	
U.S. government agencies	40.1	
Municipal governments	121.3	
Others	5.8	
Federal funds & repurchases, net[2]		7.0
Call loans on securities		15.3
	Total liquid assets:	$398.7

Spot Liabilities

Demand deposits	$329.4
Savings deposits	223.3
Federal funds & repurchases, net[2]	57.7
Total spot liabilities:	$610.5

Percentage of spot liabilities covered by liquid assets: 65.3%

Calculations are for all FDIC-insured commercial banks in the United States as of September 30, 1978 (the latest date for which figures on all banks were available in October 1980).

Figures may not agree because of rounding.

Source: *Federal Reserve Bulletin.* September 1980. pages A18 & A19. table 1.26.
[1] Deposits with non-insured, non-commercial, or foreign banks.
[2] Includes only federal funds & repurchase agreements with non-bank entities and banks that are not included in these calculations.

MATURITY BALANCE OF U.S. BANKS
(billions of dollars)

	Amount	Average Maturity (months)
Assets		
Cash items	$114.1	0
Time deposits	4.6	3
Debt securities	262.2	31.4
Loans	682.6	18.3
Federal funds & repos, net[1]	7.0	0
Total assets:	$1,070.6	

Weighted average maturity = 19.4 months

	Amount	Average Maturity (months)
Liabilities		
Demand deposits	$329.4	0
Savings accounts	223.3	0
Time deposits	360.6	9.4
Federal funds & repos, net[1]	57.7	0
Unearned interest	17.0	0.5
Miscellaneous	37.6	12.0
Total liabilities	$1,024.9	

Weighted average maturity = 3.8 months

Calculations are for all FDIC-insured commercial banks in the United States as of September 30, 1978 (the latest date for which figures on all banks were available).

The "Average Maturity" is the number of months before the item will be receivable (for assets) or payable (for liabilities).

Dollar amounts are from table 1.26 (pages A18 & A19) of the September 1980 *Federal Reserve Bulletin*. The average maturity of securities was estimated from table 1.43 (page A33) of the September 1980 issue, using 1978 data. The average maturity of loans was estimated from the category of loan shown on table 1.26. The maturities of time deposits were estimated from table 4.10 (page A69) of the November 1979 issue, using data for April 25, 1979. The maturities for "Unearned interest" and "Miscellaneous" were estimated by the authors. "Cash items," "Federal funds," "Demand deposits," and "Savings accounts" are assumed to be payable on demand. Fixed assets and capital were not included.

Figures may not agree because of rounding.

[1]Includes only federal funds & repurchase agreements with non-bank entities and banks that are not included in these calculations.

pay will rise faster than the interest rates they receive—since the deposits will be renewed more quickly than money from loans can be collected and re-lent at higher rates.

Safety Ratio

A third measure of bank reliability is the safety ratio. It focuses on loans and investments that are subject to loss—either from defaults or from rising interest rates. The safety ratio compares these risky assets with the resources the bank can afford to lose. The test determines how much of the bank's risky investments could be lost without keeping the bank from repaying its depositors.

The table on page 240 shows a figure of 12%. This means that if the value of an average bank's risky assets declined by more than 12%, the bank would be insolvent; it would no longer have enough assets to repay all depositors—even if they were willing to wait.

Understatement

Inflation has encouraged a long-term deterioration in all three categories, although there are periodic improvements in the percentages. The improvements occur during recessions—as banks feel overextended and attempt to become more liquid. But once the recessionary danger seems to have passed, the deterioration resumes.

The numbers aren't good, but even so they understate the weakness of banks.

For example, long-term bonds (which comprise about 10% of the average bank's assets) are kept on the balance sheets at the prices paid by the bank, not at the current market value of the bonds. The graph on page 228 shows that bond prices have been in a downward trend for decades. Unless a bank purchased most of its bonds just recently, the present value of the bonds is probably less than its balance sheet shows.

The same may be true of some of the other assets displayed on the balance sheet; they are valued at original cost even though the market value may have declined. This means

SAFETY RATIO OF U.S. BANKS
(billions of dollars)

	Amount	Risk Factor	Net Risk Amount
Assets			
Cash items	$114.1	0	$ 0
Time deposits at banks[1]	4.6	0	0
U.S. government securities	135.1	15	20.3
Municipal & other securities	128.7	25	32.2
Federal funds & repos, net[2]	7.0	0	0
Call loans on securities	15.3	0	0
Agricultural loans	28.1	1	28.1
Real estate loans	203.4	1	203.4
Loans to financial companies	37.1	1	37.1
Commercial & industrial loans	213.1	1	213.1
Loans to individuals	161.6	1	161.6
Other loans & leases	24.1	1	24.1
Fixed & other assets	76.8	1	76.8
Total amount at risk:			$796.6
Capital			
Equity capital			$85.5
Subordinated notes & debentures			5.8
Reserves for loan losses			7.4
Total capital:			$98.7

Percentage of risk amount covered by capital: 12.4%

Calculations are for all FDIC-insured commercial banks in the United States as of September 30, 1978 (the latest date for which figures on all banks were available in October 1980).

The "Risk factor" has been estimated by the authors. An asset with negligible risk has a risk factor of 0; an asset with a risk of complete loss has a risk factor of 1. The "Net Risk Amount" is the "Amount" times the "Risk Factor."

Figures may not agree because of rounding.

Source of data: *Federal Reserve Bulletin*, September 1980, page A18 & A19, table 1 26.

[1] Time deposits with non-insured and other banks that are not included in these calculations.

[2] Includes only federal funds & repurchases owed by non-bank entities and banks that are not included in this balance sheet.

that the safety ratio and the spot liquidity are less than the figures indicate.

Also, the figures assume that banks will be able to sell their bonds when they need to raise cash. They will, but if large numbers of banks tried to raise cash in this way (as they might during a banking crisis), bond prices would tumble. The bonds would sell for far less than their value today. Thus the true spot-liquidity ratio is less than what we have calculated.

The measurements we've made reflect the average bank. Many individual banks are far weaker and far closer to insolvency. Some are insolvent right now.

There is a great danger that the weak banks will bring down the whole system. For one thing, some of the stronger banks may have deposits in the weaker banks—deposits that would be lost if the weak banks failed.

Also, if a number of the weakest banks failed, depositors everywhere would want to find out if their banks really had the money to meet withdrawals. The resulting bank run would put a strain on all but the strongest institutions—perhaps forcing many of the average banks to close, or leading to the closing of all banks by the government. It would be small comfort to know that your bank had been stronger than the average.

HOLDING THE SYSTEM TOGETHER

Most U.S. banks are chronically illiquid—that is, there is no way they could honor withdrawal requests if all depositors asked for their money at the same time.[1]

There have been periods of illiquidity in the U.S. before. Bank runs (mass demands by depositors for withdrawals) have developed whenever depositors had any reason to won-

---

[1] A common notion is that banks have to be that way in order to earn a profit. But this isn't true; there are numerous investments that are liquid and stable, and which earn more than what banks must pay to depositors. These investments—which include Treasury bills, other short-term money market instruments, margin loans, etc.—can be liquidated at a moment's notice to meet withdrawal requests.

der if their funds were safe. Knowing they had to look out for themselves, depositors acted to protect their funds whenever they had the slightest doubt about a bank's safety.

Because all banking panics in the U.S. have been followed by depressions, the government has long had an interest in bank stability. Unfortunately, during the present inflationary era, its interest has been directed not so much at keeping banks liquid as at convincing depositors that banks don't need to be liquid.

Bank customers are offered two reassurances: (1) the fact that deposits are insured by the Federal Deposit Insurance Corporation and (2) the idea that the Federal Reserve System won't let the banks fail. We need to look more closely at each of these reassurances.

FDIC

The Federal Deposit Insurance Corporation (FDIC) is an agency of the federal government whose purpose is to prevent bank depositors from losing money.

Theoretically, there are three methods it could use to accomplish its goal:

1. It could require banks to maintain sufficient liquidity to be able to repay their depositors at all times;

2. it could collect insurance premiums from the banks or their depositors—using actuarial principles to determine the size of the premiums—and setting aside enough money to cover all losses that depositors might incur; or

3. it could try to discourage depositors from withdrawing funds *en masse*, since it is a run on a bank that usually precipitates its failure and causes depositors to lose money.

You might assume that the FDIC relies on methods one and two. But, surprisingly, the FDIC relies mostly on method three.

Resources

The bank figures we examined showed that neither the FDIC nor anyone else has used method one. A brief look at

242

the FDIC's finances will show that method two isn't being used either.

As of December 31, 1979, the FDIC was insuring $808.6 billion of deposits—or 65.9% of the total deposits in insured banks in the U.S.

To cover its commitments, the FDIC had set aside $9.8 billion, or 1.21% of the amount it was insuring. In addition, it had a standby line of credit of $3.0 billion with the U.S. Treasury, bringing its total available resources to $12.8 billion —or 1.58% of the insured deposits.[2]

These resources would be sufficient to take care of the depositors at the largest bank in the U.S. or even at the two or three largest. Thus the FDIC is well equipped to protect depositors in individual, isolated bank failures. Ironically, if your bank were especially weak and collapsed by itself, you would have nothing to worry about; the FDIC would pick up the tab.

A general banking crisis would be another matter. The FDIC's assets and credit line amount to only a small fraction of what the banks would need. Any problems extending beyond a few large banks would exhaust the FDIC's reserves.

Sticker

The FDIC doesn't protect bank depositors by making sure that banks are safe or by holding enough money to compensate the depositors. How then does it do it? Instead of protecting depositors from banks, it protects banks from depositors. It tries to dissuade depositors from testing the banks' ability to pay.

If the FDIC tried to discourage mass withdrawals by prohibiting depositors from asking for more funds than a bank felt like paying out, most people would simply stop using banks. So instead the FDIC does its job by bluffing.

---

[2] All figures regarding the FDIC's finances are from the *Annual Report of the Federal Deposit Insurance Corporation, 1979,* the latest report available when we wrote this in 1980. The reserve percentages will be lower with the raising of the coverage of $100,000 per account from $40,000.

The logic behind the bluff is as follows:

(a) A bank fails because people rush to take out more money than the bank has.

(b) People rush to take their money out because they're afraid it might be lost in a bank failure.

(c) If no one were afraid he would lose his money, no one would rush to take it out, so . . . the bank wouldn't fail, and so . . . no one would lose his money.

Keeping people from being afraid is the job of the FDIC. It does this through a careful public relations campaign to convince everyone that all deposits will be paid—when, in fact, such a thing is impossible.

The campaign relies on a sticker that is pasted on the window of each bank—saying that your deposit is insured up to $100,000 by an agency of the federal government. As long as everyone believes in this talisman, there should be no runs on banks, and the FDIC should never have to make good on its promise. As long as everyone believes, it really doesn't matter that the money isn't there.

Vulnerability

As the inflationary trend continues, the condition of the banking system will continue to deteriorate. The losses on old, low-interest loans will worsen, the potential for defaults on loans made for projects that depend on inflation will accumulate, and the number of banks operating near the edge of insolvency will grow.

Their survival and the survival of the banking system itself will depend more and more on public confidence in the FDIC sticker and less and less on the resources the banks actually possess. At some point, the FDIC's bluff will be called, and a run on the banks will be under way.

The trigger might be a flurry of bank failures that keeps FDIC personnel so busy that there are delays in repaying depositors. Or perhaps a rapid decline in FDIC assets will alarm the public. Or possibly some other government insurance fund will have well-publicized troubles. Or maybe a run by holders of large, uninsured deposits will ruin a prominent bank. Or the trigger could be a non-financial event, such as a war scare, that creates a sudden demand for cash-in-hand. But it probably will be something else, something we can't now foresee.

A showdown is inevitable. At some point someone will ask for his money and he won't get it. He'll be told that his deposit is insured by the Federal Deposit Insurance Corporation. He'll be reminded that the FDIC is an agency of the U.S. government. He'll receive a recitation of the FDIC's record of decades of success. He may even hear a plea for the "public interest." He'll listen politely; and then he'll ask for his money again.

FEDERAL RESERVE PROTECTION

The FDIC is really only in charge of tidying up. If a bank fails, the FDIC pays off depositors or arranges a merger with another bank, and does whatever else is necessary to keep the story off page one of the newspapers. The real powerhouse of government protection is the Federal Reserve.

The Federal Reserve can save a bank by lending it money, perhaps oceans of money, at below-market interest rates. The cheap credit can buy off a lot of problems. Furnishing the money is easy, since the Fed can simply print it if it needs to. But there are two restraints on the Fed's use of this power.

First, the Fed must offset each loan it makes by selling an equivalent amount of government bonds in the open market—otherwise, the money supply would grow with each loan it made. Its holdings of government bonds are large—$120 billion as of August 1980. But this amount is small compared to the deposit liabilities of all banks ($1,404 billion on the same date) and could be exhausted quickly.[3]

Second, a Federal Reserve welfare program, like any other welfare program, would attract hoards of willing beneficiaries. An open hand at the Federal Reserve would encourage banks to exaggerate their troubles in order to qualify for subsidized loans, and would reinforce the present tendency toward carelessness in lending and investing. The Fed gov-

---

[3]*Federal Reserve Bulletin,* September 1980, pages A11 and A16.

ernors know this, so they approach any bank bailout cautiously.

It might be assumed that the Fed will at least make sure that no large bank fails—in order to avoid a panic. But Franklin National Bank was the nation's 20th largest bank and after lending it $1.75 billion, the Fed gave up and let it go under in 1974.[4]

Credit Lines

Banks also have made non-deposit promises that any government bailout would have to pay for.

Many companies have established lines of credit with their banks, usually as a reserve of working capital that can be drawn down as needed. As of March 31, 1980, unsecured credit lines (unsecured meaning that the customer may borrow without collateral) exceeded $250 billion.[5]

Companies pay for these credit lines in order to have something to fall back on in an emergency. They rely on credit lines in the same way they rely on cash. Because these promises to lend money are a legally enforceable bank obligation (just as deposits are), no attempt to save a bank from failing could succeed without honoring them.

PROTECTION OF BANKS

The FDIC insurance program and the supposed omnipotence of the Federal Reserve are meant to prevent bank runs by assuring the public that the government protects bank

---

[4]*Federal Reserve Bulletin,* October 1974, page 740; *The Failure of the Franklin National Bank* by Joan Edelman Spero (Columbia University Press, 1980), page 11.

[5]An unpublished Federal Reserve survey reported unused, unsecured credit lines of $248.4 billion at banks holding 85% of the banking system's deposits. If the lines of credit are added in to the consolidated balance sheet for all banks (on the asset side as risky assets, on the liability side as spot liabilities), the spot liquidity for the banking system becomes 46%, and the safety ratio just 9%.

deposits. In addition, the government attempts to guard banks from possible runs by providing special regulatory treatment and by trying to shield banks from competition.

Silence

When a regulator in any government agency has even a suspicion that something might be wrong with a private company, the characteristic response is to issue a press release detailing the suspicion and promising a prompt and thorough investigation. If the suspicion later proves to be unfounded, the company involved is left to clean up its reputation as best it can.

With banks, the approach is exactly the opposite; difficulties at a bank aren't discussed publicly. The Comptroller of the Currency (a federal banking agency) periodically reveals the number of banks on its "problem" list—but never the names nor very much about the problems. In this regard, banking is a more sensitive topic than national defense.

Price-Fixing

The government also has assumed that banks would be safer if they didn't compete with each other in the interest rates they offer. And so it authorized the Federal Reserve's "Regulation Q"—which places ceilings on the interest rates a bank or thrift institution can pay.

Like any price-fixing arrangement, it was supposed to benefit someone. But like most such schemes, it has produced more problems than benefits for everyone involved.

So long as market interest rates were below the official ceilings, the ceilings had no effect. Later, when open market rates rose and banks needed to pay more to attract and hold deposits, the official ceilings caused banks to lose business to non-bank competitors. This led to repeated tinkering with the interest-rate ceilings, and to attempts to handicap the competitors.

The problems first surfaced in 1970 when Treasury-bill interest rates rose to 7%, while the bank savings account ceil-

247

ing was 4½%. Many depositors closed their savings accounts and bought Treasury bills. The U.S. Treasury Department came to the rescue by raising the minimum purchase of Treasury bills to $10,000 (from $1,000)—sending small depositors back to the banks and the 4½% savings accounts.

In 1973 interest rates shot upward again—high enough above the ceiling that banks lost the large customers who could easily afford the $10,000 minimum to buy Treasury bills. The Federal Reserve stopped this drain by cutting a hole in the interest-rate ceiling, but it was careful to cut a hole that only certain depositors could get through.

The hole was an exemption from interest ceilings for deposits of $100,000 or more. This figure was chosen because holders of large deposits are the first to leave when bank interest rates appear too low. A large sum makes it worthwhile for the owner to investigate alternatives to bank deposits and go to the trouble of switching into them. The exemption for large deposits was enough to stem the outflow in 1973.

Since 1977, Treasury-bill interest rates have been consistently higher than the 5¼% ceiling on savings accounts. When T-bill rates reached 9% in 1978, the Fed had to cut another carefully shaped hole in the Q ceiling by letting banks offer something called "Money Market Certificates" or "T-Bill Accounts." The account is a six-month time deposit ($10,000 minimum) that supposedly offers an interest rate equal to the rate on six-month Treasury bills.

This latest change in Regulation Q is remarkable because of the government's acquiescence in the banks' use of the "T-bill" label. In the first place, the same government that presumably fights misleading advertising allows banks to use the "T-bill" label, even though the T-bill accounts are considerably different from U.S. Treasury bills.

These accounts are discussed in more detail in the appendix on page 525, but here we simply note that:

1. A T-bill account pays less interest than a Treasury bill;
2. it is less liquid than a Treasury bill;
3. it is not an obligation of the U.S. government;
4. it is not secured by Treasury bills;

5. it lacks certain tax advantages that Treasury bills have; and

6. contrary to what many depositors have been led to believe, it is not a Treasury bill.

In the second place, it is surprising that the government would be so lax when its own product is the one being pirated. The term "T-bill" is as much a trademark as "Coca-Cola." Would the government look the other way if you began printing gummed stickers bearing the words "U.S. Postage"?

In 1979 and 1980, interest rates went higher yet—causing small depositors to flee to money market funds (discussed in Chapter 17). The government's first response was to impose (in March 1980) a 15% reserve requirement on the money market funds—even though they hold only liquid assets.[6]

Finally, however, the government seems to be throwing in the towel on Regulation Q. A banking law passed in April 1980 provides that Regulation Q will be phased out over a five-year period. Like all previous price-control arrangements, this one has finally become impossible to sustain.

Only time will tell what new efforts the government will make to protect banks from competition.

REGULATION

We have covered the bank-government relationship in detail because we think it's a mistake to believe the government is busy seeing to it that banks are safe. Something very different is going on; the government is busy seeing to it that the banks receive the protection they need to keep going. We feel safer relying on institutions that don't need that kind of help.

THRIFT INSTITUTIONS

A savings and loan association is a special type of bank. In exchange for agreeing to emphasize loans on real estate, it

---

[6]The requirement was suspended later in the year.

is allowed to attract deposits by paying slightly higher interest rates than banks may offer. Everything we've said about banks applies as well to savings and loans and other thrift institutions.

However, savings and loans have additional problems. Over 80% of their assets are in illiquid, long-term mortgages —and the collateral behind these mortgages is especially sensitive to any slowing in inflation. So the position of savings and loans is even more precarious than that of banks.

The total insured deposits of savings and loans on December 31, 1979, were $460.8 billion. On the same date, the Federal Savings and Loan Insurance Corporation, the counterpart of the FDIC, had an insurance reserve of $5.85 billion plus a credit line with the U.S. Treasury of $750.0 million— bringing total resources to $6.60 billion, or only 1.43% of the deposits insured.[7]

ALTERNATIVES

The problems of the banking system have been a long time developing, and we can't tell you when they might explode into a general banking crisis. We do know that the number of bank failures has increased with each recession—from a yearly average of 4.6 in the 1950s to an average of 8.1 in the 1970s, increasing the bill the FDIC and the Fed have to pay.[8] As inflation continues, the problems will get worse.

If rearranging your finances to withstand a banking crisis required great cost or inconvenience, the few pages of this chapter wouldn't be enough to motivate you to make the change. Fortunately, there are simple and easy steps that can put a little distance between you and the banking system— steps we'll discuss in the next two chapters.

If you have even vague doubts about your bank's ability to keep its promises, you may find that the steps are worth

---

[7]*Federal Home Loan Bank Journal*, April 1980, page 19.
[8]*Annual Report of the Federal Deposit Insurance Corporation*, 1979, page 203.

taking. And the financial cost of reducing your exposure to banks is not merely low, it may be negative—since the alternatives pay higher rates of interest than banks.

You need only to learn some new habits.

16

U. S. GOVERNMENT
SECURITIES

EVERY FOUR TO SIX YEARS, THE ECONOMY GOES THROUGH A credit squeeze.

The Federal Reserve, worried about inflation, tightens the money supply so sharply that most people feel cash-poor. For a few months, almost every investment price falls—even the so-called inflation hedges. Investors who had held some cash through the inflationary boom find bargains in nearly every market.

Once the recession gets under way, interest rates decline sharply—as credit demands fall and people anticipate a decline in inflation. At that point, safe long-term bonds rise in price, becoming the profitable exception to the fall in investment prices.

Up to now, each such episode has been followed by a renewal of monetary expansion—returning the economy to the pattern of rising inflation. But the tight-money periods provide a small-scale preview of what would happen during a deflationary depression.

In a deflation, the dollar would be king. Cash would provide security in the midst of falling values—as well as the purchasing power with which to buy the bargains that other people are forced to unload. And safe long-term bonds would provide profit—as falling interest rates sent bond prices soaring.

So far, the Federal Reserve has ended each period of tight money before a deflation could develop, continuing the familiar four-to-six-year cycles of monetary expansion and contraction that we described on page 49. If you were confident that these cycles would continue indefinitely, you might choose to ignore them.

In that case, you would hold only enough cash for personal convenience and security—and put nearly all your portfolio into gold, real estate, collectibles, or whatever else you thought would profit from inflation. You couldn't take advantage of the bargains that appear every few years, but your financial life certainly would be uncomplicated.

Unfortunately, you can't be sure the cycles of inflation and recession will continue forever. Any recession can grow into a deflation if the government fails to inflate fast enough.

A deflation would cause the collapse of many of the investments commonly purchased to protect against inflation, and it might be many years before they recovered. The safest and most profitable investments in a deflation would be long-term bonds that were safe from default; they would perform the way "growth" stocks once were expected to.

PROMISES & DEFAULTS

Providing for a deflationary depression is the primary reason for keeping dollar investments in your portfolio. So it's essential that the dollars be in a form that won't go bad at the very time you need them.

Except for currency itself, all dollar assets are promises. A bank account, bond, mortgage, money market instrument, or other IOU is nothing more than someone's promise to deliver dollars to you on a specified date. In a deflation, many such promises would be broken. The bonds of many "blue-chip" corporations could be in default—or at least under a cloud of doubt and selling at distress prices.

Buying these bonds now as a hedge against deflation would be like building a lifeboat out of lead.

WHAT IS A DOLLAR?

Since it is dollars that are to be repaid, the meaning of the word "dollar" has special importance.

The words "U.S. dollar" are, in effect, a trademark of the

U.S. government. There is a certain combination of ink color, paper size, type style, and decoration that only the U.S. government has the legal authority to use. And there is no legal limit on the number of copies it may print; the government can always print as many dollars as it owes. This makes its debts the safest dollar promises available.

The printing of new dollars reduces the purchasing power of government securities, but it also reduces the value of all other fixed-dollar investments. So the government's printing license doesn't put its securities at a disadvantage to other dollar assets; but it does make repayment of government securities more nearly certain.

So we feel it makes sense to concentrate on U.S. government securities for holding dollars. This chapter will examine the variety of dollar investments that the government issues or underwrites.

TREASURY BILLS

U.S. Treasury bills (T-bills) are short-term borrowings by the U.S. government. When issued, a T-bill normally has a life of 13, 26, or 52 weeks. The minimum size of a T-bill is $10,000; larger denominations are available in increments of $5,000—such as $15,000, $20,000, $25,000, and so on. The bills are traded in a large market where you can easily buy or sell at any time.

Interest Return

In recent years the interest on Treasury bills has been very close to the current 12-month price-inflation rate. This pattern is shown in the graph on page 222.

A Treasury bill doesn't pay interest in the same way a bond does; there are no interest coupons or payments. You receive the T-bill's face value on the maturity date. But the price at which you buy the bill is less than that. For example, you might buy a one-year Treasury bill for $9,100 when it's issued, and redeem it one year later for $10,000. The $900 difference is the interest you've earned.

This way of handling the interest payment can cause

some confusion about the true yield. In the above example, the $900 in interest from a one-year T-bill commonly is quoted as a "9% discount" ($900 is 9% of $10,000). But, in fact, you didn't invest $10,000; you invested only $9,100. So the return, or yield, was actually 9.9% ($900 is 9.9% of $9,100).

The true yield is always higher than the discount rate that's quoted. The gap is especially large when interest rates are high, and is larger for longer-term bills (52 weeks is the longest) than for shorter-term bills.

A further confusion can arise with a Treasury bill that has less than one year remaining to maturity. No matter how long the time to maturity, the discount always is quoted as an annual rate. For example, a 13-week bill might be quoted at a discount of 9% (per year), although the interest earned over 13 weeks will be only a little more than one-fourth of that. (However, if a series of four 13-week bills were purchased, one after the other, the interest would compound over the 52-week period to somewhat more than 9%.)

The interest on all Treasury securities is exempt from state and local income taxes. So, for many investors, the yield on T-bills may be closer than it appears to the after-tax yield on commercial paper, certificates of deposit, or anything else subject to state and local taxes.

The table on page 257 compares the discount rates on T-bills with the true yields. It also shows the interest rates that investors in various state and local tax brackets need to earn on taxable investments to match the yield on Treasury bills.

Buying & Selling

Many U.S. banks and most stock brokers will purchase Treasury bills for you.

Normally you'll pay a flat commission of $25 to $50. If the bills are sold before maturity, you'll pay the same commission again. In addition, there's a slight difference (about 2/10 of 1%) between the price at which you can buy and the price at which you can sell. So the total cost for buying and

TRUE YIELDS ON TREASURY BILLS
(52-week bills)

Quoted Discount	True Yield	Yield Required on Locally Taxed Securities —Tax Bracket—		
		10%	7%	3%
5%	5.28%	5.86%	5.68%	5.44%
6%	6.40%	7.11%	6.88%	6.60%
7%	7.55%	8.39%	8.12%	7.78%
8%	8.72%	9.69%	9.38%	8.99%
9%	9.92%	11.02%	10.67%	10.23%
10%	11.14%	12.38%	11.98%	11.49%
11%	12.40%	13.77%	13.33%	12.78%
12%	13.68%	15.20%	14.71%	14.10%
13%	14.99%	16.65%	16.11%	15.45%
14%	16.33%	18.14%	17.56%	16.83%
15%	17.70%	19.67%	19.03%	18.25%
16%	19.10%	21.23%	20.54%	19.70%
17%	20.54%	22.83%	22.09%	21.18%
18%	22.02%	24.46%	23.67%	22.70%
19%	23.53%	26.14%	25.30%	24.26%
20%	25.08%	27.86%	26.96%	25.85%

Quoted discount: The "bank discount" rate normally quoted for Treasury bills.

True yield: The actual yield earned on the investment over a 365-day period; the yield that should be compared with alternative investments.

Yield Required on Locally Taxed Securities: The rate that must be earned by a security that is subject to state and local income taxes (corporate bond, CD, money market certificate, commercial paper, etc.) to provide the same after-tax return as a T-bill at the "Quoted Discount" rate. The three columns in this section show the yield required according to the effective rate of combined state and local taxation.

selling might be around 1% on a $10,000 T-bill—less for a larger denomination.

It is possible to bypass the bank or broker and purchase T-bills directly from the Treasury at its weekly auction. By filling out a short form, you can arrange to buy bills from the Treasury at the average price prevailing at the auction. This approach is described in the appendix on page 521, and may be well worth the small effort it requires.

No Certificates

Until recently, a Treasury bill was a certificate—a piece of paper promising you a certain amount of money on a certain date, payable by the U.S. government. But the Treasury Department no longer issues certificates for T-bills. Instead, it simply keeps a record of your ownership. You get a receipt, but the receipt is only a memorandum; it can't be transferred, sold, or redeemed.

When you buy a T-bill through a broker (or bank), the broker's name appears in the government's records. As far as the government is concerned, the broker owns the T-bill. In turn, the broker *owes* you a T-bill.

Will the broker keep his promise? Almost certainly, yes. Even if the broker were bankrupt, his creditors would have no claim on property you had bought and paid for. It would require fraud or theft to deprive you of what's yours. It would be fraud for the broker to "sell" you a T-bill he didn't actually own. And once you had bought it, it would be theft for the broker (without your permission) to sell it or pledge it as collateral to raise cash.

The chance that you might be injured by such a crime is remote, but not quite zero. Every few years a fraud comes to light that reminds us that the outrageous and the improbable do occur. An insurance company wholesales nonexistent policies to other insurance companies, or a bank manager collects deposits without recording them.

Such events are rare, but the chance of your being a victim would be greatest at the very time you were relying most on the safety of your T-bills—during a banking crisis. In every such crisis, there are bankers and brokers who believe that if they can hang on for just a few more days or weeks, they'll be able to survive.

In desperation, some of them "borrow" investments owned by customers—hoping to return them in a few days. Only when the firm's problems become unmanageable do the customers learn that they've been robbed.

Choices

Purchasing your Treasury bills directly from the government's auction has advantages and disadvantages.

When you buy at auction, you eliminate the need to rely on the promise of a banker or broker to safeguard your T-bill and to deliver your money when the T-bill matures. You also save the commission.

On the other hand, it is a little more work to buy at the auction. And if you don't want the government to know about the transaction, you certainly can't send it your check and your name. Also, if you want to sell the Treasury bill before it matures, you'll have to have it transferred to a broker—a process that will involve some trouble and a few days' delay.

T-Bill Accounts

The "T-bill Accounts" offered by banks and savings and loans are described in the appendix on page 525. Here we'll only mention that they are not Treasury bills and they are not a good substitute for Treasury bills.

TREASURY BONDS

Treasury bonds are long-term obligations of the U.S. government. They are issued for periods of between ten and thirty years in multiples of $1,000.

The bonds are sold by the government at around face value, with a fixed interest rate. The interest is paid twice yearly. After issue, the bonds trade in a large resale market at prices that change from day to day.

Like Treasury bills, Treasury bonds begin their life at a government auction. But bond auctions are held only every three months, and you probably will find it much simpler to purchase T-bonds through a bank or broker.

Bearer & Registered Bonds

Treasury bonds are still issued as certificates, which are of two kinds—registered and bearer.

A registered bond has your name on it, and your ownership is registered with the U.S. Treasury. If you want to sell the bond, you endorse it, and the buyer sends the certificate to the Treasury and has a new one issued in his own name. A registered bond can be replaced if it is lost or stolen.

A bearer bond doesn't show your name, and your ownership isn't registered anywhere. Like cash, it is the property of the "bearer"—whoever holds it. If the bond is lost or stolen, you have no recourse. As with a $50 bill, you can describe it to the police, but they won't recover it for you.

Interest Payments

Bearer bonds have interest coupons attached to them, one for each payment date. When interest is due, you can take the current coupon to almost any bank. The bank will pay you and forward the coupon to the Treasury for reimbursement.

Registered bonds can be bought either with interest coupons attached or in "fully registered" form. Fully registered means that each semi-annual interest payment is sent by check from the U.S. Treasury to the registered owner.

Interest coupons, whether from bearer bonds or registered bonds, are themselves bearer instruments. If your registered bond is lost or stolen, no one can sell it without falsifying your signature. But the interest coupons can be presented for payment at any bank without proof of ownership. So registered bonds with coupons attached need to be protected from theft and other loss.

Choices

A bearer bond is completely private if you purchase it anonymously for cash. And, if necessary, it would be easier than a registered bond to sell at a bank or broker where you aren't known, or outside of regular financial channels.

In the event of a deflationary crisis, a bearer Treasury bond would be the most spendable investment next to cash itself. Even if all banks were closed, a bond might be welcome elsewhere—in trade or as something to pawn. Later, when the crisis eased, it would be accepted instantly at the first bank to reopen.

On the other hand, a bearer bond must be guarded like cash; if it's lost or stolen, it is unlikely to be recovered. And during normal times, a fully registered bond offers the convenience of receiving interest payments by mail.

You'll have to decide which medium is better for your purposes. But we suggest that you hold at least a small amount of Treasury bonds (such as 1% of your total assets) in bearer form in $1,000 denominations—as a kind of near-cash. They will be spendable in any circumstance short of runaway inflation. And if they are never needed in an emergency, they at least will be earning interest.

Whether you decide on bearer or registered bonds, it is best to take delivery of any bonds you buy (unless they must be used as collateral for a loan). Taking delivery means you have physical possession of the bonds, keeping them either at home or in a safe-deposit box. That way you eliminate the possibility of becoming entangled in the financial troubles of any firm you deal with.

TREASURY NOTES

U.S. Treasury notes come in between bills and bonds. A Treasury note, when issued, has a life of from one to ten years. Otherwise, everything we've said about Treasury bonds applies to Treasury notes. In fact, when a Treasury bond is within ten years of its maturity, it is virtually indistinguishable from a Treasury note.

SHORT-TERM BEARER INSTRUMENTS

As time passes, every Treasury note and Treasury bond turns into a short-term instrument. When a note or bond has just one year to go, the only difference between it and a Treasury bill is the interest coupons.

This similarity can be useful if you want to hold a short-term Treasury security in bearer form. You can do so by buying a bearer bond or note that is only a few months from maturity.

GOVERNMENT AGENCY SECURITIES

In addition to the Treasury, there are a number of government-sponsored agencies that borrow on their own. These include the Federal Home Loan Bank, the Tennessee Valley Authority (TVA), the Government National Mortgage Association (GNMA), the Federal National Mortgage Association (FNMA), and many others.

The bonds and notes issued by these agencies are traded in active markets, but the markets aren't nearly so large or active as for Treasury securities. Because the markets are slightly less liquid, the interest rate paid is slightly above that of Treasury securities—usually only a fraction of 1%.

Some, but not all, of the bonds issued by the agencies have the government's "full faith and credit" backing—meaning that the government has made an absolute promise to pay off the bonds even if the agency goes broke.

Because the yield difference between Treasury securities and most agency securities is so small, and because the agency securities are not as liquid (especially in small lots), we think it's simpler for most investors to stick with Treasury securities. But if you decide to buy an agency security, be sure to determine whether it has a full faith and credit backing.

GOVERNMENT-GUARANTEED LOANS

In addition to financing its own activities, the U.S. government underwrites the financing of private ventures that can't raise money on their own. One method it uses is to act as a co-signer for loans obtained from private sources, guaranteeing repayment.

The most prominent of these programs is conducted by the Small Business Administration (SBA). The SBA guarantees up to 90% of the principal and interest of certain loans made by commercial banks to small businesses.

A bank, in turn, often will sell the guaranteed portion of the loan to an investor. If the borrower defaults, the bank will take a loss on the unguaranteed 10% it holds, but the investor will eventually receive all the principal he advanced, plus the accrued interest.

The guarantee is a "full faith and credit" obligation of the government, but a guaranteed loan isn't the same as a direct obligation—such as a T-bill or T-bond. A Treasury security must be paid when promised, or the government will lose the ability to finance its activities. A guaranteed loan also must be paid, but not necessarily on schedule. If the borrower defaults (as is often the case), the government will pay the bill—but only after a delay.

Invoking an SBA guarantee is like foreclosing on a mortgage; you'll get your money, but there are steps to be taken. First, you must wait until the borrower is 60 days late in paying. Then you must ask the bank to repurchase the loan, giving it 15 days in which to do so. If the bank fails to repurchase it, you must apply to the Small Business Administration and wait a while longer. Then you'll get your money, including the interest that has accrued during the delay.

Under normal circumstances, the entire procedure should take no more than four months. During a financial crisis, when the government would be swamped with applications, it undoubtedly would take longer.

SBA-guaranteed loans aren't as resalable as T-bills or bonds. Because of that, and because of the possible delay in collecting your money, the loans carry higher interest rates than Treasury securities. The rate is usually 2% or so higher, after allowing for a service charge to the bank of around ¾% per year.

If these guaranteed loans are held in a portion of your

263

portfolio that will never require timely payment, the extra interest can be a true bonus. But they shouldn't be held if receiving your money on a definite date is important.

Worth of Guarantee

The government's obligation to make good on SBA-guaranteed loans provides for more safety than its obligation to a government insurance fund—such as the Federal Deposit Insurance Corporation. Although the FDIC is a creature of the government, its line of credit at the U.S. Treasury is limited.

If claims against the FDIC should ever exceed its reserves, the government might add to the reserves—but it has no legal obligation to do so and has never promised to. However, the government has promised to absorb all losses on SBA-guaranteed loans—regardless of the cost.

The long-term costs of any government program are usually underestimated or ignored entirely. When the chickens finally come home to roost, the SBA's bill probably will be much larger than anyone dreamed of in his worst nightmare. We can't predict the reaction of Congress to such a situation. The bill probably will be paid, since it would be difficult to issue Treasury bills after reneging on a full-faith-and-credit guarantee. But neither of the authors will post a bond to guarantee it.

Fixed & Floating Rates

The SBA guarantees both fixed-rate and floating-rate loans. We suggest that you stick to the floating-rate loans.

A fixed-rate loan is attractive when interest rates decline. But an SBA borrower can pay off his loan at any time, and he most likely will do so and take a new loan if interest rates drop. And if interest rates rise, he'll be glad to continue paying you a rate that's below the current market.

The usual formula for a floating-rate loan is to adjust the interest every six months to the current prime rate. The prime normally is much higher than what you can get on a low-risk investment, but this can be misleading. If the loan rate is adjusted only every six months or so, it will lag behind changes in T-bill and other open-market interest rates. The excess interest over 6-month Treasury bills will be greatest when interest rates are falling, and smallest when interest rates are rising.

Finding the Loan

SBA-guaranteed loans are not well known as an investment, and you're likely to find them only at a large brokerage firm that deals in government securities. Usually you'll pay a one-time fee to the broker of 1% to 2% of the face value of the loan.

If you purchase an SBA loan, you have to be sure you're getting what you want, because names can be misleading. The exact name for this investment is either "Small Business Administration Guaranteed Loan" or "Small Business Administration Guaranteed Loan Participation." If the investment doesn't carry one of those two names, it may be something else. Don't accept:

1. "SBA-approved loans";
2. "SBA-sponsored loans";
3. "SBA-type loans";
4. "Small Business Assistance loans"; or
5. "Small Brooklyn Bridge Association loans."

Also, many loans are called "floating rate," but be sure the interest rate is adjusted at least once each year; every six months is better yet.

In addition, you should ask the broker if he'll handle the paper work required to invoke the guarantee if the borrower defaults. Bear in mind that even if he promises to, the promise might be broken during a financial crisis when defaults become epidemic and the workload grows too large.

Investment Costs

SBA-guaranteed loans pay a higher return than Treasury securities. But to earn the higher return, you have to pay an initial cost of about 2%, you might have to handle a default, and you have to pick out a specific loan from the broker's inventory. It is up to you to decide whether the slightly higher return is worth the effort. But if you are striving for higher yields, we'd rather see you reach for SBA-guaranteed loans than for bank CDs.

There's also the psychological cost of having to do something unfamiliar. Being unfamiliar, the investment may produce the same discomfort as a risky investment—even though it has a full-faith-and-credit guarantee.[1]

SAFETY & CONVENIENCE

Treasury securities are the safest way to hold dollars. In Part Six, we'll suggest methods by which these securities can balance other investments in your portfolio.

You'll have to ponder the merits of buying T-bills at auction or through a broker, and of buying Treasury securities or guaranteed loans. As you do, remember that extra interest earned and any costs saved will compound—and may make a big difference in the portfolio's value ten years from now.

But the first consideration with dollar investments always is safety—since their main purpose is to provide for a deflation in which many dollar investments would default. So don't let a little extra interest cause you to take on an undesirable or avoidable risk.

Convenience is a less obvious consideration, but it is equally important. Stay with investments that can be handled with the time and attention you're sure you can give. If you take on something too complicated, you might fail to give it the attention it needs. And that can turn an otherwise safe investment into a liability.

---

[1]A complete description of the guarantee program is given in *Investments in Small Business Administration and Farmers Home Administration "Full Faith & Credit" Guaranteed Loan Participations,* published by Merrill Lynch. It is available free of charge by writing to: Michael Butkus, Merrill Lynch & Co., 165 Broadway, 20th Floor, New York, N.Y. 10080.

17

MONEY MARKET FUNDS

WE HAVE SAID THAT TREASURY SECURITIES ARE THE SAFEST way to hold dollars. But you can't use Treasury securities to pay your bills each month; and unless you are dealing in very large amounts, Treasury securities aren't practical for handling the day-to-day and week-to-week flow of cash. Something else is needed.

Money market funds provide a way of handling cash that is almost as convenient and flexible as a bank checking account. And some funds provide almost as much safety and interest as Treasury bills.

WHAT IT IS

A money market fund takes the legal form of a mutual fund—an investment company that continually offers new shares for sale and redeems (buys back) existing shares.

However, a money market fund doesn't invest in stocks or long-term bonds. It invests only in "money market" instruments—such as Treasury bills, commercial paper, and the other cash substitutes discussed on page 70.

All of a money market fund's investments are short-term debts—maturing in one year at the most. The market value of these investments is highly stable (unlike long-term bonds), despite changes in market interest rates. And, for the most part, the fund's investments are marketable at a moment's notice.

The share price of a stock-market mutual fund fluctuates

267

daily, as the value of its investments rise and fall. Because the value of a money market fund's assets is stable, the price of its shares also is stable. Most funds keep their share price fixed at exactly $1.00 by paying a tiny dividend every day—equal to the interest earned on the fund's investments the day before.

A day's dividend, for example, might be only $.0003 (3/100 of a cent) per share. The fund would use the dividend to purchase additional $1 shares for each investor. Thus, if you bought 1,000 shares one day, the next day's dividend might add another 0.3 shares to your holdings. At that rate, after one year, you would have 1,116 shares of $1 value—or 11.6% more than you started with.

Whenever you deposit money, it is applied to the purchase of $1 shares. When you withdraw money, the required number of $1 shares are liquidated.

There is no charge for the purchase or redemption (resale) of shares. You can withdraw money by writing, wiring, or telephoning the fund. If you wish, the money can be wired to your local bank—normally arriving there the day after the fund receives your instructions.

USE AS A CHECKING ACCOUNT

Most funds allow you to redeem shares by writing checks on the fund's bank account. The redemption check can be made payable to anyone, so you can use it to pay a bill or to deposit money into your own bank checking account. Of course, if you write a check for more shares than you have, the fund won't honor it. The usual minimum for a redemption check is $500, but some funds will handle smaller checks.

Redemption by check makes it easy to reduce your reliance on the banking system. You can keep a token amount in your bank checking account—say, $10. When you pay bills, use the bank's checks, just as you do now. At the same time, write one of the fund's checks for an amount equal to all the bank checks you've written, and deposit it into your bank checking account.

With this procedure, you can keep your cash reserve in a non-bank depository, earning interest, and still have it available in spendable form. Your cash reserve will be vulnerable only during the time that checks are in process of collection, and only to the amount of those checks. The rest of your reserve will be sitting safely in the fund.

Needless to say, a money market fund also replaces a bank savings account.

FUNDS & BANKS

Money market funds are not completely independent of the banking system. As we've seen, you withdraw money from a fund by writing a check on its account, receiving a bank check from the fund, or by having the fund wire money to your bank. The fund relies on the banking system to function. In addition, there is no branch of the fund a few blocks from your home where you could withdraw banknotes for spending money during a banking crisis.

Despite this, if there's a banking crisis, having your cash reserves in a money market fund can benefit you in two ways.

First, a banking crisis might mean the loss forever of *all* the money you have on deposit in a bank. The most that could be lost through a conservative money market fund is the small cash reserve the fund keeps in a bank—probably less than 1% of its holdings. Whenever any banks reopen, the money you've invested in a fund will be immediately available to you.

Second, it may be that some banks will remain open—even as others are failing. If so, the fund can continue to function by selling its investments through an open bank, and paying its investors with checks drawn on the open bank.

Keeping your cash reserves in a money market fund, instead of in a bank, does not guarantee that you'll never be inconvenienced. But, if you choose a fund that invests only in the safest instruments, it does mean that your money won't be lost.

FUND INVESTMENTS

Money market funds invest in cash substitutes. We suggested in Chapter 4 that many types of supposedly safe cash substitutes might not survive a deflation. Consequently, we feel it's necessary to choose a fund on the basis of its investment policy—before giving any consideration to the convenience or interest it offers.

There are seven investments a money market fund might use.

1. *Treasury bills:* Discussed in the last chapter, these are debts of the U.S. Treasury, issued for one year or less. They are direct obligations of the U.S. government that must be paid on time if the government wants to stay in business.

2. *U.S. government agency securities:* These are debts of government agencies—such as the Federal National Mortgage Association, the Federal Intermediate Credit Bank, and the Export-Import Bank—maturing within one year. Some have the "full faith and credit" backing of the U.S. government (described on page 262). Others are commonly regarded as default-proof because the issuing agency is in the business of carrying out government policies.

3. *Bankers' acceptances:* These are post-dated checks written by businesses (not necessarily major corporations) that have been "accepted" and guaranteed by a bank. Usually, the post-dating is for no more than nine months.

There are two, often three, guarantees behind a bankers' acceptance. First, the acceptance is an obligation of the bank that accepts it. Second, if the bank fails to make good, the company that wrote the check is responsible for it primarily to the investor, not to the bank. Third, the company usually pledges collateral, such as inventories or invoices for goods in shipment.

If both the bank and the company default, the collateral can be sold to pay off the acceptance. In that case, there would be a delay in collection, but most—if not all—of the money would be recovered eventually. .

We have read numerous statements that even during the Great Depression, no money was lost in bankers' acceptances —although some were paid off only after a delay. Whether this is strictly true, we don't know. However, we have uncovered no evidence to the contrary, and we believe that it is at least very close to the truth.

4. *Commercial paper:* These are unsecured promissory

notes of major corporations, maturing in nine months or less. The issues are rated, in the same way bonds are, by Moody's and by Standard and Poor. Very little is sold that doesn't have a high rating.

5. *Large negotiable certificates of deposit:* Large CDs ($100,000 or more each) are issued by banks. In the event of a general banking crisis, many banks will default on their CDs, just as they will default on other deposits. Consequently, a money market fund that invests heavily in CDs is little safer than a bank.

Although the minimum for a negotiable CD is $100,000, they are usually sold in denominations of $1,000,000 or more. So the fraction of a typical CD that is covered by FDIC insurance is very small. During a banking panic, when the FDIC sees its reserves running low, it might adopt a policy of paying off insured depositors only and leaving the others to fend for themselves. Thus the CDs that many money market funds hold are even less secure than a passbook savings account.

6. *Euro-CDs:* These are certificates of deposit issued by banks in foreign countries. Most of the Euro-CDs held by money market funds are from the London and other overseas branches of U.S. banks. These CDs are probably less safe than those issued by the banks' U.S. offices.

In desperate circumstances, some U.S. banks will be looking for commitments they can dishonor or stall on. Euro-CDs would be a good candidate, since depositors' demands could be tied up in the legal procedures of a foreign country.

As a related example, one very large U.S. bank used to have a branch in Saigon (now Ho Chi Minh City), South Vietnam—fully equipped with an FDIC sticker. After Saigon was "liberated," some depositors attempted to withdraw their money through a U.S. office of the bank, but were turned down. The depositors have sued, and the matter is now being settled by a federal court.

7. *Repurchase agreements:* In a repurchase agreement ("repo"), the fund buys an investment, such as a Treasury bill, which the seller agrees to repurchase at a later date for a stated price. If the seller were to default on his promise, the fund would take a loss only if the market value of the investment had fallen below the agreed-upon repurchase price.

271

The purpose of a repo is to turn a long-term investment into a short-term investment. For example, a fund might purchase a two-year Treasury note under an agreement calling for it to be repurchased in one week.

So long as there are no problems with the banking system, repurchase agreements—because of their short-term nature—help to protect a fund against interest-rate fluctuations. However, the dealers that offer repurchase agreements either are banks themselves or depend on banks. Consequently, a repurchase agreement is no safer than the underlying investment.

Most repurchase agreements involve short-term Treasury or government-agency securities and are very secure. But any investment might be involved in a repo. So, if a fund says that it invests in repos, it is important to find out what type of security is involved.

SAFETY OF INVESTMENTS

Except for repurchase agreements, the investments have been listed in order of safety. On a scale of 1 to 10 (with 10 the safest), we would rate their ability to survive a severe crisis as follows:

Treasury bill = 10
Agency securities with "full faith and credit" guarantee = 9.7
Agency securities without "full faith and credit" guarantee = 9.5
Bankers' acceptances = 8.0
Commercial paper = 5.0
Certificates of deposit = 1.2
Euro-CDs = 1.0

A repurchase agreement would have the same rating as the underlying security.

Interest Rates

There is competition among funds to offer the highest possible interest rates.

The graph on page 274 shows the 1971–1980 interest rates for four of the six cash substitutes we've discussed. The difference between any two interest rates on the same day reflects mostly the market's evaluation of the risks. You earn a higher rate by taking a bigger risk. Treasury bills, as the safest investment, almost always pay the lowest rate.

Since we believe that safety is the prime concern with dollar investments, we think the extra 1% or 2% you might receive from a fund that invests in risky assets is too small for the risk.

MONEY MARKET FUND vs. T-BILLS

If you decide to restrict your dollar holdings to Treasury securities, there are several considerations involved in choosing between buying Treasury bills directly and holding shares of a money market fund that invests only in Treasury bills.

1. *Minimum purchase:* If you have less than $10,000 to invest in Treasury bills, you don't have enough for one bill. So the fund is the obvious choice.

2. *Convenience:* Even if you have far more than $10,000 to invest, you may want to keep some of it (say, two months' normal expenditures) in a money market fund—so that you can conveniently make small deposits and withdrawals as needed or use the fund's check-writing privileges.

3. *Fund costs:* A money market fund has yearly operating costs that come to about 1% of its assets. After paying those costs, a fund will be able to pay you an interest rate that is about 1% less than you could earn by buying T-bills directly.

4. *Taxes:* Treasury bills are exempt from state and local (but not federal) income taxes, while the income from money market funds is not exempt from any taxes. The importance of the tax consideration will depend upon your local tax rate.

As an extreme example, an investor living in New York City faces a maximum state and city tax rate on interest income of 19.3%. This means the after-tax yield of a money market fund will be almost 20% less before anything else is considered.

On the other hand, if you don't have to deal with state

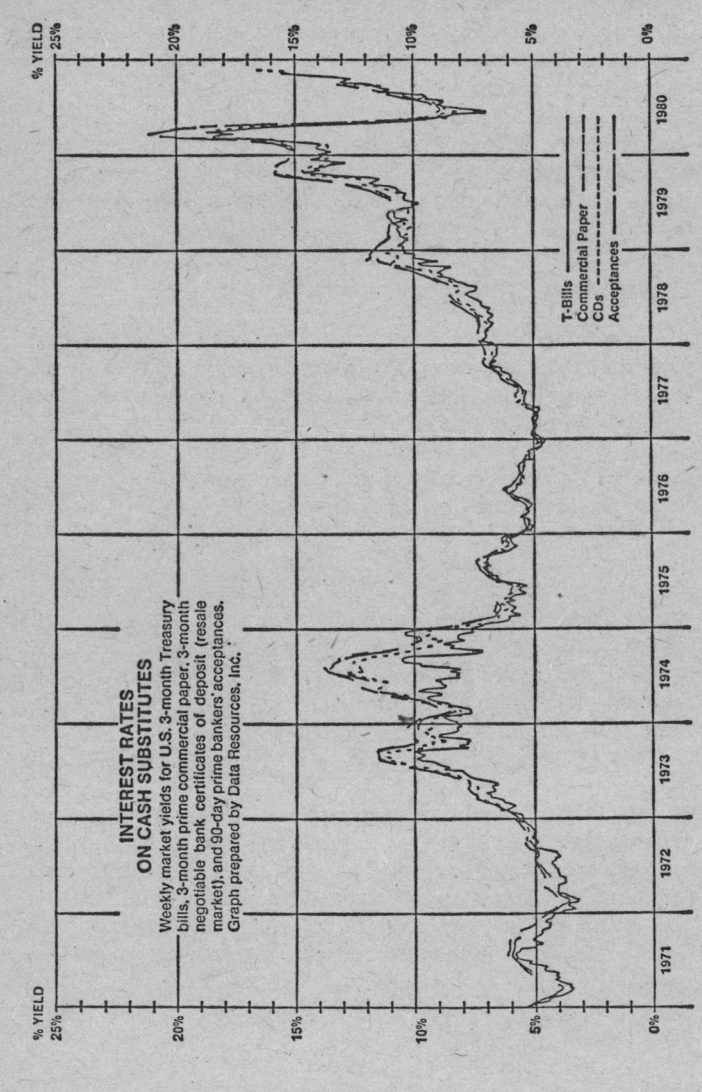

INTEREST RATES
ON CASH SUBSTITUTES

Weekly market yields for U.S. 3-month Treasury
bills, 3-month prime commercial paper, 3-month
negotiable bank certificates of deposit (resale
market), and 90-day prime bankers acceptances.
Graph prepared by Data Resources, Inc.

T-Bills
Commercial Paper
CDs
Acceptances

and local income taxes, or if the interest income is sheltered, the T-bill exemption won't matter.

5. *Safety:* Every additional person or institution you have to depend upon reduces an investment's overall safety. Investing through a money market fund means that you're depending on the reliability of one more intermediary than if you buy the T-bills yourself.

The risk of losing your money in a money market fund that invests only in Treasury securities is very remote, but not nonexistent. The considerations involved when you leave securities with a bank or broker (described on page 258) are present when you invest in a money market fund.

OLD & NEW FUNDS

The money market fund alternatives were muddied a bit in March 1980 when the U.S. government unveiled its umpteenth anti-inflation program. As part of the new program, money market funds were required to deposit 15% of additional assets received after March 14, 1980, in a non-interest-bearing account with the Federal Reserve.

The effect of this rule was to reduce the yields on additional money market fund investments by about one-sixth. A fund that had been earning 12% could earn only 10% on new money—since one-sixth of the new money could not earn anything at all. To avoid short-changing existing investors, many funds closed their doors to newcomers. That way, all money in the fund would continue to earn interest without the one-sixth dilution.

To accommodate new investors, many funds then created twin brothers—that differed from the originals only in that they would be fully subject to the 15% reserve requirement. The twin fund would earn one-sixth less interest, but would be open to anyone, while established investors in the old fund would continue to earn full interest.

In May 1980, the reserve requirement was reduced and, two months later, it was suspended entirely. Since then, most of the twins have announced plans to merge with their brothers.

CHOICE OF A FUND

There were 78 money market funds open to the public in March 1980, prior to the Federal Reserve's imposition of reserve requirements. Most of them, including some of the largest and best known, invest heavily in bank CDs, and we would avoid them.

There are a few, however, that emphasize safety. The table on page 277 describes five funds that either invest only in Treasury securities or offer some other reason for consideration.[1]

Capital Preservation Fund and Merrill Lynch Government Fund invest exclusively in U.S. Treasury securities and repurchase agreements for Treasuries. Capital Preservation was one of the first money market funds, and for many years the only fund that invested exclusively in T-bills. Funds for Government Investors holds Treasury securities and U.S. government agency securities.

First Variable Rate Fund invests in Treasury bills and SBA-guaranteed loans. The yield on the loans is greater than on Treasury bills; but, due to the loans' inferior liquidity, there's a small chance that during a banking crisis the fund would have trouble meeting redemption requests. When the dust settled, however, the fund's assets probably would be intact.

In addition to its Government Fund, Merrill Lynch sponsors a second fund, CMA Money Trust. "CMA" stands for Cash Management Account.

The fund's portfolio is mostly CDs. However, it is possible to use some of the fund's services, which are unusual, without making more than a token investment.

An investment in the CMA trust is made in conjunction with a normal customer account at Merrill Lynch. The account can be used to buy and sell stocks, bonds, and other investments. Any Treasury bills (and most stocks and bonds) that you leave on deposit can be used as collateral for a short-term margin loan.

---

[1] *Donoghue's Money Fund Report* (described on page 481) publishes a weekly and a monthly report showing the investment portfolios of all money market funds.

SELECTED MONEY MARKET FUNDS

Fund & Address	Telephone	Minimum To open	Minimum Addition	Check	% of Portfolio in Treasury	% of Portfolio in Other	Size	Yield
Capital Preservation Fund 755 Page Mill Road Palo Alto, CA 94306	(800) 227-8996 (800) 982-6150	$1,000	$ 0	$ 500	60%	40%	756	12.0%
First Variable Rate Fund for Government Income 1700 Pennsylvania Ave., NW Washington, DC 20006	(800) 424-2444 (202) 328-4000	1,000	250	500	66%	34%	453	11.8%
Fund for Government Investors 1735 K Street, NW Washington, DC 20006	(202) 861-1810 (collect)	2,500	500	500	42%	58%	409	11.3%
Merrill Lynch CMA Money Trust 55 Water St. – 36th Floor New York, NY 10080	(800) 221-4146 (800) 522-5510	0	0	0	0%	21%	2,809	12.2%
Merrill Lynch Government Fund 125 High Street Boston, MA 02110	(800) 225-1576 (617) 357-1460	5,000	1,000	500	100%	0%	153	11.3%

Minimums shown are those required to open an account, for each addition to an existing account, and for a withdrawal made by writing a check on the fund's account. There are no minimums for withdrawals by other means.

Portfolio percentages shown are for U.S. Treasury securities, and for other U.S. government securities (including securities of U.S. government agencies, as well as repurchase agreements covering Treasury and agency securities).

Size of fund is in millions of dollars as of October 1, 1980.

Yield is average of 12-month period through August 31, 1980.

Source of data: *Donoghue's Money Fund Report*, October 6, 1980; *Donoghue's Money Fund Directory*, Spring 1980; and inquiries at funds.

When you write a check on CMA Money Trust, the check is paid for by redeeming shares—just as with any other money market fund. But if your check is bigger than your CMA Money Trust holdings, Merrill Lynch will honor the check by making a margin loan. Later deposits that you make will be used to repay the loan—with any excess going into shares of CMA Money Trust. So, if you have Treasury bills (or other securities) on deposit, you needn't invest more than a token amount in the money market fund to be able to write checks.

For example, suppose you want to hold $30,000 in Treasury bills. You can open a CMA account and purchase $30,000 worth of Treasury bills plus a token number of shares in the CMA Money Trust (there is no minimum initial investment). When you need to spend, say, $4,000, you would write one or more CMA withdrawal checks. Merrill Lynch would honor the check and charge your margin account for $3,000 ($4,000 less the $1,000 in the fund). You would pay interest on the $3,000 until the loan was repaid, either directly by you or from the proceeds of maturing Treasury bills.

Even if CMA Money Trust lost every penny on its investments, you would suffer only a small loss, because you would own mostly Treasury bills, and only a few shares in CMA.

An additional advantage of CMA is that there is no minimum for check writing—giving you even more independence from your local bank. Most funds will not honor withdrawal checks for less than $500.[2]

Other Possibilities

Two additional possibilities are Fidelity Government Fund and Treasury Note Trust.

Fidelity Government Fund is not quite a money market

---

[2]Merrill Lynch Government Fund and CMA Trust should not to be confused with Merrill Lynch Ready Assets Trust, which invests primarily in CDs, and doesn't offer the margin-loan services of CMA Money Trust.

fund by the conventional definition, since the average maturity of its investments (in June 1980) is about two years. Because the portfolio is longer-term, the value of a share can fluctuate slightly from day to day. The value will deteriorate mildly during periods of rapidly rising interest rates and appreciate mildly during periods of rapidly falling interest rates.

But Fidelity has two important advantages. First, because of its longer-term portfolio, it would not fall under reserve requirements of the type described on page 273. Second, unlike all the other funds, Fidelity is organized not as a corporation, but as a limited partnership.

When you invest in Fidelity, you don't become a shareholder, you become a partner. Under most state laws, income you receive from a partnership is taxed as your share of whatever the partnership did to earn the money. In the case of Fidelity, the partnership earns money by investing in Treasury securities, so the interest you receive as a partner is exempt from state income tax—just as though you had invested in the Treasury securities directly.

Although Fidelity Government Fund allows withdrawals by bank wire, it does not provide a check-writing service. Consequently, Fidelity would not be a good first choice as a money market fund. However, it is a good second choice, especially if you are in a high state and local tax bracket.[3]

The managers of Capital Preservation Fund recently formed the Treasury Note Trust, which is similar to Fidelity Government Fund. It invests in Treasury notes maturing in one to four years, and would avoid reserve requirements of the type described on page 273.

Because it is a trust, and not a corporation, it has applied for rulings from various state governments that the earnings it pays out to shareholders are exempt from state income taxes. Some states are resisting, but the legal questions may be settled by the time you read this.

---

[3]Fidelity Government Fund, 82 Devonshire St., Boston, Mass. 02103; (800) 225-6190. This shouldn't be confused with Fidelity Daily Income, a money market fund that invests primarily in certificates of deposit.

DIVERSITY

Diversity is valuable not only in choosing investments, but also in choosing the media through which to handle investments. By using several media, you lessen your vulnerability to any one event that might catch you by surprise.

You could hold some dollars in one-year Treasury bills, purchased at Treasury auctions and replaced automatically; some dollars in two-year Treasury notes held in bearer form; some dollars in a money market fund that invests only in T-bills or other short-term government securities; and still other dollars in a fund that earns higher interest by investing in government-guaranteed securities.

Not only does this spread the risk, it means that some dollars are in convenient form for transactions, others are earning higher interest, and others are in the safest possible form.

Diversity reduces your risk. Don't put yourself into a position of needing everything to go perfectly. Diversity allows something to go wrong without your plans collapsing.

18

BORROWING

A VERY POPULAR INVESTMENT CLICHÉ SAYS THAT THE WAY TO beat inflation is by borrowing as much money as you can, investing it in equity investments that rise with inflation, and eventually paying off the debt with "cheaper dollars"—dollars that have less purchasing power and are easier to come by. Variations of this cliché are "leverage is power" or "always work with other people's money."

Like most investment slogans, this one is only half true—at best. There are at least three good reasons to be cautious about borrowing to "beat inflation."

First, borrowing had more validity six to ten years ago—when few people expected inflation to approach the levels we've seen recently. At that time, inflationary expectations were low, interest rates were low, and there wasn't a widespread expectation that the so-called "inflation hedges" would go up in price. Anyone who borrowed then to invest in gold or real estate, for example, probably did well. But he did well because his expectations proved to be more realistic than those of other people.

Today, however, inflationary expectations are high, interest rates are high, and the "inflation hedges" are very popular. This means the interest rate you pay is based on the assumption that inflation will get worse. And many "inflation hedges" sell at prices that already include next year's inflation and the inflation of the year after that.

If future inflation matches what is implied by today's interest rates and investment prices, you may do little more than break even on the investment. If inflation fails to match the expecations, you'll probably lose money.

If borrowing to buy "inflation hedges" is the current rage, it's unlikely that you'll profit from doing so. Most investment slogans tout approaches that worked well in the past (when they were unpopular and you could obtain bargains) but have outlived their usefulness.

Second, inflation won't last forever. If it culminates in a runaway inflation, the dollars for repaying loans will be virtually free. But if it culminates in a deflation, the debts will be a heavy burden.

And third, even a continuation of inflation doesn't mean that *your* dollars will be "cheaper." Inflation doesn't push up every price and wage together; it affects the economy unevenly, as new money stimulates one area at the expense of another.

If you borrow to buy consumption items, expecting to repay with cheaper dollars, you have to be sure that *your* income will be larger next year—not just that inflation will continue.

If you borrow to make an investment, the mere expectation that inflation will be greater next year doesn't guarantee a profit for *any* investment—nor is it a sufficient reason for taking on the risk of too much debt.

You can't build a portfolio on investment slogans. You have to recognize your own circumstances and appraise each investment and strategy on its merits.

REASONS FOR BORROWING

There are four reasons that might prompt you to borrow money for an investment:

1. *Speculation:* When you believe you've found an attractive investment, you may want to borrow money to buy more of the investment than you could pay for out of your own pocket.

2. *Tax reduction:* Most interest payments are a tax-deductible expense. Borrowing can reduce your current tax bill and, if the investment is successful, the loan will finance profits that won't be taxed until later—perhaps as capital gains.

3. *Favorable rates:* It may be possible for you to borrow at below-market interest rates—from an insurance policy or a credit union. Even if you have nothing more elaborate in mind, it could be to your advantage to borrow and put the money into Treasury bills.

4. *Risk reduction:* Depending on what else is in your portfolio, borrowing may accomplish the opposite of speculation; it may reduce your overall risk.

This chapter will discuss the four investment reasons for borrowing—discussing the conditions under which borrowing may be wise or foolish.

SPECULATION

If you have a strong opinion about an investment, borrowing allows you to purchase more than you could have otherwise. If your opinion turns out to be correct, your profit will be magnified and a mistake will be more expensive.

If you're rushing to borrow money to capitalize on a sure thing, we hope you'll first reread pages 91–92 of this book—dealing with sure things.

In deciding whether to borrow, however, we believe it's a mistake to focus on the debt incurred for any single investment. It's more important that you have the right amount of each investment in your portfolio. Your debts are important only because they help to determine your *net* position in dollar investments you own minus the dollar debts you owe.

If your overall dollar position is satisfactory (for your expectations and objectives), the amount you owe against any one investment is irrelevant. But if your net dollar position is too low, it's no help that a given loan is only a small percentage of the value of its collateral.

We'll come back to this point several times in this chapter and in Part Six.

TAX REDUCTION

The second possible reason for borrowing is to reduce taxes.

283

The interest on the debt is deductible from ordinary income as it is paid each year; but the investment (if it is successful) appreciates year after year, unmolested by the Internal Revenue Service. When the investment is finally sold, the profit may be taxed at capital-gain rates, which are lower than ordinary income tax rates.

Inflation increases the tax motive for borrowing. And the higher inflation goes, the stronger the motive becomes.

First, interest rates usually rise with inflation, so the interest deduction is greater. If the investment seems to rise with inflation also, its appreciation is expected to overshadow the after-tax interest expense.

Second, when money is depreciating, every year that a tax payment can be postponed decreases the purchasing power of the eventual payment. Delay is valuable by itself, even if it doesn't lower the total tax you pay over the years. Since the interest payment reduces the tax you have to pay this year, it is a form of tax delay.

Because the tax benefits of borrowing are so attractive, they can easily lead to a highly speculative, imbalanced portfolio—even if that wasn't the intention. The borrowed money goes to purchase equity investments—such as stocks, real estate, gold, or something else not denominated in dollars. The result is that the investor owes many more dollars than he owns—so that his portfolio depends too much on continuing inflation.

Real estate is a prime example. It's possible to finance as much as 80%, and sometimes even 90%, of a real estate purchase with borrowed money. With such high leverage, each year's interest and depreciation on the property will exceed any rental income. This creates a yearly loss that reduces the investor's income tax—even if the market value of the property is rising.

Such a tax strategy can be irresistible to someone who faces a 50%, 60%, or 70% tax rate. But it is very risky when his real estate holdings or his debts exceed 100% of his net worth—since he could be hurt badly by a decline in inflation.

When inflation moderates, real estate prices don't just rise more slowly, they fall. If inflation eased for an extended period, even without a deflation, the real estate investor who had borrowed too heavily would be wiped out.

Tax strategies are important, but they should never overrule prudent investment strategy. And it isn't prudent to have more than 100% of your net worth riding on one investment.

FAVORABLE RATES

The third reason for borrowing is the availability of especially low-cost credit.

If you purchased a life insurance policy many years ago, it may contain a clause allowing you to borrow against the cash value at an interest rate well below today's rates. A 5% rate isn't uncommon in policies that were written twenty years ago. If Treasury bills are paying a rate 2% or more above the interest rate at which you can borrow, it's worth the effort to borrow the money and buy T-bills.

An insurance loan has a fixed interest rate and can be repaid whenever you want. You can borrow when open-market interest rates are high. If interest rates fall, you can pay back the loan by selling the T-bills.

If you borrow the cash value from your life insurance, the company will subtract the unpaid loan before paying the beneficiaries. However, if the borrowed money is invested in Treasury bills and available to your beneficiaries, your net estate will remain unchanged.

Insurance loans are the extreme example of below-market interest rates, but there are others. You may belong to a credit union that lends money at below-market rates. You might get a loan commitment from a bank just before interest rates move upward. Or, if you have no scruples about dealing with the government, your children might be eligible for a subsidized student loan or you may be eligible for a low-cost loan as a farmer.

If the loan conditions don't prevent you from using the money in the way you want, you may as well take the loan—even if you don't need it. The borrowed money allows you to acquire cash that can go into Treasury bills, and you can collect the difference between the T-bill rate and the loan rate —while your *net* position in dollars remains unchanged.

RISK REDUCTION

Although borrowing often adds to your risk position, it is also possible to reduce risk by borrowing.

A portfolio becomes more risky to the extent that all the assets are pointed in the same direction—whether toward more inflation or less inflation. The risk lessens as different kinds of assets are introduced that offset each other. Sometimes a portfolio weighted too heavily in one direction can be balanced through borrowing.

Suppose, for example, that you've retired on a pension. If the pension provides a fixed number of dollars yearly, the purchasing power decreases as inflation proceeds. To balance this, you might buy a small rental house, financing the purchase with a 20-year mortgage.

If inflation gets worse, your pension will be worth less. But the mortgage will be repayable in dollars of the same value as those you receive from your pension—while the market value of the house and the income from it should rise. If inflation slows, the real estate investment, by itself, will turn out poorly. But the pension dollars will have more purchasing power than expected and will be comparable to the dollars owed on the mortgage.

The usefulness of this approach will depend on what else is in your portfolio. But it is one way of offsetting a fixed-dollar pension that doesn't fit your plans.

Another example might concern stock in the company for which you work. Suppose you were able to buy the stock at a bargain price, as a fringe benefit, but you had to agree to keep it for at least ten years—and there are still three years left in the agreement.

If you're afraid of what might happen to the stock's value during the next three years, you could borrow money to purchase gold bullion. Over long periods, stocks and gold generally move in opposite directions. Owning both of them can be less risky than owning only one or the other.

FIXED vs. FLOATING RATES

Your risk position is affected also by the type of loan contract you make.

In general, a floating-rate loan (with an interest rate that changes periodically) is safer if you have large holdings of real estate, gold, or other investments that tend to do well in times of rising inflation—and especially if you owe more dollars than you own.

If inflation rises, the interest rate will go up, but you expect this to be overshadowed by the rise in the value of your investments. On the other hand, if inflation declines, the investments may decline—but you won't have the additional burden of a fixed-rate, high-interest loan.

If the interest rate is fixed, an unexpected rise in open-market interest rates is unprofitable for the lender and profitable for the borrower. The opposite is true if interest rates fall unexpectedly; the lender profits and the borrower suffers.

So if your investments are heavily weighted toward more inflation, you worsen the imbalance by borrowing with a fixed-rate loan. But if you feel under-protected against inflation, a fixed-rate loan will help to reduce the risk.

Put another way, if you need more protection from inflation, a fixed-rate loan will add to the portfolio's balance. If you already have enough protection against inflation, a floating-rate loan is probably a better choice.

Prepayment Privilege

Some fixed-rate loan contracts, especially mortgages, allow you to pay off the loan early without incurring heavy penalties. This gives you the best of fixed and floating rates. If interest rates rise, you can continue to pay the old, lower interest rate. If interest rates drop, you can pay off the loan early and acquire a new loan with a lower rate.

Walking Away

A loan might reduce your risk by transferring some of the risk to the lender.

In some states, if the market value of a foreclosed property is less than the unpaid balance, a mortgage lender cannot collect the difference from the defaulting borrower. If so, and if real estate prices fall drastically, you can walk away from the property—letting the lender take it over.

It may not be your style to use the law to take advantage of someone. However, if the state law specifies that the home-owner isn't responsible for the unpaid balance after a fore-closure, it is necessarily an implied clause in every contract. The lender knows it, and the interest rate he charges reflects it. And in some cases, the loan agreement itself might spell out this provision. The principal disadvantage is the effect on your future credit rating.

A walk-away mortgage is the same as having a put option on the property—the opportunity, but not the obliga-tion, to sell the property to the lender for the balance due on the loan. The higher the mortgage (as a percentage of the property), the more valuable the option will be—because you will have less equity to lose in a market downturn.

If this kind of option fits your thinking, it would be especially valuable if you're too vulnerable to a deflation. However, since the lender recognizes the risk (even if he may underestimate it), he will require a higher interest rate if the mortgage is an especially large fraction of the property's current market value.

One way to minimize your overall interest cost is to take two mortgages on the property. The first mortgage would be for an amount that doesn't create a special foreclosure risk. Then take a second mortgage, for five years or so, for as much as you can get.

You'll pay a higher rate on the second mortgage—because of the foreclosure risk to the lender. But you'll be paying the higher rate on only part of the total amount bor-rowed, and only for a short period.

It is likely that by the end of five years either (1) you will have abandoned the property in a real estate crash or (2) inflation will have carried the value of the property high enough that there is little risk of it later falling below the amount owed.

MARGIN LOANS

A margin account is a readily available source of floating-rate loans. A margin account uses an investment (such as stocks, bonds, or commodities) as collateral for a loan. Its essential features are:

1. The lender keeps the investment in his custody as assurance that the loan will be repaid.

2. The lender may change the interest rate at any time. In practice, margin interest rates rise and fall with other short-term interest rates. The interest rate might change two or three times a month; there are periods when it will change two or three times a week.

3. There is no repayment schedule and no fixed due date on the loan. The borrower may repay the loan at any time, and the lender may require repayment at any time.

4. If the investment's market value declines and drops too close to the amount of the loan, the lender may (and almost certainly will) issue a margin call—asking the borrower to reduce the loan balance. If the borrower doesn't respond, or if the investment's value is dropping too fast to allow the lender to wait, the lender can sell all or part of the investment—using the proceeds to reduce the loan.

Because the interest rate can be altered at any time, and because the lender faces virtually no risk of default (since he holds the collateral), interest rates on margin loans are quite low. So if you have the appropriate collateral, a margin loan may be the cheapest kind of floating-rate loan available.

Usually, a margin loan finances the purchase of an investment, with the investor borrowing through his broker. But this doesn't have to be the case. The loan can be taken on an investment you own already, and the loan can be obtained at a bank—where margin interest rates are often lower than brokers' rates.

The Federal Reserve sets limits on the size of margin loans made against stocks or corporate bonds. Since January 3, 1974, the limit for stocks and convertible bonds has been 50% of the market value. And the lender must demand partial repayment if the market value declines to where the loan equals 70% of the value. For non-convertible corporate bonds, the lending limit is 90% of the value.

There are no legal limits for margin loans on commodities, but the lender will establish limits of his own. After the wild rise and fall in gold and silver prices in early 1980, few banks will lend as much as 50% of the value of precious metals—and 25% is more likely.

Diversified Collateral

If you use a margin loan as a way of raising money, you can reduce the chance of a margin call by pledging a diversified group of investments as collateral.

Any single stock or other investment could drop by 30% very quickly—prompting a margin call. But if the margin loan covers several stocks, for example, there is less chance that the value of the entire group will drop quickly.

The total value of the collateral will be even less likely to drop rapidly if it includes a counter investment, such as gold. A sharp fall in stock prices is often accompanied by a rise in the price of gold—which would keep the collateral's overall value more stable.

To borrow on a diversified group of investments requires that one lender have custody of all of them. And you may have trouble finding a U.S. bank or broker that will lend money on both stocks and gold. Swiss banks (discussed in Chapter 9) do this as a matter of course, but gold is a relatively unfamiliar investment in the U.S.

Since margin loans are less expensive than most other loans, you may want to keep them in mind when you borrow. One drawback is that any investment you would like to keep private cannot be used as collateral in the U.S.—nor can you take an interest deduction on your tax return for a margin loan on an investment you're keeping to yourself.

BORROWING FROM YOURSELF

One source that's easy to overlook is borrowing from yourself.

In Part Five, we'll describe some relatively simple ways by which you may be able to set up your own pension plan and postpone taxes into the far future. Once you have such a plan (or if you have one already), it may be possible to gain the tax advantages of borrowing without adding to your risk.

Suppose, for example, that your pension plan holds dollar assets such as Treasury bills. And suppose that, between pension plan holdings and personal holdings, you have more dollar assets than you need. You could sell some of the pension plan's T-bills and buy gold with the proceeds.

But it would make more sense to have the pension plan sell the T-bills and lend you the money—which you would use to buy gold for your personal account. Overall, your portfolio has the same position either way—but the tax consequences are better with the loan. The pension plan will pay no tax on the interest it earns on the loan, while the interest you pay the plan is tax-deductible for you.

DOLLARS & DEBTS

You may think of a pension plan as a safe refuge for the future—a nest egg you shouldn't borrow from, especially to buy gold. But what is important is the total portfolio—everything you own and owe, inside and outside a pension plan. The pockets in which you place various assets depend upon such considerations as taxes and privacy, but the placement will have little effect on your overall risk.

You might dislike the idea of being in debt. We, too, respect the danger of owing too much money. But borrowing is not the same as being in debt. If you own, either directly or indirectly (as through a pension plan), a larger number of dollars than you owe, you are not a debtor and you are not exposing yourself to the grief a deflation can bring a debtor.

The same principle is true in reverse. Suppose you owe nothing personally, but owe money indirectly through the debts of a limited partnership or your own corporation. If those debts exceed the dollars you own, you're vulnerable to a deflation. Your risk may be limited to the net value of your interest in the corporation or partnership, but the risk isn't eliminated. A rise in the purchasing power of the dollar will hurt you.

It is your overall *net* holdings of dollars (what you own minus what you owe) that determines how exposed you are to inflation or deflation. And the net position isn't affected by your purpose in borrowing or by the collateral you have pledged. The dollars you owe reduce your net worth and represent an obligation that might turn out to be difficult to meet.

If you owe too many dollars, you will need to make some important changes to protect your portfolio against a deflation. And if you hold too many dollars, you may need to borrow in order to reduce the risk of rising inflation.

PART V

AVOIDING TAXES

19

DEFERRING TAXES

INFLATION MAKES IT EXPENSIVE TO HOLD DOLLARS AND profitable to be in debt. The higher the inflation rate, the faster a cash reserve or a debt depreciates in purchasing power. Now that high inflation rates are the norm, most people have responded by reducing their cash holdings (measured in purchasing power), and many have borrowed heavily.

This makes the economy brittle. With cash reserves low, even small problems could cause many people to feel cash-poor—creating a widespread increase in the demand for money and triggering a deflation.

As a result, investors are caught in a conflict. Inflation sets the stage for a deflation, against which dollars would be the best protection, but inflation makes dollars unprofitable to own.

Even if they earn interest, dollar investments are eroded by the combination of inflation and taxes. When inflation is running at 10%, an investor in a 50% tax bracket will lose half the purchasing power of a Treasury-bill investment in 15 years.

While inflation continues, three things are needed for low-cost deflation protection: (1) Your portfolio must contain dollar assets that will be safe against default even during a deflation, (2) the dollars must earn interest at a rate close to the inflation rate, and (3) the interest must be tax-deferred—that is, taxes on the interest income must be postponed indefinitely. If the three requirements are met, preparing for deflation will be inexpensive.

Even so, the dollars won't be a profit-making investment so long as inflation continues; they are only a precaution against what many lie ahead. But tax deferral lessens the cost of taking the precaution.

The chapters in this part will offer methods by which taxes, especially taxes on interest income, can be deferred or reduced. This chapter will introduce the concept, and the following chapters will describe specific tax-deferral plans and other methods of avoiding taxes.

BENEFITS

A tax-deferral plan isn't an investment. It's a legal device for delaying and reducing taxes on profits or income from investments. Such a plan offers several possible benefits:

1. *Reduction of taxable income from sources outside the plan:* With some plans, you can deduct the capital you put into the plan from your current taxable income. Thus you can invest before-tax dollars, rather than after-tax dollars, and have the extra amount working for you.

2. *Deferral of investment income:* Profits and interest earned inside the deferral plan aren't taxed, so the earnings can compound at a faster rate. Even the money that eventually must be paid in taxes can be producing income for as long as the deferral program continues.

3. *Lower tax rates:* In some cases, when the deferral ends, investment earnings will be taxed at capital-gain rates—even if the earnings have come from interest or dividends. In other cases, the earnings will be taxed eventually at special low rates applicable to the particular plan. And in still other cases, the deferral can continue indefinitely—avoiding both income and estate taxes.

4. *Tax payment at more favorable times:* Income tax rates might be lower someday—or you might be in a lower tax bracket (after retirement, for example). Many deferral plans can be liquidated at almost any time you choose, so you can pay the tax whenever tax rates seem most favorable.

DEFERRAL POWER

Deferring taxes is not procrastination. It achieves more than simply putting off the pain of writing a check to the government.

Tax deferral is like getting an interest-free loan equal to your tax bill. Until the loan is repaid (when the deferral ends), the money is invested for *your* benefit—earning an interest rate that allows a fund of dollars to maintain its purchasing power.

As an example, the graph on page 299 applies the principle to $1 invested in Treasury bills. The broken line shows the amount that accumulates if taxes are paid on the interest each year at a 43% rate (for joint returns, the marginal rate on income over $35,200) and the remainder is reinvested in more T-bills. The solid line shows the result if no income tax is paid and all the interest is left to compound. The tax-deferred investment grew to $3.11; the pay-tax-as-you-go investment grew to only $2.29.

The dotted line shows the progress of the Consumer Price Index during this period. The tax-paying investment fell behind it at a noticeable rate. The tax-deferred investment ran ahead of consumer prices until 1974 and has appreciated since then at approximately the same rate as the Consumer Price Index.

The higher inflation and interest rates go, the more useful each dollar in a tax-deferral plan becomes. If you're in a 50% tax bracket and T-bills are earning 10%, tax deferral saves you 5 cents per year for every dollar in the plan. But if inflation and interest rates go to 20%, you'll save 10 cents per year per dollar in the plan.

For investors in lower tax brackets, the results from deferral are less dramatic but should be no less welcome.

DEFERRAL EXAMPLE

The Keogh plan, a pension plan for self-employed individuals, will be described in detail in the next chapter. It isn't the most powerful deferral plan available, but we'll summarize it here to show how valuable tax deferral can be.

In its simplest version, a Keogh plan allows you to put up to $7,500 per year into an investment account that is earmarked for retirement. The money going into the account is deductible from current taxable income, and no tax is due on the profits or income earned until the money is withdrawn.

Almost everyone has heard of a Keogh plan, but many people may have ignored it for one reason or another: (1) For someone with a large income $7,500 is too little to bother with; (2) taxes will have to be paid eventually anyway; (3) privacy is impossible; (4) the kinds of investments that can be made through the plan are unattractive; or (5) retirement is too far away to worry about or has already been provided for. But these objections may be misplaced.

First, the $7,500 deduction reduces this year's taxable income by that much, and the deduction can be repeated year after year. The money deducted can generate profits or income that won't be taxed—even if an investment is sold. Nothing is taxed until you withdraw money from the plan. The yearly deductions and accumulated interest can increase your tax-exempt investment fund to $130,000 or so in ten years. So don't ignore a tax advantage just because it appears to be small.

Second, when the plan is liquidated, you can choose to have the money taxed under special rules that may be very attractive. For an accumulation of $200,000, for example, you can withdraw the money all at once and pay a tax of only 24.8%, regardless of your tax bracket for other income. The plan can reduce your taxes as well as delay them.

Third, privacy is important, but it's doubtful that you should keep every investment out of sight. In fact, nothing could attract more attention to you than for all your assets to disappear. Some of your investments need to be out in the open—and the Keogh plan can hold them.

Fourth, there are almost no investments that may not be held by a Keogh plan. Although dollar investments need tax deferral the most, the choice of what to hold in the plan is up to you.

And fifth, don't confuse tax labels with reality. A tax-deferral plan may bear the label "pension," but you don't have to have retirement in mind to exploit it. Some plans can

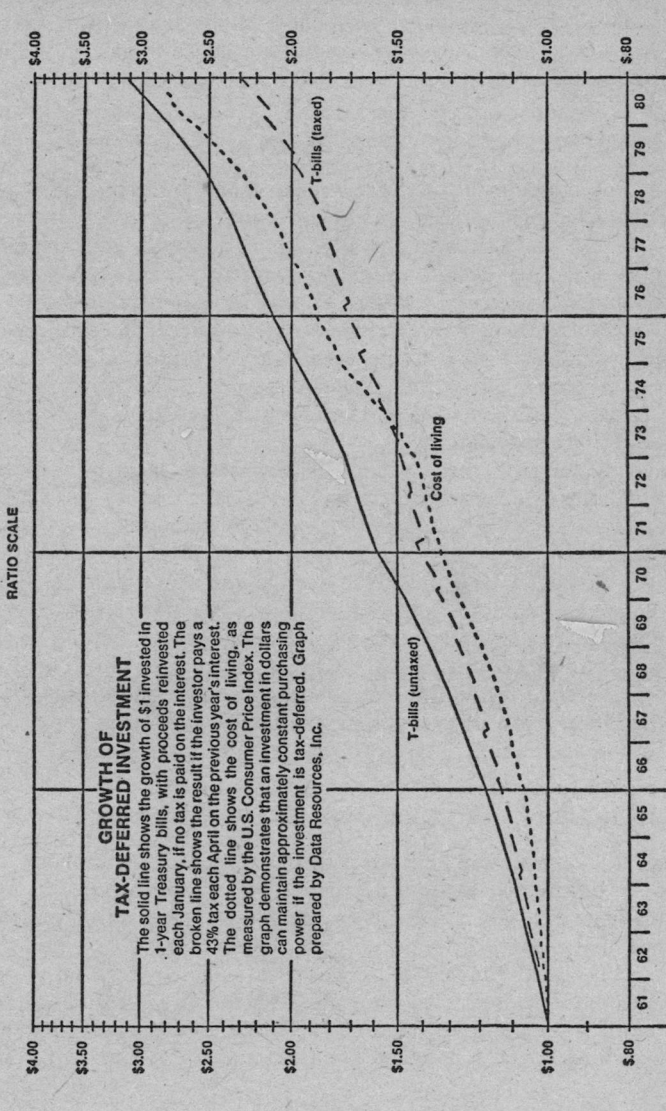

RATIO SCALE

GROWTH OF
TAX-DEFERRED INVESTMENT

The solid line shows the growth of $1 invested in 1-year Treasury bills, with proceeds reinvested each January, if no tax is paid on the interest. The broken line shows the result if the investor pays a 43% tax each April on the previous year's interest. The dotted line shows the cost of living, as measured by the U.S. Consumer Price Index. The graph demonstrates that an investment in dollars can maintain approximately constant purchasing power if the investment is tax-deferred. Graph prepared by Data Resources, Inc.

T-bills (taxed)

T-bills (untaxed)

Cost of living

be liquidated without penalty whenever you want; with others, the penalty may be relatively small. And you would probably have other assets outside the plan that you could draw on if you needed cash, so you wouldn't need to break into the Keogh plan until those assets had been used up.

INVESTMENTS IN THE PLAN

A tax-deferral method is most valuable if you use it to shelter the right investments.

The first step is to decide what should be in your overall portfolio. Then decide where each item should be kept—using a tax deferral refuge for the investments that need it most.

Gold, silver, warrants, and dual-purpose funds attract no taxes until they're sold, and even then the profits are taxed as capital gains. The same is nearly true of Swiss francs, low-dividend stocks, and real estate—since income is secondary to capital appreciation.

Among all your investments, dollars are most in need of sheltering—because interest income is taxed every year and at rates up to 70%. Protect the dollars from taxes and you have solved most of your investment tax problems.

Tax deferral is profitable even if you don't want to hold dollars as deflation protection. You can lower your tax bill by holding Treasury bills inside a deferral plan and offsetting them with money borrowed personally, outside the plan. The interest earned inside the plan attracts no immediate taxes, but the interest you pay on the money you've borrowed personally is tax-deductible.

DEFERRAL ALTERNATIVES

The following chapters will describe various methods to defer or reduce taxes. In general, we'll concentrate on the methods that are available to the largest number of people and that require little or no legal assistance.

The next chapter will cover three types of pension plans that you can create for yourself. Chapter 21 will discuss the use of a personal corporation to handle investments. Chapter 22 will show how deferred annuities can serve a similar purpose for people who can't use either a pension plan or a corporation. Chapter 23 will provide a miscellany of other possibilities. Chapter 24 will explain why we believe municipal bonds are far from the ideal way to avoid taxes. And Chapter 25 will examine tax-haven countries and equity-type tax shelters—such as oil-drilling ventures and cattle-feeding programs.

The equity tax shelters don't shelter interest income; to the contrary, they often are based on borrowing. Some of them can reduce your tax bill to zero if you're willing to invest enough. But large doses of these investments are dangerous, since the common thread running through them is a dependence on inflation. Either the investment reduces taxes because it's financed with borrowed money, or its value will hold up only if inflation continues—or both.

Thus it's safe to use equity tax-shelter investments aggressively only if you hold enough dollar investments elsewhere to protect against deflation. But the interest earned on the dollars must be shielded from taxes if your overall tax plan is to succeed.

So no matter what your approach, the key to a low-tax, *balanced* portfolio is tax deferral for interest income. Achieve that deferral and most tax problems can be handled without exposing yourself to large risks.

With tax deferral, you can afford to hold dollar assets. With dollar assets, you're protected against a deflation. With deflation protection, you can afford the risks involved in equity tax shelters or other inflation-oriented investments.

20

CREATING YOUR OWN PENSION PLAN

In the name of "retirement," the tax law allows you to divert money from your taxable income, put it into a "pension plan," make investments with it, and shield the investments' earnings from all taxes. The tax deferral on the investment income continues until you withdraw the money from the plan—which may be many years from now.

Generally, you can create your own pension plan if you are self-employed, operate a business, have a professional practice, *or* work for a company that hasn't provided a pension plan. You cannot set up your own plan if you work for a company that has already provided a pension plan for you (unless you have earnings from a separate business or profession), or if you have no occupational income at all.[1]

If the company you work for has a pension plan, you probably can't control how your share of the money is invested. Even so, finding out the kind of plan you have and what assets are in it is important. If the pension fund invests in a way you consider risky, you might be able to offset your share of that risk by the way you handle your own investments. This chapter may help you to understand how your

---

[1]However, there may be ways to adapt yourself to the rules. See the remarks on page 328 concerning incorporation of certain investment activities. And if you are not self-employed, see the comments on page 323.

pension plan works and to know how much value it has for you.

Not an Investment

A pension plan is not itself an investment. It's a special compartment of your portfolio that might hold any investment, protecting its earnings from taxes.

You'll make the best use of a pension plan if you view it as a device (a very powerful device) for avoiding taxes. It's a mistake to think of it as a retirement plan. If the plan is properly designed, you can remove money from it before you retire (though there are penalties in some cases), and you can keep money in the plan after you retire. "Retirement" is merely the label that prompted Congress to grant favorable tax treatment.

TYPES OF PLANS

There are three basic types of tax-qualified pension plans. Which one you can use depends on your employment status.

1. *Keogh plan:* This plan is for unincorporated, self-employed individuals, including sole proprietors and partners. Using a Keogh plan works best if you have no employees (other than yourself), since the law requires that any pension arrangements you make for yourself be made for your employees, too. But it can serve a purpose even if you have employees.

2. *Corporate pension plan:* This plan is for employees of corporations—which can include a self-employed individual who has incorporated his business or professional practice. This is the most high-powered of the three types of pension plans, but it is also the most complicated to handle. In addition to the pension advantages, incorporating has other tax benefits—which are the subject of the next chapter.

3. *IRA (Individual Retirement Account):* An IRA is for anyone who works, but whose employer has not established a Keogh or corporate pension plan for him. It is the

least powerful of the three plans, but should be used if nothing else is possible.[2]

The three types of plans have many similarities and several differences. Most of this chapter will be a description of various features and rules, explaining how they apply to each of the three types of plans.

HOW IT WORKS

We'll begin with a brief look at how a pension plan operates.

Suppose you have a Keogh plan that permits you to contribute $7,500 to it each year, a local bank is the trustee for the plan, and you've decided that the pension plan is the best way to hold Treasury bills.

Sometime during the current tax year (which for most people is the calendar year), you'll send checks to the bank —totaling up to $7,500. With each check, you'll enclose a note instructing the bank to buy one-year Treasury bills for your Keogh plan. Or you may already have given the bank instructions to place all Keogh funds in one-year T-bills, and to replace them with new bills as they mature.

At the end of the year, the bank will send you a statement—showing how much you've contributed to the plan. On your tax return, you'll deduct this amount from your taxable income. You'll have invested before-tax dollars in T-bills, rather than reducing the investment by paying taxes first.

Thereafter, the interest generated by the T-bills can be ignored for tax purposes. It will accumulate and compound —without being diluted by taxes.

Sometime in the future, you'll begin withdrawing money from the plan, and the withdrawals will be taxable. But because of the favorable tax rules applicable to pension plans, you'll probably pay tax at a lower rate than you would pay now.

This is the essence of a pension plan. There are variations—the investments you choose or the amount of the year-

---

[2]Page 323 offers suggestions for upgrading to a Keogh or corporate plan.

ly deposits, for example. The various options available are described in this chapter.[3]

COVERAGE FOR ALL EMPLOYEES

If you're not the only employee of your company, it can establish a Keogh or corporate pension plan only if the plan covers all permanent, full-time employees on the same terms.

This rule may make a pension plan less attractive. Ways to avoid paying for unwanted participants are discussed on pages 321–323.

CONTRIBUTIONS TO PLAN

The money contributed to a pension plan each year is deductible from taxable income. For corporate and Keogh plans, the company makes the contribution and takes the deduction. For an IRA, the employee makes the contribution and takes the deduction.

The pension plan pays no taxes on the dividends, interest, or profits made on its investments. The money is taxed only when, eventually, it is withdrawn from the plan—which may or may not be when the participant retires.[4]

MAXIMUM YEARLY CONTRIBUTION

There is a maximum tax-free amount that can be put into the plan each year.

For an IRA, the limit is 15% of each year's gross income from wages and salary—up to a maximum of $1,500. This

---

[3]For simplicity, our example used Treasury bills as the investment, although T-bills require a minimum purchase of $10,000. The same position could be obtained with Treasury notes or bonds that mature within one year, and which have minimums of only $1,000, or by buying shares of a money market fund that invests only in T-bills.

[4]The profits *are* currently taxable if the pension plan borrows money to purchase an investment.

low maximum makes the IRA the least attractive of the three plans. If your spouse is not working and is not covered by a pension plan, the limit is increased to $1,750. If your spouse is working but not covered by a pension plan, she can establish her own IRA—with her own $1,500 yearly maximum.

For Keogh or corporate plans, the rules are a little less simple. The maximum contribution depends on whether the plan calls for contributions tied directly to the participant's salary ("defined contribution") or for contributions needed to finance a specified pension ("defined benefit"). We'll explain the two types.

Defined-Contribution System

With a defined-contribution plan (corporate or Keogh), the amount contributed to the plan each year depends on your salary and, perhaps, on the company's profits.

The maximum yearly contribution for a defined-contribution Keogh plan is 15% of your income from self-employment—but no more than $7,500 in any year.

The yearly ceiling for a corporate plan is 25% of an individual's compensation (salary and bonuses), up to a maximum of $36,700. The latter figure was effective in 1980, but the dollar-ceiling is adjusted every year by the inflation rate.

The amount a company contributes to a Keogh or corporate plan for an employee is a matter, like salary levels, to be negotiated between the two. Up to the legal maximum, it can be any percentage of each employee's salary, or it can be a share of the company's profits distributed among employees in proportion to their salary. In either case, the percentage must be the same for every employee covered by the plan.

With a defined-contribution system, you can, if you choose, establish a separate investment account for each participant. Each person chooses his own investments and tells the trustee (described on page 316) how to invest the money. When the employee retires or leaves the company, he'll collect whatever his investment account has accumulated. With this system, you, as a participant, need to consider only your own desires when choosing investments.

307

Defined-Benefit System

The second alternative is a defined-benefit plan—which specifies the pension the employee will receive each year after he retires. The yearly contribution to the plan is whatever is needed to finance the promised pension. The yearly pension usually is equal to a given percentage of the employee's current salary or his average salary over a given number of years.

This year's contribution is determined by (1) the number of years until the retirement age indicated in the plan, (2) an assumption about the rate of return the plan will earn on its investments, and (3) the amount of money already accumulated by the plan. The calculation will be made by the plan's trustee (discussed on page 316).

For a defined-benefit Keogh plan, the maximum yearly contribution, as of 1980, is $16,000—no matter what benefit is specified. This figure is adjusted yearly in accordance with inflation.

For a corporate plan, the benefit established cannot exceed either $102,000 per year or 100% of the employee's current or average salary. But the contribution can be any amount reasonably required to produce that benefit.

Generally, a defined-benefit system will call for a larger contribution if you're now over 35, while a defined contribution system will have a larger maximum if you're under 35. This is only a rough rule of thumb, however. When you set up the plan, you can determine which method permits larger contributions.

Two Plans

A corporation can establish both a defined-contribution plan and a defined-benefit plan. In that case, every permanent, full-time employee is covered by two plans.

The contribution rules covering dual plans are quite complicated, but they allow a larger yearly dollar contribution than would be possible with only one plan. The table on page 310 shows the percentage of your salary your corporation could contribute during the first year of a dual plan, depending on the age at which you start.

VOLUNTARY CONTRIBUTIONS

An employee covered by a defined-contribution plan (Keogh or corporate) is allowed to make additional, voluntary contributions to his own account in some cases. (Voluntary contributions aren't applicable to an IRA, since the employee makes all contributions anyway.)

In most cases, the ceiling on voluntary contributions is between 6% and 10% of the employee's current annual salary, depending on how much the employer is contributing.

Voluntary contributions are not deductible from anyone's taxable income. But once inside the plan, the money can produce earnings that escape current taxation. And voluntary contributions can be withdrawn from the plan at any time without penalty.[5]

With a Keogh plan, a participant may make voluntary contributions (which are applied to his own account) only if there's more than one person in the plan. If you're self-employed and have no employees, then you're the only participant and you cannot make voluntary contributions.[6]

With a corporate pension plan, you can make voluntary contributions even if you're the only participant.

Any rights to make voluntary contributions accumulate through the years; that is, you can decide this year to make voluntary contributions that you were entitled to make in earlier years. However, there's an overall ceiling applied to employer and voluntary employee contributions together each year. If the employer is contributing the maximum allowable, there may not be much room for the employee to catch up on voluntary contributions he failed to make in earlier years.

No income tax is paid when you withdraw money that was deposited as a voluntary contribution, because this money was taxed before it went into the plan. However, income or

---

[5]Other withdrawals are covered in the next section.
[6]One way to get around this is discussed on page 320.

DUAL PENSION PLAN
MAXIMUM FIRST-YEAR CONTRIBUTION
(per $1,000 of Salary)

| Age | | Contributions to Plans | | | % of |
Current	Retirement	Defined Benefit	Defined Contribution	Total	Salary
25	55	$163.30	$100.00	$ 263.30	26.3%
35	55	351.10	100.00	451.10	45.1%
45	55	979.90	100.00	1,079.90	108.0%
55	65	821.80	100.00	921.80	92.2%
65	75	636.90	100.00	736.90	73.7%

The calculations show examples of the maximum contribution possible (per $1,000 of salary) in the first year of an employee's pension-plan coverage when both a defined-benefit and a defined-contribution plan are used.

The "% of salary" applies up to a salary of $110,000 per year. Above that level, ceilings on contributions will reduce the percentage of salary that can be contributed.

The defined-benefit plan calculations assume a pension of 100% of current salary and a rate of return of 6.0% per year on the plan's investments.

The calculations are for the first year of coverage for the first year of employment. If the employee has been with the corporation longer, it may be possible to increase the contribution to allow for past salary payments.

profits earned by voluntary contributions will be taxed when the earnings are withdrawn.

WITHDRAWING THE MONEY

The rules governing withdrawals are similar for all three types of pension plans.

Voluntary contributions can be withdrawn whenever you choose, without liquidating the plan and without incurring any penalty. The tax-deductible contributions can be withdrawn only by liquidating the plan.

One way or another, you can liquidate your plan at any time. However, penalties are applied if you do so before the "normal" retirement age named in the plan. To satisfy the IRS, the plan may permit you to withdraw the money as early as age 59½, and a Keogh plan or IRA must require withdrawals by age 70½—even if you won't retire then.

There are no penalties if a participant in a corporate plan withdraws his share when he ends his employment. So if the owner-employee of a corporation resigns or fires himself, he can collect most or all of the pension plan proceeds without penalty. A Keogh plan remains in force even if the company is dissolved. An IRA remains in force if the individual changes jobs.

This section will discuss the tax consequences of normal and early liquidations.

Normal Liquidation

The tax paid on a normal liquidation will depend on the choice you make between two methods of withdrawing the money.[7]

The first method is an annuity—by which the pension plan pays you a fixed yearly sum for life or for a specified number of years. The pension plan can make the yearly pay-

---

[7]The current rules apply to money accumulated by a pension plan after December 31, 1973. For money placed in a plan before then, its owner has the choice of having the money taxed by the current rules or as a long-term capital gain.

ments directly to you, or it can purchase an annuity from an insurance company. The yearly payments you receive will be added to whatever other earned income you have for that year and taxed at earned-income rates (the maximum rate is 50%).

The second method is a lump-sum payment—by which you receive all the money from the pension plan during one year. In this case, the money is considered to be "unearned" income, like interest or dividends, for which the maximum rate is 70%.

However, this higher maximum is offset by two advantages. First, the money is taxed separately from all other income received that year; it doesn't push other income into a higher bracket.

Second, the tax rate on the lump-sum distribution is calculated by a special formula ("Special Ten-Year Averaging Method") that creates a tax rate roughly equivalent to the rate assessed if you were receiving only one tenth as much money. For example, if the proceeds are $200,000, the average tax rate is only 24.8%—making a one-time tax of $49,590.

The table on page 313 shows the tax rate for lump-sum distributions of various sizes.

You don't need to make the choice between a lump-sum settlement and an annuity until you decide you want the money. At that time, the decision will be affected by the amount of money in the plan, your taxable income from other sources, and your life expectancy. Expectations regarding estate taxes are involved also, because money not yet paid to you by an annuity settlement can go to your heirs outside of your taxable estate.

Early Liquidation

You can liquidate a Keogh plan or IRA before age 59½, but the money withdrawn will be added to your taxable income for that year. In addition, you must pay a penalty tax of 10% of the amount withdrawn, and you may be prohibited from participating in any pension plan for five years.

EXAMPLES OF TAXATION ON LUMP-SUM PENSION PLAN DISTRIBUTIONS

Amount in Plan	Tax	Average Tax Rate	Tax Rate on Next Dollar
$100,000	$ 19,150	19.2%	24%
200,000	49,590	24.8%	34%
300,000	89,740	29.9%	44%
400,000	138,320	34.6%	55%
500,000	193,320	38.7%	55%
600,000	253,920	42.3%	63%

The calculations show the tax paid (under rules applying in 1980) at selected amounts of distribution. Since the tax is progressive (as with normal income tax), amounts between the figures shown in the first column will be taxed at marginal rates between those shown in the last column; the marginal tax rate for the first dollar above each amount is shown in the last column.

The same rules apply to a corporate pension plan, but you can withdraw the money without penalty if you leave the corporation's employment (by resigning or being fired).

Whether the 10% penalty would make you regret creating a pension plan depends on four factors. The plan becomes more valuable : (1) the longer the money is in the plan before withdrawal, (2) the higher your tax bracket while the plan is in force, (3) the lower your tax bracket in the year of the withdrawal, and (4) the higher the rate of return the investments earn.

For example, if you're in a 20% tax bracket, you hold Treasury bills that earn 10%, and then liquidate the pension plan the following year when you're in a 40% bracket, you'll have less after paying taxes than if you had not had the pension plan. But if you're in a 50% tax bracket, the Treasury bills are earning 15%, and you liquidate the plan five years later when you're in a 35% tax bracket, you'll be way ahead even after paying the penalty.

It's very unlikely that the penalty for early liquidation would make you regret putting money into a pension plan. Because the tax benefits of leaving money in the plan are so great, you would choose to withdraw the money only in truly desperate circumstances—in which case you probably would be in a low tax bracket, and thus liable to little tax beyond the 10% penalty.

BORROWING FROM A CORPORATE PLAN

You're not permitted to borrow money from a Keogh plan or an IRA. But you can borrow money from a corporate plan, and the remarks in this section apply to corporate plans.

There are three reasons you might borrow money from your corporate pension plan. First, perhaps your personal need for spendable cash is so great that you can't afford to take the smaller salary that would be left after your corporation made the maximum contribution. If so, your corporation can still make the maximum contribution, and you can borrow back from the plan the amount you couldn't afford to go without. Thus you get the tax advantage of making the maximum contribution without saving more than you care to.[8]

Second, in following years, you'll pay interest on the loan, which you can deduct from your personal taxes—while the pension plan pays no tax on the interest it receives. So you create a tax deduction for yourself without an offsetting tax increase elsewhere—and do so without, on net, going into debt.

And third, if the loan carries a higher interest rate than the plan could earn elsewhere, the extra interest you pay is a way of getting additional money into the tax shelter.

Since the interest is deductible from your own income tax, it's to your advantage to pay the *maximum* plausible interest rate if you have a defined-contribution plan and your own separate investment account. But if you share a common investment fund with other participants in the plan, the interest you pay will accrue to their benefit as well as yours; so you should pay the *minimum* plausible interest rate.

With a defined-benefit plan, the excess interest it receives from you will reduce the size of the allowable corporate contribution the following year. So paying high interest may not increase the ultimate size of the plan by much, but it does allow the money going into the plan to be deductible sooner. And it allows you, rather than the corporation, to take the deduction; and you probably will be in a higher tax bracket than the corporation.

To make loans, the pension plan must have rules in its charter allowing it to do so. If you already have a corporate plan, and it does not allow borrowing, the rules can be amended.

To satisfy the government, the plan's rules must place some restrictions on borrowing. The basic requirement is that any loan made to you must be on a basis that would be reasonable between two unrelated parties—such as between a bank and its customer. You can't simply grab money out of

---

[8]While you can "catch up" on voluntary contributions in later years, you can't do so with tax-deductible contributions; the yearly allowable contribution isn't cumulative.

the plan and call it a loan, and you can't simply pour money into the plan and call it interest.

The loan rules should specify the maximum size of a loan and the uses to which it can be put. For example, loans might be restricted to "secured loans equal to no more than 80% of a participant's vested interest [the current value of your holdings], and only for home and auto loans, loans for educational, medical, or other productive purposes, and short-term loans of up to 12 months for personal emergencies."

Without these limits, the government might conclude that the money is available to you whenever you want it, and so the pension plan really isn't a pension plan at all. But the rules won't cramp your style if they permit borrowing for the kinds of expenditures you're likely to make.

TRUSTEE

The pension plan (corporate, Keogh, or IRA) must have a trustee. The trustee is the individual or institution that purchases and holds the investments, and makes certain reports to the government.

The choice of the trustee is important, because the costs and arrangements differ with the type of institution you choose. Generally, you can choose among banks, savings and loans, pension administrators and their affiliates, and the trustees provided by many mutual funds. And with a corporate plan, you can be your own trustee. We'll discuss each of these possibilities.

Bank Trustee

A bank will serve as trustee without charge if all the plan's funds are kept as deposits in the bank. We think this arrangement is neither safe nor profitable.

Some banks have established their own investment funds (similar to mutual funds) in which pension-plan holdings are placed. As it's highly unlikely that your investment strategy will include the investments the fund would make, it's best to avoid these arrangements also.

A few banks will allow you to set up a *directed trust*—

which allows you to tell the bank which investments to buy. If a local bank will accept a directed trust at a reasonable charge, there's no reason not to use it.

If several banks near you allow directed trusts, choose the one with the lowest trustee fee. Two firms that provide low-cost, directed-trust services for Keogh plans and IRAs are listed on page 478. The trustee doesn't have to be near you.

Savings & Loan Trustee

Many savings and loan associations will retain a bank or trust company to act as trustee for your Keogh plan or IRA if all the money is kept as deposits with the savings and loan. As with banks, we believe this is neither safe nor profitable.

Trustee Provided by Mutual Fund

Most mutual funds, including money market funds, have a standing arrangement by which a bank acts as trustee for Keogh plans and IRAs. The bank is the trustee, but it invests all the pension plan's assets in the fund.

This method is the simplest approach, although it generally is available only for defined-contribution plans. If you want all the funds in Treasury bills, for example, you can do it through a money market fund that invests only in Treasury bills. Every dollar placed in the plan is immediately covered by Treasury bills. If you buy the T-bills yourself, you can do so only when $10,000 (the price of the smallest T-bill) is accumulated.[9]

With a money market fund, the custodial fees are usually only $10 per year or so. However, you indirectly pay your share of the fund's operating expenses, typically about 1% yearly of the fund's assets, reducing your net earnings by that much. (If the pension plan's assets are worth $10,000,

---

[9]However, it's possible to have the same investment position by buying Treasury notes or bonds that mature within one year. The minimum amount for a note or bond is $1,000.

you're paying about $100 per year toward the fund's operating costs.)

Pension Specialist

There are "financial planning" and other firms that specialize in establishing and administering pension plans. Such a firm may be the trustee or will provide one. Although they generally choose the investments for the client, some of them permit you to have a directed trust by which you choose the investments.

Self Trustee

The owner of a corporation may be the trustee for the company's pension plan. If you're the plan's only participant, this is the best arrangement. You can hold the plan's investments in a custodial account at a bank, keep the books yourself, and choose the investments you want.

If you're not the only participant, there is one danger. Other participants could sue you for any investment losses, on the grounds that you've made "imprudent" investments. However, it's unlikely that Treasury bills would be considered an imprudent investment—even if their purchasing power is destroyed through a runaway inflation.

You cannot be your own trustee with a Keogh plan or an IRA.

Custodial Safety

Whoever is the trustee, the pension plan's investments are required by law to be segregated from the assets of the trustee. This means the solvency of the trustee shouldn't affect you, but see our remarks concerning custodial safety on page 258.

MAXIMUM CONTRIBUTIONS

A pension plan can be a powerful device for reducing taxes and deflation-proofing your portfolio. Unless your circumstances are unusual, it probably would be advantageous to divert every dollar possible into the plan.

If the maximum allowable contribution is more than you wish to save in a given year, it makes sense to make the contribution anyway. You can sell an equivalent amount from the investments you hold outside the pension plan. Your total portfolio will be the same as with a smaller contribution, but more of it will be sheltered from taxes.

If you run out of assets to sell, borrow what's needed to allow you to make the maximum contribution. If it's a corporate plan, you can borrow from the plan itself for your personal needs and take a smaller salary. Your taxable income in the current year will be less. And in future years, the interest you pay will be tax-deductible while the interest earned by the plan will compound tax-free.

Force-Feeding

If you believe you should get the maximum amount possible into the plan, there are a number of ways to force-feed a Keogh or corporate pension plan.[10]

1. *Choice of plans:* If your age is over 35, the maximum allowable contribution will be greater if you use a defined-benefit plan (see page 308). A defined-contribution plan is easier to visualize when you're making decisions, and it's easier to keep track of, but the larger contribution allowed by a defined-benefit plan may be enough incentive to warrant the extra effort.

2. *Benefit assumptions:* A defined-benefit plan has to compute each year the contribution that will produce a given pension benefit later. The computation has to assume how soon the participant will retire (the sooner the retirement, the larger the contribution) and how much the investments will earn (the lower the earnings, the larger the contribution needed). To get the largest contributions, assume a low rate of return—say, 6%. And assume a retirement age of 55, or 10 years older than you are now, whichever is higher.

---

[10]There's no way to force-feed an IRA.

This won't greatly affect the total amount the plan eventually accumulates, because the contributions will slow down as the promised benefits become almost fully funded. But it will allow you to make the tax-deductible contributions sooner.

3. *Two plans:* As described on page 308, you can usually make a larger yearly contribution if you have two plans—one with a defined contribution and one with a defined benefit.

4. *Voluntary contributions:* If the company hasn't contributed the maximum possible to a defined-contribution plan, you can make up the difference with voluntary contributions (see page 309). A voluntary contribution isn't deductible from your current taxable income, but the investments it can make will be tax-sheltered. And a voluntary contribution can be withdrawn at any time without penalty.

5. *Spouse on payroll:* If you're the only participant in a Keogh plan, you're not allowed to make voluntary contributions. But if you hire your spouse, and make her the second participant in the plan, you can make voluntary contributions.

6. *Borrow with high interest rates:* If you can borrow from a defined-contribution corporate plan, do so and pay the highest plausible interest rate. The interest you pay will be a tax-deductible transfer of funds from outside the plan to inside the plan. (See the qualifications for this on page 315.)

7. *Early contributions:* Make contributions to the plan as early in the tax year as possible, so the money can be earning tax-free interest as soon as possible. Don't buy Treasury bills outside the plan if you haven't yet made the year's maximum contribution to the plan. Instead, put the money into the plan and make the investment there.

8. *Boosting salary:* If you have a corporate plan, increase your own salary and personally pay tax-deductible occupational expenses—such as travel, entertainment, and auto expenses—rather than having the corporation reimburse you. The after-tax expense won't change for either you or the corporation, but your higher salary will increase the contributions the corporation may make to the pension plan.

320

OTHER EMPLOYEES

An IRA is established by an employee for his sole benefit. Neither his employer nor his fellow employees are involved.

A corporate pension plan or a Keogh plan is established by an employer for his employees. If you have no employees, the plan is solely for yourself. In that case, there probably is no reason that you shouldn't start exploiting the tax benefits immediately.

If you have employees, the decision is not so simple. You cannot have your own pension plan without providing a similar plan for every permanent, full-time employee, and your company must make all the contributions.

If each employee would consider pension-plan contributions to be part of his pay (and you assume future employees would, too), there's no reason not to establish a plan in lieu of giving raises. But if you have many employees, and if they wouldn't think of the contributions as part of their pay, the cost may be too great.

If you want a pension plan for yourself but not for your employees, there are some loopholes to examine. One or more of these might work for you.

Independent Contractors

If you have only a few employees, one approach is to reorganize your company so that you have no formal employees—or at least no permanent, full-time employees.

This converts each person who works for you into an independent contractor, in business for himself, who sells his services to you. For example, your secretary would become a secretarial service, billing you weekly or monthly for services rendered.

As an added benefit, this eliminates payroll taxes and withholding. And in many cases, when employees no longer punch a time clock, they find that they can produce more in fewer hours.

However, it isn't enough just to start calling your employees self-employed. The Internal Revenue Service is concerned about a trend in this direction, and it applies certain tests to see whether someone really is self-employed. The key element is that the individual must decide for himself how to produce the result asked for, rather than following an employer's instructions.

If it's practical for you to let your workers decide how they'll do their work, and if you can let them work the hours they choose and be satisfied merely that the work is done competently and on time, you may be able to convert them into separate, one-man firms.

You need to be cautious with this approach. You should consult an attorney who's familiar with the rules to be sure that your plan will hold up before you go to the trouble and expense of implementing it. If you carry out a plan that won't hold up, the tax consequences can be disastrous.

Part-time & Short-term Employees

You're not required to include a part-time employee (someone who works less than 1,000 hours per year) in a pension plan. And you can establish a waiting period before a new employee is included in the plan (normally, no more than three years).

If You Have Employees

If there's no way to avoid having employees in your Keogh or corporate plan, it can still be practical if the employees understand that the pension contributions are part of their compensation.

Explain to them what they're getting. Point out that it allows their savings to grow without being diminished by taxes. Keep the plan simple so that the explanation will be simple. That generally means sticking to a defined-contribution plan that promises each employee a contribution equal to a specified percentage of his salary.

Let each employee select his own investments. Offer to help anyone who doesn't understand how to do it, or is unsure what the investments should be. Provide a simple investment plan, such as Treasury-bill holdings, for anyone who doesn't want to make investment decisions. Don't try to explain exotic concepts, such as the value of gold in today's world.

If it's a corporate pension plan, make the borrowing rules as liberal as possible, so each person can borrow back from the plan any sums beyond what he wants to have in it.

IF YOU'RE THE EMPLOYEE

If you're employed by a company, your pension-plan options are quite restricted, but there may be ways by which you can have a pension plan that suits you.

If your employer has established a Keogh or corporate plan for you, see if you have a separate investment account. If you don't have your own account, see if you can do so. A separate account allows you to choose the investments, make voluntary contributions, and have pretty much your own pension plan.

Another alternative is to try to be taken off the payroll and treated as an independent contractor (see the discussions on pages 321 and 328). If this can be done, you can set up your own Keogh (or possibly even corporate) pension plan. In addition, a self-employed person usually can claim more tax deductions for occupational reasons than can an employee.

As a last resort, if your employer hasn't provided a pension plan for you, you can set up an IRA for yourself.

GETTING STARTED

The table on page 324 provides a brief summary of the distinctive features of the three types of pension plans.

Of the three, the most troublesome to get started is the corporate plan. If you don't have a corporation already, you'll need an attorney to help you incorporate. And you'll need an attorney or a company that administers pension plans to establish the plan.

The mechanics of an IRA or a defined-contribution Keogh plan are comparatively simple. The following remarks apply to both plans.

During the first few years, the amount of money in the

323

HIGHLIGHTS OF PENSION PLANS

	IRA	Keogh	Corporate
Who may use	Employee not otherwise covered	Self-employed person	Any corporation with employees
Maximum yearly contribution			
Defined contribution plan	15% or $1,750	15% or $7,500	25% or $36,700
Defined benefit plan	Not available	$16,000	100% or $102,000
Voluntary contributions allowed	No	Yes	Yes
Must cover all permanent employees	No	Yes	Yes
Separate account possible for each employee	Automatically	Yes	Yes
Permissible to borrow from plan	No	No	Yes
Participant can be trustee	No	No	Yes
Withdrawal allowed without penalty when . . .	Retirement*	Retirement*	Retirement* or end of employment

This table provides a quick view of the differences between the three types of plans. For details, see the text of this chapter.

*If retirement is at the age specified in the pension plan. When the plan is created, it may specify any age between 59½ and 70½ as retirement age.

plan will be small, so the easiest and most economical way to start is with a money market fund. If this is your choice, select a fund from those described on pages 276–280 of this book. Write to the fund and say that you want to establish a Keogh plan or an IRA, using the fund for your investments. The fund, or a trustee it selects, will send you the application forms and information you need. From then on, simply send the pension contributions to the fund.

When the plan's assets grow beyond $20,000 or so, you may want to find your own trustee. Call a few banks and savings and loans in your city. Find a bank that handles Keogh plans (or IRAs) with a *directed trust*—whereby you choose the investments.

When you begin, the trustee will provide the forms you need as well as any up-to-date information concerning such things as the maximum allowable yearly contribution. All you have to do is to make the contributions.

PENSION PLANS

The tax advantages of a pension plan would be valuable even in a world without inflation. The presence of inflation increases the plan's value in several important ways.

First, inflation pushes you into a higher tax bracket, where a larger percentage of your income is taxed away.

Second, inflation raises interest rates without raising the real (after-inflation) return you receive on interest-bearing investments. Taxes take larger and larger amounts of the true interest you're earning.

And third, inflation increases the potential for a deflation—for which dollars are the best protection. But unless you shelter the interest earned from dollar investments, you'll pay a stiff price for deflation protection. A tax-sheltered plan reduces the cost of protection.

21

TAX BENEFITS FROM INCORPORATION

THE CORPORATE PENSION PLAN IS THE MOST POWERFUL OF the plans discussed in the previous chapter. The desire to have such a plan is often the primary reason for incorporating a business.

But a corporation offers additional tax advantages. By shifting your business activities to a corporation, you can convert some of the income that otherwise would be taxed to you into corporate profits that are taxed at a lower rate. This would increase the number of after-tax dollars available for investment. And in the following years, the investments' earnings would be taxed at the corporation's low rate.

In addition, a corporation offers opportunities to reduce estate taxes.

These and other possibilities will be discussed in this chapter. The chapter is not meant to be a complete guide to corporate tax planning. We'll concentrate on what you need to know if you intend to use a corporation to accumulate interest income at a lower tax rate.

WHO CAN INCORPORATE

The legal costs of incorporating a small business and setting up a pension plan are in the range of $1,000 to $3,000. So the initial cost is less important than the question of whether incorporating will actually help.

For a corporation to succeed as a tax shelter, there must

be a business activity to incorporate. In general, incorporation makes sense if you're in one of the following categories.

1. *Small business*—wholesale, retail, service—anything lawful.

2. *Professional practice*—doctors, dentists, attorneys, and so forth.

3. *Independent contractor*—providing consulting, sales, or other services to companies or anyone else.

4. *Partner:* If you're a general partner in an unincorporated business or professional practice, it may be practical for you to incorporate your own activities. The corporation (with you as its primary employee) would take your place as a partner in the present business. Nothing would change but the legal framework.

5. *Key employee:* If you're an important person in the company where you work, you may be able to incorporate yourself, with the new corporation selling your services to the firm that employs you now. If you're not a key person, your employer probably wouldn't cooperate with a plan to change your name to a corporation.

6. *Lending activity:* If you frequently lend money (such as on mortgages or for any other purpose), it might be to your advantage to incorporate your lending activities as a finance company or loan broker. Part of what is now interest income to you could be diverted to a pension plan, or to salary income or corporate profits—to be taxed at lower rates.[1]

7. *Income properties:* If you own rental properties, you could establish a corporation, hire the corporation to manage the properties for you, and have the corporation employ you to do work. Part of what is now rental income could become salary income, pension-plan contributions, or corporate profits. You would continue to own the properties.[2]

In each of these cases, you would be both a stockholder

---

[1]However, only interest in excess of what you could earn from passive investments (such as bonds) can be diverted in this way without an IRS complaint that you're paying yourself an unreasonable salary.

[2]The fees you pay your own corporation cannot safely exceed what an unrelated company would charge for the same services.

and an employee of the corporation. And the situation is best if you are, or would be, the only full-time employee.

Generally, incorporation is a way to shelter large amounts of income only for people who are in one of the five categories we've described. The benefits are likely to be smaller if you're in either of the last two categories. This chapter may help you decide whether incorporation is a possibility worth investigating.[8]

To understand how a corporation works, we need to look at five features of the tax code—covering (1) tax rates, (2) liquidation (going out of business), (3) pension plans, (4) retained earnings, (5) personal holding companies. We can find our way through these tax rules by dealing with them one at a time.

As we proceed, keep in mind that we're talking about a corporation with one stockholder and one employee—who are the same person.

TAX RATES

Each dollar that a corporation earns through your efforts can be used in one of two ways. It can pay the dollar to you in salary, in which case you'll pay tax on the dollar at personal income rates. Or the corporation can retain the dollar as profit, in which case it will be taxed at corporate rates. Either way, the dollar will be taxed; your choice of which tax to pay will depend first on a comparison of your personal tax rate with the corporation's tax rate.

The corporation pays a tax each year of:

17% on the first $25,000 of profit
20% on the next $25,000 of profit
30% on the next $25,000 of profit
40% on the next $25,000 of profit
46% on profits exceeding $100,000

If your personal tax rate is above 17%, it may be possible to divide income between yourself and the corporation

---

[3]If you don't fit into any of the categories we've described, you may want to skip over to the next chapter, on page 339.

so that both of you are in a lower tax bracket than you are now by yourself. No matter how large the corporation's profits may be in any one year, the first $25,000 of profit will be taxed at 17%. So for the first $25,000, it can keep 83 cents of each dollar.

Thus the corporation may have more after-tax money to invest than you would have after paying personal income tax. Later, as the investments produce interest income, the corporation will pay tax on the interest but, again, perhaps at a lower rate than you would have to pay.

In addition, a corporation can deduct 85% of the dividends it receives from other U.S. corporations before paying taxes. However, it must pay capital-gain taxes on stocks it sells at a profit.

LIQUIDATION

Eventually, you (or your heirs) will want to get the money out of the corporation.

The simplest way to do so, when the time comes, is to liquidate the corporation by selling all its assets and distributing the cash to the stockholder(s). You'll receive all the accumulated after-tax profits of the corporation, and you'll pay tax on them—but as capital gains at a maximum rate of 28%.

With a 17% tax rate, the corporation can keep 83 cents of each dollar of the first $25,000 it earns every year. At liquidation time, the 83 cents may be reduced by up to 23 cents by the capital-gain tax. So even if you liquidate soon after incorporation, you'll net at least 60 cents after taxes—which may be more than if you had received the earnings directly as personal income.

The tax advantage becomes greater, the longer the corporation keeps the money before liquidating. It can invest the money and pay a lower tax rate on the profits or interest—allowing more interest to compound year after year.

The table on page 332 shows what happens to $1 that you earn as salary and invest on your own. It compares this with the results for $1 retained as profits and invested by the corporation. The comparison varies with the length of time involved and the respective tax rates, but the corporation can produce a greater net return even after just one year if your personal tax rate is above 39%.

PENSION PLAN

So far, it seems better to have the corporation keep at least the first $25,000 of earnings, rather than pay it to you in salary. But the presence of a pension plan adds another dimension.

The corporation can deduct contributions to the pension plan from its taxable income. And once in the plan, the money can accumulate and compound with no yearly taxes to slow it down—in other words, at a tax rate of zero. So there's an incentive to get every dollar possible into the pension plan.

However, the deductible amount the corporation can put into the pension plan is based on what it pays you in salary, and you'll have to pay tax on the salary you receive. The pension plan complicates your decisions, but only because it offers additional opportunities.

The decision concerning how much to retain in profits involves three tax rates: (1) the pension plan's 0% tax rate; (2) the tax rate on your salary, which will be between 0% and 50%; and (3) the corporation's tax rate, between 17% and 46%.

There's more to consider than just this year's tax bill, however. In succeeding years, the pension plan's investment earnings will be tax free, while the corporation's investment earnings will be taxable. In addition, you need to consider the respective tax rates you'll face when you liquidate the corporation and the pension plan.

Each year, there will be an optimum split of the corporation's earnings. Some or all might be kept by the corporation as profits; some or all might be paid to you in salary and to the pension plan. There's no simple formula that tells what the optimum would be in a given case. Before the end of each taxable year, you have to calculate how best to divide the profits.

WHAT $1 IN EARNINGS GROWS TO AFTER TAXES WHEN INVESTED BY YOUR CORPORATION VS. BY YOURSELF

Years	By Corporation Before Liquid.	By Corporation After Liquid.	By Yourself at Personal Tax Rate Shown 24%	26%	30%	34%	39%	44%	55%	70%
0	.830	.598	.760	.740	.700	.660	.610	.560	.500	.500
1	.899	.647	.818	.795	.749	.704	.647	.591	.523	.515
2	.973	.701	.880	.854	.801	.750	.687	.624	.546	.530
3	1.054	.759	.947	.917	.858	.799	.729	.659	.571	.546
4	1.142	.822	1.019	.985	.918	.852	.773	.696	.596	.563
5	1.237	.890	1.096	1.057	.982	.909	.820	.735	.623	.580
6	1.339	.964	1.179	1.136	1.051	.968	.870	.777	.651	.597
7	1.450	1.044	1.269	1.220	1.124	1.032	.923	.820	.680	.615
8	1.571	1.131	1.366	1.310	1.203	1.101	.980	.866	.711	.633
9	1.701	1.225	1.469	1.407	1.287	1.173	1.039	.914	.743	.652
10	1.842	1.326	1.581	1.511	1.377	1.251	1.103	.966	.776	.672
15	2.745	1.976	2.280	2.159	1.931	1.721	1.483	1.268	.958	.779
20	4.089	2.944	3.289	3.085	2.709	2.370	1.994	1.665	1.206	.903
25	6.092	4.387	4.744	4.409	3.799	3.262	2.680	2.187	1.503	1.047
30	9.077	6.535	6.842	6.300	5.329	4.490	3.604	2.871	1.873	1.214
35	13.523	9.737	9.868	9.003	7.474	6.181	4.846	3.771	2.334	1.407

The calculations assume that the investment earns a constant 10% yearly return before taxes. The results are more favorable for the corporation at interest rates higher than 10%, less favorable at lower interest rates.

The "Years" column shows the number of years the investment is held. The "0" row shows the amount remaining after paying tax on the earned income, but before earning interest on the investment.

The "Before Liquid." column under "By Corporation" shows the after-tax amount the corporation will accumulate if it earns $1, pays tax on the earnings, and invests the remainder at 17% (the rate applicable to a corporation's first $25,000 of annual earnings) on both the original earnings and the investment interest.

The "After Liquid." column shows the amount left for the stockholder if he liquidates the corporation in the year shown, and pays a long-term capital-gain tax at the maximum rate of 28%.

The "By Yourself" columns show the after-tax amounts you will accumulate (at various tax rates) if you earn $1 personally, pay tax on it (at no more than the maximum rate of 50% applicable to occupational income), and invest the remainder at 10% yearly.

The bold-face number in each column shows the first year in which the corporation produces a higher-after-tax return (after liquidation) than you could earn on your own.

Results are shown to 1/10 of a cent.

Unless you're familiar with all the rules, an accountant should make the calculation. And he should give you a precise calculation, not a sweeping generality.

When he makes the calculation, he needs to consider eight factors: (1) your personal tax bracket; (2) the corporation's tax bracket; (3) the relationship between your salary and the amount that can be contributed to the pension plan; (4) how long before you'll liquidate the pension plan and the corporation; (5) the taxes you'll have to pay when they're liquidated; (6) your investment goals; (7) how much of your living expenses need to be covered by salary from the corporation; and (8) the estate benefits of retaining profits (if your planning allows for estate taxes).

He'll also have to consider two rules we have yet to cover—regarding accumulated earnings and personal holding companies. These two rules were enacted by Congress to limit the ability of corporations to shelter investment income; they call for careful planning.

ACCUMULATED EARNINGS

At some point, the yearly split between profits and salary may be affected by the tax rules governing accumulated earnings.

If, over the years, the corporation accumulates more than $150,000 in profits, and it doesn't have a plausible business reason for keeping that much, it may receive a bill from the IRS for an "accumulated earnings" tax computed at a rate between 27½% and 38½% of the amount retained (adding to the tax already paid on these earnings).

Thus, at some point, the corporation could be forced to stop retaining profits. All further earnings would have to be paid to you and the pension plan. The only alternative is worse—that the earnings be paid out as taxable dividends when they've already been taxed as corporate profits.

The $150,000 limit applies only to money the corporation has earned and kept. Neither the original capital nor money the corporation has borrowed are counted toward the $150,000.

The limit may be exceeded if the corporation needs

money for a business purpose. However, the concept of a "business purpose" is a little vague, and has led to a great deal of litigation between corporate taxpayers and the IRS.

Some purposes for accumulating earnings are generally safe. A corporation may assume earnings to pay off debts, to provide financing for customers, or to have money available for purchases of inventory or equipment that it can reasonably expect to need.

It also may accumulate funds to finance a future business venture. But for the IRS to accept it, the business venture must be plausible. You can't say you're accumulating earnings to finance your 150-year program to colonize Venus.

Whatever the amount you're entitled to accumulate, retained earnings can be kept in Treasury bills or bonds or in any other investment; they don't have to be held in a bank account.

PERSONAL HOLDING COMPANY

An additional consideration is the possibility that the corporation's investment earnings might become large enough to alter the nature of the corporation.

If its investment income amounts to 60% of its adjusted gross income, the corporation will be labeled a personal holding company, and any investment income it retains will be taxed at a rate of 70%.

In most cases, adjusted gross income amounts to the corporation's receipts minus the cost of products sold. In some service businesses, there are no products sold, and so the adjusted gross income is the same as total receipts. Adjusted gross income isn't the same as profit; salaries and other operating expenses are not deducted in calculating it.[4]

At the beginning, it may seem impossible that investment income will ever amount to 60% of your corporation's adjusted gross income. But as investment income compounds,

---

[4]Investment income includes interest, dividends, rents, and royalties—and is counted as part of adjusted gross income in making the calculation. Capital gains and losses are not counted in investment income or in adjusted gross income.

it could overwhelm business income. So if you're planning a long period of accumulation, you should estimate now what your investment earnings may eventually amount to.

Some types of business, such as finance companies and surety companies (that underwrite loans), are exempt from the rules governing personal holding companies. If your corporation's income comes mainly from interest on loans (as opposed to interest on passive investments such as Treasury bills), the corporation may qualify as a finance company and be exempt from the personal holding company rules.

Whatever you do, don't stumble into the problems of a personal holding company without a plan for avoiding the punitive tax. If investment earnings begin to dominate the corporation's income, you should review your plans with an attorney.

ESTATE BENEFITS

We've assumed that you'll eventually liquidate the corporation and pay tax on the capital gain. But the corporation can outlive you, delaying the capital gain still further and reducing estate taxes as well. To make this possible, you can organize (or reorganize) the corporation with two classes of stock—"common" and "non-cumulative preferred."

Preferred stock has a prior claim on dividend payments each year; no dividends can be paid on the common stock until the preferred stock has been paid a specified amount. Preferred stock also has first claim on the corporation's assets. When the corporation is liquidated, the preferred stockholders must be paid a specified sum, and the common stockholders receive only what is left over, if anything.

You can organize (or reorganize) the corporation so that nearly all the corporation's starting value is owed to the preferred stockholders—leaving the common stock with very little value. You can keep the preferred stock for yourself, and give the low-value common stock to your prospective heirs (or to a trust for their benefit) without incurring sizeable gift taxes. Or they can buy the common stock at a small price.

As the corporation accumulates earnings, the value of

the common stock will grow, while the value of your preferred stock remains fixed. To help the corporation accumulate profits, you can have it declare dividends only in years when you actually need the money.

When your estate is settled, only the preferred stock will be a part of it. The common stock, which represents the value of the accumulated earnings, will already be the property of your heirs and will escape estate taxes. To get the accumulated earnings into their own hands, your heirs will have to pay capital-gain taxes (as you would have done if you'd liquidated the corporation during your lifetime), but only when they sell the common stock or liquidate the corporation.

You don't have to lose control of your business with this technique. Just give the preferred stockholders (you) the right to elect a majority of the corporation's directors.

WHETHER TO INCORPORATE

The tax advantages of a corporation and its pension plan can be enormous. If you don't now operate as a corporation, you may want to find out if you can do so.

If there's no business or professional activity to incorporate, the corporation won't be a tax shelter; it will be a personal holding company. But if you have an unincorporated business or professional practice, or if your investments involve an element of business activity, you can probably profit from incorporation.

If you haven't looked into this possibility, it may be because you know the tax code is immensely complicated. However, incorporating a small business or professional practice isn't an exotic area of tax planning that requires high-priced legal talent.

Unless your situation is unusually complicated, a consultation with a tax attorney, costing no more than a few hundred dollars, should tell you whether incorporating is practical. Just be certain the attorney knows how you intend to use the corporation.

If you do incorporate, have the attorney review the situation every year or so—to be sure you're exploiting all the possibilities, and to be sure you're not bumping into any of the rules. If something you're contemplating can't stand up to the rules, it's better to find out early—before the IRS starts running a vacuum cleaner through your bank account.

22

DEFERRED ANNUITIES

DURING A TIME OF INFLATION AND HIGH INTEREST RATES, TAX deferral is more important for dollar investments than for any others, since high interest rates mean that dollar investments will be producing more taxable income. Thus a device for deferring taxes will be especially valuable if it can be used to shelter assets denominated in dollars.

The pension plans we discussed in Chapter 20 are the most efficient tax-deferred methods in common use, and they can easily be used to hold almost anything. If you can't create a pension plan for yourself, or if your plan isn't large enough yet to hold all the dollar investments you need, a deferred annuity is another possibility.

Like a pension plan, a deferred annuity shields interest income from taxation—although you can't invest before-tax earnings in an annuity, as you can with a pension plan. The annuity's interest rate usually will be lower than for Treasury bills, but probably higher than what you would net if you had to pay current taxes on T-bill interest.

This chapter will explain how a deferred annuity works, and will describe some of the plans being offered by insurance companies.

ANNUITIES

An annuity can be like a savings account. The dollars you put into it earn interest until the day you withdraw them.

However, unlike a savings account, the interest earned inside an annuity is not taxed until you withdraw it.

You buy the annuity by making a single payment. When you decide to close out the annuity, you can take all the money at once, receive yearly payments, or choose one of the other alternatives discussed later in this chapter.

To meet the legal definition of an annuity, the insurance company must promise to eventually pay the owner or someone else an annual income. But the contract can include other options, so that the annual income is merely one of several possibilities available to the annuity owner.

The key option in the annuities we'll examine is the right to withdraw all or part of your investment whenever you want. This makes the annuity a tax-sheltered savings account. You deposit money that you can withdraw at any time, and the interest earned is free of taxes until it's withdrawn.

FLOATING-RATE ANNUITIES

Traditionally, the interest rate on an annuity was fixed at the time the contract was purchased; but inflation has made fixed interest rates unattractive. So a number of insurance companies have introduced floating-rate annuities that have two valuable features:

1. The insurance company can raise or lower the interest rate whenever it wishes, subject to a minimum; and

2. The owner of the annuity can cash it in any time—maintaining pressure on the company to keep its interest rate competitive.

The result is an interest rate that moves up and down along with open-market rates. The annuity rates are usually below the inflation rate, but well above the rate on savings accounts and, for most people, the after-tax return on bonds.

FEATURES

There are numerous deferred annuities available on the market, and each has its own features. However, these terms are typical:

1. You make a one-time deposit of at least $1,500.

2. There is no explicit sales charge for the annuity. Your entire investment earns interest.

3. The company guarantees that the interest rate will never fall below a certain level, but the minimum is small—only 3% to 4% or so.

4. The company also provides a guaranteed minimum interest rate covering the next three months or the next year.

5. The company is free to raise or lower the interest rate at any time—as long as it doesn't go below the minimums covered in #3 and #4 above.

6. During the first five years of the contract, you can withdraw up to 6% of the annuity's current value each year without paying a penalty.

7. If you withdraw larger amounts during the first five years, you pay a penalty of about 4% of the amount of the withdrawal—more in the first year, less in the fifth year. However, the penalty can't be more than you've already earned in interest, so you can't lose any of what you've deposited.

8. After five years, there's no penalty for withdrawals of any amount.

9. You can transfer into an annuity issued by another insurance company at any time, although transfers are governed by the withdrawal terms given in #6, #7, and #8.[1]

10. When you close out the annuity, you can choose whether to receive the principal and interest as a lump sum, in yearly payments, or according to the other options discussed on page 343.

The actual details vary from company to company, but these terms are representative.

One important detail is the sales charge. All insurance companies have selling costs, but most of them do not levy an explicit sales charge. This is the reason for the penalties on early withdrawals. But a few companies do make an explicit sales charge at the outset—and then allow unlimited withdrawals without penalty.

---

[1]Under the tax rules, this is an exchange of "like kind" assets, so no gain is realized and the accumulated interest isn't taxed. The deferral continues without interruption.

EXAMPLES OF DEFERRED ANNUITIES

Policy Name	Company	Interest Rates		Early Withdrawals			A.M. Best Rating
		Permanent	Current	Free Limit	Penalty	Years	
An-Plan	Anchor Life	3%	8.75%[1]	6%	5%	5	A+
Q-Plan	Anchor Life	3%	9.51%[2]	6%[5]	5%[6]	—[6]	A+
Securannuity	Capitol Life	4%	9.00%[3]	6%[7]	7%[7]	—[6]	A
Charter	Crum & Forster	4%	11.40%[1]	7%	7%[8]	7	A
Executen	Executive Life	7½%[4]	11.50%[1]	7%	7%[8]	8	A+
SPDA	Great West Life	3½%	9.55%[1]	7%	7%[8]	6	A+

All information is current on October 27, 1980, and is subject to change at any time.

More detailed information on any policy should be obtained before purchase

These policies are shown as examples of what is available. A stockbroker or insurance agent can give you further details of these policies and details of other policies available.

None of the annuities shown has a sales charge

Securannuity allows additions in minimums of $1,000 after the purchase has been made. The other annuities allow no additions

Securannuity charges a $20 annual fee on all annuities, as does Great West on annuities under $10,000. None of the others has an annual fee.

Interest Rates: "Permanent" rate is the guaranteed minimum for the life of the annuity. "Current" rate is the rate being paid on October 27, 1980. Footnotes: (1) Guaranteed for first year of contract. (2) Guaranteed for first 3 months of contract. (3) Guaranteed for first 5 years of contract. (4) Permanent guarantee is 4%, but 7½% is guaranteed for first 10 years of contract. In some cases, the interest rate is reduced if the annuity is cashed in prematurely.

Early Withdrawals: "Free Limit" is the amount that can be withdrawn yearly without penalty during the first few years of the contract. "Penalty" is the charge assessed against withdrawals above the free limit (the penalty can never be more than the interest already earned, however). "Years" is the period to which the free limit and penalty apply; there are no limits or penalties after this period. Footnotes: (5) 6% is total amount that may be withdrawn during the life of the contract. (6) Penalty and limits apply for the life of the contract. (7) 6% withdrawal may be made once in each of 3 of any 7 consecutive years of the contract. $5 fee on any withdrawal. (8) Penalty rate declines from figure shown to 0% during number of years limit is in force.

No single policy is licensed for sale in every state. A stockbroker or insurance agent can tell you which policies are available in your state

Source of data: Financial Planners Equity Corporation, Larkspur, Calif. Information is believed to be correct, but is not guaranteed.

This arrangement is the exception, but it benefits the customer. It puts a little more pressure on the company to pay a competitive interest rate, since the company knows there's no "exit fee" to discourage a dissatisfied customer from cashing in.

Contracts also vary in their minimum and current interest rates.

A sampling of what the market offers is shown on page 342. Current details for each plan can be obtained from insurance agents and some stockbrokers—who also sell the annuities.

WITHDRAWALS & TAXES

The money you deposit in an annuity is not taxed when you withdraw it; only the interest is taxable income. And the tax rules regard "isolated" withdrawals from an annuity as simply a return of your own capital—until the total withdrawn exceeds the amount deposited.

For example, you could put $100,000 into an annuity and withdraw an average of $6,000 per year for 16 years without paying any taxes. During that period, the amounts not yet withdrawn would continue to earn interest. Once the withdrawals totaled $100,000, subsequent withdrawals would be taxed as interest income.

However, if you make "systematic" withdrawals, the tax code assumes that part of the money withdrawn is interest—and you're taxed accordingly. To remain tax-free up to the amount of your deposits, the withdrawals must appear to be "isolated"—random and unsystematic.

To keep the withdrawals random, don't withdraw money every year; don't withdraw an amount equal to the interest earned during the year or since the last withdrawal; don't make withdrawals on the same days of the year; and don't make more than one withdrawal in any year.

SETTLEMENT OPTIONS

When you decided to end the contract, there will be four general methods of settlement you can choose from.

1. Lump-Sum Settlement

If you receive all the principal and accumulated interest in one payment, the contract is closed out.

All the interest earned over the life of the contract will be taxed in a single year. The tax rate (a maximum of 70%) will depend on the amount of the interest and your other taxable income.[2]

2. Installment Payments

A second alternative allows you to receive the principal and accumulated interest in annual installments over the number of years you choose.

As each payment is made, the money still in the account continues to earn interest—at a rate that may or may not be fixed at the beginning of the installment period. If the rate is fixed, the contract loses its protection against inflation.

With installment payments, the tax burden is spread over the entire period of payments, with part of the interest taxed each year.

If you die before the installment payments are completed, the payments continue to your beneficiary on the same schedule. The balance yet to be paid will be subject to estate taxes, and your heirs will pay income tax on interest from the contract as they receive it.

3. Income for Life

The conventional annuity settlement provides a fixed yearly dollar income for the rest of your life—however long that turns out to be. When you die, nothing is left in the account.

The yearly payment will depend on the amount of money in the account and on an actuarial estimate of how long you'll live. Because it promises an income of a fixed number of dollars, there's no inflation protection.

---

[2]The tax rules for income averaging apply to annuity income in the same way as to most types of income. However, in most cases, an installment payout will produce a lower tax bill.

Only the part of the yearly payment that comes from interest is taxable; the rest is a return of your capital.

4. Interest-Only Settlement

The fourth alternative provides a yearly payment of just the interest earned each year. Because the interest rate continues to float, the inflation protection continues—but without the benefit of tax deferral. The payment is completely taxable because it is all interest.

If the contract is still in force when you die, your beneficiary will receive the principal plus the interest that accumulated before payments began. The annuity will be subject to estate taxes, and the accumulated interest will be subject to income taxes as it is paid out.

Combination Settlement

The four methods of withdrawing money from a deferred annuity can be used in combination, if you wish. For example, you might withdraw all of your original investment after ten years (tax-free), leaving the accumulated interest inside the annuity to continue to compound. Later, when you retire, you could take a lifetime annuity, based on the accumulated interest, or you could take an interest-only settlement.

EXTENDED DEFERRAL

Taxes on the interest are deferred until the interest itself is withdrawn, and most contracts allow you to wait until age 75 or 80 to do so. However, it's possible for the deferral to continue beyond your lifetime.

When you buy an annuity, you are its owner. Usually, you'll name yourself as the *annuitant*—the person who supposedly will receive the annual income from the contract. But you can, if you wish, name someone else as the annuitant—even your two-year-old grandchild. You'll be the owner of the annuity with the right to take a lump-sum settlement at any time. But if you don't cash in the contract, the tax deferral will

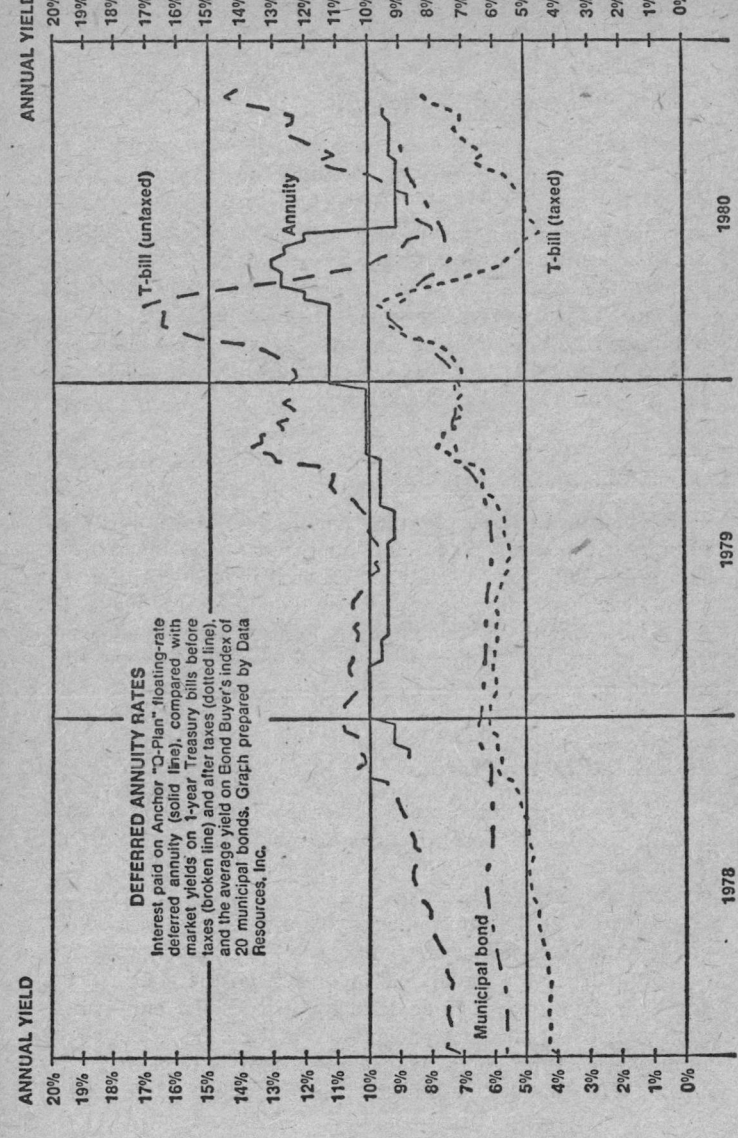

ANNUAL YIELD

20% 19% 18% 17% 16% 15% 14% 13% 12% 11% 10% 9% 8% 7% 6% 5% 4% 3% 2% 1% 0%

DEFERRED ANNUITY RATES

Interest paid on Anchor "Q-Plan" floating-rate deferred annuity (solid line), compared with market yields on 1-year Treasury bills before taxes (broken line) and after taxes (dotted line), and the average yield on Bond Buyer's index of 20 municipal bonds. Graph prepared by Data Resources, Inc.

T-bill (untaxed)

Annuity

T-bill (taxed)

Municipal bond

1978   1979   1980

ANNUAL YIELD

20% 19% 18% 17% 16% 15% 14% 13% 12% 11% 10% 9% 8% 7% 6% 5% 4% 3% 2% 1% 0%

continue beyond your lifetime until the annuitant reaches age 80.

However, the value of the annuity will be included in your taxable estate at the time of your death, and will be subject to estate taxes.

INFLATION PROTECTION

A deferred annuity has two inflation-proofing features: (1) an interest rate that moves upward with open-market interest rates; and (2) the tax deferral that allows the interest to compound without tax erosion.

The graph on page 346 compares the interest rate on one deferred annuity (Anchor Q-Plan) with the rate on one-year Treasury bills, before and after taxes, and the rate on municipal bonds.

The annuity's interest rate rises and falls with open-market rates, but the annuity rate is below the before-tax return on Treasury bills. A tax-deferred investment in Treasury bills will do better than a deferred annuity, but the annuity will outperform a T-bill investment that isn't tax-deferred.

The annuity also outperforms municipal bonds—so long as the deferral continues. But the annuity will attract taxes eventually, while the municipal bonds are tax-free forever.

Your circumstances will determine how attractive an annuity is to you. If your tax bracket is less than 20%, your after-tax return on Treasury bills will be as good as the annuity return—and there will be no taxes to pay later. If you expect your tax rate always to be at 70%, municipal bonds will outperform annuities in the long run. And if you expect your tax rate always to be around 50%, you shouldn't buy a deferred annuity unless you intend to hold it for at least 25 years.

But if your tax bracket is above 30% now, and you expect it to drop substantially when you retire, a deferred annuity is an attractive option—especially if you intend to keep it for ten years or more.

Another factor to consider is that annuity rates should become gradually more competitive if inflation continues to

347

rise. Floating-rate annuities have been actively promoted by insurance companies only since about 1976. With higher inflation and interest rates, the market for annuities will expand and more companies will enter the field. Competition should narrow the gap between T-bill rates and the rates earned on annuities. And with floating rates, today's policyholders will benefit along with new customers.

DEFLATION PROTECTION

A floating-rate annuity has two deflation-proofing features: (1) It provides a way of holding dollars without a prohibitive loss of purchasing power; and (2) a deflation could make the guaranteed minimum interest rate extremely valuable.

Most companies offer a very low minimum rate—3% or 4%. But one company, Executive Life, promises a minimum of 7½% for the first ten years on its Executen annuity. The minimum isn't important so long as open-market rates are higher. But a deflation would send T-bill interest rates down to the 1%–2% range, and the 7½% minimum would provide a return that couldn't be equaled elsewhere.

DEFERRED ANNUITIES

A deferred annuity isn't the ideal way to hold dollars as a protection against deflation and general uncertainty. But it should be carefully considered if a better alternative isn't available.

Because you can cancel the policy at any time and receive at least what you've deposited, you needn't fear that changing conditions will make you regret today's purchase later. You can't get locked into a lifetime bad deal.

A deferred annuity won't quite keep up with inflation. Nevertheless, a balanced portfolio needs some dollar assets for protection against deflation. The practical question is how they can be held most cheaply.

Of more concern than the slight loss in purchasing power is the fact that an annuity is a paper promise. The terms of the contract, attractive or unattractive, merely define the promise. And inflation leads to many broken promises.

If a deferred annuity makes sense otherwise, we suggest the following guidelines for reducing the risk:

1. Don't use deferred annuities as your only dollar investment. Keep at least 5% of your net worth in Treasury bills or in a money market fund that invests only in Treasury bills.

2. Don't invest more than 10% of your net worth in any company's annuity—even if that means using a second company, whose terms are less attractive.

3. Use only those companies with a A. M. Best rating of A+ or A, even if other companies offer terms that are more attractive.[3]

4. Check the Best ratings at least once each year. If a company with which you're dealing loses its A rating, transfer to another company that has at least an A rating.

5. If you find it difficult to sleep nights because large companies are going bankrupt, withdraw your original investment (which will involve no taxes) and split the proceeds between Treasury bills and 20-year Treasury bonds. If you're still worried, withdraw the interest as well and pay the necessary taxes.

With these safeguards in reserve, you may be able to put a deferred annuity to good use.

---

[3]The A. M. Best Company rates the ability of insurance companies to keep their promises. An insurance agent or stockbroker will probably have the latest issue of *Best's Review* (*Life, Health edition*), or you may find it at a large library.

23

MISCELLANEOUS INTEREST SHELTERS

THIS CHAPTER WILL DESCRIBE FOUR TECHNIQUES THAT RE-
duce taxes on interest income. They may be useful if the
plans described in the preceding three chapters can't shelter all
the interest on the number of dollars you want to keep.

Because the techniques involve special situations, no one
of them will be applicable to everyone; and for many people,
none of them will apply. So you may want to read the chapter
quickly, slowing down only if you run across something you
can use.

1. COVERED FORWARD SALES

The first technique is useful if you want to reduce your
holdings of gold or silver and increase your holdings of dollars.

It makes it possible, for a year or two, to earn interest on
the new dollar investments in a form that will be taxed as a
capital gain, rather than as ordinary income. And it delays the
payment of any capital-gain tax due on the sale of the gold
or silver.

These results are accomplished by selling the excess holdings "forward" instead of outright.

The Forward Market

Most commodities (including gold and silver) are traded
in two types of markets—the spot market and the forward

351

market. Spot sales are settled immediately—on the spot; the money is paid and the commodity is delivered then and there.

The forward market involves a contract to trade something at a later date. For example, you might purchase gold to be delivered to you one year from today—at a price determined today. The contract price remains fixed no matter what happens to the open-market price during the intervening year. The gold will be delivered to you at the end of the year on the agreed-upon terms.

With a perishable commodity, the forward price reflects market estimates of future supply and demand. The current supply has little effect on prices for the future—because the current supply will perish before the future arrives. So the forward price may be higher or lower than the spot price.

But with a precious metal, the forward price almost always will be higher than the spot price, because there's usually a large stock-pile of the metal available for future needs. The forward price will exceed the spot price simply by the cost of holding the metal for the time involved in the forward contract. Most of that cost is the interest that's lost by tying up cash in owning the metal.

So the forward price exceeds the spot price by a percentage that's close to the current rate of interest. Thus, if the price of gold today is $500 per ounce and the current interest rate is 10%, the price of gold for delivery one year from today will be about $550 ($500 + 10% of $500).

Capital Gains Instead of Interest

If you have gold (or silver) to sell, you can use the difference between the spot and forward prices to your advantage.

By selling the gold forward (instead of outright), you turn the gold into a dollar asset—because the buyer promises to pay you a fixed number of dollars. That number is larger than what you would have received by selling the gold outright, and the excess is equivalent to the current rate of interest. But, although you're earning interest on a dollar asset, the earnings will be taxed as a capital gain.

For example, suppose you sell one ounce of gold outright for $500 and put the proceeds into Treasury bills. At a 10% interest rate, the $500 will earn $50 over the next year —which will be taxed as unearned income at rates up to 70% (if it isn't sheltered in some way).

Suppose instead that you sell the gold *forward* for delivery one year away. A year later, you'll receive $550. The extra $50 will be considered to be part of the profit earned on the gold investment—and will be taxed at a maximum of 28% as a long-term capital gain.

And (in this example) if you paid $550 or more for the gold, there's no tax at all because there's no profit. In that case, the forward sale eliminates all the tax on what would have been the first year's interest from a dollar investment.

In addition to turning interest income into a capital gain, the forward sale delays for a year or more the payment of the capital-gain tax on any gold profit. If the profit is very great, the delay may be as important as the tax saving on the interest income.

The gold you sell forward reduces your effective gold holdings by that quantity—because the sale carries a fixed price, even though you won't deliver the gold until later. Your portfolio position will be the same as if you had sold the gold outright and invested the proceeds in Treasury bills. Only your tax bill will be different.

Conditions

There are two conditions that must be satisfied to get long-term capital-gain treatment on the forward sale.

First, you must have held the gold for at least one year and one day *before* making the forward contract. If you sell forward something you've owned for one year or less, the money you earn will be taxed as a short-term capital gain— even if the forward contract is for more than one year.[1]

---

[1]Net short-term capital gains (in excess of capital losses) are taxed at rates up to 70%, like interest income. The method of calculation is shown on page 534. Also, see the explanation of "unearned income" on page 514 in the Glossary.

Second, if you have a long-term capital gain on the gold you want to sell, don't use this technique unless you're sure you won't want to buy gold again during the life of the forward contract. If you buy more gold, your tax position might become worse, not better. Of the gold sold forward, the profit earned on a quantity equal to what you then buy will be taxed as a *short-term* capital gain. Not only would you fail to turn interest income into a long-term capital gain, you would lose the long-term capital-gain treatment for part of any prior profit on the gold.

If you didn't have a long-term gain on the gold, buying more during the life of the forward contract wouldn't hurt you so much. You'd have the same tax result as if you had sold the gold outright and invested the proceeds in Treasury bills.

Except in very special circumstances, a forward sale will reduce your tax bill if you've held the gold for over one year before making the sale, and if you buy no additional gold during the term of the forward contract.[2]

Where to Do It

When making a forward sale for a commodity you don't own, you're required to post a deposit of 10% to 50% of the value of the commodity—to assure that you'll live up to your end of the bargain. And if the spot price goes up during the time of the forward contract, you may be asked to increase the deposit (a margin call).

However, if you do own the commodity you've promised to deliver, and if the institution handling the sale has possession of it, no deposit is required. The transaction is a "covered" forward sale; your promise is covered by the presence of the commodity you've agreed to deliver.

If the metal is stored at a Swiss bank, just tell the bank how much you want to sell forward, and for what period of

---

[2]Although we've used gold as an example, the technique can apply to silver or to any other metal for which a large stockpile exists.

time. Forward sales are practical for gold bullion, bullion-type gold coins (such as Krugerrands), and silver bullion.

If the metal is stored with a dealer in the U.S., the dealer may be able to arrange the forward sale for you. But be sure the difference between today's price and the forward price he offers is close to the current interest rate on Treasury bills.[3]

If the metal is in your possession, you can make the sale through a U.S. commodity futures exchange. The metal will have to be delivered to an approved warehouse and may have to be assayed. And the rules of the futures markets require that you post a deposit (and maybe increase the deposit if the price moves upward before the contract expires) even if the commodity to be delivered is in an approved warehouse. A commodity broker can arrange everything for you. The U.S. futures markets handle gold bullion, silver bullion, and silver coins.

In each of these cases, there's a minimum quantity that can be sold forward. Through a futures exchange, the minimum is 100 ounces of gold bullion, 5,000 ounces of silver bullion, or 10 bags of silver coins. Among Swiss banks, the minimums and terms vary, but each bank has a minimum of some kind. A U.S. coin dealer might accommodate any size sale, but you may have trouble getting a good price on a small quantity.

Length of Contract

No minimum period is required for the forward sale to gain the tax advantage; but the longer the period, the more interest you'll earn that's taxable as a capital gain. Forward sales through banks are rarely made for longer than two years—and most forward sales are for one year or less. Sales through a U.S. futures market can be for as far away as 22 months.

---

[3]To calculate the interest rate implied by the forward price: (1) divide the one-year forward price by the spot price; (2) subtract the number 1; (3) multiply by 100.

Currencies

This technique sometimes will work if you want to sell holdings of a foreign currency and invest the proceeds in dollars.

However, the forward price of a currency is not necessarily higher than the spot price. In general, the difference between the two prices will be roughly equivalent to the difference in interest rates between the two countries. If the foreign currency has the lower interest rate, the forward price will be higher than the spot price—and vice versa.

Thus, if the current interest rate on Swiss francs is about 5% and the interest rate on dollars is 12%, the one-year forward price for Swiss francs will be about 7% higher than the spot price (12 — 5 = 7).

In such a case, if you sell the francs *forward* for one year and earn 5% interest on the francs during the year, the 5% will be taxed as interest income and the 7% forward premium will be taxed as a capital gain. If you sell the francs *outright* and invest the proceeds in dollars, you'll earn 12% interest which will be taxed wholly as interest income.

There's no advantage to a forward sale unless the price is higher than the spot price. If the forward price is higher, you'll need to calculate the after-tax result from a forward sale and compare it with the after-tax result from selling the foreign currency outright and investing the proceeds in dollars.

The calculation must consider (1) the percentage amount by which the forward price exceeds the spot price; (2) the tax rate you'll pay on long-term capital gains in the year the forward contract ends; (3) the interest you can earn on the foreign currency before the delivery date of the forward contract; (4) the interest you can earn on dollars; and (5) the tax rate you'll pay on the interest income, whether from the foreign currency or dollars.

A forward sale converts the difference between the forward price and the spot price from interest income into a capital gain. For a metal, that difference is approximately the interest rate on dollars—so a forward sale makes sense. But for a foreign currency, the difference between the forward and spot prices often isn't enough to justify using the technique.

2. USING CAPITAL LOSSES

The second technique uses capital losses from the current or previous tax years to reduce taxes on interest income.

The tax rules governing capital gains and losses are shows on page 534. One important rule is that no more than $3,000 in net capital losses can be deducted from ordinary income in any one year. Losses in excess of $3,000 must be deducted in future years—$3,000 at a time.

Because of this, it may take many years before a large capital loss is fully deducted. In each of those years, you have a large potential tax deduction that isn't being used.

If you have a capital loss from previous years or if selling something now would create one, you can use the capital loss to reduce taxable interest income. As with the first technique, it involves the use of covered forward sales (described on page 351). This is how it's done:

1. With the dollars that are to produce interest, buy gold instead of Treasury bills. Store the gold with the bank or dealer that sells it to you.

2. At the same time and with the same dealer, sell the gold forward for delivery on the most distant date possible.

3. You have two positions in gold—but zero interest in the future prices of gold (as far as this transaction is concerned). Any gain or loss on the gold you buy will be offset by a loss or gain on the forward sale.

4. The forward price at which you sell will exceed your purchase price by roughly the same percentage as the current interest rate on dollars.

5. Because you haven't met the conditions we described on page 353, the difference between the forward price and the purchase price will be a short-term capital gain (no matter how long the transaction lasts). For the taxable year in which the forward contract ends, this gain will be canceled out by unused capital losses from previous years—even if the amount is over $3,000.

Had you invested the money directly in Treasury bills,

the interest earned would have been taxed as unearned income. Instead, the profit on the forward sale is a short-term capital gain that's offset by the unused capital losses you already have—resulting in no tax at all.

You shouldn't use this technique if you expect to have other capital gains that will use up the old losses. Without the old losses to offset it, the short-term capital gain from this transaction would be taxed at "unearned income" rates of up to 70%—just as though it were interest.

DIVERTING INCOME TO LOW-BRACKET TAXPAYERS

If you have children or other dependents who are in low tax brackets (or who pay no tax at all), it is sometimes possible to transfer assets to them—so that the income earned by the assets is taxed at a lower rate, perhaps a much lower rate.

The assets will continue to affect your portfolio if the income eventually will buy something for the dependent that you'd pay for in any case (such as a college education), because the income earned will reduce the amount you'll have to take from your pocket later. But for tax purposes, the investments will belong to the dependents, and the income will be taxed at rates applying to their income levels.

You won't be taxed on the income unless it's spent on things you're legally obligated to provide for the dependents (such as food, clothing, housing, medical care, basic education, and modest amenities). If the investment is held by someone you're not legally obligated to support, the investment income can be used for any purpose.

The rest of this chapter is devoted to two techniques that allow you to divert interest income to a lower-bracket taxpayer. And they may have the additional virtue of avoiding gift taxes.

3. NO-INTEREST LOANS

The simplest method of diverting taxable income is with a no-interest loan. If you lend money to your children (or anyone else), they can invest it in Treasury securities (or anything else). They, not you, receive the income and pay taxes at their lower-bracket rates.

The loan to your children will be a dollar asset in your portfolio. Because it's secured by the Treasury bills the children buy, it's safe from loss through default. And the interest earned on the T-bills will accrue to your benefit if it will pay for things you otherwise would pay for out of your own income.

The loan should be in the form of a demand note (with no specific due date but repayable whenever you say so) because of the flexibility it provides. You can add to the loan if you want to increase the income flowing to your children, or demand a partial repayment whenever you want to reduce their income. And when enough income has been accumulated for your purpose, or if you need the money back, you can demand full repayment. Then the children would sell the Treasury bills and repay the loan.

The loan can remain unpaid until you die—at which time it will have to be settled as part of your estate.

The IRS has challenged no-interest loans repeatedly. Most of the cases it has won have been on the basis of considerations that apply only to *term* loans—loans with a definite repayment date. The IRS also has had no success in levying gift taxes on properly structured demand loans, even when the income seems to be an obvious gift to the borrower.

However, to stand up to attack by the IRS, a no-interest loan (term or demand) must satisfy your state's rules regarding the enforceability of a debt. Some states have statutes of limitations for debts; if no interest or principal is paid for a certain number of years, the loan obligation may become legally unenforceable. And most states restrict the enforceability of loan contracts with minors.

If it turns out that your loan cannot be legally enforced, the IRS will treat it as a gift. So, before you make such a loan, check with a tax accountant or tax attorney to confirm that your plan will work.

Under any circumstances, stick with a demand loan. If the rules change after you make a no-interest loan, a demand note allows you to demand repayment immediately and look for another interest shelter.

Borrowing to Lend

It's also possible to borrow the money you lend to your children. The interest you pay will be roughly offset by the interest they earn on their investments. But the interest you pay is deducted from your higher-rate income, while the interest they earn is taxed at lower rates.

This has to be handled carefully. The IRS will disallow the interest deduction if it's obvious that you've borrowed to finance a no-interest loan. Consequently, the two transactions —borrowing money and lending money—should be kept as separate as possible.

As an example, suppose you own $50,000 worth of gold that you want to keep. You could borrow $25,000, using the gold as security, and lend the $25,000 to your children. But it would be fairly obvious that the two loans were connected. To muddy the relationship, you can:

1. Sell the gold for cash (in this example, $50,000).
2. Simultaneously, buy an equal amount of gold in the forward market (explained on page 351) for delivery a few months later. Use $25,000 of the proceeds of the cash sale as a deposit for the forward purchase.
3. Lend the other $25,000 to your children.
4. You'll continue to have the same financial interest in gold, since the holdings you've sold will be replaced when the forward contract expires.
5. When the forward contract expires, take delivery of the gold—arranging for it to be held in a margin account with a loan of $25,000.

The net result is that you've borrowed $25,000 on your gold to finance a loan to your children. But the two loans will be separated in time, and the immediate source of the money lent to your children will be the proceeds of a sale—not the proceeds of a loan. You can use this technique with any investment you own for which there is both a forward market and a spot (cash) market.

However, you should first make sure that the sale of the original investment won't produce an unwanted tax liability.

Notice that borrowing to lend to your children doesn't add to, nor subtract from, your net dollar holdings. It merely reduces your tax bill by changing the character of the dollar holdings.

4. CLIFFORD TRUST

A somewhat fancier device for diverting income is a Clifford trust. An attorney is needed to create such a trust, and it's not as simple as some of the other techniques we've described.

A trust is an agreement by which you transfer control of some of your assets to a trustee for a special period of time. The agreement states that the trustee is to use the income from the investments to benefit a specific person or group of persons (the beneficiaries) for purposes stated in the agreement—such as to pay for their education.

At the end of the trust period, the assets are returned to you. To qualify as a Clifford trust, the period must be at least ten years.

During that time, you pay no tax on the income earned by the trust on its investments. Instead, the tax is paid by the beneficiaries (if the income is paid to them each year) or by the trust (if it holds on to the income). Either way, the income can be diverted to a lower-bracket taxpayer.

The advantages of a Clifford trust are:

1. Its legal status is well defined and isn't likely to be changed by a new IRS ruling.

2. Since the investments revert back to you after the trust expires, you'll benefit from any appreciation in, for example, long-term bonds—while the interest on the bonds goes to the beneficiary of the trust. Thus, you can have an investment that would profit from deflation without losing most of the interest to taxes while inflation continues.

3. The trust assures that the income will be used for the purpose you intend—spelled out in the trust agreement. If you use a no-interest loan to divert income, the beneficiary can use the money as he pleases when he becomes an adult —and that might be contrary to your intentions.

The disadvantages of the Clifford trust are:

1. The trust involves legal and, sometimes, administrative expenses that other techniques avoid.

2. Once established, the trust is irrevocable. You can't take back the assets until the trust expires, so you should deposit with the trust only the amounts you're confident you won't need for the term of the trust.

3. The right to receive the investment income is a gift from you to the trust and may attract gift taxes. The attorney who sets up the trust for you can let you know whether gift taxes apply in your case.

INTEREST SHELTERS

The techniques we've described don't tell you how many dollars you should have in your portfolio. They are merely methods by which you might be able to lower your tax bill on the dollars you decide to hold.

Each technique is useful only in a special situation. As such, it may or may not be appropriate for you.

24

MUNICIPAL BONDS

THE APPEAL OF MUNICIPAL BONDS IS SIMPLE AND COMPELLING: the interest they pay is exempt (not just deferred) from federal income tax. With municipal bonds, you avoid the work involved in shielding or deferring interest income in other ways.

The interest rate on high-grade municipal bonds is roughly 65% of the interest rate on bonds of comparable quality. So a bond buyer in a tax bracket over 35% ($29,900 in net taxable income) obtains a higher after-tax yield by buying municipals. And in most states, the interest on municipal bonds issued within the state is exempt from state income taxes.

But despite the obvious appeal, there are three reasons that we believe municipal bonds are a poor choice for almost anyone's portfolio: (1) the large risks involved; (2) the depreciation in purchasing power; and (3) the availability of other ways to reduce taxes.

This chapter will examine those reasons. It also will provide guidelines for choosing municipal bonds—in case you're not convinced by our reasons.

SAFETY

Our first concern is the safety of municipal bonds. Just as with many industries, governments are direct or indirect beneficiaries of inflation, and inflation isn't going to continue forever.

In Part I, we said that many business projects survive only

363

because a rapid expansion of the money supply makes credit artificially cheap.

These projects depend on the kind of subsidized financial irrigation that only a loss-motivated institution such as the U.S. government is likely to provide. Eventually, the irrigation system will dry up—either through a deflation or a total breakdown in the currency. When that happens, a lot of subsidized industries will collapse.

It's impossible to trace all the byways along which new money and government subsidies travel. So it isn't possible to say with much precision which companies or even which industries will be hurt the most. But inflation has proceeded so far and for so long that there's good reason to believe the list of casualties will be lengthy.

Not only companies will be in trouble, but municipal governments as well. We don't know the city names either, but they'll be the cities that depend on inflation-sponsored industries and that have been the least careful about their own finances.

Most municipal governments probably will make it through without formal bankruptcy. But those that do survive will give their creditors plenty of uneasy moments. Interest payments and principal redemptions will be delayed, and the market value of the bonds will nose-dive because of the uncertainty. And for some cities, there will be outright defaults.

The U.S. government bailed out the New York City government in 1975—reassuring bondholders of other cities and encouraging local governments to keep borrowing. But such help enjoys less political support now than it did in 1975. And when the day of reckoning comes, the U.S. government won't have the resources to support all the large corporations and municipal governments that are in trouble.

It's hard to imagine a city government going bankrupt, since governments usually don't go out of business. The bankruptcy probably would take the form of a moratorium on debt payments that continued until the city's tax revenues caught up with its obligations. The debts might be paid in full eventually, but "eventually" could be ten or more years later.

We believe it's a mistake to consider a municipal bond to

364

be safer than a corporate bond. As with corporate bonds, some will escape default and some won't; a few may hold their value throughout the crisis, but most won't.

PURCHASING POWER LOSS

Our second concern is that municipal bonds are already a losing proposition. The tax exemption merely makes the loss smaller than if taxes had to be paid.

The graph on page 366 adjusts the Bond Buyer municipal bond index for changes in the Consumer Price Index. The two lines show the result if the interest is reinvested in new bonds and if it isn't. In either case, the capital invested in municipal bonds has suffered a steady erosion in purchasing power. The tax exemption is small comfort when the investment itself provides a steady loss.

There's good reason to have dollars in your portfolio. But the tax exemption has led many people to have more dollars (in municipal bonds) than needed for protection against deflation and uncertainty. Keeping too much in municipal bonds throws your portfolio out of balance and causes purchasing power to be eroded. And it doesn't even reduce your tax bill—since non-dollar assets avoid taxes as effectively.

Gold, silver, warrants, and dual-purpose investment funds provide no current taxable income that needs sheltering. You can defer profits indefinitely simply by not selling. And when you do sell, the profits are long-term capital gains with a maximum tax rate of 28%. Swiss francs and real estate are similar, since any large profits they produce will be through appreciation rather than income.

It may seem that you need interest-bearing assets to provide income for living expenses. If so, a 7% tax-free return on municipals can be attractive—since it takes a 23% yield on taxable bonds to produce the same after-tax return (for a 70% tax bracket).

But you also can get an after-tax return of 7% with a capital gain of only 10%. And you can provide a cash flow for living expenses by selling a small portion of your non-dollar assets each year. So long as they appreciate by an aver-

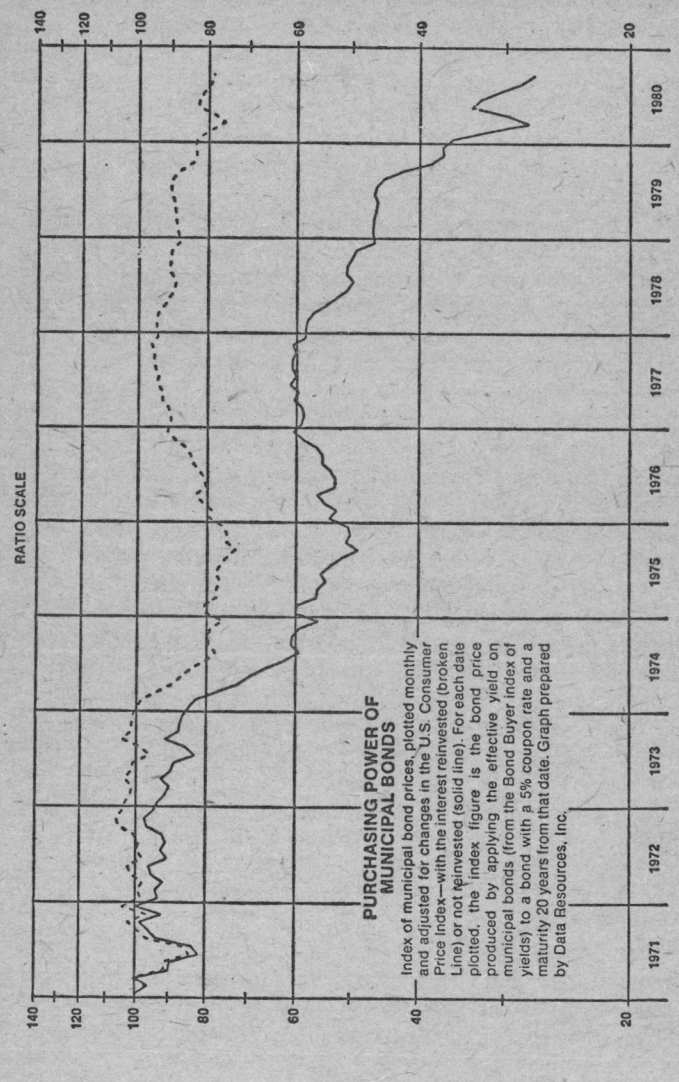

RATIO SCALE

PURCHASING POWER OF
MUNICIPAL BONDS

Index of municipal bond prices, plotted monthly
and adjusted for changes in the U.S. Consumer
Price Index—with the interest reinvested (broken
Line) or not reinvested (solid line). For each date
plotted, the index figure is the bond price
produced by applying the effective yield on
municipal bonds (from the Bond Buyer index of
yields) to a bond with a 5% coupon rate and a
maturity 20 years from that date. Graph prepared
by Data Resources, Inc.

age of 10% per year or better (over several years), you can sell 10% of your holdings yearly and the portfolio's dollar value won't decline.[1]

So a portfolio properly balanced with non-dollar assets can provide the spending money you need, and it will be much safer and more profitable than one overloaded with municipal bonds.

ALTERNATIVES

If there were no way to beat taxes other than through municipal bonds, you would have to decide whether the tax exemption was worth the default danger and the loss of purchasing power inherent in municipal bonds. Fortunately, there are alternatives.

First, if your net taxable income is less than $30,000 per year, buy Treasury bonds. Even unsheltered, their after-tax yield will be better than the return on municipals.

Second, if you have a pension plan, use it to hold dollar investments that provide a better return and are safer than municipal bonds.

Third, if you don't have a corporation, find out whether you can incorporate your business or some aspect of your financial activities. By retaining profits and establishing a generous pension plan, you can hold tax-deferred dollar investments that will outperform municipals.

Fourth, if neither of these devices is available and you expect to be in a lower tax bracket later (after you retire, perhaps), buy a deferred annuity with dollars you won't need for at least five years. (If you assume you'll always be in a high tax bracket, an annuity won't provide the after-tax benefits of a municipal bond.)

Fifth, don't hold more dollars than a balanced portfolio requires. Beyond that quota, buy non-dollar investments that have no tax problems.

---

[1]This system is discussed in more detail on pages 402–404 and 471–472.

CHOICE OF BONDS

If we've failed to convince you that you can live without municipal bonds, perhaps we can at least help you to reduce the risk. Here are a few suggestions:

1. Purchase only bonds rated AAA or AA.

2. Put no more than 2% of your net worth into the bonds of any one issuer.

3. Don't leave municipal bonds with your bank or broker —especially if they are bearer bonds. Bearer bonds are as un-traceable as a $20 bill, and are the investment most likely to disappear mysteriously during a financial crisis. For double protection, have the bonds issued to you in registered form and store them in a safe-deposit box.

4. If you believe you should hedge against deflation, put half your bond budget into long-term bonds—20 years or more to maturity. These bonds could skyrocket in value as in-terest rates fall during a deflation. However, don't buy a bond that could be redeemed early at a price close to your purchase price. Buy only bonds that are selling at a deep discount from par, and can't be called for many years, or that can't be called at all.[2]

MUNICIPAL BONDS

It's hard to say how much the interest rate on municipal bonds should exceed the after-tax return for Treasury securi-ties to justify the higher risk. But we doubt that the present premium on municipals is high enough.

The next ten years will provide numerous surprises. So we think you'll be better off if you overestimate the risks than

---

[2]Some bonds have call dates in addition to maturity dates. If so, the bond issuer has the right to pay off the bond anytime between the call date and the maturity date. If interest rates drop during a deflation, bond prices will rise, creating profits for holders of bonds. But if the bond can be "called" in the near future, the market price of the bond isn't likely to rise above 100 (the par or face value of the bond). The pricing of bonds is described on pages 221 and 224.

if you underestimate them, even if that increases your tax bill slightly.

If municipal bonds still seem to be part of your future, we suggest that you:

1. determine how many dollars your portfolio should have *before* you think about tax exemptions;

2. explore every other avenue for holding dollars and deferring taxes before buying municipal bonds; and

3. at the most, invest only part of your dollar budget in municipal bonds, using the guidelines offered on page 368.

25

TAX HAVENS
& TAX-SHELTER
INVESTMENTS

DESPITE OCCASIONAL TAX REDUCTIONS, THE INFLATION OF THE past 20 years has pushed most people into higher tax brackets —making tax avoidance more popular than ever.

Two widely publicized devices for avoiding taxes are tax shelters and tax havens. A tax shelter is an investment that seeks to delay or reduce taxes by exploiting loopholes in the tax code. A tax haven is a country whose tax laws can be used to reduce the taxes of people who don't live there.

We'll begin with tax shelters.

TAX SHELTERS

The tax code contains loopholes because a tax system that simply collected a percentage of everyone's gross income, without regard to business or investment expenses, would destroy the economy on which the government feeds.

At the least, there have to be deductions for expenses incurred in the process of generating income. And because the tax system is administered by thousands of people, there must be written rules for them to follow in determining just what is income and what is an expense.

The rules necessarily are imperfect. There's no way to write them so that they define income accurately and in all circumstances—or reliably distinguish business expenses from consumption. Is the trip to Hawaii to attend a "business conference" really a business expense or a nice vacation? Is the $2,000 mahogany desk in your office a business expense or a personal pleasure? Is the company car necessary to your business activity or is it disguised consumption? Is income earned when an investment appreciates or only when it is sold?

In addition, various economic groups ask for special treatment, and much of what they ask for is written into the rules. They want deductions for consumption expenes (such as the interest expense on a home mortgage), they want business expenses to be deductible before they occur (such as the accelerated depreciation expense on buildings and equipment), or they want tax credits for "socially desirable" investments (such as installing thermal insulation or restoring old buildings).

Thus the tax rules are the end result of a multitude of conflicting considerations and pressures. Inevitably, the rules are complicated, but still do not express the intentions of the people who framed them.

Because it's impossible to define income and expenses precisely, and because in some respects the government doesn't try, taxpayers have opportunities to arrange their affairs so that *measured* income is less than *true* income. Tax-shelter investments are designed to exploit these opportunities.

Most tax shelters work by exaggerating expenses (especially interest expense), by understating income (deferring it and perhaps turning it into capital gains), or by piling up tax credits. We'll see how each of these is accomplished.

Interest Expense

Interest expense is deducted in measuring the profit or loss of any business. But high inflation converts interest payments into repayments of a loan's purchasing power, rather than a true expense—thereby causing the profits of the business to be understated or perhaps turned into a loss.

So it's no surprise that many tax shelters are based on debt financing. With enough debt, an economic profit can be represented as a tax loss. The workings of this process in real estate are described on pages 161–162.

Expenses & Capital Gains

Many tax shelters are based on expenditures that contribute to the capital value of an asset, but which can be deducted as an expense from current income. This has the effect of understating income, since the appreciation in value isn't noticed for tax purposes until the asset is sold.

For example, money spent to feed livestock is treated as a current expense, even though the food adds to the capital value of the animal that eats it. Or an oil-drilling program deducts drilling costs as an operating expense, even though the drilling produces a capital asset (an oil and gas well) that may be sold and taxed as a capital gain.

Just as with the use of interest, the expense reduces current taxes, but increases the tax when the investment is finally sold; the taxes are delayed, not eliminated. However, as explained on page 296, delay by itself is very useful—especially when inflation rates are high. And the current expense can be deducted from ordinary income, while the eventual profit may be taxed as a capital gain.

With real estate, an investor can deduct interest expense from current income that would be taxed at rates up to 70%. But a building's appreciation doesn't add to taxable income until the property is sold—and then the profits are taxed as a capital gain, at a maximum rate of 28%. The principle also applies to expenses and profits involved in raising livestock, avocados, timber, and many other things.

In many cases, the investment is sold before it starts producing net business income, so the investment is never taxed at ordinary income rates.

Tax Credits

Another loophole exploited by many tax-shelter investments is the tax credit that can be earned by purchasing equipment for business use. The credit isn't a mere deduction from income; it's a dollar-for-dollar reduction of the investor's tax bill.

Any purchase of equipment for a business (other than merchandise to be resold) is eligible for a tax credit if the useful life of the equipment is at least three years. The tax credit is between 3% and 10% of the cost of the equipment, depending on the equipment's expected life; if the useful life is seven years or more, the credit is 10%.

The investment tax credit plays an important part in equipment leasing programs. The investor buys a piece of equipment on credit (perhaps in partnership with others), and leases it to a business that needs it. If the equipment is bought with a 50% down payment and qualifies for a 10% tax credit, 20% of the cash investment comes back to the investor as a tax credit. And the tax credit will be in addition to deductions for interest and depreciation.

Some tax shelters depend almost entirely on the investment tax credit; interest and depreciation expenses play only a small part. The heart of such a program is an exaggeration of the value of the equipment being purchased. We can illustrate this with a far-fetched example.

Suppose someone offers to sell you a shovel for $1,000. The shovel is obviously overpriced, but you're in the excavation business, so the shovel seems to qualify for a tax credit that would reduce your tax bill by $100 (10% of the purchase price).

To make the investment attractive, the seller agrees to accept a down payment of only $50 and an IOU for $950. And the IOU contains an escape clause, stating that the $950 balance will be due only when the shovel has produced enough income to cover it—even though both you and the seller know this will never happen.

The shovel cost the seller only $15—giving him a $35 profit just on the $50 down payment. And the tax credit, based on the nominal purchase price, reduces your current taxes by $100, while you pay out only $50. You both come out ahead.

Of course, this scheme would never survive an IRS audit. If the matter went to court, it would be decided on a question of fact: Do shovels really sell for $1,000 in the open market?

But there are capital goods for which the market value is difficult to establish. Such goods present the opportunity to exploit the tax-credit rules in the same way (although not to the same degree) as in the shovel transaction. One currently popular example is lithographic (or litho) plates.

A litho plate is an original work of art, etched in metal, that can be used to print a limited number of copies. If the buyer is in the business of producing art prints, the plate qualifies for a tax credit. If the price of the plate is high enough, the tax credit can be very large. But how does one determine the value of a one-of-a-kind work of art?

The plate's ultimate value will depend on the subjective judgment of art lovers who may or may not buy the reproductions printed from it. If an investor pays $5,000 for the plate (putting only $500 down), who can say that $5,000 is too much? Even the failure of the plate to earn back the $5,000 would not prove that the price was unreasonable at the time; any speculative investment can fail to pay off.

The IRS is currently attacking a number of litho-plate shelters in the courts. It's likely to win at least some cases, in which the taxpayer is asking the court to believe the unbelievable about the worth of a plate. More cautious litho-plate deals may survive.

Whatever the outcome, there undoubtedly will be other deals invented to exploit the tax credit by exaggerating the value of a capital good.

Portfolio Problems

With the variety of tax-shelter investments available, it isn't too difficult to reduce your taxable income to zero. Any tax-shelter sales will show you how.

Some tax-shelter investments even reduce your current taxable income by more than your cash outlay, which can make a pension plan seem like pretty dull stuff. And anyone can invest as much as he pleases in tax shelters, without regard to the size of his salary income.

But if you care about risk, you can't approach tax planning in isolation from portfolio planning. A prudent tax-shelter investment must make sense first as an investment, second as an element in your portfolio, and only third as a tax shelter. Otherwise, your plan to avoid taxes will throw your portfolio badly out of balance.

An overdose of tax shelters will unbalance your portfolio because most tax-shelter investments depend on inflation. A majority of shelters are built around the heavy use of debt financing, for which inflation is expected to transform the interest expense into a repayment of the loan's purchasing power. But if inflation slows appreciably, the interest expense will turn out to be a real cost.

And even without debt financing, the underlying investment usually is one that depends on inflation. Any prolonged slowing in inflation would be ruinous for real-estate tax shelters. And unless the slowing was part of a soft landing, it would be harmful for tax shelters based on oil drilling, equipment leasing, and other operating businesses. You could lose a lot more on the investment than you had saved in taxes.

Shelter Evaluation

If a tax shelter qualifies both as a good investment and as a method of tax reduction, and if it won't make you overly dependent on inflation, there's no reason not to use it.

But make sure you understand how much of a liability, if any, you're incurring beyond your cash investment. The liability is part of your portfolio—just like the mortgage on a piece of property—and it shouldn't be ignored.

And before you buy the tax shelter, we think it's wise to look first at the tax-deferral methods described in Chapters 20 to 23. They not only lower your tax bill, they make it inexpensive to hold the dollar assets that are the safest balance to the inflation-oriented tax shelters.

And as a final precaution, when someone tells you that a given tax shelter will pass IRS scrutiny without question, it wouldn't hurt to get a second opinion.

TAX HAVENS

Tax havens have a different kind of appeal.

Some countries tax income at very low rates, or not at all. A country with very low tax rates is called a tax haven if its laws can be used to reduce the taxes of people who don't live there.

Many investors find the idea of taking financial refuge in a tax haven extremely appealing. And in days gone by, tax havens were fairly simple to exploit, especially for accumulating interest income. But things are no longer so easy.

The U.S. government has enacted laws that cripple any straight-forward investment use of tax havens. Tax havens aren't dead, but now only the more intricate arrangements have any chance of success.

One effect of the changes in U.S. tax laws has been to make international tax planning the Barbary Coast of the tax profession. The opportunities are good, but the rules are unsettled. It's easy for a newcomer to be misled, and the mistakes he might make can be costly.

The international tax-planning field seems to be divided between a few very aggressive advisors who can devise plans that withstand IRS attack (or lawfully avoid IRS scrutiny), and a handful of others who create ornate versions of tax fraud. There are few guidelines for distinguishing between the two groups, so you need to exercise more than the usual degree of skepticism in evaluating any plan based on tax havens.

Still, there are valid, lawful tax-haven opportunities open to investors who can bear the legal and administrative expenses of using them. But there's no profitable way to use tax havens that is both simple and legal.

A U.S. citizen can't avoid taxes lawfully just by holding his investments in a tax haven, because the U.S. government taxes all his income—no matter where he lives and no matter where in the world the income is generated. However, it's sometimes possible to have a corporation or trust in a tax haven accumulate income on your behalf without paying current U.S. taxes. Thus you would have a tax-deferral device for holding dollars—like a pension plan with no limits on the contributions.

But there are considerable obstacles in the way of such a plan. So for most readers, our comments may serve only to alert them to the drawbacks of the schemes they might be offered.

Foreign Corporations

A typical approach is to establish a corporation in a tax haven such as the Bahamas.

The Bahamian government doesn't levy income taxes of any kind, so the corporation could simply buy U.S. Treasury bills and accumulate the interest. Eventually, you could liquidate the corporation or sell your stock in it—treating the profit as a capital gain.

Unfortunately, the U.S. tax laws include two roadblocks.

First, because you, a U.S. citizen, own more than 50% of the corporation, and since most of its income comes from investments, the IRS will call it a *foreign personal holding company*—similar to a closely held U.S. corporation that receives its income primarily from investment (rather than business) activities.[1]

Because the IRS can't tax the foreign corporation directly, it will add the corporation's investment income to your personal income each year, and tax you on the total at a rate up to 70%. Failure to report your share of a foreign personal holding company's investment income on your tax return would be tax fraud.

The second roadblock is that your company may be deemed by the IRS to be a *controlled foreign corporation*, since a U.S. person (you) owns a majority of the voting stock. This creates the same personal tax liability on investment income as a foreign personal holding company.

So, while it may seem clever, simply establishing a foreign corporation to hold your investments won't reduce your taxes.

Foreign Investment Company

The situation is better if you share the corporation with other stockholders (excluding family members), at least some of whom are not U.S. citizens or residents.

If the foreign investors own at least 50% of the *voting*

---

[1]Domestic personal holding companies are described on pages 334–335.

stock (and certain other requirements are met), the company won't be a controlled foreign corporation. And if there's no combination of five U.S. shareholders that own more than 50% of the *value* of the corporation, it won't be a foreign personal holding company.

Instead, your corporation probably would be a *foreign investment company*—so labeled because the bulk of its assets are investments. You're not taxed personally on the income of a foreign investment company, so it could accumulate interest income indefinitely.

However, when you sell your stock, your share of the company's accumulated investment income is taxed as ordinary income, not as a capital gain—no matter how long you've held the stock. This is because the corporation does nothing but invest in securities. So this device would delay your taxes, but not necessarily reduce them.

In principle, there are some investors who can profit from the use of a foreign investment company (which they don't control) to accumulate interest income. The technique is similar to a deferred annuity—helpful to an investor who expects to be in a substantially lower tax bracket later in life.

Putting the principle to work won't be easy, however. Since you can't control the foreign corporation yourself, you have little alternative but to find an existing foreign investment company in which you'd be willing to participate. There are foreign money market funds that accumulate their interest income, but all the funds we've discovered invest heavily in Eurodollar certificates of deposit.[2]

Foreign Bank

An improvement on the foreign investment company is to establish your own foreign bank.

A foreign bank can be exempt from the rules we've described. As long as it doesn't do business inside the U.S., it can accumulate tax-free the interest it earns on loans. And when you liquidate the bank or sell your stock in it, the profit achieved will be taxed as a capital gain.

---

[2]Our concern about Euro-CDs is expressed on page 271.

You can't just call your corporation a bank, however. It must actually be in the banking business—making loans, not just holding Treasury bills. And to be a good investment, it would have to be extremely careful about the loans it makes.

There's also a problem of scale. A bank will have start-up costs and operating expenses. If you create it with an investment of $10,000 or $100,000, the tax savings will be much less than the expenses. It would take a minimum investment of $2 million or so to produce enough income to exceed both the overhead and the after-tax income you could earn without the bank.

Since foreign banks can be exempt from the rules we described earlier, you could in principle own all the stock in the bank; no cooperation with other investors would be needed. But, regardless of what the rules say, the reaction of the IRS to a specific bank is by no means assured.

You would be on safer ground if foreigners had voting control of the bank and if ownership were spread among a number of shareholders. Then, even if the IRS insisted that the bank was a foreign investment company, its income wouldn't be added to your taxable income each year. The worst that might happen would be that, when you sold your stock, the profit would be taxed as ordinary income, rather than capital gains.

To achieve this safety, you have to find foreign investors whom you can trust and who share your vision of how a foreign bank should fit into an inflation-proof portfolio.

Foreign Trusts

Tax-haven countries also provide favorable conditions for trusts.

A trust is an entity that's created and financed by one person (the grantor) for the benefit, usually, of another person (the beneficiary). A third party (the trustee) holds the trust's assets and promises to use them for the purpose originally specified by the grantor.

A U.S. citizen or resident who creates a foreign trust is required to pay U.S. taxes on any income the trust retains. So the opportunities for gain are very narrow unless the trust is granted by someone who isn't a U.S. taxpayer.

But if a foreign person establishes a trust in a tax-haven country, and if the trustee is also a foreigner and has the formal authority to apportion benefits among the beneficiaries, no one in the U.S. will be taxed on the income. So if a foreigner happened to spend a few thousand dollars, as a kindness, to establish a trust for you and your family, the trust could be used to accumulate investment (or even business profits) tax-free.

The original endowment of the trust could be an amount as little as $2,000 and still be practical. But it could cost from $5,000 to $50,000 for legal work that would assure that the trust is defensible in a U.S. court.

The trust would begin operating with the money deposited by the grantor. It would then be up to you to build up the assets of the trust without making direct contributions to it. You could do so through business transactions with the trust that were legitimate, but which favored the trust.

For example, you could sell a property to the trust at a price equal to a low (but not unreasonable) appraisal of its value. The sale would be made for a small down payment plus a mortgage at the lowest interest rate currently being charged by banks. Not only would this give the trust a good chance to make an above-average profit when it sells the property, it could decrease your taxable income at the same time.

After the trust had accumulated money through transactions that were tilted in its favor, it could lend money to you at high (but not unreasonable) interest rates. Its tax-exempt income would grow, while your taxable income continued to decline.

Later, when you want to withdraw money from the trust, the process would be reversed. You and the trust would have business transactions that favored you. It might lend money to you at low interest rates. Or if you had a piece of property or a business to sell, it would pay a high (but not unreasonable) price. A year or two later, it would sell the property, perhaps at a loss.

The trust could simply make a gift to you or to any other

beneficiary. But, depending on the age of the beneficiary and on how the trust acquired the money, the gift might be taxable at confiscatory rates. If the money returns to you in exchange for something you sell, it takes the form of a capital gain.

A trust can continue for no longer than 21 years after the death of the longest surviving beneficiary who was alive at the time the trust was created. By that time (or perhaps much sooner), the trust should have returned to you or your heirs most of the money it took in. Any accumulated income that remained in the trust when it expired would have to be distributed to the beneficiaries and taxed as ordinary income (at rates up to 70%), with possible surtaxes.

For a foreign trust to be useful, you must not have any formal, binding authority to control the trust's investments or to direct the trustee to make payments to beneficiaries. Otherwise, you'll be taxed on the trust's income. Nevertheless, you'll have *effective* control if the grantor of the trust has appointed you as the "trust protector," with the authority to change the trustee. So long as you don't ask the trustee to violate the terms of the trust, you can expect him to consider your requests in all matters, since he doesn't want to lose the trust as a customer.

The grantor can also name you as the "appointing beneficiary"—which allows you to choose in advance how the trust's assets will be used when you die. The proceeds can be distributed to the beneficiaries you select (from among persons named as beneficiaries in the trust), can go into other trusts for them, or can continue to be held by the trust. Having this choice (which can take effect only when you die) doesn't make you personally liable for taxes on the trust's income.

Foreign trusts are so attractive that some U.S. taxpayers have been tempted to pay a foreigner to grant a trust naming the U.S. taxpayer and his family as beneficiaries. This is a straightforward approach, but it is tax fraud and is pointless. If you're going to deceive the U.S. government, you can save the expense of creating a trust by simply hiding Treasury bills in a Swiss bank. The only reason to use a foreign trust is to avoid taxes without committing a crime.

To be valid, the trust has to be granted by someone as a

pure gift, with nothing in return. To avoid suspicion, it has to be created by a foreigner who has a plausible reason for, in effect, giving you money. It would have to be a relative, a devoted friend, or a person who's grateful to you for an act of kindness in the past, for example. A relative is better than a friend, and a rich relative is best of all.

Someone you sat next to on the beach in the Bahamas would not qualify, nor would a mysterious benefactor who just happened to come along after you had paid a large fee to an attorney in the Cayman Islands.

Problems

Our discussion of foreign corporations and trusts has covered only the tip of the iceberg. Most tax subjects are immensely complicated, but this area is especially so.

Perhaps this chapter will at least warn you that the subject is more involved than you might have believed. The idea that you can spend $100 or $1,000 for someone's plan and suddenly be liberated from the U.S. tax code is a false dream. If a foreign corporation or trust is going to avoid taxes successfully, it will be only after extensive and careful legal work that concentrates on the details of your circumstances.

And, unfortunately, this is an area in which you can easily receive bad advice. A tax advisor can remain in this field despite many unsatisfied customers, because investors interested in tax havens generally value privacy. Even if the investor intends to remain within the law, he doesn't want to call attention to himself and trigger a tax audit or an expensive legal contest with the IRS. So he won't complain too loudly when he discovers that the plan he paid for was based more on the advisor's imagination than on his knowledge.

Some attorneys and investment advisors exploit the situation by assuring the client that whatever he wants to do is workable and will produce the desired tax consequences. Instead of designing a plan that will satisfy the tax laws, the advisor throws together a plan that satisfies the client's fantasies.

All the client really gets is the grounds for claiming that he thought what he was doing was legal. He won't go to jail, but he may lose everything in taxes and penalties.

Our suggestion is that you exploit all the simple methods first. If your tax burden is still unbearable, then look into the possibilities with tax havens. But be prepared to spend enough money to get two legal opinions—one from the firm that would handle the actual transaction, and another from an established U.S. firm that is hired only to evaluate the plan.

PART VI

CREATING A PORTFOLIO

26

THE INVESTMENT MENU

THIS PART OF THE BOOK IS INTENDED TO HELP YOU DESIGN A portfolio that matches your expectations for the next ten years or so—without being vulnerable to the surprises that will inevitably occur during those years. Once chosen, the portfolio should be able to take care of itself, without constant surveillance on your part.

This chapter reviews the various investments you might include in such a portfolio and summarizes our opinion of how each one should respond to the five inflation possibilities. More detailed discussions of the investments are given in the appropriate chapters of Parts Two and Three.

POSSIBILITIES

In Part One, we identified five possible futures for inflation. One of them will prove to be the economic course of the 1980s:

1. a leveling off of inflation, with the rate staying somewhat constant;

2. an inflation that continues to rise in an irregular pattern, as it has been doing for the past 20 years;

3. a runaway inflation with rates of 100% or more, possibly leading to the total destruction of the dollar;

4. a soft landing, in which inflation slowly declines to zero; or

5. a deflationary depression, in which inflation ends abruptly.

As we examine each investment in terms of the five possibilities, bear in mind that no investment is simply an "inflation hedge," a "deflation hedge," or a "prosperity hedge." Although inflation is a dominant factor today, each investment has its own character. No investment's future depends on inflation alone.

For example, we've seen that stocks have been hurt by the combination of inflation and the tax rules for depreciation allowances. By itself, a rise in inflation would add to the problem. But a change in the tax rules would help stocks—even if inflation continues to rise.

It's important to know what inflation tends to do to an investment, so that you can construct a portfolio in line with your expectations for inflation, and so that you can select investments that will rescue your portfolio if your expectations turn out to have been wrong. But tendencies are not certainties. If you realize that many factors will influence each investment's profitability, you'll be encouraged to diversify within each broad investment category.

MARKETABLE EQUITY INVESTMENTS

The first group we'll review are investments that don't have a face value of a fixed number of dollars, and which can be bought and sold quickly without large transaction costs.

Gold Bullion & Coins

The term "inflation hedge" is a common but misleading description for gold. Gold is a hedge against chaos of any kind, including the chaos and uncertainty that comes from a rising or unpredictable inflation rate.

To the extent that inflation influences the gold price, the prospects for a gold investment are:

Fair if inflation levels off at a somewhat constant rate;
Excellent if inflation continues its gradual rise;
Excellent if there's a runaway inflation;
Poor if there's a soft landing; and

Good in the early, most dramatic stages of a deflation, but very poor in the later stages.

Bear in mind that the market for gold is worldwide, and the price is affected by inflation rates in other countries—as well as by political, social, and military conditions, and by economic events unrelated to inflation.

Silver Bullion

At a price around $15 per ounce, it appears that the output from silver mines still is less than the amount being consumed by industry. This deficit gives silver an upward bias —as the market attempts to find a price that will reduce consumption to the level of production.

So long as the deficit continues, its effect will be bullish—regardless of what inflation is doing. But the extreme possibilities of deflation or runaway inflation might reduce industrial consumption enough to eliminate the gap.

The outcome for a silver bullion investment would tend to be:

> Good to excellent if inflation levels off at a constant rate;
> Good if inflation continues to rise;
> Mediocre in a runaway inflation;
> Good to excellent in a soft landing; and
> Poor in a deflationary depression.

Despite the upward bias created by the production deficit, silver is no longer the sure-thing investment it was at $2 or $5 per ounce.

U.S. Silver Coins

During a runaway inflation, U.S. silver coins (pre-1965) would be more reliable than paper money as a medium of exchange—and would take on special value. If we don't have a runaway inflation, silver coins will move in step with silver bullion.

Other Commodities

Because most commodities are perishable, they can't be considered for a long-term portfolio.

The metals are an exception, but even a metal should be included in a long-term portfolio only if you have a special reason for expecting it to appreciate faster than most other things. We aren't aware of any metal, other than gold or silver, that qualifies.[1]

The Swiss Franc

Changes in the price of the Swiss franc depend on differences in inflation rates between the U.S. and Switzerland. If inflation is greater in the U.S., the franc will rise. Assuming that Swiss inflation will continue to be low (under 5%), the franc's *average* yearly rise will be a little less than the U.S. inflation rate.

This means the franc should:

> Appreciate slowly if U.S. inflation levels off where it is now;
>
> Appreciate faster if U.S. inflation continues to rise;
>
> Rise rapidly if the U.S. has a runaway inflation;
>
> Level off or drop a little if the U.S. has a soft landing; and
>
> Fall sharply against the dollar during a U.S. deflation.

If the Swiss inflation rate rises, the franc will do less well. If Swiss inflation returns to about 0%, where it was from 1976 to 1978, the franc should rise by approximately the rate of U.S. inflation. And if Switzerland should undergo a deflation, the franc would rise sharply.

Because the Swiss franc is a traditional refuge for frightened money, it rallies whenever there's a political or military crisis in the world. These rallies (and the reactions that follow) are temporary phenomena—deviations that a long-term

---

[1]Which, of course, doesn't mean that no other metal will turn out to have been a good investment.

portfolio can ignore. In the long run, comparative inflation rates—and nothing else—will determine the franc's price.

Other Currencies

The future of any currency depends on how its inflation rate compares with U.S. inflation; the Swiss franc isn't special in this regard. We've singled out the franc for investment because the Swiss government's economic and monetary policies have been the most realistic of the major countries, and are the least likely to change quickly.

There are other countries with reputations for low inflation. We don't believe their monetary conservatism is as strong as it is reputed to be—and is likely to be forgotten if economic conditions become difficult. However, if you want a second foreign currency in your portfolio, we would choose from among the German mark, the Austrian schilling, the Belgian franc, and the Netherlands guilder—in that order.

U.S. Stocks

The U.S. stock market has been hurt by the *combination* of inflation and the wording of the tax rules. Because of the way the tax rules are written, inflation has the effect of raising the effective tax rates on business profits. The higher inflation goes, the worse the problem becomes. Assuming there are no changes in the tax rules, the stock market's long-term performance will tend to be:

> Mediocre to good if inflation levels off;
> Poor to mediocre if inflation continues to rise;
> Poor if there's a runaway inflation;
> Excellent if there's a soft landing; and
> Very poor if there's a deflationary depression.

Changes in the tax rules that eliminated imaginary profits, or a fundamental improvement in the government's attitude toward business, would benefit the stock market no matter what happens to inflation. But it would help the most if inflation continues to any degree. And it wouldn't prevent a deflation from bringing on a stock market crash.

ILLIQUID EQUITY INVESTMENTS

An illiquid equity investment (such as real estate) is one that doesn't have a face value of a fixed number of dollars, and which can't be bought and sold quickly.

Regardless of how these investments might respond to the various inflation possibilities, they should be approached with caution. In a time of uncertainty, no illiquid investment should dominate your portfolio.

A Business

Unless you're in an unusual line of business (such as an auction house that would benefit from forced liquidation), your prospects depend on the same considerations as those for the stock market.

The ideas in Part One of this book may give you a small edge in anticipating difficulties, but they won't enable you to dodge them entirely. If you expect the stock market to have trouble, you should assume your business will be having serious problems of its own. And if the stock market is going to explode upward, your business may have the opportunity to make exceptional profits.

Real Estate

During a polite inflation, real estate benefits from its ability to turn today's interest deductions into tomorrow's capital gains.

Any substantial decline in the inflation rate would reduce the efficiency of this tax-avoidance machinery and would injure real estate prices. An abruptly higher inflation rate might also hurt real estate, since the ensuing disorder would threaten the property rights of real estate investors.

The prospects for real estate are:

> Mediocre if inflation levels off;
> Good if inflation continues a gradual rise;
> Mediocre but uncertain if there's a runaway inflation;

Poor if there's a soft landing; and
Very poor if there's a deflationary depression.

With any of the inflation possibilities, real estate is also vulnerable to changes in the tax laws that would put an end to its tax advantages or extend new privileges to other investments.

These prospects apply generally to all types of real estate —residential or business, urban or rural. However, rural and small-town real estate might be a little less affected by social disorders resulting from the extremes of deflation and runaway inflation.[2]

Tax Shelters

The investment results for tax shelters based on real estate will tend to be the same as for real estate itself. The results for tax shelters based on operating businesses (oil drilling, equipment leasing, etc.) will tend to be similar to the results for the stock market.

Collectibles

The term "collectibles" includes all rarities—postage stamps, numismatic coins, art works—rare anythings.

Since it's difficult to borrow against collectibles, they aren't affected by the tax laws as intensely as real estate. But we believe they would respond to the inflationary possibilities in much the same ways (described on the facing page).

LIQUID DOLLAR INVESTMENTS

The next investment group includes assets that promise to pay a fixed number of dollars, and which can be bought and sold quickly with small transaction costs.

The result for any dollar investment will depend not only

---

[2]To the best of our knowledge, this distinction was first made by Howard Ruff in *How to Prosper During the Coming Bad Years.*

on the course of inflation but also on the ability of the issuer to survive and to keep its promise, and on whether the interest income is sheltered from taxes.

Short-Term Instruments

Short-term interest rates for marketable assets (such as Treasury bills and other money market instruments) should continue to move with the rate of inflation.

At current inflation levels, Treasury-bill interest is roughly the 12-month inflation rate, while less secure investments pay interest about equal to inflation or a little above. At higher inflation rates, the small gap between inflation and T-bills would widen slightly, and at lower inflation rates, T-bills should run slightly ahead of inflation.

Assuming that the interest income from an investment in T-bills (or other very high-grade, short-term IOUs) is protected from taxes, the outcome should be:

> A standoff if inflation levels off;
> Mediocre if inflation continues to rise;
> Very poor if there's a runaway inflation;
> Mediocre to somewhat good if there's a soft landing; and
> Good if there's a deflationary depression.

The results are similar, but less attractive, for a T-bill investment that isn't sheltered from taxes and for high-grade, short-term tax-exempt securities.

For lower-grade investments, such as commercial paper and certificates of deposit, the results will be dominated by the threat of default. Except in a deflation, these investments should do a little better than Treasury bills—although even a soft landing would cause isolated defaults. But in a deflation, T-bills and the lower-grade investments would part company; the results for Treasury bills would be good, while the results for the lower-grade investments would be very poor.

A money market fund will be almost as safe as the investments it holds.

Long-Term Dollar Instruments

Long-term interest rates also move with the rate of inflation, although they are slower to respond. But unlike a short-term security, a long-term security with a fixed rate of interest declines substantially in price when inflation and interest rates rise.

For Treasury bonds and other very high-grade investments, the results should be:

> Mediocre to somewhat good if inflation levels off;
> Poor if inflation continues to rise;
> Very bad if there's a runaway inflation;
> Good in a soft landing; and
> Excellent in a deflation.

For middle-grade corporate bonds and municipal bonds, the results will be slightly better in all cases except a deflation. If there's a deflation, these bonds will perform very poorly.

As with short-term instruments, the results with long-term bonds are improved considerably if the interest income is sheltered from taxes.

LESS LIQUID DOLLAR INVESTMENTS

This group includes investments denominated in a fixed number of dollars, and which cannot be sold at a moment's notice.

Mortgages

Unless it amounts to less than half the value of the property, a mortgage owed to you can be the worst of all possibilities. Only a steady inflation rate or a soft landing would be favorable for it, and there's no chance for a large profit in return for the risk.

If inflation and interest rates rise, a mortgage loses value. In a runaway inflation, the mortgage could be paid off with a day's wages.

A deflation would jeopardize the collectibility of the mortgage, since the property that serves as collateral might end up being worth less than what is owed to you. In a fore-closure, you would, in effect, be buying the property at a price above its market value.

A mortgage responds to inflation much like a medium-grade, long-term bond—but with one important difference. A bond is liquid and can be sold easily when you see conditions turning against you. A mortgage can't be unloaded so easily.

Life Insurance, Annuities & Pensions

You're promised a fixed number of dollars by such things as cash-value life insurance policies, annuities with a fixed interest rate, and employer pensions from which you've started receiving payments. Except for the fact that they can't be sold, they all are similar to a long-term bond in responding to inflation.

Constant or rising inflation rates will diminish the value of these promises. Runaway inflation will wipe them out. A soft landing would increase their value. And a deflation would increase the purchasing power of what was promised—but reduce the chance that the promise can be kept.

Deferred Annuities & Other Floating-Rate Assets

A deferred annuity, a bond, or any other instrument that has a floating interest rate will respond to changing interest and inflation rates much like a short-term dollar investment.

OTHER INVESTMENTS

There are an infinite variety of investments and variations on investments; we can't cover them all. In Parts Two and Three of the book, we explained the reasons for our opinions about the investments we've covered. If you agree with our thinking, you can apply those reasons to any investment you own.

DEBTS

Your liabilities are as much a part of your portfolio as your assets, and need to be examined just as carefully.

Generally, your debts will affect your portfolio in the opposite way from what we've described for dollar investments that you own.

If the debt has a fixed interest rate, a constant rate of inflation leaves the dollar virtually unchanged, while it reduces the purchasing power. A rising inflation rate reduces the dollar value of the debt and erodes its purchasing power at an ever-faster rate. A runaway inflation would, in effect, wipe out the debt. In a soft landing, money would depreciate at a slower pace than you now expect—making the debt more burdensome. And a deflation could make the debt terribly expensive to repay.

If the debt has a floating interest rate, the dollar value of the debt will hold steady, but its purchasing power value will decline at a rate equal to inflation, or rise in a deflation.

In evaluating your own liabilities, don't rely too heavily on the general relationships between inflation and debt. The common advice to borrow during an inflation and pay back with "cheaper dollars" ignores the fact that inflation doesn't affect everyone equally. A rise in the rate of inflation doesn't necessarily mean that dollars will be cheaper for you to obtain. Your own circumstances must be considered.

And there are two respects in which debts owed to you are not symmetrical with debts you owe.

First, debts that are owed to you and debts that you owe might not be of the same quality. The fact that someone defaults on his debt to you won't relieve you of your obligations. And since bankruptcy probably would be the only alternative to paying your debts in full, you have to think of your own debts as being as secure as Treasury securities. So unless the dollar assets you hold are very secure, they won't offset your own debts exactly when calculating your net dollar position.[3]

Second, unless there's been a grave error in your plan-

---

[3] A partial exception is a walk-away mortgage—one for which you don't have a binding legal obligation to make up the difference between what is owed and what the lender can recoup in a foreclosure sale. But even if your formal liability is limited, your credit will suffer if you default.

ning, the interest on the debts you owe will be tax-deductible. But the interest on dollar investments may escape immediate taxation if, for example, they're held in a pension plan or a deferred annuity. So in some cases it can make sense to enlarge your dollar position on both sides of the ledger—increasing both your dollar assets and your debts—to reduce your tax bill.

ELEMENTS OF A PORTFOLIO

You can't evaluate an investment solely in terms of your expectations for inflation. But this is the starting point, because your expectations for inflation tell you the *kind* of investments to emphasize.

From the menu we've reviewed, we're ready now to select the items needed for a balanced portfolio.

27

THE IDEAL PORTFOLIO

OVER THE NEXT TEN YEARS, ONE INVESTMENT WILL DO BETTER than all the others; no mix or combination of investments will be able to beat it. If you think you've identified that investment, you may be tempted to put all your money into it.

Unfortunately, none of us knows for sure what the big winner will be. Each of us may make a guess—and, because there are so many of us, some of the guesses will turn out to be right. But that won't mean that anyone *knew* the future—only that a few people estimated shrewdly or guessed well.

Uncertainty is a fact of life. The world is too complicated for anyone to be able to project all the details of the present into the future and predict where the world will be ten years from now.

But that shouldn't make you feel helpless—only humble. With a little understanding and with a good deal of financial diversification, you can prepare for the unknown. Understanding the economic principles that are at work will shield you from expectations that are based only on hope or habit—including some expectations that are widely held.

And financial diversification can protect you from what can't be foreseen. A diversified portfolio should reflect your expectations by emphasizing the investments you believe will do best. But it should also include what appear to be second and third best investments, as well as small amounts of hedges that probably will lose money if your favorites pay off. It isn't

399

easy to put money into hedges you don't expect to do well, but there are two reasons that you should.

First, the future may not match your expectations. If it doesn't, the hedges will save you from a disastrous loss.

Second, even if the world ten years from now is about as you expect, the road from here to there won't be a straight line. Your favorite investment will have ups and downs along the way—and each time it's down, you may wonder if it will ever get up again. The hedge investments provide comfort and security during those times by partially offsetting the temporary losses on your favorites.

The surprise factory in Washington will continue to be the main source of investment uncertainty—as the government looks for new ways to paper over old problems. You can't anticipate what the government will do next year or even next month—although some actions will be less surprising than others. And even if you knew what the government would do, you still couldn't be certain of the investment effects or of their timing.

If you have opinions about the future, you should act on them. But it's a mistake to confuse opinions with knowledge. Our purpose in this chapter is to design a portfolio that emphasizes your expectations while arming you against surprises.

TWO PORTFOLIOS

We think it's valuable for most investors to have two portfolios—what we call a Permanent Portfolio and a Variable Portfolio.

The Permanent Portfolio relies on balance and on a long-term perspective. It contains investments that should do well in differing circumstances; thus it should have some winners no matter what happens.

Since it's designed to cover a long period—perhaps five to fifteen years—the investments won't change. They're chosen to fit your broad expectations for the next decade or more, without regard for the ups and downs that will occur along the way—but with respect for the possibility that your long-term expectations may be mistaken.

Once a Permanent Portfolio is established, it calls for little further attention. New money may flow into it from your business or salary income, or money may flow out of it for you to live on. And, as investment prices change, small purchases and sales will be made every year or so to reestablish the percentage breakdown that you originally decided on. But such transactions are mechanical; they aren't prompted by your opinion of short-term investment trends.

The Variable Portfolio is an investment budget devoted to short-term investments. It might be used to buy gold if gold appears to be entering one of its periodic two-to-four-year bull markets. Or you might have various budgets within the Variable Portfolio for short-term speculations in a variety of markets that interest you.

The Variable Portfolio's purpose is to take advantage of what you believe to be the current trends in the markets. And any investment made from it will be sold as soon as the trends seem to have changed—which may be tomorrow or three years from now.

The distinction between the two portfolios is important. For example, you might hold some gold as a fixture in the Permanent Portfolio. And during the times you expect the gold price to rise, you might have gold in the Variable Portfolio as well. When the temporary uptrend seemed to have ended, you would sell the gold from the Variable Portfolio. But you wouldn't sell the gold from the Permanent Portfolio; it remains there to protect against surprises that might send the gold price soaring.

The Permanent Portfolio is your financial fortress—designed to protect you from all the hazards and uncertainty of the next decade. If your expectations for the decade prove to be generally correct, the purchasing power of the Permanent Portfolio will increase, but it probably won't create a new fortune for you.

The Variable Portfolio is your opportunity to profit from shifting trends. If you manage it well, it might make you rich. But if your trading decisions are wrong, it will lose money— and you'll be glad you have the Permanent Portfolio to back you up.

Division Between Two Portfolios

The division of funds between the two portfolios depends solely on how well you believe you can manage the Variable Portfolio.

For some people, the Permanent Portfolio should have all of their assets and the Variable Portfolio none—because these investors have no interest in making short-term investment decisions. Others might have three quarters in the Permanent Portfolio—or one third or one eighth. It depends on your attitude toward risk and on the confidence you have in your ability to succeed where others often fail.

The division is up to you. The only breakdown we believe makes no sense at all is to have everything in the Variable Portfolio and nothing in the Permanent Portfolio. We think everyone needs a Permanent Portfolio of some size—as a backstop against a run of bad short-term investments.

One benefit of having two portfolios is that it clearly limits the money available for short-term trading. There will be only so much you can lose if the markets go against you. If the Variable Portfolio does lose money, it should be replenished only with new funds that become available—not by transferring money from the Permanent Portfolio.

When you have the Permanent Portfolio to back you up, you can afford to act more decisively with the Variable Portfolio—knowing that you aren't risking everything you have. This may improve your trading decisions by freeing you from any sense of desperation.

So you must first decide how much of your assets, if any, to risk in the Variable Portfolio. The rest of your net worth is the Permanent Portfolio—which is our only concern in this book.

INVESTMENT INCOME

As we choose the investments that belong in the Permanent Portfolio, there will be no reference to investment income. It's as though income didn't matter—and it doesn't when making investment decisions.

It is common for someone who's retired to choose investments that will earn enough interest and dividends to cover living expenses. We think this approach is misguided, and it may lead to the wrong investments.

Your first consideration should be the safety of the capital that's precious to you. If the capital is lost, your income will be zero.

The second consideration should be the total return—income *plus* the growth of capital. The form the total return takes, whether mostly income or mostly capital appreciation, doesn't matter—except as it affects your tax bill. And your tax bill almost certainly will be lower if the return is in the form of capital appreciation.

It isn't the traditional advice, but we believe you should choose your investments without regard to the need to cover living expenses. You can provide the necessary income with a mechanical arrangement *after* you decide which investments make the most sense.

Suppose, for example, that you have $100,000 and you need $10,000 per year (before payment of income taxes) to live on. The traditional approach is to invest the $100,000 so that it earns $10,000 in interest and dividends. But the only requirement is that $10,000 be available to you; it doesn't need to come from interest and dividends.

Suppose that instead of basing your plans on income, you invest the $100,000 in investments that pay no interest or dividends at all, but which appreciate over the long term at an average of 10% per year. You can cover your living expenses just by selling some of the investments each year. In any year, the investments may appreciate by more or less than 10%. All that's needed is that they appreciate by an *average* of at least 10% per year.

"Living off capital" may sound like living beyond your means, but it needn't be. If you don't sell assets for living expenses faster than your portfolio is appreciating, your capital won't shrink—and it may even grow. What you can afford to spend without diminishing your capital is its total return—income plus appreciation—not the amount that comes to you marked "interest" or "dividends."

In fact, it may be imprudent and extravagant to treat interest and dividends as spending money. If, for example, you

403

have your entire portfolio in Treasury bills, your income may be 10% per year. But if you spend it all, you're really dipping into capital. Even though the face value of the T-bill holdings is steady, the purchasing power is declining from year to year.

The table on page 405 shows what would have happened had you divided $100,000 equally among gold, an annuity, and stocks at the end of 1969, and sold 10% of the gold and stocks each year during the following decade. Ten years later, your portfolio would have been worth $240,931, with purchasing power of $118,317 in 1969 dollars.

And you would have withdrawn a yearly average of $10,497 during the period—equal to 10.5% of the original investment. By comparison, an interest-paying initial capital of $100,000 would have declined by 50.9% in purchasing power during the same period and could not have safely paid a return anywhere close to 10% annually.[1]

A further benefit of "living off capital" is that the money withdrawn from your portfolio is taxed at capital-gain rates rather than unearned-income rates. And even if you withdraw an amount equal to all the portfolio's appreciation for the year, part of the proceeds of what you sell will be a tax-free return of capital. If half the proceeds are investment profit, for example, the effective tax rate on what you spend can't be more than 14%—because the maximum capital-gain rate is 28%.

Of course, you must choose the investments carefully. But you'd have to do that even if you restricted yourself to income-paying investments—and you'd have less of a selection from which to find the right investments.

MODEL PORTFOLIOS

One of the stock features of investment books is the model portfolio—a program recommended for everyone of a

---

[1]The table illustrates the concept of living off the total return from your investments, rather than just the "income." But the illustration doesn't mean that the investments used are the ones you should have held during the last decade—or should hold in the next. The purpose of the table is merely to show that you don't need interest and dividends to arrange for spending money.

INCOME FROM EQUITY INVESTMENTS

Year	Prices Gold	Prices Stocks	Total Value	Withdrawal	Remainder
1969	$ 35.20	800.36	$100,000	$ ----	$100,000
1970	37.37	838.92	105,661	7,033	98,628
1971	43.63	890.20	108,005	7,055	100,950
1972	64.90	1020.02	123,892	8,419	115,473
1973	112.25	850.02	145,407	10,332	135,074
1974	186.50	616.24	177,320	13,271	164,049
1975	140.25	852.41	146,671	9,939	136,733
1976	134.75	1004.65	140,171	9,005	131,166
1977	164.95	831.17	144,396	9,127	135,270
1978	226.00	805.01	162,875	10,656	152,219
1979	512.00	838.74	261,068	20,137	240,931

Average yearly withdrawal = $10,497 or 10.5% of original investment. Net appreciation in portfolio (after deduction of withdrawals) = $140,931 or 140.9% of investment.

This table shows how a balanced portfolio can provide money for living expenses even if it includes no investments that produce immediate dividends or interest.

A hypothetical investment of $100,000 was divided equally between gold, stocks (represented here by the Dow Jones Industrial Average), and a deferred annuity on December 31, 1969. The annuity accumulated value (at a hypothetical constant rate of 6%) during the following 10 years, but no money was withdrawn from it. Instead, at the end of each year, 10% of the gold and stock holdings were sold to provide cash for the investor to spend. It is assumed that none of the stocks paid dividends.

Although the investments rose and fell in value, the balanced portfolio was able to support yearly withdrawals of 10.5% of the original investment, while appreciating by 140.9%.

Source of prices: International Monetary Fund *International Financial Statistics* and *The Dow Jones Investor's Handbook, 1980.*

given age, wealth, income, marital status, or other description —as though the advice were coming from the Census Bureau. We doubt that belonging to one of these stock categories signifies anything about what to do with your money.

A bad investment is bad—no matter who owns it. If utility stocks are a bad investment, for example, they don't become a good one in the hands of a retired person who believes he needs the dividends.

And the models can be dangerous; doing what's recommended for the "middle-aged businessman"—just because you are one—may give you a false sense of security.

In many important ways, you have nothing in common with anyone else in the world. The considerations that should dictate your investment choices are unique to you; they shouldn't be overruled by an author's discovery that you belong to a certain demographic herd. Among the things to consider, four in particular should be stressed.

1. *Expectations:* You have expectations about the future; at the least, you have general opinions about the course of inflation and the economy. And there are certain dangers that concern you more than others. You won't be comfortable with your investment portfolio if it doesn't reflect these expectations and concerns.

2. *Risk:* Only you know what chances you're willing to take. What you can afford to lose without changing the way you live will depend on your net wealth, your income, and how much you need to live on. These things are measurable. But there's no way to measure the grief you'd feel from a loss or how painful it would be for you to worry about the possibility of a loss. And only you know what you're willing to risk in order to increase your wealth.

3. *Taxes:* If one or more of the tax-deferral methods we've described are available to you, you can afford to hold enough dollars to be properly prepared for a deflation. If no tax-deferral methods are available, deflation protection will be costly; you might decide to skimp on dollar holdings and take your chances, or you might choose to pay a higher tax bill as the price for greater security.

4. *Personal effort:* You won't be comfortable with your investment plan if it demands more of your time and atten-

tion studying the economy and the markets than you're willing to give. You may enjoy watching investments and betting on your opinions—or you may find the subject and the risk a burden. An investment plan may be brilliant, but it won't be profitable if you won't devote the attention needed to make it work.

These considerations are mostly subjective. They involve feelings that can't be reduced to numbers and that prevent anyone but you from saying reliably the kind of investor you are. Model portfolios are for Monopoly money.

CREATING THE IDEAL PORTFOLIO

It would be presumptuous for us to say we know how you should invest your money. We don't know anything about you.

We've found that it requires a minimum of two hours of conversation with a client just to get a picture of his attitude and circumstances. We can't make suggestions until we've asked enough questions to understand the client's objectives, attitude toward risk, expectations for the economy, tax problems, and many other factors. And very often, the answers to early questions are amended as the discussion digs deeper.

Obviously, we can't do that here, but there's much that we can do. Any consultation with a client is a joint effort; we make suggestions and call attention to realities (as we've tried to do in this book), but the client always makes the final decision—just as you must make the final decision.

And the final decision is always based on one essential test. Before designing an investment program, you need to know the characteristics of the various investments on the menu and how to buy each investment; you need to crystalize your attitude toward risk and your opinions about the future; and you have to consider the tax consequences of any changes you make. But when these considerations have been integrated into a first draft of a portfolio, the essential test must be applied. And that test is simply: *How comfortable do you feel about the plan?*

If an investment in the portfolio makes you uneasy, maybe it should be reduced in size or replaced by another that serves the same purpose. If you feel you're not taking advantage of an opportunity you see, perhaps the budget for certain investments should be increased. The portfolio must be adjusted until you *feel right* about it—until you feel that it provides the combination of safety and opportunity you want.

You don't have to be a financial expert to do this. Expertise might allow you to orient your portfolio more toward profit and less toward safety, but you don't need expertise to determine whether you're comfortable with a given program. Even if you have no idea what the markets will do in the coming years, you can arrange your portfolio to cover all the possibilities—thus assuring that you won't lose much of what you have now.

YOUR PORTFOLIO

We can begin now to create the portfolio.

To start with, we're not interested in what you own. For now, you need only to determine roughly how much you're worth. If you sold all your present investments for cash today, approximately how many dollars would you have? Only a rough figure is necessary. $5,000? $40,000? $200,000? $1,000,000? $50,000,000? Without spending more than a couple of minutes, calculate your approximate net worth (your assets minus your liabilities).

The next step is to imagine that you've sold all your present investments, and the proceeds are now sitting in dollars in a bank—waiting to be invested.

Determine how much you want to allot to the Variable Portfolio. How much, if anything, are you willing to risk on your judgment of short-term trends? Whatever it is, set aside a budget for it (with no concern now for particular investments), and subtract that amount from your net worth. The remaining money is for the Permanent Portfolio.

You have a pile of dollars available for the Permanent Portfolio. How will you invest it? With the money in cash, nothing can stop you from achieving the combination of safety and opportunity you want. You don't have to wait for any investments to recoup their losses; there are no unrealized capital gains to discourage you from selling something; you have no investments on which you've staked your reputation or self-esteem; you have nothing to consider except how best to invest a pile of cash.

What would you buy? Gold, silver, stocks, foreign currencies, oil leases, commodities, real estate, T-bills, bonds, annuities, second mortgages, debentures, convertible bonds, rare art, fried-oyster franchises? What would you buy? You have the whole world from which to choose.

Make a list of the investments you'd purchase with that imaginary pile of cash. And next to each investment, write the percentage of your Permanent Portfolio you want it to have.

In making these choices, what you already own isn't important. How much income you need from your portfolio isn't a consideration. What friends, relatives, and investment advisors are buying isn't important. You're making a fresh start, and the direction you take is up to you alone.

There is only one consideration: If you had the money in cash right now, with no constraints on your investment choices, what combination of investments would make you feel most comfortable?

In no more than five minutes, you'll have the first sketch of your new portfolio. Then you might make some changes. When no more changes seem possible, put the sheet of paper aside. Take another look at it tomorrow. You'll probably make one or two more changes. And perhaps again the next day. After a few days, no more changes will seem possible or necessary. You'll have created the ideal portfolio.

The next step is to make a list of what you own now and its present value (covered in the next chapter). Then sell the amount by which any item exceeds the percentage budget you gave it in the new portfolio. With the proceeds of these sales, buy what's necessary to have enough of each item you listed in the ideal portfolio.

Of course, the transition from what you have now to what you want may not be simple. You may have investments that can't be sold easily, and you may be reluctant to pay capital-gain taxes on investments you no longer need. We won't ignore those problems; we'll deal with them in Chapter 29. But you won't get close to the ideal unless you begin by defining it—without worrying about the hurdles.

It may seem that our approach is too simple; your present assets may be spread over a multitude of investments and among a number of pockets. If there seem to be too many complications to handle, it's only because you're concentrating on where you are now, not on where you want to be.

That's why you must start with the imaginary pile of cash. Only then will you be able to look past the results of the piecemeal decisions you may have made over many years.

You *do* have a fresh start; you can make it any time you want by saying, "Sell." Your portfolio can be as simple or as complicated as you want it to be—but the choice shouldn't be dictated by what you happen to have now.

GETTING STARTED

Once you have some figures on paper, ideas for changes will come to you faster and faster. You'll remember things that are important to you, and some of the investments that once seemed necessary may no longer be so attractive.

But it may be difficult to get started, to write down the first group of figures. To provide a starting point, page 411 lists six sample portfolios. None of them can possibly match all the considerations that should dictate your choice of investments. But one of the six portfolios will come close to your general expectations for inflation.

There is one portfolio weighted toward (but not totally committed to) each of the five inflation possibilities we've discussed. If you have an opinion about the future of inflation, begin with the corresponding portfolio; if you have no opinion about the future of inflation, use the sixth portfolio.

Copy the portfolio you select onto a piece of paper. Then study it. What don't you like about it? What does it overlook that's important to you? What does it include that seems to be too involved or too risky?

Change anything that seems wrong—anything you don't understand, anything that seems to have no place in your plans, anything for which you believe you have a superior replacement, anything that seems too risky. Then change the figures again—and again—until you've found the arrangement you can live with, until the portfolio appears to have been

SAMPLE PORTFOLIOS EMPHASIZING INFLATIONARY EXPECTATIONS

Item	Level Inflation	Rising Inflation	Runaway Inflation	Soft Landing	Deflation	Uncertain
Gold coins & bullion.........	25%	35%	50%	20%	20%	30%
Silver bullion	15%	12%	0%	15%	0%	8%
Silver coins	1%	3%	10%	1%	1%	2%
Swiss francs	10%	15%	20%	9%	4%	15%
Stock market investments	15%	10%	5%	25%	5%	15%
Real estate	15%	20%	20%	5%	5%	10%
Cash[1]	-	-	-	-	-	-
Short-term dollars[1]	14%	15%	10%	15%	25%	15%
Long-term dollars	5%	(10%)	(15%)	10%	40%	5%
Miscellaneous[2]	0%	0%	0%	0%	0%	0%
Total	100%	100%	100%	100%	100%	100%

Each of the first 5 portfolios emphasizes an expectation concerning inflation for the next 10 years: Level inflation, that inflation will level off at some rate; Rising inflation, that inflation will continue to rise in waves as it has for the past 20 years; Runaway inflation, that inflation rates will reach 100% or more; Soft landing, that inflation will ease gradually down to 0% without an economic crash; and Deflation, that there will be a 1929-type deflationary crash. Each of these portfolios emphasizes its expectation but still hedges against other possibilities. The Uncertain portfolio assumes no particular expectation regarding inflation.

Silver bullion percentages assume a silver price of $10 per ounce or less. The figures shown should be reduced by 1/3 if the price is between $10 and $15, by 2/3 if the price is between $15 and $20, and eliminated if the price is over $20. If the budget is reduced, the difference should be spread evenly among the other items.

Silver coins are U.S. pre-1965 90% silver coins or 1965-1970 Kennedy half-dollars.

If other foreign currencies are desired, they should be part of the Swiss franc budget.

The stock-market budget is for warrants, dual-purpose investment funds, leveraged stocks, equity in your own business, or interests in business partnerships other than real estate. For the runaway inflation portfolio, only warrants are suggested.

Collectibles and real estate partnerships, if any, should be allocated from the real estate budget.

Long-term dollars include long-term Treasury bonds minus long-term fixed-rate debts (such as mortgages). Figures in parentheses are negative (more owed than owned).

[1] Short-term dollars include cash, checking accounts, Treasury bills, money market funds, and floating-rate dollar assets minus short-term debts and floating-rate debts. A separate budget should be assigned to cash (including checking accounts and money market funds), but the amount to assign is a consideration of the size of the total portfolio, personal preference, and whether money will be drawn from the portfolio for living expenses.

[2] The miscellaneous budget is for items not otherwise listed—such as gold stocks, foreign stocks, Social Security, etc. While we are not suggesting any of these items, a budget of up to 10% will not distort the emphasis in any of the portfolios.

modeled on your view of the future and with your concern for safety and opportunity.

Eventually, you'll have the ideal portfolio.

You may want to finish reading the book before trying to work out the portfolio. But we suggest that you stop for five minutes or so right now, and make your first outline.

THE IDEAL PORTFOLIO

It isn't difficult to create the right portfolio for yourself. But it won't be the right portfolio unless *you* make the choices. No investment advisor nor anyone else (even if he's sure he knows what's best) will share your losses with you.

You have to make the decisions because you will live with the consequences.

28

WHERE YOU ARE NOW

WE HOPE THE PREVIOUS CHAPTER HELPED YOU SETTLE ON THE proportions for an ideal portfolio. How close you actually get to your ideal will depend on several matters yet to be covered. But at the least, you'll probably acquire a portfolio that's much more like the ideal than what you currently hold.

The next step in the process of getting to where you want to be is to determine where you are now. This means drawing up a balance sheet—an inventory of what you own and owe. The result will tell you the exact size of that pile of cash we asked you to imagine in the last chapter.

This chapter will explain how to enter each asset and liability on the balance sheet. The process is not overly complicated, because you probably don't have more than a dozen or so items to enter. Unfortunately, we don't know what those items are—and there are other readers to consider. So the chapter has to explain everything we can think of that anyone might need to include.

To make your job easier, the chapter is divided into sections. The first paragraph or two of each section tells which items should be included in the investment category covered. If you don't own any of the items mentioned, feel free to skip to the next section.

WHAT TO INCLUDE

To evaluate your holdings, you need to list all the assets and liabilities that are part of your Permanent Portfolio. However, you probably haven't separated your investments into two portfolios before now, so you'll have to sort out Variable Portfolio items as you go along.

An investment is part of your Variable Portfolio if it represents a trading position—if you intend to sell it as soon as you believe short-term trends have changed. The Variable Portfolio should also include any cash you're holding as a buying reserve for such investments. The Permanent Portfolio includes everything you intend to hold for several years, regardless of short-term market trends, plus any cash not allocated to the Variable Portfolio.

You need to know how much of your net worth is currently devoted to the Variable Portfolio; it may be more or less than the amount you decided on when reading the last chapter. So, although our attention is focused on the Permanent Portfolio, you should make a separate list of Variable Portfolio investments and cash as we go along. Don't include these items in the balance sheet for the Permanent Portfolio.

If you've already separated your investments between the two portfolios (by whatever names you call them), or if you intend to have 100% of your funds in the Permanent Portfolio, you won't need to make a list of the Variable Portfolio investments.

Non-investment items shouldn't be included in the balance sheet. Ignore such things as autos, furniture, appliances, etc.—as well as any loans incurred to pay for them. However, your home (if you own it) and any mortgage on it should be included, because it will be a significant part of your net worth.

Other than Variable Portfolio investments, no investment should be excluded from the balance sheet—even if you know you aren't going to sell it. Every investment affects the character of the total, and needs to be included in order to determine how well your portfolio is balanced.

Trusts, Pension Plans & Company Programs

You need to include the investments of a pension plan you control and any assets you've transferred to a trust. Also include a company profit-sharing or other employee benefit plan that gives you an interest in a pool of investments (but doesn't promise you a fixed pension).

If the investments held by any of these entities will contribute to your direct or indirect benefit, think of the investments as though they were in your own hands. If other people are covered by any of these plans, determine your percentage share of the plan and include only your share of each investment.

Investment Items

If you're reading this chapter for the first time, you might decide to delay making the balance sheet until you've finished reading the book. But if you're drawing up the balance sheet now, look closely at each item we discuss; it might remind you of something you need to include.

There's a sample form for the balance sheet on pages 416–417. Make a copy of it—ignoring the hypothetical examples that are show in italics. Use ledger paper if you have it; if not, lined paper will do. Enter everything in pencil, so that it will be easy to make changes.

We'll approach your holdings by broad groups or categories—covering equity investments first, then dollar assets and liabilities, then miscellaneous investments, and finally the handling of specialized compartments for holding investments, such as corporations, limited partnerships, and pension plans.

As we go through the balance sheet, make the entries that are called for, but leave extra lines to handle items you might think of later. You may have to go through the entire list twice to catch everything you own and owe.

Values to Use

The value to be listed for each asset is what it would fetch on the open market. You should use the current market price; the price you paid for the item doesn't matter.

Enter the *gross* market value—not the equity remaining after paying off a margin loan, mortgage, or other indebted-

BALANCE SHEET

(1) Item	(2) Denomination	(3) Quantity	(4) Current Price $	(5) Market Value $	(6) Category Value $	(7) Category Share %
Gold						
Bullion	ounces	31	625	19,375		
Krugerrands (bought at less than $400)	coins	7	655	4,585		
Krugerrands (bought at more than $400)	coins	8	655	5,240	29,200	10.7%
Silver bullion	ounces	500	17.00	8,500	8,500	3.1%
Silver coins						
90% silver	bags	1	12,240	12,240		
40% silver	bags	1.3	5,015	6,520	18,760	6.8%
Foreign currencies						
Swiss franc accounts	francs	12,340	.6412	7,912		
German mark accounts	marks	2,180	.5760	1,256		
Swiss franc bonds	francs	5,000	.6240	3,120		
Swiss franc annuity	francs	15,000	.6412	9,618		
Margin loan in francs	francs	(4,702)	.6412	(3,015)	18,891	6.9%
Stock market investments						
Stocks - gainers	—	—	—	21,200		
Stocks - losers	—	—	—	4,680		
Stocks - no large change	—	—	—	8,112		
Ajax Mutual Fund	shares	1,000	6.12	6,120		
Business assets	—	—	—	35,000	75,112	27.4%
Real estate & collectibles						
Home (gross value)	—	1	80,000	80,000		
Real estate partnership	—	—	—	40,000		
Stamp collection	—	—	—	6,000		
Numismatic coins	—	—	—	5,500	131,500	48.0%

All entries are hypothetical examples.

BALANCE SHEET (Cont'd.)

(1) Item	(2) Denomi- nation	(3) Quantity	(4) Current Price $	(5) Market Value $	(6) Category Value $	(7) Category Share %
Cash						
Cash in hand	dollars	—	—	800		
Checking accounts	dollars	—	—	4,300		
Savings accounts	dollars	—	—	5,200		
Money market fund	shares	3,100	1.00	3,100	13,400	4.9%
Short-term dollar items						
Treasury bill	dollars	—	—	10,000		
Time deposit	dollars	—	—	2,000		
Deferred annuity	dollars	—	—	7,600		
Business payables	dollars	—	—	(11,000)		
Margin loan - gold	dollars	—	—	(6,226)		
Margin loan - stocks	dollars	—	—	(4,137)		
Call loan at bank	dollars	—	—	(1,200)	(2,963)	(1.1%)
Long-term dollar items						
Treasury bonds	dollars	5,000	.83	4,150		
Mortgage on home	dollars	—	—	(57,000)		
Company pension	dollars	—	—	31,000		
Current annuity	dollars	—	—	14,000		
Real estate partnership liabilities	dollars	—	—	(35,000)	(42,850)	(15.6%)
Miscellaneous						
"Deep Mine" gold stock	shares	300	6.40	1,920		
Swiss franc stocks	—	—	—	1,496		
Social Security	dollars	—	—	21,000	24,416	8.9%
GRAND TOTALS:					$273,966	100.0%

All entries are hypothetical examples.

Items in parentheses are negative amounts.

ness. All debts you owe will be listed separately further along.

Your present financial position is affected by the amount of a debt—not by your reason for incurring it. If you look only at your equity in an investment (current market value minus what you owe on it), you might not realize how much of your net worth the investment represents.

Grouping Assets

Groups of assets that are highly similar can be represented on the balance sheet by a single entry. By "highly similar," we mean that all investments in the group would be equal candidates for sale if you should decide to reduce your holdings.

For example, if you own ten different stocks of U.S. companies, all of which are listed on exchanges and none of which is worth significantly more or less than you paid for it, make a single entry for "U.S. stocks."

You'll have to list them on a separate sheet of paper to total their value, but making a single entry on the balance sheet will save it from becoming cluttered with details that are unnecessary and which may be distracting. Keep any separate lists for reference later.

Combining similar assets into groups is a matter of convenience only. If you have just two stocks, for example, it would be simpler to enter each one on the balance sheet, rather than make a side calculation.

Make separate entries for groups of assets that differ in any way that might affect your decisions about what to sell—such as differences in marketability. And assets with large gains or losses should be separated because the prospect of capital-gain taxes might influence your selling decisions. For our purposes, a "large gain" or "large loss" means that the current price is at least 30% above or below your purchase price. An investment lying between these two boundaries can be treated here as though there were no gain or loss to consider.

So if you own stocks (for example) with a wide range of gains and losses, you'll need three entries—one for stocks with large gains, one for stocks with large losses, and one for those in the middle.

We're ready now to make an inventory of your investments. We'll go through the list, category by category.

QUOTED EQUITY INVESTMENTS

The first items to be listed are quoted equity investments —assets for which you can easily determine the current market value and which are *not* promises to pay you a fixed number of dollars.

The current market price of an asset in this category may be listed in the daily newspaper. If not, try *The Wall Street Journal* or *Barron's,* either of which can be found at any large newsstand. If the price doesn't appear in any of these sources, you can get a current market quote from a broker or dealer who handles the item.

Enter the gross value on the balance sheet, even if there's a loan against the investment. Loans will be handled later.

Gold

This section covers gold bullion and the low-premium "bullion" coins shown in the table on page 112. Any other gold coins are numismatic, and will be covered with "Collectibles" on page 424.

If some of your gold holdings are short-term (because you're betting on one of gold's temporary uptrends) note them only on your list of Variable Portfolio investments. All other gold holdings belong on the balance sheet for the Permanent Portfolio.

For gold bullion, enter "Gold bullion" in column 1, the word "ounces" in column 2, the number of ounces you own in column 3, and the current gold price in column 4.

Gold coins require a separate entry for each *type* of coin you own—Krugerrand, Austrian crown, etc.—because each will have a different weight and price. And if you purchased one type of coin at different times and prices, you may need two or three entries for that one type—grouping the coins by large gains or losses (see the explanation on page 418).

Enter the name of the coin in column 1, the word "coins" in column 2, and the quantity you own in column 3. If you know the current price at which dealers are buying the coins, enter it in column 4. If you don't have a current quote, enter the current price of gold bullion adjusted by the number of ounces in one coin.[1]

Silver Bullion

Enter "Silver bullion" in column 1, "ounces" in column 2, the number of ounces you own in column 3, and the current price in column 4.

Silver Coins

This listing covers "junk silver"—U.S. silver coins dated prior to 1965 (or half-dollars dated prior to 1971) that have no numismatic value. Numismatic silver coins fall under "Collectibles" on page 424.

If you have both pre-1965 coins of 90% silver and 1965–1970 Kennedy half-dollars of 40% silver, make separate entries.

Column 2 should show the word "bags," and column 3 should show the number of bags of $1,000 face value that you own. The "bag" is the customary trading unit. If you have an odd number of coins, determine the face value by multiplying the number of dimes by $0.10, the quarters by $0.25, and the half-dollars by $0.50. Then divide the result by $1,000 to determine the number of bags—which probably will be a fraction. Enter that quantity in column 3.

The price relationship between silver coins and silver bullion can fluctuate widely. So, for accuracy, you should determine the current market price of the coins.

---

[1]To make the adjustment, multiply the current bullion price by the number of ounces in one coin (shown in the table on page 112). Thus, if you own British sovereigns and the current bullion price is $500, you would multiply .2354 times 500, making a price of $117.50 per coin. This method ignores the small premium that the bullion coins usually command. One-ounce coins require no adjustment; just enter the current bullion price per ounce.

The Wall Street Journal (and possibly a local newspaper) carries the price of 90% coins on the commodity page. In a table titled "Cash Prices," there's a listing "Coins, whol $1,000 face val" under the heading "Precious Metals." You can also call a coin dealer and ask for the price at which he'll purchase one bag of 90% (or 40%) coins.

If you can't obtain a current coin price easily, estimate the price per bag by multiplying the current silver bullion price times either 720 (for pre-1965, 90%-silver coins) or 295 (for 1965–1970, 40%-silver Kennedy half-dollars).

Other Commodities

This section is for any other commodities you own (excluding forward and futures contracts, which are covered on page 432).

In column 1, list each commodity owned. In column 2, show the unit in which the commodity's price is normally quoted (ounces, pounds, tons, bushels). Enter the number of those units you own in column 3. In column 4, enter the price per unit.

Foreign Currencies

This section covers foreign currency holdings in the form of bonds and banknotes, as well as bank deposits that are either current (checking) accounts or liquid savings accounts. Include other foreign currency assets, such as time deposits and certificates of deposit, if they mature within one year. Do not list foreign stocks here (they're covered on page 431). Foreign-currency annuities should be listed here, and are explained on the next page.

Each currency you own requires a separate line. But within each currency, all banknotes and bank deposits can be a single entry (if there isn't a large profit or loss difference within the group).

For banknotes and demand deposits, enter the name of the currency (such as "Swiss francs") in column 1, repeat the unit name (such as "francs") in column 2, and the number of units you own (such as "12,340") in column 3. In column

4, enter the current price in dollars for one unit of the currency (such as $.64). The current price is listed in most daily newspapers, and in *The Wall Street Journal* and *Barron's*.[2]

If you own foreign-currency bonds, each bond will have its own price, so you'll have to calculate the value of each one individually. If you own a large number of different issues, you can calculate their total value on a separate page and enter the result in column 5 of the balance sheet, leaving columns 2 to 4 blank.

If you own only two or three different issues, enter them on the balance sheet individually. And don't combine bonds unless they're denominated in the same currency.

On either the balance sheet or the separate page, identify each foreign-currency bond in column 1 and skip column 2. In column 3, enter your total holdings of the bond—in face value (for example, 5 bonds each with 1,000 francs' face value would be entered as 5,000).

You'll need to determine the bond's current market price (in the foreign currency). If you can't easily obtain a current quote, you can use a price quoted to you within the last month or so.

Convert the bond price to a decimal figure (a price of 82 becomes .82 and 103 becomes 1.03). Multiply that figure by the dollar price of one unit of the foreign currency. The result is the price in dollars per unit of face value, and should be entered in column 4.

Annuities in Foreign Currencies

An annuity denominated in a foreign currency is an equity investment because the number of dollars you'll eventually receive isn't fixed; it will depend on the future value of the foreign currency.

If you're already receiving payments from the annuity,

---

[2]Make sure the price quoted is for one unit of currency; if the quote is "per 100," divide the quote by 100. If the price you obtain is in units of foreign currency per one dollar (such as 1.65 francs per dollar), divide it into the number 1 (for example, 1 ÷ 1.65 = .606) to get the price in dollars of one unit of the foreign currency.

use the instructions on page 430 for a "current annuity" to determine its value. If the annuity hasn't begun paying, use its surrender value.

In either case, you'll have the current value in terms of the foreign currency. Convert that to a dollar figure by following the instructions given for currency conversion on page 421.

Enter the name of the annuity in column 1 and the current value in dollars in column 5.

Foreign Currency Liabilities

If you have a debt that's denominated in a foreign currency (and if the debt isn't one you're carrying as part of the Variable Portfolio), enter it here. Name the debt in column 1 and skip columns 2 to 4. Determine the price of one unit of the foreign currency, using the method shown on page 421, and multiply that by the number of units of the foreign currency you owe. Enter that figure *in parentheses* in column 5.

U.S. Stock Market Investments

This category includes U.S. stocks, warrants, and mutual funds. It doesn't include foreign stocks that happen to be purchased in the U.S. (they are handled on page 431). Short sales of stocks are covered on page 432.[3]

If you have only two or three items, make a separate entry for each, naming it in column 1. In column 2, enter the word "shares," "warrants," or "options," and enter the number owned in column 3. Find the current market price in the daily newspaper or *The Wall Street Journal,* and enter it in column 4.

If you own a large number of different stocks, warrants, mutual funds, or call options, total their value on a separate sheet of paper, and enter them as one item. But make separate entries for issues with large gains or losses.

---

[3]Call options on stocks should be included in the Permanent Portfolio balance sheet only if the options are continually rolled over as a permanent investment position. If so, enter them here.

ILLIQUID EQUITY INVESTMENTS

An illiquid equity investment is one that doesn't promise a fixed number of dollars and can't be bought or sold quickly.

By definition, you won't find the price of an illiquid investment quoted in the daily newspaper or in any financial journal, so it won't be easy to determine current values. You may have to make estimates, and it will be important not to be too optimistic. If you decide to sell something and get much less than you estimated, you'll be unable to pay for all the investments you had planned to buy.

Real Estate

Every piece of real estate you own should be included here. That includes your own home—even if you have no intention of selling it, and even if you don't think of it as an investment. The fact that you own the house may influence what you should do with other assets.

Make a separate entry for each property you own, naming it in column 1. Column 2 will be blank, and the quantity shown in column 3 will be "1."

Enter your estimate of the current market value in column 4. Don't enter the price you're hoping you can get, the price you could get under ideal conditions, or the price that an agent said you could get when he asked you to put it on the market. Enter what you're confident you'd receive in a quick sale, after subtracting a reasonable allowance for selling costs.

Enter the estimate as the gross value. If there's a mortgage on the property, it will be handled separately on page 428.

Collectibles

This category includes postage stamps, numismatic coins, art works, anything that has value because of its rarity. It also includes any gold or silver items that don't fit the descriptions given for gold and silver investments on pages 419–421.

The price you originally paid for a collectible is a poor

guide to what you could get for it now. A large part of the price you paid covered the dealer's services—maintaining inventories, alerting you to what's available, and selecting and displaying the particular piece you bought. No matter how much you believe collectibles in general have appreciated, you don't know for sure that you could even recoup what you paid.

An insurance estimate or a courtesy estimate by a dealer is of little value. The only accurate figure is a dealer's firm offer to buy, and then only if the dealer believes you're willing to sell. Try to get such an offer.

You may not like what the dealer says, but it's better to hear it now—when you need accurate information on which to base your plans—rather than later, when you might be expecting money that isn't forthcoming.

If you won't go to the trouble of getting an offer, you'll have to estimate the value yourself. A rough method (not very accurate but better than nothing) is to subtract 50% from the price you paid, and then add 10% (of the 50%) for every year since the purchase. If you've held the item for three years, for example, your estimate would be 65% of what you paid.

That may not conform with what the salesman said when you were buying, but it conforms roughly with our own knowledge of the market. And it assumes that you bought the item at what collectibles salesmen call a "wholesale" price. One result of this calculation may be to motivate you to go out and get an offer from a dealer.

If you have only a few items, list each one. If you have many, group the entries by appreciation or depreciation, as described on page 418. For group entries, leave columns 2 to 4 blank, and enter the estimated value of the whole group in column 5.

CASH, & SHORT-TERM DOLLAR ITEMS

The next items in the roll call are denominated in a fixed number of dollars. They include cash, short-term and long-term dollar assets, and debts.

Cash

Enter here the value of checking and savings accounts, money market funds, credit union share accounts, brokerage accounts, and U.S. currency. An asset should be included as cash only if its face amount is fixed and if it can be converted into currency on demand.

Don't include cash and checking accounts devoted to current living expenses (as opposed to a reserve for investment purposes). And don't include cash that's reserved for the Variable Portfolio, but note it on the Variable Portfolio list.

Write "Cash" in column 1, skip columns 2 to 4, and enter the amount in column 5. If you want to lump all cash items together, list them on a separate sheet so you'll know what you've included.

Short-Term Liquid Dollar Assets

This group includes assets (other than cash) that promise to pay you a fixed number of dollars within one year from today, but which can be sold or liquidated immediately if you so desire. These include:

1. Treasury bills, commercial paper, and bankers' acceptances;
2. time deposits and CDs that aren't subject to large withdrawal penalties;
3. marketable bonds or notes maturing within one year *or* with floating interest rates;
4. deferred annuities with floating interest rates; and
5. "call" loans you can collect whenever you want.

Columns 2 to 4 can be left blank. If there are only a few such items, make a separate entry for each, writing its name in column 1 and the face value in column 5. If there's a large number of short-term assets, write "Short-term dollar assets" in column 1, and enter the total in column 5.

Although some items may sell at a discount in the market, the short time to maturity assures that the discount will be small enough to ignore in drawing up a balance sheet.

For a deferred annuity, enter the lump-sum redemption value in column 5.

Short-Term Illiquid Dollar Assets

This group includes promises to pay you dollars—if the promises mature during the next 12 months, and if you cannot liquidate them now or sell them easily in the open market.

These include time deposits subject to large penalties for early withdrawal; unmarketable bonds, notes, or mortgages due within the next 12 months; and any other debts owed to you which will be paid within a year and which can't easily be sold or collected early.

If the principal will be taxed when collected (such as with deferred compensation from an employer), subtract an allowance for taxes.

Make a separate entry for each item. Name the item in column 1 and enter the face value of the asset in column 5—skipping columns 2 to 4.

Short-Term Dollar Liabilities

This group includes any debts *you owe* that will mature within a year from today, debts that carry a *floating* interest rate, and debts that must be paid whenever demanded. These include margin loans on securities and other investments, as well as call loans at a bank. Do not include loans incurred for non-investment purposes, except for a floating-rate mortgage on your home or other property.

Many floating-rate mortgages have ceilings on the interest rate. If you owe such a mortgage, and if the ceiling is less than 3% above the current interest rate, think of it as a fixed-rate obligation (since the rate can't float much higher). If it will be more than 12 months before the mortgage is paid off, enter it under "Long-term dollar liabilities" (covered on page 428); otherwise, enter it here.

Don't lump the items in this category together. Make a separate entry for each loan—using one item for a margin loan on securities, another line for a call loan at the bank, and so on. Name the loan in column 1, skip columns 2 to 4, and enter the loan balance in column 5. Put *parentheses* around the figure—for example, "($5,000)"—to show that it is money you *owe*.

LONG-TERM DOLLAR ITEMS

The next category covers items denominated in dollars which won't mature for a year or more.

Long-Term Liquid Dollar Assets

Here you should include marketable assets that promise to pay a fixed number of dollars on a date over one year away. These include mainly the bonds and notes of governments and corporations.

Because each bond has its own price, you'll have to calculate the value of each one separately. If you own the bonds of many different issuers or maturities, you can calculate their total value on a separate page and enter the result in column 5 of the balance sheet, leaving columns 2 to 4 blank. If you own only two or three different issues, enter them on the balance sheet individually.

On either the balance sheet or the separate sheet, identify each bond in column 1 and skip column 2. In column 3, enter your total holdings of the bond—in face value. For example, five bonds with $1,000 face value each would be entered as $5,000.

Convert the current price of a bond to a decimal figure (85 becomes .85—and 103 becomes 1.03), and enter the decimal figure in column 4. The current price may be listed in *The Wall Street Journal;* if not, you can obtain it from a stockbroker.

If the calculations are done on a separate page, multiply column 3 by column 4 for each bond, and enter the result in column 5. Add up all the column 5 results, and enter the total in column 5 of the balance sheet.

Long-Term Dollar Liabilities

This category includes any dollars *you owe* that are not repayable for a year or more, and which have a *fixed* interest rate. This category probably will include only mortgages. A loan with a freely *floating* interest rate should be treated as a short-term loan (covered on page 427, not here) no matter how many years it has to run.

Make a separate entry for each debt and name it in column 1. Skip columns 2 to 4. Enter the current value of the loan in column 5 *in parentheses*—for example "($25,000)."

If the interest rate on the debt is close to the rate that would be charged on similar borrowing today, the current loan value is the same as the principal due on the loan.

If interest rates have changed more than 1% since you took the loan, the current value will be different from the balance due on the loan. If each payment you make is applied to both interest and principal (the usual case with a mortgage), use the mortgage table on page 530 to determine the current value. For interest-only loans (with the principal repaid in a lump sum at the end of the loan), determine the present value of the interest payment by using the table on page 530, and determine the present value of the balloon payment by using the table on page 532. Add the two results together and place the answer *in parentheses* in column 5.

Long-Term Illiquid Dollar Assets

This section is for dollars *owed to you* with a specific due date more than a year away, and which cannot easily be turned into cash.

Examples are a mortgage that's owed to you; a bond or note for which there's no resale market; a personal debt owed to you by your family or friends (if it's connected in some way with your investment position); an annuity (denominated in dollars); and a pension that promises a fixed number of dollars and doesn't have a cost-of-living clause.[4]

You shouldn't include any pension if you're indirectly responsible for paying the amount promised—as is the case with a pension from a corporation you own. Instead, each asset the pension plan owns should be included as a separate item in the appropriate category of the balance sheet.

---

[4]A pension with a cost-of-living clause (including Social Security) is covered on page 430.

For the items that belong here, use a separate line for each item; name it in column 1, skip columns 2 to 4, and enter the value in column 5. How you determine the value will depend on the nature of the asset.

With any item in this section, if you have the option of collecting a reasonable sum today that would wipe out the debt to you, enter that amount in column 5. For example, if you're covered by a company pension plan (and you don't own the company), and if the plan promises to pay you a fixed pension, enter your vested interest—the amount you could collect if you quit tomorrow.

If you own an annuity that hasn't begun paying money to you (a "deferred annuity") and that doesn't have a floating interest rate, use the annuity's surrender value.[5]

If you don't have the option to collect a single sum today that would liquidate the asset, you'll have to estimate its current value. For a mortgage owed to you, use the table on page 530. For an annuity that has already begun paying a fixed number of dollars yearly for life (a "current annuity"), use the table on page 529 to determine your life expectancy, and then use the mortgage table on page 530 to find the current value for that number of years.

MISCELLANEOUS

The sections that follow are for investments that don't fit any of the general categories we've covered up to now. Check the beginning of each section to see if you own anything it includes.

Cost-of-Living Pensions & Social Security

A cost-of-living pension is one that increases its payments as the cost of living goes up; it is protected (or has been promised protection) from changes in inflation and interest rates. Thus the pension is not a dollar asset; the cost-of-living

---

[5]Floating-rate annuities are covered on page 427. Foreign-currency annuities are covered on page 422.

clause means the promise is denominated in purchasing power.

Use the life-expectancy table on page 529 to find the number of years the payments should last. Then find the current value by using that number of years and the 3% column in the table on page 530.[6]

Social Security is a cost-of-living pension. But if you're under 45 years of age, we believe you're better off ignoring the value of Social Security benefits (unless you're already receiving them), because we don't have much faith in the promises.

If you're at least 45 years old, and haven't yet started receiving Social Security payments, you can estimate the current value of what you've been promised by doing the following: (1) Call a Social Security office and ask what the monthly payments would be for someone age 65 with your salary history. (2) Determine how many years you can expect to receive those payments by finding your life expectancy on page 529 and subtracting the number of years until you'll be 65 (if you're now 51 and male, for example, you can expect to live 23 years, less 14 years until 65, resulting in 9 years of payments). (3) Use the mortgage table on page 530 to determine the value the payments would have if you were already 65 (using the number of years determined in step #2). (4) Use the table on page 532 to discount that value for the number of years remaining until you'll be 65. In steps #3 and #4, the interest-rate column to use depends on the confidence you have that you'll be paid. If you expect to collect everything promised to you, use the 3% column. If you suspect, as we do, that the government will have to renege on some of its promises, use the 6% column.

Foreign Stock Investments

List here any stocks of foreign companies.

If there are many different stocks, you may want to make

---

[6]The 3% figure is the interest rate we assume would prevail in a world without inflation. For the past 75 years, 3% has been the approximate average after-inflation return on high-grade bonds.

the calculations on a separate page. But you should have at least one entry on the balance sheet for each country.

On the balance sheet or on the separate page, identify the stock in column 1. Write "shares" in column 2, and enter the number of shares in column 3.

If the price of the stock is quoted in U.S. dollars, enter the price per share in column 4.

If the stock price is quoted in a foreign currency, convert it into U.S. dollars. Determine first the price in dollars of one unit of the foreign currency, using the method shown on page 421. Multiply that figure by the current foreign-currency price per share. This gives you the price in U.S. dollars; enter it in column 4.

Gold Stocks

For the reasons discussed on page 113, gold stocks should be listed under "Miscellaneous," not in the group of gold investments. If their prices are quoted in dollars, enter them by the same method shown for "U.S. Stock Market Investments" on page 423. If their prices are quoted in a foreign currency, use the method shown for "Foreign Stock Investments" above. In either case, enter them in the "Miscellaneous" category.

SPECIALIZED ITEMS

The next groups of items involve special handling, and will be entered at various places on the balance sheet.

Futures, Forwards & Short Sales

This section covers futures or forward positions in commodities and financial instruments, as well as short sales on stocks.

Usually, such a position is geared to current market trends and is part of the Variable Portfolio. But if your case is an exception and you plan to hold the position indefinitely as part of your Permanent Portfolio (perhaps because it hedges an oversized item in the Permanent Portfolio), the position should be included in the balance sheet. Otherwise, skip over to "Compartments" on page 435.

Each position you hold requires two entries—because it represents both an asset and a liability. One of the two entries is a dollar item—the dollars you owe if you've bought long, or the dollars owed to you if you've sold short. The other entry will be the investment involved; it will be an asset if you've bought long or a liability (measured in ounces, shares, etc.) if you've sold short. The entries will be located in two different parts of the balance sheet.

If you've *bought* a forward or futures position (gone long), make an entry in the section covered by that investment (a commodity is entered under "Gold Bullion," "Silver Bullion," or "Miscellaneous," for example). Name the item in column 1 as "Forward [or Futures] position in [name of item]." In column 2, enter the unit in which the item is traded. In column 3, enter the number of those units (not the number of contracts) you hold. In column 4, enter the current price per unit. The current price for the delivery month your contract covers may be in the newspaper; if you have a forward contract, use the price for the delivery month nearest to the delivery date of the forward contract.

In the section "Short-Term Dollar Liabilities" (covered on page 427), enter in column 1 the name "Liability for futures [or forward] contract of [name of item]." Columns 2 and 3 carry the same information mentioned in the preceding paragraph. Enter the price in column 4. In the case of a futures contract on a U.S. exchange, use the current price. In the case of a forward contract (with a dealer or bank), use the price fixed in the contract. Enter the figure *in parentheses,* because this line represents a liability.

If you've *sold* a forward or futures position *short,* or have sold stock short, make an entry for each position in the appropriate section of the balance sheet (stocks sold short under "U.S. Stocks," for example). In column 1, name the item "Short sale on [name of item]." In column 2 enter the unit in which the item is traded—"shares," "ounces," and so forth. In column 3, enter the quantity of those units (not the number of contracts) involved in the sale. In column 4, enter the current price (not the price at which you sold). Enter this figure *in parentheses;* it represents something you owe—and the current price indicates what it would cost you to meet the obligation today.

In the section "Short-Term Dollar Assets" (covered on page 426), enter in column 1 the name "Proceeds to be received for sale of [name of item]." Column 2 and 3 carry the same information as in the preceding paragraph. In column 4, enter the price. In the case of a futures contract or a stock sold short, enter the current price. In the case of a forward contract, enter the price fixed in the contract. This is a dollar asset promised to you.

For each position we've discussed, you make two entries. One is an asset, the other a liability in parentheses. By subtracting the figure in parentheses from the other figure, you know the current value of the position. But it's important to enter the position as two separate items. Your liability isn't limited to the margin you deposited. And your potential gain is not reflected by your net equity position; it's measured by the gross value of the investment, because every unit of the investment will be affected fully if the price rises.

Be sure to enter, in the relevant section of the balance sheet, the assets you've deposited with the broker or dealer as margin for your investment position. If you've deposited cash, enter the balance under "Cash" (covered on page 426). If you've deposited securities, enter the items in the appropriate section. In the case of a futures contract or a short sale of stock, your cash balance will have changed as the market has changed, and you should enter the current balance of the margin account. If your position is a forward contract, enter the total you've deposited as margin for this position.[7]

---

[7]If your transaction took place on a U.S. futures exchange (Chicago Mercantile, Comex, Chicago Board of Trade, etc.), you have a futures contract. If your transaction is with a bank or dealer (Swiss Credit Bank, City National Bank, Monex, etc.), you have a forward contract.

Compartments

The balance sheet should include any company, trust, or other entity in which you have an interest. Rather than simply enter the value of your interest in the "Miscellaneous" section, the balance sheet will be more accurate if you treat the entity as a compartment inside your portfolio that holds assets you own (and that may have incurred liabilities on your behalf).

The remaining sections will deal with these specialized compartments.

A Business

This section covers any business you own, in whole or in part, whether or not it's incorporated. It doesn't cover limited partnerships; they're treated separately on the next page.

Everything your business owns and owes should be included on your balance sheet. If you own only part of the business, apply the percentage you own to each asset and liability to determine your share.

In the "Stock Market Investments" section of the balance sheet, enter "Business assets" in column 1. These include equipment and machinery at liquidation value, inventory at liquidation value, patents and copyrights, and goodwill (the difference between what your business could be sold for and the net value of its tangible assets). Total these items on a separate sheet, and multiply the total by your percentage ownership of the business. Enter the result in column 5 of the balance sheet—leaving columns 2 to 4 blank.

In the same way, enter your share of buildings and land, at current market value, in the "Real Estate" section of the balance sheet. And your share of cash and long-term and short-term dollar assets should be entered in those dollar categories.

Your share of the business liabilities should be included in the balance sheet—even if the business is incorporated and you're not personally liable for them—because the liabilities affect what the business is worth to you. Your percentage share of the liabilities should be entered as "Business Liabilities" in the sections for long-term and short-term dollar liabilities. Enter your share of the amount *in parentheses* in column 5, skipping columns 2 to 4.

If you're not personally responsible for the debts, and if the business is so highly leveraged that a depression or other misfortune could push it into bankruptcy (giving practical significance to the limitation of your liability), put an asterisk (*) after the amount of each debt in column 5.

If the business has earned profits for which a significant tax is yet to be paid, estimate your share of the tax bill and enter it *in parentheses* under "Short-term Dollar Liabilities."

Limited Partnerships

This section covers limited partnerships that are formed for investment purposes.

There are no active resale markets for most limited-partnership interests, so you can't get a market quotation. You have to estimate the value by determining your share of the partnership's assets and liabilities.

If the partnership was organized to make short-term trades in investments (such as a commodity fund), simply subtract its liabilities from its assets. Then multiply the result by your percentage share. In the "Miscellaneous" section of the balance sheet, enter the name of the partnership in column 1 and your share of the value in column 5. The kinds of assets and liabilities are unimportant, since they'll change frequently; your investment is in the manager's trading skill.

Even though the partnership changes its investments frequently, your investment is part of the Permanent Portfolio if you don't intend to sell your interest as short-term trends change.

If the partnership operates a business (oil drilling, cattle feeding, equipment leasing, etc.), or if it was formed to hold an asset (such as an apartment house), you'll need to obtain a copy of its balance sheet and determine your percentage share of the assets and liabilities. Enter each one on your balance sheet in the appropriate section.

Enter machinery, inventory, patents, oil wells, etc. as "Business assets" in the "Stock Market Investments" section of the balance sheet. Enter your share of land or buildings in the "Real Estate" category. Enter your share of any cash or long-term or short-term dollar assets in the appropriate dollar sections. In each case, name the item in column 1 and put your share in column 5.

If the partnership has debts, enter your share in the appropriate long-term or short-term dollar liability section *in parentheses*. The debts should be entered even though you, as a limited partner, aren't personally liable for them. However, if you aren't personally liable and if there's so much debt that the partnership couldn't survive a depression, place an asterisk (*) after the amount of the debt in column 5.

The partnership's gross assets and liabilities (rather than just your cash investment) are entered in the balance sheet to reflect the leverage achieved by the partnership's borrowings.

With a real estate partnership, for example, a $10,000 cash investment is not the same as a $50,000 purchase financed with $40,000 in debt. If the value of the property rises 5%, the value of a cash investment rises by 5%; with financing, the value of the investment rises by 25%. And if the property depreciates by 5%, you lose 25% of your leveraged investment.

The leveraged investment gives you a bigger stake in the future of real estate than a cash purchase would. And the mortgage means that you have a bigger stake in the future of the dollar than with a cash purchase.

Controlled Pension Plan

If you control your own pension or profit-sharing plan (either corporate, Keogh, or IRA), enter its investments in the appropriate sections. If there are other participants in the plan, enter only your percentage share of each asset.

Other Employee Benefit Plans

If your employer has established a profit-sharing or other plan that gives you an interest in a pool of investments without promising you a fixed pension, enter your percentage share of the plan's investments in the appropriate sections of the balance sheet.

Trusts

If you've contributed property to a trust, and if the trust supports something you'd pay for if the trust weren't able to (whether a charity, your children, or your own consumption), enter each asset and liability of the trust in the appropriate section of the balance sheet. If someone else has established a trust for your benefit, enter its assets in the same way.

OTHER ITEMS

You may have assets or liabilities that we haven't included. If so, try to determine the categories in which they best fit. If no other category seems right for an investment, enter it under "Miscellaneous."

SUMMARY OF WHERE YOU STAND

The next step is to consolidate these many assets and liabilities into a summary of where you stand.

To begin, fill in any empty space in column 5 by multiplying column 3 by column 4; if the figure in either column 3 or column 4 is in parentheses, the result in column 5 also should appear in parentheses.

Then total the amounts in column 5 for each category; if a number is in parentheses, subtract it. Enter each category total in column 6 on the last line for that category; if it's a negative number (if you owe more than you own), put it in parentheses.

Next, total the numbers in column 6, subtracting any number that's in parentheses. Put the total at the bottom of column 6. This grand total is the net worth of your Permanent Portfolio.

Variable Portfolio Total

Determine the net worth of the Variable Portfolio by adding up its assets and subtracting its liabilities. Compare the net worth of the Variable Portfolio with that of the Permanent Portfolio.

If the Variable Portfolio is too large for comfort, decide how much it should be reduced. Enter that amount in the "Miscellaneous" section of the Permanent Portfolio—calling it "Receivable from the Variable Portfolio." Then increase the total in column 6 for the "Miscellaneous" section, and the grand total for the balance sheet, by the same amount.

This means you'll be selling something from the Variable Portfolio to make cash available to the Permanent Portfolio.

If the Variable Portfolio seems too small, enter the amount by which you want to increase it as a liability (in parentheses) in the "Miscellaneous" section of the Permanent Portfolio's balance sheet—calling it "Payable to the Variable Portfolio." Then reduce the total in column 6 for the "Miscellaneous" section, and the grand total for the balance sheet, by the same amount.

This means you'll be selling something from the Permanent Portfolio to make cash available to the Variable Portfolio.

Permanent Portfolio Breakdown

To see how the Permanent Portfolio holdings are distributed among various investment categories, divide each category total (from column 6) by the portfolio's grand total and multiply the result by 100. This is the percentage of the portfolio that's devoted to each category. Place each percentage in column 7. If the dollar total in column 6 was in parentheses, the percentage figure in column 7 should also be in parentheses.

To check your calculations, total the percentages in column 7—subtracting any figure in parentheses. If the answer isn't 100, you've made an error either in totaling column 6 or 7, or in calculating the percentages.

The results might shock you. An investor who believed he had a small investment in real estate, gold, or stocks may find that he has over 100% of his net worth exposed to the future of that investment. In these cases, the use of financing has unbalanced the portfolio, and the balance sheet probably shows large negative figures for long-term or short-term debt.

It's easy to think of an investment only in terms of the cash you put into it. But the fact that a loan was received for a specific investment doesn't change the loan's impact on your overall portfolio. It is money owed. By buying more of an investment than a cash purchase would have permitted, you're more exposed to a particular market—and equivalently exposed to the future of the dollar by the amount of your loan.

Comparison with Ideal

The next step is to compare your present situation with where you want to be.

Page 441 shows a "Changes" form for comparing the ideal portfolio with your present balance sheet, filled in with hypothetical figures as examples. Every category you listed in either the ideal portfolio or your balance sheet should be entered in column 1.

Any percentage figure shown in the ideal portfolio should be converted to a decimal (25% becomes .25, for example), and multiplied by the total dollar value of the Permanent Portfolio. The result is the dollar amount you want that category to have in the ideal portfolio. Enter the figure in column 2 of the "Changes" form on the line for that category.

Next, transfer each net category figure from column 6 of the balance sheet to column 3 on the appropriate line of the "Changes" form.

Then, for each line on the "Changes" form, compare columns 2 and 3. If column 2 is larger, enter the difference in column 4. If column 3 is larger, enter the difference in column 5.[8]

---

[8]Of any pair of figures in columns 2 and 3, if one is in parentheses, the other is the "larger" figure, no matter what the numbers, and the two numbers should be *added*, not subtracted. If both numbers are in parentheses, the smaller number is "larger"; it should be subtracted from the other number and placed in column 4 or 5. No number in column 4 or 5 of the "Changes" form will be in parentheses.

CHANGES TO BE MADE

(1) Investment Category	(2) Ideal Portfolio	(3) Present Portfolio	(4) To be Bought	(5) To be Sold
Gold	$ 95,888	$ 29,200	$ 66,688	$
Silver bullion	32,876	8,500	24,376	
Silver coins	8,219	18,760		10,541
Foreign currencies	41,095	18,891	22,204	
Stock market investments	27,397	75,112		47,715
Real estate & collectibles	54,793	131,500		76,707
Short-term dollar items[1]	41,095	10,437	30,658	
Long-term dollar items	(27,397)	(42,850)	15,453	
Miscellaneous	0	24,416		24,416
Totals:	$273,966	$273,966	$159,379	$159,379

All entries are hypothetical examples.
Items in parentheses are negative amounts.
[1]Includes cash.

When you're finished, column 4 will show the amounts you must buy, and column 5 the amounts you must sell, to achieve the ideal portfolio. To check your calculations, total column 4 and total column 5. If your arithmetic has been correct, the two totals will be the same.

You now know what changes are needed to reach the ideal you imagined in the previous chapter. At first glance, you may seem to be far away from your goal—but don't despair. There are ways to get there. And we won't ask you to sell three rooms of your house just because you have too much real estate.

The remaining chapters in this part will discuss how to get from where you are to where you want to be.

29

GETTING FROM HERE TO THERE

GETTING FROM WHERE YOU ARE NOW TO WHERE YOU WANT TO be will involve some easy decisions and, for many investors, some hard ones.

Rather than let the hard ones intimidate you, start with what's easy. If you reach a point beyond which you can't go, you'll at least be that much closer to your ideal. And most likely, once you're in motion—taking care of the easy matters —the hard ones won't seem as difficult as they did before.

This chapter discusses ways to identify the easy decisions and to handle the hard ones—planning around' immovable objects, controlling capital-gain taxes, and handling other matters involved in making the transition to the ideal portfolio.

SELLING LOSERS

Up to now, we've been dealing only with generalities— the dollar amounts and percentages devoted to categories of investments. But to reduce the excess in any category, you'll have to choose specific items to sell.

All other things being equal, you should sell the items that will attract the smallest tax. Start with the big losers, followed by the smaller losers. If still more must be sold, sell the winners with the smallest gains. Put off paying taxes on the big winners as long as possible.

In discussing the balance sheet, we suggested treating gains of 30% or less as no gain at all. The purpose of the 30% figure is to separate gains that are small enough to ignore when deciding whether to sell something. Even if you're in the top tax bracket, a profit of 30% will produce a tax of only 6.5% of the proceeds of the sale.[1]

SELL LIST

The "Changes" form tells you how much needs to be sold from each investment category. Now we need to draw up a list of particular items to sell.[2]

Start by scanning column 5 of the "Changes" form. You need to make sales from any investment category with a number in that column. For each such category, look on the balance sheet (or the separate pages on which you grouped investments for the category), and pick out items that will be easy to let go.

They'll be the items that are fully marketable and for which a sale won't mean a large tax. Put these candidates for sale at the top of your "Sell" list. If the easy sales add up to the amount shown for that category in column 5 of the "Changes" form, put a check mark there—indicating that you're finished with that category.

When you've gone through all the categories on the "Changes" form, the "Sell" list will have all the items that both need to be sold and can be sold without hesitation.

If you plan to borrow, because you want to reduce your net dollar holdings and there are no marketable dollar assets to sell, enter the amount of the borrowing on the "Sell" list. Like the investments you're selling, borrowing will make cash available to buy the investments you want. And the borrowing is a sale—the sale of your IOU to the lender.

Now total up everything you've entered so far on the "Sell" list.

---

[1]An item bought for $100 and sold for $130 would incur a maximum capital-gain tax of $8.40, which is 6.5% of the $130 proceeds. The method of figuring the tax liability is shown on page 534.

[2]We wanted to call this *The Book of Lists,* but the title was already taken.

BUY LIST

If the list represents everything covered in column 5 of the "Changes" form, your work is almost done. All that's left is to make the sales and use the proceeds to buy the items you need. Otherwise, the total from the "Sell" list is only your initial budget. In either case, the things you're going to purchase with it go on a "Buy" list.

But before deciding on any purchases, see if anything listed on the "Sell" list triggers the repayment of a debt—such as a mortgage or a margin loan against an investment being sold. If there's a loan to be repaid, enter "Repay loan on [name of item]" and the amount at the top of the "Buy" list. This part of the sale proceeds will be spent buying back your IOU.

You may want to repay other debts, too, if the "Changes" form calls for you to increase your net dollar holdings. The decision to do so, rather than use the funds to buy dollar assets, depends primarily on interest rates. If the interest rate on a debt is greater, after taxes, than the after-tax rate you can earn on a secure dollar investment, you're better off repaying the debt—provided there are no prepayment penalties.

If your "Sell" list includes an asset you'll be selling on an installment contract, include the amount of the unpaid balance on the "Buy" list. In effect, you'll be using part of the sale proceeds to buy someone's IOU.

Next, go through the "Changes" form to find the categories that have figures in column 4—indicating that purchases are necessary. You don't need to name specific things to buy yet, but you do have to decide which categories will get the money that's being made available by the easy sales.

On your first run through column 4, pick out the most pressing needs—the categories that cause you to feel vulnerable because they're undersized. For example, you might feel you need to get some Treasury bills right away (even though it might be a month or two before you can set up a method for sheltering their income). Or it may be a purchase of gold that's most urgent.

When you've entered the most pressing items on the

"Buy" list, total the amounts on the list so far. If the total is less than that for the "Sell" list, enter more purchases from categories specified in column 4 of the "Changes" form.

If the total on the "Buy" list is already greater than the total on the "Sell" list, you'll either have to wait on purchases that seem urgent or speed up the sales that are more difficult to make.

HARD CHOICES

If the "Sell" list doesn't include everything listed in column 5 of the "Changes" form, it's time to look at what's holding you back. Examine the investment categories that require sales, but for which you haven't entered enough items on the "Sell" list.

There's a reason you consider these items difficult to sell, and it will help to identify the reason. Usually, it's one of four —poor marketability, potential liability for a large capital-gain tax, a reluctance to take a loss, or a reluctance to sell a single large investment that can't be split up for a partial sale. We'll discuss each of these possibilities.

Poor Marketability

Poor marketability simply means that the asset can't be sold quickly and easily, and possibly that a sale would involve large selling costs.

Although selling an illiquid asset is never much fun, it has to be sold—now or sometime in the future. No investment is meant to be kept forever; you buy only to sell later. So any difficulty involved in selling now will apply as well to a future sale.

Because this item puts you over the budget you allocated for its category in the ideal portfolio, you need to get rid of it. And if poor marketability is a problem now, it will be an urgent and more difficult problem if you're ever forced to sell. It may be wiser to sell now, when you can do so without pressure.

You might object that you can't unload a non-marketable asset—because it isn't marketable. But marketability is a matter of degree. Nothing in your portfolio is absolutely non-marketable. Someone, somewhere, will pay you some price for anything you own.

You may be afraid that you won't get a "fair" price. But the only fair price is what the market will pay—not what *you* paid, not what you'd hoped to get, and not what the item "should" be worth by some abstract standard. There's no guarantee that it will ever be worth what you'd like. And if you get rid of it now, you won't have to worry about its marketability any more.

While our general advice is to sell anything you haven't chosen for the ideal portfolio, there are a few cases in which foot-dragging is understandable. These involve assets that produce income far out of proportion to what they can be sold for. They include such things as a patent, a business that few people understand, or a mortgage you're sure the borrower will repay but which a potential buyer would evaluate as very risky. In some cases, such an asset may even produce a yearly income equal to its market value.

If owning such an asset keeps your portfolio out of balance by only a few percentage points, there's no reason not to keep it. But if owning the asset throws your portfolio far out of balance, you need to do something about it. One alternative is to acquire another investment that offsets it. We'll discuss that possibility on page 451.

If you have a number of such assets, another alternative is to sell some of them—even if you have to take a poor price—and keep the others. What you get for some of them will help finance the purchase of something you need more. Or you may be able to sell a partial interest in a single large asset that's overwhelming your portfolio.

Capital Gains

A second reason for reluctance to sell an asset is that doing so will attract large capital-gain taxes.

Like the investments with poor marketability, the big gainers will have to be sold someday—and we trust you aren't waiting until you can avoid the tax by selling them at a loss.

If you have capital losses to offset the gains, the tax bill on the sales will be smaller—and there may not be any tax at all. There are three possible sources of such losses.

1. *Previous losses:* You may have capital losses carried forward from previous years. If so, they can offset gains from the items to be sold.

2. *Current losses:* Any losing investments you sell now as part of the transition will help to reduce the tax liability on the winners. Being aware of this might make it easier for you to sell losing investments despite their illiquidity.

3. *Tax switches:* There might be losing investments you intend to keep. If so, you may be able to sell them and rebuy similar assets that serve the same purpose. You'll register a capital loss for tax purposes without changing the character of your portfolio. It's particularly easy to sell one company's stock and replace it with the stock of a similar company, or to replace one gold coin with another. It may not be so easy to do with other kinds of assets.[3]

If you still have a net gain after offsetting all the losses, find out how large the tax will be—so you'll know how large the hurdle is. Check the tax table on page 535, find your tax rate, multiply it by the net capital gain (after deducting any losses you'll have), and multiply the result by 40%. Then you'll know how many dollars you'll have to pay in taxes to get rid of the excess assets.

To put the potential tax liability in perspective, divide the amount of the tax by the value of all the investments to be sold. This will show you the size of the tax bill as a fraction of the sale proceeds—the per-dollar tax cost of getting rid of what you don't want.

Remember that the tax will have to be paid eventually. We've said that tax delay is valuable—but only if the money you hold back from the government is used in a way that benefits you. It makes no more sense to hold on to an un-

---

[3]Under the "wash sale" rules of the tax code, you can't take a tax loss on a stock if you rebuy the same stock within 30 days after the sale. But you can buy the stock of any other company. The wash sale rules apply only to securities; there's no problem when switching commodities or currencies.

wanted investment to avoid taxes than it would to accept an interest-free loan to buy an investment you don't want.

Reluctance to Take a Loss

The third reason that may make it hard to sell an asset is that it's in a loss position, and you want to recoup what you paid before you get rid of it.

Whatever its psychological power, this reason has no merit. If you let it influence you, you'll probably never have the ideal portfolio.

The fear of "taking a loss" is misguided. If the price today is lower than the price you paid, you *already* have a loss. Keeping the investment won't make the loss less real. If the investment depreciates further, you'll have a larger loss.

Successful investors are not characterized by an absence of losses on their records—but by the ability to take a loss when they see that an investment shouldn't be kept.

An investment is either right or wrong for you. The rightness isn't determined by the fact that you already own it or by what you paid for it. That's one reason we asked you to picture your net worth as a pile of cash (rather than as specific investments)—to help isolate you from past decisions that should be disregarded in making your plans now.

That pile of cash is yours to invest in any way you choose. Use it to acquire the investments you think will contribute most to your well-being—the ones you included in the idea portfolio.[4]

Single Property

A fourth reason you might find it difficult to make the sales called for by the ideal portfolio is the presence of a single property—usually real estate—that can't be split up for sale.

---

[4]If you've decided never to sell a losing investment unless it recovers, and never to sell a successful investment because of the tax bill, you've constructed a trap for yourself from which there's little chance of escape.

The investment makes your real estate budget far larger than you want it to be, but you're reluctant to sell the property because its prospects seem so good.

You may not realize fully how vulnerable this situation makes you. If you have a single property that dominates and unbalances your portfolio, you shouldn't hedge against it; you should sell it.

Holding one large investment of this kind not only keeps you from the ideal portfolio, it's foolhardy by almost any standard of portfolio planning.

A single investment that amounts to two or three times your net worth isn't really an investment as we normally use the word; it's a business. Unless you're in that business, it's foolish to be so exposed. People who have several times their net worth tied up in one position don't work at another job and play with the investment in their spare time; they spend most of their working hours managing it.

Even if you could justify holding several times your net worth in one type of investment, it shouldn't all be in one property—causing your future to depend on the success of a single building. You're vulnerable not only to a deflation, but to a change in the property values of the neighborhood, a new urban renewal project, an earthquake (or just the discovery of an earthquake fault), or any of a hundred other common events that could destroy you financially almost overnight.

If you're determined to hold a large position in one investment category, at least spread the investment among several items. We don't presume to know how everyone should invest his money, but we can't think of any reason that justifies an investor staking his future on a single asset.[5]

MORE SALES & PURCHASES

With the difficult choices, you'll have to weigh the costs of selling against the benefits of selling.

The costs are the transaction costs of unloading a poorly marketable asset, the tax cost of realizing capital gains, the

---

[5]Although we've used real estate as the example, the principle applies to a single large asset in any investment category.

psychological cost of accepting losses, or the possible loss of opportunity when selling a single, dominating investment.

The benefits are profit and safety. By selling, you can generate the cash to buy the investments you think will do best during the coming decade and the investments needed to balance your portfolio.

Add to the "Sell" list any additional items you've decided to let go. Add up their value. Then refer to column 4 of the "Changes" form to pick out more investments you can buy with the proceeds from the sales.

Eventually, either (1) you'll have decided to sell everything that doesn't fit into the ideal portfolio and buy what you want; or (2) you'll have gone as far as you feel you can, but with the portfolio still out of balance.

If you've made it all the way to the ideal portfolio, congratulations. If you haven't, you need to consider how to handle the imbalances that remain.

OUT OF BALANCE

The most common problems that throw a portfolio out of balance are too much real estate, too much money tied up in a business, and too many illiquid dollar assets.

In each of these cases, too much of one thing will mean that you have too little of others—too little of the investments you wanted in the ideal portfolio. The answer is to use the marketable portion of the portfolio in the way that best offsets the imbalance.

We'll look at each of the three common problems.

Too Much Real Estate

If the value of your home alone is greater than your net worth, a radical solution would be to sell the house and rent. Most people won't want to do this—because they're especially comfortable where they are now, or because the income-tax deductions for interest and property taxes make it cheaper to own than to rent, or simply because they get a stomachache whenever they see a moving van.

The problem also may arise with leveraged real estate

451

partnerships that can't be liquidated. Or perhaps we've made you uneasy about real estate without persuading you to sell.

Whatever the reason for being stuck with too much real estate, you can lessen the risk somewhat by handling the other investments properly.

With too much real estate, you're overprepared for polite inflation—inflation that rises slowly enough to avoid general disorder. And you're underprepared for other possibilities, probably badly underprepared for deflation. Consequently, you should avoid any additional investment that's aimed toward polite inflation.

The closest category is collectibles; if you own too much real estate, don't make matters worse by investing in art and antiques. And keep investments in silver and foreign currencies to a minimum; they, too, are exposed to a deflation. Stock market investments should be relatively small; you should hold only high-leverage hedges like warrants and dual-purpose funds.[6]

Gold, on the other hand, will respond profitably to the kind of chaos that would endanger real estate investments—whether the disorder comes from inflation or any other source. If you have too much real estate, gold is the only investment (of those that respond positively to inflation) that should be emphasized in the portfolio.

The put option program described in Chapter 13 might be useful. Although we discussed it as a hedge against business problems, it would reduce (but not eliminate) the risk caused by overinvestment in real estate. The annual contribution to the put program should equal 1% of your excess real estate holdings.

The put option program will pay off if your real estate holdings are hurt by a deflation, but understand that both the put options and real estate would lose in a soft landing.

If the gross value of your real estate exceeds your net worth, you're already too deeply in debt. So try to get rid of all other debts, and don't borrow for any new investment purpose.

In summary, if you're overinvested in real estate and

---

[6]Explained on pages 187–193.

don't want to sell what you have, give extra emphasis in your portfolio to gold and dollars. Eliminate collectibles and avoid new debts. Keep stock market, silver, and foreign currency investments to a minimum and, of course, don't buy any more real estate.

Too Much Business Equity

Another problem is caused by having too much tied up in your own business, in tax shelters that operate businesses, or in stocks you can't sell.

The put option program described in Chapter 13 was designed for this problem and can reduce your risk considerably. It should work especially well if you can acquire puts against stocks in the industries in which your business is involved. But remember that no hedge can do as thorough a job of reducing risk as simply getting rid of the excess investments that create the risk.

With the money available for other investments, stay away from real estate, silver, and Swiss francs, but purchase the full budget—or more—for gold.

Keep debts to a minimum, because they would be heavy burdens during the same deflationary conditions that would hurt your business. Have a small position in long-term Treasury bonds (but not corporate bonds), since the T-bonds would profit during a deflation. Hold a good supply of safe short-term dollar assets and cash—to offset the liquidity missing in your business position.

Don't buy any stocks, since you're already invested in this direction.

If you're tempted to expand your business, bear in mind that you'll be depending on more than just your own skill as a businessman; you'll be depending on the health of the economy.

Too Many Dollars

A different type of problem is created by having too many dollars.

The problem may be caused by pension claims or other

dollars owed to you—assets that can't be sold or collected early. If so, borrowing can reduce your net position in dollars. We discussed this approach on pages 285–286.

If you borrow, a long-term loan with a fixed interest rate will do the most to balance your dollar position. With too many dollars, you'll be hurt by further inflation, while a fixed-interest debt will be valuable during rising inflation and interest rates.

However, you shouldn't borrow if the after-tax interest cost is too large to make the transaction worthwhile. The lowest cost fixed-rate loan readily available is a mortgage secured by real estate.

The lowest cost floating-rate loan is a margin loan—using gold, silver, or stocks as collateral. If you decide to take a margin loan, don't borrow more than one third of the value of the investment collateral—to lessen the chance of a margin call.

Before you borrow, give careful thought to just how much the dollar assets you hold are really worth. If they should default, the debts you incur now to offset them won't disappear with them. Review the discussion on page 397 questioning the symmetry of dollar assets and liabilities.

If your too-many-dollars situation seems desperate, using gold options as a hedge (described on page 115) may be a partial solution.

Altering the Buy List

If your portfolio is out of balance because of too much real estate, too much business equity, too many dollars, or too much of anything else that can't be sold, review the ideal portfolio and the "Buy" list—to see whether you should change the shopping list and acquire items that will help to offset the imbalance.

IDENTIFICATION FOR TAX PURPOSES

We've said you should sell losers first—in order to minimize your tax bill. To make sure you get the tax effect you want, you have to handle the sale carefully when you sell only part of a holding—such as only some of the shares of stock of one company or only some of one kind of gold coin you own.

One ounce of gold bullion is just like every other ounce; one Krugerrand is like every other; and one share of General Motors stock is no different (except for the serial number on the certificate) from any other GM share. In these cases, there are tax rules governing partial sales.

For example, suppose you're going to sell Krugerrands. If you bought all the coins at one time and you sell some of the coins now, the matter is simple. All the coins have the same purchase price, so the tax will be the same no matter which of the coins are sold.

But suppose you bought 50 coins at a price of $300 and 50 coins on another occasion at $400. If you want to sell 30 coins now, your tax bill will be lower if you sell from the coins bought at $400. If the two purchases were made and stored at different places (such as two banks or dealers), sell the coins from the $400 supply. The cost (the price you paid) will be obvious for tax purposes.

If the same dealer holds coins that were purchased at two different prices, the IRS will apply the "first in, first out" rule unless you handle the sale carefully. The rule assumes that the first coins you sell are the first coins you bought—and the first price paid will be the purchase price that determines the tax gain.

However, you can avoid the "first in, first out" rule by observing a simple formality. Specify in writing to the dealer that he's to sell the coins that were purchased on a given date at a given price. Ask the dealer to give you written confirmation that the coins sold were the coins originally purchased on the date and at the price you specified. You can then use the higher purchase price as the basis for computing the capital gain.

The same rules and procedures apply for stocks and bonds held on account with a broker. In addition, stock and bond certificates have serial numbers. So if the certificates are in your possession, you can designate which item is being sold by the particular certificate you sign over to the broker to complete the sale.

These tax rules apply to multiple holdings of any investment—bonds, coins, commodities, shares of stock—where the value of one item is the same as that of the others. It does not apply between shares of stock of two different companies, bonds of different companies or maturities, or different types of coins.

GETTING THERE

We hope this chapter has made the task of getting to the ideal portfolio seem a little less intimidating. Whether or not it has, you'll probably find the job to be less formidable once you start doing the easy things.

Sell the easy items first—the losing, most marketable investments. Then take what you can get for the unmarketable investments, and pay whatever tax is required to sell the winning investments that have grown too large for your portfolio. And if the portfolio is still out of balance, find hedges that will help to offset your vulnerability.

The next two chapters will discuss some unfinished business—how to allot investments to a pension plan or other compartment in your portfolio, arranging for income from the portfolio, assuring marketability and diversification within categories, and maintaining the portfolio once it's set up.

But you'll be pleased to know that we're through with the difficult parts.

30

WHAT TO HOLD &
WHERE TO HOLD IT

UP TO NOW, OUR PORTFOLIO DECISIONS HAVE BEEN AIMED AT categories of investments—choosing the categories that deserve a greater share of your net worth and those that need to be reduced.

With those decisions behind you, you still need to select the specific items that each category will hold. If you need more stocks, which stocks? If you don't have enough gold, should you add bullion or coins? And you need to decide where to hold each investment—in the U.S., in Switzerland, or elsewhere.

The chapters in Parts Three and Four described the investments available for each category, and include our suggestions for choosing among them. Here we'll offer additional ideas, but of a more generalized nature—ideas about diversification within categories, the importance of holding marketable investments, and safe storage. We'll also suggest ways to make the best use of a tax-deferral plan by allocating the right investments to it.

DIVERSIFICATION

We've said many times that none of us can be sure how the future will unfold. We've stressed the need for enough diversification to provide profit and protection no matter which of the inflation possibilities dominates the 1980s.

This calls for a broad portfolio containing several investment categories that balance each other. But it's just as important to spread the risk *within* each investment category.

The coming decade will be full of surprises. An investment that, viewed abstractly, should profit from what happens may fail to—because someone defaults on a promise or because the government changes the rules. The only way to insure against this is to spread the risk—to diversify your holdings within each investment category so that no single surprise, or even group of surprises, can undo your plans.

We could draw up a long list of surprises that might upset any investment or approach, but the endeavor would be futile. No matter how long the list, we'd fail to anticipate most of what actually is going to occur. It's better simply to accept the idea that you're going to be surprised, and that you need to place a variety of bets on each inflation possibility.

Our advice is simple: Don't take anything for granted—not a promise, not a policy, not a prediction. Nothing can be counted on for certain.

This means spreading your stock market budget among the stocks and warrants of several different companies; and if you buy dual-purpose funds, buy all of them. It means keeping some dollars in Treasury bills and some in two or more money market funds. If practical, it also means having more than one brokerage account, more than one bank account, and so on.

And it means dividing gold holdings between a Swiss bank (or two) and gold coins in your own possession. If you use safe-deposit boxes to keep coins (or other valuables), try to have two, three, or more boxes. And store some coins outside a safe-deposit box, if you find it practical to do so.

Your best defense against surprises is diversification.

MARKETABILITY & SAFETY

As you look at each investment category, pay special attention to marketability.

Having assets that can be sold easily is essential as your portfolio grows—and as *you* grow, develop new insights, and attempt to adapt to changing circumstances. You may change your definition of the ideal portfolio next year or five years from now; you'll be able to act on new judgments only if what you own can be disposed of quickly and without large selling costs.

In addition, the next chapter will explain the need to make small purchases and sales once a year to keep your portfolio in balance—and, if you wish, to draw off money for living expenses. The program is simple and automatic, but you won't be able to use it if you don't have assets that are easy to sell.

For each category, there are investment media that are more marketable than others.

Gold: Most likely all the gold you own is easily marketable. But if most of your gold is in jewelry or in small bars, you don't really have the protection that gold affords, since you can't sell small amounts quickly and privately—even during orderly conditions. At least 75% (if not 100%) of your gold should be either (1) stored with a Swiss bank that will handle orders to sell small amounts of bullion or coins, or (2) held by you in the form of low-premium bullion coins.[1]

Silver: Silver coins should always be under your own control—since they are there primarily as protection against a breakdown in normal market conditions. If you have other silver investments, at least 50% (if not 100%) should be in silver bullion—rather than in medallions, commemorative coins, jewelry, or irregular-size bars (less than 100 ounces). The safest place for the bullion is in a Swiss bank.

Swiss francs: At least one third of your franc investment should be in banknotes or in a current account at a Swiss bank. The rest can be in bonds or a deposit account. The only non-marketable franc investment you're likely to make is a Swiss franc annuity. If you like the privacy and tax deferral an annuity affords, buy one; but put no more into it than the minimum you expect to hold in francs for the next several years.

Stocks & business equity: If everything in this category is tied up in your own business or in investment partnerships, you won't be able to take profits when the economy is in a

---

[1] A list of bullion coins is given on page 112.

boom phase. And if you decide there's an urgent need to reduce your exposure to the economy, you won't be able to do so.

With half or more of this budget in marketable stocks, warrants, or dual-purpose funds, you'll have plenty of room to maneuver. In addition, warrants, dual-purpose funds, and high-leverage stocks allow you to take profits during a stock-market boom, and their leverage reduces your exposure to surprises by allowing you to have only a small amount invested.[2]

To safeguard against the failure of your stockbroker or his custodian, take delivery of certificates for stocks, including dual-purpose funds. But leave warrants with the broker, since a financial crisis most likely would make them totally worthless anyway—while if you keep them yourself, you might allow a valuable warrant to expire unnoticed.

Real estate: By its nature, real estate isn't readily marketable. But you can restrict your holdings to the kinds of properties that are easiest to sell. Generally, middle-class, single-family houses are the most marketable, while specialized commercial or industrial properties are the most illiquid. It will help also to have your budget spread among as many properties as possible—instead of depending on only one.

Collectibles: Rather than nag you further about collectibles, we suggest that you try selling some. We've met many investors who were happy with their purchases, but few who were happy with their sales.

Long-term dollar assets: At least half should be in marketable bonds. Take delivery of the bond certificates or leave them in a Swiss bank—but not with a U.S. bank or broker.

Short-term dollar assets: Safety and marketability are especially important here, since the virtue of these assets—stability of dollar value—is largely wasted if you don't have the freedom to sell whenever you need to tap the value. And the stability is imaginary if there's a substantial risk of a default occurring during a credit crisis or a deflation.

---

[2]This is discussed on page 187–188.

Rely on intermediaries as little as possible. Take physical delivery of Treasury notes, and have at least a small amount in bearer form. If practical, buy Treasury bills at the weekly auction, rather than through a bank or broker.

If you do hold non-marketable, short-term dollar assets, such as second mortgages, try to stagger the maturities so there's always one about to fall due.

Cash: Because a single day without access to spendable cash could result in great hardship and loss, make an effort to design a cash reserve that will resist any shock. You might consider the following approach.

1. Hold enough currency, stored outside of a bank, to cover one month's personal expenses.

2. Divide most of the remaining cash between two money market funds that invest primarily in U.S. government securities.

3. Keep two checking accounts (at separate banks).

For bookkeeping convenience, route all your transactions through one of the checking accounts and one of the money market funds. Let the second account and the second fund lie dormant until they are needed.

USING A PENSION PLAN EFFECTIVELY

If you control your own pension plan, you need to decide which investments it should house.

The general rule is that it should hold the investments that produce the most current income—which usually means interest-earning dollar assets.

There's no need at all for the pension plan's investments to be balanced or diversified. Diversification matters only for the overall portfolio—everything you own. Once you've decided on the composition of the overall portfolio, only tax considerations should influence which investments go into the pension plan.

It's a mistake to use a pension plan to hold gold, silver, currencies, low-dividend stocks, or anything else that's purchased primarily for long-term appreciation. When the plan is liquidated, the money you receive will be taxed as ordinary income, even if the plan earned the money as capital gains. So putting appreciating assets into a pension plan will turn capital gains into ordinary income—a kind of reverse alchemy.[3]

The pension plan is most useful as a place to hold interest-earning dollars. If the plan is worth more than the amount you want to hold in dollars, you can offset the excess amount by borrowing an equivalent amount for your personal account, using the proceeds to buy the investments you want. These investments will be taxed only as capital gains; at the same time, you'll have personal tax deductions for interest, and the pension plan will earn tax-sheltered interest. And your overall portfolio still will be balanced in the way you choose.

If you have a corporate pension plan, you can borrow directly from the plan. Otherwise, you must borrow elsewhere to offset the effects of the plan's dollar assets on your portfolio.

Gold & Pension Plans

The desire for privacy presents a special reason to keep gold out of a pension plan. Because gold is the security of last resort, it's the asset you least want anyone to know about.

Under the present rules, very little needs to be reported about a pension plan's investments. But the plans are a creature of the law—which could be changed at any time to require you to report what the plan owns.

In the past year or so, a number of investment companies have offered Keogh plans and IRAs that invest in gold, silver, and rare coins. Whatever the merit of the investments, they don't belong in a pension plan.

Annuities & Pension Plans

Many pension plans hold annuities; this, too, is a mistake. The attraction of an annuity is its ability to defer taxes

---

[3]However, a pension plan is a good place to hold Variable Portfolio investments on which you're hoping for *short*-term capital gains.

on interest income. But a pension plan can do this on its own, without using an annuity. And there are interest-earning investments the pension plan can buy, such as Treasury bills, that are safer and pay a higher interest rate than an annuity.

If you have a deferred annuity in your pension plan, cash it in and invest the proceeds in Treasury bills. Even after paying any liquidation cost that may be charged, you'll be ahead with Treasury bills.

A deferred annuity should be considered only if you don't have a pension plan or other way to defer taxes on as many dollars as you want to hold.

OTHER COMPARTMENTS

The pension plan is just one example of a portfolio compartment; your portfolio may have others. In assigning investments to compartments, keep three principles in mind:

1. No compartment, by itself, needs investment balance or diversification.

2. Investments that produce the most current income should go into the compartments that are subject to the lowest tax rates (a pension plan, for example, has a tax rate of zero).

3. You can alter the present allocation of investments to various compartments without modifying your overall portfolio, since the investment sold by one compartment can be bought by another.

Here is a list of the compartments your portfolio might have—starting with the compartments that are subject to the lowest tax rates on current income.

Compartment Order

1. Tax haven corporation or trust.
2. Pension plan, defined contribution.
3. Pension plan, defined benefit.
4. Children's investment account (if the money is to be used to buy things you would provide anyway).
5. Clifford trust.

6. Personal corporation (if there are no problems with the rules regarding personal holding companies and accumulated earnings).

7. Personal holdings.

Next is a list of investments your portfolio might have—ranked in order of their propensity to produce taxable income:

Investment Income Order

1. Treasury securities and other interest-producing assets.

2. High-dividend stocks. (However, a personal corporation may be the ideal place to hold these stocks, because of the corporate dividends-received deduction; see page 33).

3. Low-dividend stocks and interest-earning holdings of low-inflation currencies.

4. Deferred annuities, dual-purpose funds, no-dividend stocks—anything that produces no current income but someday might.

5. Silver, gold, foreign currency holdings that earn no interest, warrants—anything that produces no current income and never will.

6. Tax-shelter investments, including highly mortgaged real estate. These produce negative taxable income; they reduce taxes, rather than add to them.

From the Compartment Order, find the highest-ranked compartment you have. Keep in that compartment the investments you own that are ranked highest on the Investment Income Order. When you've filled the first compartment you have, go to the next highest compartment you have, and so on down the list—adding the remaining investments that are highest on the Investment Income Order. Finally, you'll have some investments left that will be part of your personal holdings.

Don't waste the power of a tax-deferral compartment by putting the wrong investments in it. There may be an easy, no-risk arrangement of your holdings that will provide dramatic tax savings.

464

Adjusting Compartments

If your investments are now in the wrong compartments, you can rearrange them.

An investment in the wrong compartment should be sold by that compartment and purchased by the compartment that should be holding it. The composition of your overall portfolio need not be affected; you're simply moving assets from one pocket to another.

For example, suppose you now have $20,000 worth of gold in a pension plan and $20,000 in Treasury bills that you hold personally—and that these amounts are in keeping with the ideal portfolio. Have the pension plan sell the gold and buy T-bills with the proceeds. At the same time, sell the T-bills from your personal account and buy gold with the proceeds.

The gold sale won't attract any taxes—since the pension plan is making the sale. In the years that follow, the pension plan can accumulate the interest on the T-bills without yearly taxes. And if the gold you hold appreciates, it will produce a capital gain—not ordinary income—only when you sell it.

You can make similar adjustments in your holdings for any combination of investments that are currently in the wrong place.

In some cases, a compartment will have to sell an investment on the open market while another compartment is buying the same thing. In other cases, one compartment may be able to trade directly with another.

HOLDING INVESTMENTS

Through diversification, marketability, and proper choice of compartments, your portfolio can be safe, profitable, and relatively immune to surprises—all while you keep your tax bill under control.

Lastly, we need a way to keep the portfolio in balance through the years; and if you live off your investments, you'll need a way of producing spending money. These are the subjects of the next chapter.

31

PORTFOLIO HOUSEKEEPING

AFTER YOU'VE CHOSEN THE IDEAL PORTFOLIO, PICKED OUT THE specific investments for it, assigned each investment to the right compartment, and made the necessary purchases and sales, the portfolio should take care of itself.

Until the day you believe that the portfolio's basic plan should be changed (which might not be for many years), no further decisions are required. And you don't even need to look at the portfolio more than once a year.

The once-a-year look is to take care of one, or maybe two, housekeeping details—preserving the balance you chose for the portfolio and, if desired, drawing spendable cash from it. These two details are the subject of this chapter.

ANNUAL ADJUSTMENTS

As soon as you have your portfolio in balance, the investment markets will begin to undo your work. Investment prices change daily—and as they do, the shape of your portfolio will change.

For a simple example, suppose the price of gold rises by 30% in 1982, while the prices of your other investments remain about the same. Because of its increased value, the gold you own will be a larger percentage of your new net worth than what you chose for the ideal portfolio. And the other investment categories will now represent smaller percentages of your net worth than you chose.

Such disturbances are inevitable. But there were reasons

for choosing the percentages you did, and the reasons won't change just because the prices have changed.

At least once each year, update your balance sheet to determine your new net worth. Sell a portion of any investment that has come to represent a greater percentage of the portfolio than you originally chose for it. With the proceeds of the sales, buy investments whose share of the portfolio has shrunk.

An example of this procedure appears on page 469.

Notice that these purchases and sales involve no investment judgment on your part. They are automatic. You simply sell and buy whatever is needed to restore the original percentages.

By following this policy, you will—to a certain extent—be practicing the secret art of buying low and selling high. You'll be selling portions of investments that have appreciated—taking profits—and adding to other investments after they've dropped in price.[1]

Restoring the investment percentages would be necessary in any era. But it will be especially profitable if the markets are as volatile during the next decade as we expect them to be. Prices of some investments will rise dramatically one year, only to drop dramatically the next year. By making the annual adjustment, you'll collect large profits and buy attractive bargains. Thus the market turmoil that will be a source of worry to other investors can work to your advantage—without your having to make short-term investment judgments.

Real Estate Adjustments

Since you can't break a real estate investment into small pieces, you won't be able to adjust your holdings to the precise amount in the ideal portfolio each year.

If the discrepancy between the ideal and the actual holdings (as a percentage of your net worth) is no more than

---

[1]Although it's not likely to happen with a balanced portfolio, if all your investments depreciated (or appreciated) in the same year, you'd still need to make adjustments—because all the investments wouldn't depreciate (or appreciate) by the same amount.

ANNUAL PORTFOLIO ADJUSTMENT
(Hypothetical Example)

	(1)	(2) Beginning Portfolio Value in $	(3) Price	(4) Price	(5) One Year Later Value in $	(6) %	(7) Ideal in $	(8) Need to Buy	(9) Need to Sell
Item									
Gold	30%	$ 30,000	$ 500/oz.	$ 670	$ 40,200	36.4%	$ 33,166	$	$7,034
Silver coins	1%	1,000	13,000/bag	14,500	1,115	1.0%	1,106		9
Swiss francs	10%	10,000	.6100/fr.	.5625	9,221	8.3%	11,055	1,834	
Stocks[1]	10%	10,000	7.25/sh.	6.90	9,517	8.6%	11,055	1,538	
Real estate[2]	25%	25,000	25,000	27,000	27,000	24.4%	27,638	638	
Short-term dollars[3]	19%	19,000	1.00	1.00	19,000	17.2%	21,005	2,005	
Long-term dollars	5%	5,000	.80	.72	4,500	4.1%	5,528	1,028	
Totals:	100%	$100,000	—	—	$110,553	100.0%	$110,553	$7,043	$7,043

Column 1: The percentage of the portfolio devoted to each investment, as defined by the ideal portfolio.

Column 2: The dollar amount allotted to each investment when a $100,000 portfolio is established—as required by the percentage shown in column 1.

Column 3: The price of the investment at the time the portfolio is established.

Column 4: The price of the investment at the end of the first year.

Column 5: The value of the investment at the end of the first year.

Column 6: The investment's new value as a percentage of the new value of the total portfolio.

Column 7: The dollar amount that *should* be devoted now to each investment in order to restore the original percentages (column 1).

Columns 8 & 9: Purchases and sales needed to restore the original percentages (column 7 minus column 5).

All figures (including the ideal portfolio) are hypothetical, and are shown only to illustrate the concept of making annual adjustments. Figures may not agree because of rounding.

[1]The stock-market budget is assumed to be invested wholly in one dual-purpose investment fund for simplicity.

[2]Includes collectibles.

[3]Includes cash.

10% or so, don't try to adjust it. Instead, distribute the difference among holdings of gold (¼), Swiss francs (½), and Treasury bills (¼).

For example, if your real estate holdings fall short of the ideal allocation by 8%, you would add 2% to your budget for gold, 4% to Swiss francs, and 2% to Treasury bills. Or if your actual real estate holdings exceed the ideal by 8%, you would make subtractions from those categories.

If you don't hold all three of these investments, you may prefer to distribute the discrepancy evenly among all other investments in your portfolio (although this may change the portfolio's balance).

If the real estate holdings differ drastically from the percentage in the ideal portfolio (by 10% of your net worth or more), purchases or sales will be necessary—or hedging of the sort described on page 451 will be required.

Frequency of Adjustment

We suggest that the adjustment be made once a year, but it can be made more frequently. The choice depends largely on how much of a chore you find it to be. The choice depends also on the size of your portfolio; if its value is no more than, say, $50,000, it won't be practical to make changes involving only 1% or so.

If you make the adjustment once a year, we suggest you make the calculations in December. Then you can choose whether to make the sales and purchases in December or January—choosing the tax year that's better for the gains or losses.[2]

No matter how often you choose to make the periodic adjustment, there may be occasions when it would be valuable to make it early. Dramatic moves in gold, silver, and stock prices can occur within a period of a few months. Between January and March 1980, for example, the price of gold rose by 67% and then dropped by 45%.

---

[2]If your taxable year isn't the calendar year, make the calculations in the last month of the taxable year.

Such moves can throw your portfolio far out of balance. If you're aware that one of your investments has had a large price move, it would be valuable to readjust the portfolio ahead of schedule. A rule of thumb would be to adjust all investments whenever one investment has risen or fallen by 30% since the last adjustment.

These special adjustments will reduce your risk and reinforce the practice of buying low and selling high—thus making the portfolio safer and more profitable. But you don't need to feel under pressure to make the adjustments more often than once a year if you'd prefer to ignore your investments entirely for 364 days at a time.

When making adjustments, review the comments on pages 454–456 regarding the identification of assets for tax purposes. The rules explained there may help to lessen capital-gain taxes—and to assure that you take a *long*-term (rather than short-term) gain.

CASH FLOW

On pages 402–404, we pointed out that you don't need interest and dividends to provide cash for living expenses. So long as some of your investments are liquid, you can generate cash just by selling a small portion of your holdings each year.

This is another reason for making sure that you have plenty of marketable investments, and that they're spread among many small units—such as many gold coins rather than one bar of gold bullion.

The easiest way to meet your need for spending money is to allow a sufficient budget for the cash category of the ideal portfolio—an amount equal to at least one year's net expenditures (what you spend in a year minus the interest, dividends, and salary you receive). During the year, draw down the cash (probably from a money market fund) as you need it. At the end of the year, replenish the cash fund as part of the annual portfolio readjustment.

However, you may prefer not to leave the living expenses sitting in cash throughout the year. If so, you can make small sales every three months (or any other period you choose), generating the cash you need for the following three months. If you do this, spread the sales over several investment categories—selling some gold, some stock investments, etc.—or take it all from an investment that has appreciated by a large amount since the last sales.

There will be times when the overall portfolio hasn't appreciated since the last sale by as much as you're going to sell now. But there will be other times when you'll be withdrawing much less than the appreciation. To keep the capital intact, the portfolio needs only to appreciate over the years by the *average* amount you withdraw.

When you sell portions of investments that have appreciated, you'll incur a tax liability. However, after the investments have been held for one year, the profits will be long-term capital gains. And some part of what you sell will be a return of capital and won't be taxed at all.

Follow the guidelines given on pages 454–456 to achieve the lowest tax bill whenever you sell.

HOUSEKEEPING

Once you've arranged the ideal portfolio, almost everything flows automatically. Other than making the annual adjustment, there's little for you to do. You don't have to watch the markets, there's no need for stop-losses, you don't have to stay on top of prices.

Your investment work is done, and you can turn your attention to areas of your life that interest you more.

32

WHERE TO GO
FOR HELP

THERE'S NO SHORTAGE OF PEOPLE OFFERING TO HELP YOU
with your investments. You name it—and there's sure to be
someone willing to buy it, sell it, find it, recommend it, or
write about it.

The services that the investment industry offers can make
the job of arranging your portfolio much easier. But you'll
need to apply a measure of skepticism in evaluating the help
you're offered. We don't mean you should disbelieve everything you hear—only that you'll have fewer disappointments
if you apply common sense and dismiss any proposal that
violates your standards of plausibility.

Is it really possible that a broker will sell you something
without commission? Or that an investment is *sure* to appreciate by 40% per year? Or that an advisor has called "all
the turns"? Or that some simple legal formality can relieve
you of all taxes? Or that someone will lend you money at an
interest rate below what he can get on Treasury bills? Or
that someone is in the investment business only to save his
customers or (in the case of the really big thinkers) only to
save the nation?

If you approach them properly, the services of the
investment industry, including financial books and newsletters,
can save you a lot of time finding the answers and investments
you want. But if you ignore the fact that the people who
provide the services have their own objectives, you may find
yourself paying for disservices.

In this chapter, we list a few dealers, publications, and

other sources we've found to be helpful. We have no way of knowing what their policies will be next year or how you'll react to what they provide or the way they provide it. We list them only in the hope of saving you some time. Except for the sources in which our names are mentioned, we have no financial interest in any of the companies other than, in a few cases, as customers.

We'll list coin dealers, newsletters, tax planning services, investment advisors, services that can help you open and maintain a Swiss bank account, sources of annuities, and other places to find help and investment and economic data.

Since the focus of this book is the Permanent Portfolio and not short-term investment decisions, we've left out many worthwhile sources that are geared to short-term trading.

COIN DEALERS

There are coin dealers in most U.S. cities. You can usually locate them under "Coins" in the Yellow Pages. The four companies listed here buy and sell gold coins and silver coins nationwide by telephone and mail. Except for Investment Rarities, they also sell over the counter.

Monex International, Ltd.
4910 Birch St.
Newport Beach, CA 92660
(800) 854-3361
(714) 752-1400

Numisco Inc.
175 W. Jackson Blvd.
Chicago, IL 60604
(800) 621-5272
(312) 922-3465

Investment Rarities
One Appletree Square
Minneapolis, MN 55420
(800) 328-1860
(612) 853-0700

Deak-Perera Group
29 Broadway
New York, NY 10006
(212) 635-0515

The Deak-Perera Group also sells foreign banknotes (cash). The company has offices in many American cities; a

474

list can be obtained from the head office or from the currency exchange counters Deak operates in many U.S. airports.

INVESTMENT NEWSLETTERS

There's no shortage of newsletters, and every one has its admirers and its detractors. Although each of the authors receives a number of helpful publications, we'll confine our listings to those that might augment the material in this book.

Harry Browne's Special Reports

Harry Browne writes most of the newsletter, and Terry Coxon has been a consultant and occasional writer since its inception. The newsletter provides short-term trading ideas for the Variable Portfolio and continuous coverage of the Permanent Portfolio topics discussed in this book. A typical issue runs 15 to 30 pages, and includes an introductory Front Page, an update of investment suggestions, two or three feature articles, and a summary of news and prices.

The newsletter isn't published on a calendar schedule, but only as there's something to say—which usually turns out to be eight to ten issues per year. A subscription is for the next ten issues and costs $195 ($225 after April 1, 1981). You can purchase the current issue with updated investment suggestions for $5 (one time only). *Harry Browne's Special Reports*, Box 5586B, Austin, Texas 78763.

Free Market Perspectives

Written by Alexander Paris, this monthly 8-page newsletter applies free-market economic theories to the endless streams of data that flow from the government and other sources. Particularly valuable is the perspective it provides regarding where we are in the four-to-five-year credit cycle at any time. This can help you realize that we may not be heading into a runaway inflation when inflation is at 20%, and that a deflation may not be just around the corner when

475

a severe recession is under way. *Free Market Perspectives,* Box 471, Barrington Hills, Illinois 60010; monthly, $50 per year.

Inflation-Proofing Update

The manuscript for this book was finished in November 1980, and a lot may have happened between then and the time you read this. There may be changes in the economy, changes in tax laws and other rules, new investment products and services, and new ideas.

To bring you up to date, we'll publish a one-time supplement during the latter part of 1981. The update will advise you of any important changes, answer *some* of the questions we've received from readers, and provide our afterthoughts on what we've written. You can order a copy of the *Inflation-Proofing Update* for $15 from Harry Browne's Special Reports, Box 5586B, Austin, Texas 78763. Or you can reserve a copy by calling (512) 458-1866.

Personal Finance

This is a helpful biweekly 8-page newsletter that publishes a range of investment opinions and information about investment products. Many of the articles are written by outside contributors and although they often are written by someone in the business of selling the investment being covered, the articles can expose you to opportunities you may have overlooked. *Personal Finance,* 901 N. Washington St., Alexandria, Virginia 22314; $65 per year for 26 issues.

TAX PLANNING

The publications listed in this section can help you understand the tax rules as they now stand and alert you to important changes.

Tax Planning for Investors

This is a book, but it's updated every few years as the tax laws change. It is a compact, easy-to-understand application

of the tax laws to investments. *Tax Planning for Investors,*
Dow Jones-Irwin, 1818 Ridge Road, Homewood, Illinois
60430; $6.95.

Tax Angles

The companion publication to *Personal Finance* (mentioned previously), this 8-page monthly newsletter is written
for the layman to help him understand the possibilities and
the pitfalls of tax-saving strategies. *Tax Angles,* 901 North
Washington Street, Alexandria, Virginia 22314; $44 per year
for 12 issues.

Research Institute Recommendations

A subscription to this publication brings two weekly
newsletters. One is four pages of conventional chitchat about
business conditions and other news you've probably already
heard. The other is a thoroughly researched and carefully
written guide to tax planning. It emphasizes practical applications, but does so without oversimplifying the rules being applied. *Research Institute Recommendations,* Research Institute
of America, 589 Fifth Avenue, New York, New York 10017;
$36 per year for 52 issues.

Master Federal Tax Manual

This annual encyclopedia of the tax rules covers just
about everything any layman would want to know. Its
thorough index will help you find anything you're looking for.
Master Federal Tax Manual, Research Institute of America,
589 Fifth Avenue, New York, New York 10017; annual,
$9.95.

Master Tax Guide

An annual tax reference guide that's similar to the preceding entry. They make good companions—because what
you can't find or can't understand in one may be better han-

dled in the other. *Master Tax Guide,* Commerce Clearing House, 4025 West Peterson Avenue, Chicago, Illinois 60646; annual, $9.

PENSION PLAN TRUSTEES

Many banks will serve as a trustee for a Keogh plan or IRA, but they differ in the degree of investment flexibility they allow and in the fees they charge. There are a few institutions that will handle a directed trust (allowing you to name the investments) and that also charge low fees. Two such firms are described here.

Farmer's Bank of Delaware

The Farmer's Bank offers Keogh plans and IRAs in cooperation with numerous stockbrokers. The broker furnishes the papers for the customer to fill out, and then the Keogh plan or IRA can buy any investment that the broker handles. The bank will serve as trustee for both defined contribution and defined benefit Keogh plans; but for a defined benefit plan you'll also need an actuary to tell you the exact amount to contribute every year.

The annual fee charged by Farmer's Bank is just under ⅛ % (0.12%) of the cumulative amounts contributed to the plan, or a minimum of $40. There are small additional fees if you purchase an investment from a source other than the cooperating stockbroker.

You can obtain a list of the bank's cooperating brokers by writing to Farmer's Bank of Delaware, Box 8853, Wilmington, Delaware 19899, or by calling (302) 421-2181.

Stockcross

Stockcross is a discount stockbroker located in Boston. It has established an arrangement whereby the State Street Bank serves as the directed trustee for Keogh plans (defined contribution only) and IRAs. Your plan can hold any investment that Stockcross deals in—including stocks and Treasury bills (but not Treasury bonds).

The trustee fee is $25 per year regardless of the plan's size. Write to Stockcross, One Washington Mall, Boston, Massachusetts 02108; (800) 225-6196 (out of state), (800) 392-6104 (within Massachusetts).

INVESTMENT ADVISORS

As with a newsletter, your reaction to an investment advisor will be subjective, since a large part of the success you have with an advisor will depend on how well you hit it off personally.

Terry Coxon

Terry Coxon offers an investment advisory and tax planning service that helps individuals design and establish a Permanent Portfolio. Many of the ideas in this book were developed by him in the course of assisting his clients. His main office is located in San Mateo, California (near San Francisco). You can contact him by calling (415) 343-7161, or by writing to Private Investors, 7 Fourth Street, Suite 14, Petaluma, California 94952.

Douglas Casey

Douglas Casey is another advisor who is familiar with both conventional and hard-money investments, and who can help you design a portfolio that respects uncertainty. By reading his book, *Crisis Investing* (described on page 516), you can get an idea of how well his thinking matches your own. Douglas Casey, Box 23177, L'Enfant Plaza Station, Washington, D.C. 23177; (202) 462-3574.

Economic Research Counselors

Economic Research Counselors (ERC) helps investors establish Swiss bank accounts and guides them in long-term investments—primarily in gold, silver, and Swiss francs. Although the company is perennially bullish on these investments, it can provide a good deal of information and guidance to anyone interested in hard-money alternatives. Economic Research Counselors, Suite 2-12, 585 Sixteenth St., West Vancouver, British Columbia, V7V 4S2, Canada; (604) 926-5476, (800) 426-5270.

SWISS BANKS

The table on page 152 lists six small, exceptionally liquid Swiss banks that deal with North Americans by mail. The table on page 153 provides information on the "Big Five" Swiss banks.

The *Swiss Financial Yearbook* is the only English-language source we know of that lists the names, addresses, and other information for every Swiss bank. It can be ordered from Elvetica Edizioni, P.O. Box 694, CH-6830, Chiasso, Switzerland; $55 (includes airmail delivery to the U.S.).

The *Complete Guide to Swiss Banks* by Harry Browne is a reference book containing information for opening and maintaining a Swiss account, and is described on page 516.

SWISS ANNUITIES

Two brokerage firms specialize in arranging Swiss franc annuities for North Americans. Each will respond to inquiries with information on the types of annuities available and a form to fill out. The form will help the broker decide which insurance company and which type of policy would best suit you.

Assurex SA
Posfach 1295
CH-8033 Zurich
Switzerland

International Insurance
  Specialists
Case Postale 949
CH-1211 Geneva 3
Switzerland

DEFERRED ANNUITIES

Deferred annuities are available through many stockbrokers and insurance agents. One firm that specializes in deferred annuities, and can deal with customers by mail, is Seel & Seel Financial Planners, 51 Picardy Court, Walnut Creek, California 94596; (415) 932-2677.

MONEY MARKET FUNDS

A list of selected money market funds, with pertinent information, is given on page 277.

William E. Donoghue publishes two periodicals about the funds. One is a 22-page *Money Fund Directory*, published twice-yearly; $10 per issue. The other is a monthly 8-page summary of funds' portfolios, with comments about the funds, costing $49 per year. A sample copy will be provided free of charge. *Donoghue's Money Letter,* 770 Washington Street, Holliston, Massachusetts 01746.

U.S. GOVERNMENT SECURITIES

The *Handbook of Securities of the U.S. Government* is published every other year. It contains extensive information about the securities issued by the U.S. Treasury and numerous government agencies. Published by First Boston Corp., 20 Exchange Place, New York, New York 10005; $10.

Current prices of most government securities are published daily in *The Wall Street Journal* and weekly in *Barron's* (both described on page 482).

WARRANTS & STOCKS

Using Warrants by Terry Coxon is a 36-page booklet that explains warrants and dual-purpose investment funds. It's available from Investor's Perspective Publishing, Box 1187, Burlingame, California 94010; $10.

Value Line Options & Convertibles covers most publicly traded warrants, giving the current prices and a full description of the terms of each one. It's published on the first four Mondays of every month. Arnold Bernhard & Co., 711 Third Avenue, New York, New York 10017; $345 per year; 8-week trial subscription, $29.

The Value Line Investment Survey is a weekly service covering 2,000 stocks. Each issue provides a beta rating (defined on page 499), which can help in identifying leveraged stocks for a long-term portfolio. Arnold Bernhard & Co., 711 Third Avenue, New York, New York 10017; $330 per year; 10-week trial subscription, $33.

The No-Load Investor is an 8-page quarterly newsletter that rates the performance of mutual funds and categorizes their investment policies. This may be helpful in selecting a group of mutual funds for the stock budget in a long-term portfolio. Published by The Hirsch Organization, Box 283, Hastings-on-Hudson, New York 10706; $20 per year for 4 issues. The company also publishes *Mutual Funds Almanac*, an annual listing of data on most mutual funds; $20.

ECONOMIC DATA

A good source of summary U.S. economic data is the *Federal Reserve Bulletin;* monthly, $20 per year; single copy $2. Much the same data is repeated in graph form covering the past eight years in the *Federal Reserve Chart Book;* quarterly, $7 per year; single copy $2. Both publications are available from Publications Services, Board of Governors of the Federal Reserve System, Washington, D.C. 20551.

Principal economic indicators (inflation rates, money supply, etc.) for over 100 countries are given in *International Financial Statistics,* published by the International Monetary Fund, Washington, D.C. 20431; monthly, $35 per year.

CURRENT PRICES

The two most extensive sources of current investment prices are the two newspapers published by Dow Jones—the daily *Wall Street Journal* and the weekly *Barron's.* All listed U.S. stocks, warrants, bonds, and options are included, as well as U.S. Treasury securities, currencies, many unlisted stocks, most large mutual funds, some foreign stocks, and many other prices and economic indicators.

Both are usually on sale at large newsstands or can be received by mail subscription. *The Wall Street Journal,* 200

Burnett Road, Chicopee, Massachusetts 01021; 35 cents per copy; annual mail subscription $63; 26-week subscription $33. *Barron's*, 22 Cortlandt Street, New York, New York 10004; $1.00 per copy; annual mail subscription $43.

BOOKS

A number of books that augment the material in this one are described in the Suggested Reading on page 515.

EPILOGUE

33

INFLATION-PROOFING YOUR INVESTMENTS

IF YOU'VE READ EVERYTHING IN THE BOOK UP TO THIS POINT, we're grateful for the attention you've given us. There's been a lot to cover and it's taken a good deal of your time.

We would have preferred to tell our story in half the space. But if we'd tried to, we wouldn't have been able to give you the material we believe is necessary to make intelligent decisions. Prudent investing doesn't lend itself to light, quick reading—or to slogans, clichés, and tidy models. You'll live comfortably only with a portfolio you've chosen for yourself, and you can't pick the investments for it without knowing a great deal about them.

One reason for the size of the book has been our goal of helping you design a durable, long-term plan. We hope you'll acquire a portfolio you can live with easily for many years. But a long-term portfolio has to allow for several possible futures, which means it needs several ingredients—and each one leads us into a number of additional topics.

For example, unless you hold some dollars, you might become anxious every time the economy slips into a recession —as you wonder whether the business slowdown will deteriorate into a deflation. But while inflation continues, dollar investments lose purchasing power—unless the interest income is sheltered from taexs. Although there are several ways to create the shelter, no single approach is practical for everyone. Thus we've had to examine a variety of shelters.

On this and other subjects, one thing has led to another —resulting in a lot of material for you to digest.

PREDICTIONS

In the process of covering everything we believe is essential, we've tried to convince you that you don't have to predict the future to have a safe investment program. Not only are predictions unnecessary, we think it's dangerous to rely on them—because they can lure you into gambles you can't afford to lose.

While some advisors have made spectacularly successful predictions in the past decade or two, it's doubtful that anyone's investment profits can be attributed to those forecasts alone. Accompanying each advisor's successful predictions were others that didn't bear out nearly as well. And even correct predictions, by themselves, won't always lead to investment profits—because many contrary things can happen while the faithful await the predicted event.

The authors of this book have had their share of winning forecasts. But we'd be insulting your intelligence if we said that investors who acted on our forecasts never suffered an uneasy moment or an investment loss.

We hope we've made it clear as well that you don't have to agree with our views of the future to use our approach to portfolio planning. In fact, you couldn't agree completely with "us" because we don't fully agree with each other. We've been able to cooperate in writing this book because we've concentrated on what you need to know to make your own decisions—rather than on selling you our expectations for the future.

We've referred repeatedly to the five inflation possibilities, and we've encouraged you to respect your own view of what's likely. But we haven't told you what our expectations are, because there's no need for you to act on them. They are, after all, only two men's opinions.

But because you might be curious, and to show that agreement on expectations isn't needed for the task at hand, here are the probabilities each of us sees for the next ten years.

	Browne	Coxon
Level inflation	5%	5%
Rising inflation	40%	40%

Runaway inflation	10%	5%
Soft landing	5%	20%
Deflation	40%	30%

Each percentage figure indicates the probability (from one person's point of view) that a particular pattern will characterize the next decade. Since rising inflation is what we have now, its percentage is the probability that the pattern won't change—that inflation will continue to rise in waves.[1]

The two authors don't have exactly the same view of the future, but they can agree on what it takes to create a balanced portfolio. And you can create the kind of portfolio you need without agreeing with either of us about the future.

ALARMS

If you choose a balanced portfolio, there's no reason for you to distrust yourself when you read or hear predictions that are contrary to your thinking. Rest assured, you'll hear many of them.

The principal source of forecasts will be, as always, the government. You'll be told that the economy is going to be prosperous next year, that inflation is on the way out (especially if a bold new program is implemented), and that our problems will be solved by the latest method for preventing people from living their own lives. Since, of all institutions, the government has the worst record for forecasting and problem-solving, it won't be hard to disregard its announcements —no matter who is currently heading the government.

More unsettling, however, will be the forecasts of people who seem to know what they're doing—and whose previous predictions were right (or appear to have been right).

From such sources, you may hear that we'll surely have a

---

[1]Note that the probabilities cover only the next ten years. Both authors have given a low probability to runaway inflation. Each of us believes a runaway inflation is a threat but that it will require more time to develop—that, most likely, we won't reach it within ten years. The other possibilities can develop more quickly.

runaway inflation within two years (or one year or five years); that the deflationary collapse is about to begin; that the government will replace the dollar with a new currency within 18 months; that gold will double in price by the end of the year, and so on.

When you hear these forecasts, it may be difficult to stick to the investment plan you've created for yourself. If the predicted event is going to happen, why not get rid of the investments that will lose and make a killing on the investments that will gain?

Ironically, the best protection against alarming forecasts is to listen to them all—because when you've heard enough of them, you'll no longer take them seriously.

Eventually you may decide that a balanced, long-term portfolio eliminates the need to evaluate anyone's forecast— because a portfolio that reflects your hopes, your expectations, and your fears will provide the protection you'll need on the day some frightening prediction turns out to have been correct.

In fact, a good test of the soundness of your portfolio is whether you can hear a convincing prediction of trouble without feeling vulnerable. If you've built the right portfolio, you'll know that you're protected no matter how the forecast proves out.

CYCLES

Even so, as the long-term inflationary trend continues, it becomes harder to remain aloof.

The investment markets are one battleground in a war between the government on the one hand—and producers and consumers on the other. As the government tries to divert wealth and resources to people and enterprises it favors, the marketplace attempts to redirect the resources back toward the production of goods and services that most people want more.

One manifestation of this struggle is the familiar inflation-recession cycle. During the inflation phase, the government creates new money to direct resources to politically favored projects. During the recession phase, everyone else—acting in the free market—attempts to undo what the government has done. But the government, still struggling, prevents the adjustment from reaching completion. As a result, we get the turmoil of a recession without enjoying the benefits that would follow its natural completion.

As the long-term inflationary trend continues, these cycles become more violent; inflation rates go higher and recessions become worse. There's a great danger that, eventually, a cycle will erupt into a runaway inflation or a deflation.

And the violence of the cycles can encourage you to believe the eruption is imminent. When inflation reaches a new high, it's easy to think it will keep going straight up. When the bankruptcies and investment calamities accumulate during a recession, it's easy to fear that the bottom really will fall out. And there's never any shortage of people to encourage these thoughts.

We know it's difficult to isolate yourself from such worries. But we hope that the right portfolio will help to reduce your anxiety. It has for us.

We know, too, that either of the extreme events would change your life considerably, but you at least can ignore the investment implications if you've created the right portfolio. If you've achieved the balance we've been urging, you aren't going to be forced into destitution—even if the extreme event is opposite to what you've been expecting.

One of these days (or years or decades) the damage may be irreparable, and the economy will collapse. But it may not happen for ten or twenty years—and, possibly, not at all. We can't assure you that the bottom won't fall out next year—or even next month. But we think that once your affairs are in order, you'll be better off assuming that the end isn't just around the corner.

You can't afford to make that assumption until you've created a portfolio that allows you to relax. Until then, you'll have good reason to be frightened by each swing in the economy. Only the individual who has faced up to the problems of today can ignore them with impunity.

But once your house is in order, you can try to ignore the excitement around you. There's more to life than counting gold coins.

We couldn't begin to know what kind of society will accompany or follow the ultimate end of inflation. It might be considerably different, and less attractive, from what we have now. If that's possible, it's all the more reason to enjoy what we have today while it's still available. The price of doing so prudently is first to prepare for what may lie ahead.

RELAXATION

Our purpose in this book hasn't been to frighten you; quite the opposite. Fear comes from vulnerability, and we've tried to help you remove the vulnerabilities you felt before you picked up the book. Our success in the endeavor can be measured only by the extent to which your worries have been reduced.

If we haven't succeeded in that, please accept our apologies for taking so much of your time.

If we have succeeded, you'll probably spend the few days needed to create an investment program that suits you. Then we hope you can turn your attention to things that interest you more.

You won't be able to ignore the economy or the investment world completely. You'll hear plenty of forecasts, advice, and admonitions. There'll be more than enough people ready, willing, even demanding to tell you what's good for you—what you must do with your money.

Unfortunately, those people won't pay your losses if the future doesn't live up to their imagined certainty. That's why only you can create the investment program you need.

But along with the responsibility to take care of yourself comes the freedom to do so. You don't have to satisfy anyone's standards but your own. You don't have to prove to anyone how financially smart you are. You don't have to justify your investment decisions to anyone. You need act only on what you believe.

We hope that's what you do. We hope you'll prevail in

creating what you need—no matter what someone else thinks best.

And we hope that you then can relax and enjoy the good things life has to offer.

Harry Browne
Zurich   *November 13, 1980*

Terry Coxon
Petaluma, California

APPENDICES

A

GLOSSARY OF ECONOMIC & INVESTMENT TERMS

Here are definitions of many of the terms used in the book, plus other terms you might come across when studying the economy and the investments we've discussed.

A definition isn't authoritative; its purpose is to make communication more intelligible. In most cases, we've defined a word in the way it's generally understood in the investment and economic worlds, or as we've used it in the text.

A term appearing in **boldface** within a definition is itself defined elsewhere in the Glossary.

ADR (American Depository Receipt): A receipt issued by an American bank for shares of stock in a foreign company. The underlying stock certificates are deposited in a bank (usually a foreign affiliate of the U.S. bank), and the ADRs are traded in their stead.

Agency security: A debt **instrument** issued by an agency of the U.S. government other than the U.S. Treasury Department.

Agio: Premium.

Annuity: A contract, usually with an insurance company, that promises to pay someone a fixed amount periodically (monthly, yearly, etc.) over a given period of time or for the rest of the person's life.

Arbitrage: The purchase of an **asset** in one market accompanied by a simultaneous sale of the same (or a similar) asset in a different market, to take advantage of a difference in price. The arbitrage principle can be applied to simultaneous buying and selling of related currencies, commodities, or securities, the same commodity with different delivery dates, and so on. An arbitrager makes such pairs of trades if he believes that a pair of related prices are temporarily ill-matched and offer an opportunity for profit.

Ask price: The price at which a **dealer** offers to sell.

Asset: Anything of value on which a price can be placed.

At the bank's risk: In describing an investment, this means that the bank, not the customer, assumes most of the risk.

At your risk: In describing an investment, this means that the bank's customer will bear any loss—whether from government confiscation, exchange controls, default, price decline, or other cause.

Austrian school of economics: An approach to economics based on the theory of **human action;** it places special emphasis on the actions of individuals in studying aggregate economic activity, and is generally skeptical of government involvement in the economy.

Bag: In U.S. silver coin investments, the basic unit of trading —composed of 10,000 dimes, 4,000 quarters, or 2,000 half-dollars ($1,000 face value).

Balance of payments: The sum total of a country's commercial and financial transactions with the rest of the world.

Balance sheet: A financial statement showing a firm's or individual's **assets, liabilities,** and **capital.**

Bank holiday: A period during which banks are legally permitted or required to deny withdrawal requests from depositors.

Bank run: An epidemic of withdrawal requests motivated by doubts about a bank's solvency and **liquidity.**

Banker's acceptance: A post-dated business check, usually for $50,000 or more, that has been "accepted" (guaranteed) by a bank and sold to an investor.

Banknote: Currency in paper form, as opposed to a bank deposit.

Bankruptcy: The inability to pay debts or other obligations. Also, a formal recognition of the inability.

Bear market: A period during which the price trend is downward.

Bearer instrument: Any certificate of ownership (stock, bond, note, etc.) that isn't registered or made out to a specific name—and thus is effectively owned by whoever possesses it.

Beta: A composite measure of a stock's volatility and its tendency to move in harmony with the average of stocks in general. A beta of 1.0 may represent a stock that moves in a one-to-one correspondence with the general stock market. A higher beta indicates that the stock is much more volatile than the averages, but tends to move in the same direction. A beta lower than 1.0 (but greater than 0) means the stock's movements are somewhat independent of, and perhaps less volatile than, the averages. A beta lower than 0 means a stock tends to move counter to the general market.

Bid price: The price at which a dealer offers to buy.

Big Three: The three largest Swiss banks: Swiss Bank Corporation, Credit Suisse, and Union Bank of Switzerland. (The "Big Five" includes Bank Leu and Swiss Volksbank as well.)

Bill of exchange: A short-term debt secured by a commodity or product that is in production or in transit.

Book value: An estimate of a firm's net worth derived from its balance sheet: the difference between stated tangible assets and stated liabilities.

Borrowing short, lending long: Usually in reference to a bank, the practice of making long-term loans with money that's owed to depositors short-term.

Broker: One who acts only as a middleman between buyers and sellers; unlike a dealer, he doesn't buy and sell for his own account.

Bull market: A period during which the price trend is upward.

Bullion: Bars of refined gold, silver, or other precious metal.

Bullion coin: A gold or silver coin that normally sells at a price close to the value of the metal in the coin.

Call loan: A loan for which the creditor can demand repayment at any time, although a period of notice may be required.

Call option: The right to purchase a specified investment at a fixed price on a specified date or, in some cases, any time prior to a specified date.

Call privilege: The right of a bond issuer to repay his bond prior to its **maturity** date.

Capital: (1) The sum of money paid into a company by its shareholders. (2) The net **assets** of a person or firm.

Capital gain: A profit made from a change in the price of an investment.

Capital good: A product that is utilized to produce other products.

Carat: A measurement of the percentage of gold in an alloy; 24 carats equal 100%, 12 carats equal 50%, and so on.

Carrying charges or **carrying cost:** The interest and storage costs of owning an investment.

Cash: (1) Money in coin, paper, or other spendable form. (2) Paid for without credit.

Cash flow: The payments received during a given period.

Cash substitute: A liquid investment with a nearly constant dollar value that is held in place of cash.

Cash value life insurance: Life insurance that, in addition to paying benefits in the event of death, accumulates value that the owner can borrow against or can receive by **liquidating** the policy.

CD: Certificate of deposit.

Central bank: A bank, usually created by a government, that's licensed to issue **legal-tender** money.

Certificate of deposit: A deposit represented by a certificate that is transferable.

CH: The international postal abbreviation for Switzerland (Confederation of Helvetia); it appears in a Swiss address just before the postal zone number.

Claim account: A bank account representing the right to receive a commodity (as distinct from actual title to, or ownership of, the commodity itself).

Clifford trust: A **trust** calling for the return of its **capital** to the **grantor** after a period of at least ten years and the payment of its income to the beneficiaries on or before the day the capital is returned.

Closed-end investment company: A company that invests its stockholders' money in **securities,** and that does not continually issue new shares or redeem existing shares (as a

500

mutual fund does). Its shares are traded in the open market. It is also called a Publicly Traded Investment Fund.

Collateral: An asset that is pledged for a loan, to be forfeited if repayment is not made.

Collectible: An article valued for its artistic merit, natural beauty, or historical associations.

Commercial paper: A marketable, short-term IOU, usually for $100,000 or more, of a well-known corporation.

Consumption: (1) The use or enjoyment of a product or service as an end in itself, rather than as a means to a further end. (2) The using up of something.

Content: The precious metal in a coin, medallion, or token.

Controlled foreign corporation: According to the U.S. tax laws, a foreign corporation, a majority of whose voting shares are owned by five or fewer U.S. citizens or residents.

Convertible currency: A currency that can be easily converted into (1) another currency in the open market or (2) gold or silver at a fixed rate of exchange.

Convertible security: Any security that can be exchanged for another security, on fixed terms, upon the demand of the holder.

Coupon rate: The annual rate of interest, as a percentage of the **face value,** paid by a bond.

Covered forward sale: The sale of a commodity the seller actually owns—for delivery and payment at a later date.

Credit: (1) Borrowed money. (2) On a bank statement, an entry that is to your favor (as opposed to a **debit,** which is to the favor of the bank).

Currency: (1) Any money in common circulation. (2) **Banknotes** and coins, as opposed to bank deposits.

Current account: (1) A bank account allowing the depositor to withdraw any or all of the funds at any time. (2) A nation's exports of goods and services less its imports of goods and services. (See also **Balance of payments** and **Trade balance.**)

Custodial account: An account under which a bank stores property owned by a customer.

Custodian: An agent, usually a bank, that stores investments.

Custody account: A custodial account.

Cycle: A recurring pattern of reversals.

Dealer: One who offers to buy and sell a given instrument at quoted prices; unlike a **broker,** he owns the investments he offers to sell.

Debit: On a bank statement, an entry that is to the bank's favor (as opposed to a **credit,** which is to the customer's favor).

Debt instrument: An IOU—bill, note, mortgage, debenture, or bond.

Default: Failure to keep a promise.

Deferral: See **Tax deferral.**

Deferred annuity: An **annuity** that promises to begin making payments at a future time.

Defined-benefit plan: A pension plan that specifies the size of the pension the beneficiary will receive or a rule for determining it; contributions to the plan are determined by estimates of what is necessary to produce the benefit.

Defined-contribution plan: A pension plan that specifies the size of the periodic contribution to be made or a rule for determining it; the benefit will be whatever results from investments purchased with the contribution.

Deflation: A fall in the general price level—caused by a growth in the **demand for money** that isn't offset by a comparable growth in the **money supply,** or by a decline in the supply of money that isn't offset by a comparable decline in the demand for money.

Demand deposit: A bank deposit that can be withdrawn without penalty at any time; a **current account.**

Demand for money: The portion of a person's wealth that he wants to hold in the form of **money.**

Demand loan or **demand note:** A loan or note that is payable immediately on demand.

Deposit account: A bank account for which there are withdrawal restrictions. Normally, it earns a higher rate of interest than a **current account.**

Depreciation: (1) A loss of value. (2) A reserve to facilitate the replacement of an **asset** when it wears out.

Depression: A prolonged period of declining standards of living.

Deutschmark: The German mark, the currency of West Germany.

Devaluation: A government's dishonoring of its promise to redeem its currency at the stated rate of exchange—lowering the currency's value in relationship to gold or other currencies. A devaluation can't occur during a time of floating exchange rates, because the floating rates mean that there's no promise to dishonor.

Directed trust: A trust, such as for a pension plan, for which the owner may direct the trustee in the choice of investments.

Dirty float: See Floating exchange rate.

Discount: (1) The amount by which an asset is priced under its face value or its book value, or under the price of another asset that is comparable in some way. (2) The amount by which a forward price is below the spot price. (3) The amount by which a coin is priced under the value of its metallic content. (See also Premium.)

Discount rate: The interest rate charged by a Federal Reserve Bank on a loan to a commercial bank.

Discretionary account: An account for which the owner empowers a bank, broker, or advisor to make investment decisions.

Disinflation: A period during which the price inflation rate declines without going below zero.

Diversified common stock fund: An investment company that normally holds a diversified portfolio of stocks; the value of its shares tends to move up and down in the same direction as the general stock market.

Dual-purpose investment company: A closed-end investment company that issues both (a) income shares, whose owners receive all the interest and dividends earned by the fund, and (b) capital shares, whose owners realize all the long-term profit from the fund's investments.

Earned income: For tax purposes, income from wages, salary, or self-employment. (See also Unearned income.)

Economics: The study of how people use limited resources to achieve maximum well-being (whether on a personal, commercial, national, or international scale); the art of making decisions.

Equity: The current market value of an investment less all claims against it (from creditors or option holders).

Equity investment: An investment that does not promise to pay a specific number of dollars to the investor.

Euro-CD: A Eurodollar certificate of deposit.

Eurocurrency: A deposit in a bank located outside the country in which the currency of the account was issued (such as a U.S. dollar account in a Swiss bank or a Swiss franc account in an English bank).

Eurodollar certificate of deposit: A certificate of deposit denominated in dollars, issued by a bank outside of the U.S.

Excess equity: Excess margin.

Excess margin: In a margin account, equity that is above the amount required by the bank or other lender; it normally can be withdrawn or used to finance an additional investment.

Exchange control: A government regulation restricting or prohibiting the exporting or importing of banknotes, bank deposits, or other monetary instruments.

Exchange rate: The price of one currency expressed in units of another.

Exercise price: Striking price.

Exercise value: For a warrant or a call option, the amount by which the price of the underlying investment exceeds the striking price. For a put option, the amount by which the striking price exceeds the price of the underlying investment.

Face value: (1) The legal-tender value of a coin, banknote, or other token. (2) The amount promised to a lender at the maturity of a bond, note, or bill.

Fed: The Federal Reserve System.

Federal Reserve System: A system of 12 Federal Reserve Banks, supervised by a Board of Governors, that acts as a central bank in the U.S.

Fiat money: Currency that is not convertible into either gold or silver, and is declared to be legal tender by government fiat or edict.

Fiduciary account: (1) A custodial account. (2) Among Swiss banks, an account owned by a non-Swiss for which all the investments are made outside of Switzerland.

Fineness: The degree to which bullion is pure gold or silver, expressed as a decimal fraction. Gold bullion of .995 fineness means that 99.5% of the total weight is pure gold.

"First in, first out" rule: The convention that the units of an investment sold were the first units of the investment purchased—so that, for determining taxable gains, the cost is the price of the first lot purchased.

Fixed deposit account: A time deposit.

Fixed exchange rate: An exchange rate that is maintained within a prescribed narrow range—usually by government purchases and sales in the open market of the **currencies** involved. (See also **Floating exchange rate**.)

Fixed interest rate: An unchanging interest rate on a **debt instrument**.

Floating exchange rate: An exchange rate that is allowed to fluctuate, not influenced by government purchases and sales. A *dirty float* occurs when the government influences the exchange rate through purchases and sales, but does not announce an official, **fixed exchange rate;** the dirty float has been the exchange-rate system used by major governments since 1973.

Foreign exchange rate: See **Exchange rate**.

Foreign investment company: Under U.S. tax rules, a foreign corporation, the majority of the value of whose stock is owned by U.S. citizens or residents, and a majority of whose assets are securities.

Foreign personal holding company: A foreign corporation of which five or fewer U.S. citizens or residents own more than 50% of the value of the stock, and which derives the majority of its income from investments. (See also **Personal holding company, domestic**.)

Forward contract: A contract for delivery of an **asset** in the future at a price determined in the present.

Forward price: The price of an **asset** to be delivered and paid for on a given date in the future. (See also **Spot price**.)

Fractional reserve banking: A system in which money that is payable upon demand to depositors is invested or lent to other bank customers; thus, a system in which the bank maintains less than 100% cash **reserves** against **demand deposits**.

Free market: Any arrangement for voluntary transactions.

Fundamental analysis: A system of investment analysis that considers only sources of supply and demand that are independent of investment opinions. (See also **Technical analysis.**)

Fundamental value: The capital value of an asset—derived from the use or income value and applicable interest rates.

Fungible: Interchangeable.

Futures contract: A forward contract with standardized specifications, traded on an organized exchange.

Gold exchange standard: A gold standard in which only foreign governments and central banks may convert a currency into gold.

Gold standard: A condition in which a government promises to convert every unit of its currency into a fixed quantity of gold on demand.

Government: The dominant institution of coercion in a given area.

Grain: In weights and measures, .0648 grams or .002 troy ounces; there are 15.432 grains in a gram, 480 grains in a troy ounce. (The abbreviation *gr* normally means gram.)

Gram: The unit of weight in the metric system. There are 31.1035 grams to a troy ounce; one gram equals .03215 troy ounce. A kilogram is 1,000 grams or 32.15 troy ounces. A metric ton is 1,000 kilograms or 32,151 troy ounces.

Grantor: The person who endows a trust.

Hard-money investments: Gold and silver. The designation sometimes includes currencies, such as the Swiss franc, that have been subjected to less than average monetary inflation.

Hedge: A relatively small investment purchased to offset possible losses in one's principal investments.

Human action theory: The premise that every human action is motivated by an individual's desire to increase his mental well-being or to prevent a decrease in his well-being. The foundation of the Austrian school of economics.

Ideal portfolio: The portfolio an individual would select if all his wealth were currently in cash.

Illiquidity: The inability to turn assets or investments into cash easily, without paying a penalty for haste.

In the money: The condition of a **call option** or **warrant** when its **striking price** is less than the price of the **underlying investment.** The condition of a **put option** when the striking price is higher than the price of the underlying investment.

Income (investment): Payments received that do not represent a depletion of **capital.**

Income account: A portion of a **portfolio** set aside to hold spending money.

Inconvertibility: The contrary to convertibility. (See **Convertible currency** and **Convertible security.**)

Individual Retirement Account: A tax-sheltered pension plan for an employee whose employer has not provided a pension plan.

Inflation: An increase in the **supply of money** that isn't offset by a corresponding increase in the **demand for money**—resulting in a **depreciation** of the value of money and a corresponding increase in the monetary prices of goods and services.

Installment sale: The sale of an **asset** in exchange for a series of payments.

Inter-bank rates: Prices or interest rates that apply only to transactions between banks.

Interest differential: (1) The difference between two interest rates. (2) The net **carrying charges** incurred during a period of time.

Investment company: A company that places its stockholders' money in other investments (usually in **securities**).

IRA: Individual Retirement Account.

Kaffir: Any South African gold mining company.

Keogh plan: A tax-sheltered pension plan for self-employed individuals.

Kilogram: See **Gram.**

Legal tender: A form of **money** that an individual is legally required to accept in payment of debts.

Leverage: Any arrangement (such as a **margin** purchase or an **option** contract) that amplifies the effect of a price change.

Leveraged hedge: An investment that has the potential to produce a gain far out of proportion to its purchase price, and can be used as a low-cost balance against one's principal investments.

Leveraged stock: A stock that has the potential to produce a gain far out of proportion to its purchase price.

Liability: A financial obligation—actual or potential.

"Like kind assets": Two assets that are sufficiently similar that the sale of one and the purchase of the other is considered, for tax purposes, to be no sale at all.

Limited partnership: A partnership in which some of the partners have only a limited liability for the partnership's obligations.

Liquidation: (1) The sale of an asset. (2) The closing out of a company, annuity, pension plan, or other investment or enterprise.

Liquidity: (1) The ability to turn an asset into cash quickly without a penalty for haste. (2) The relationship of a firm's liquid assets to the liabilities, actual or potential, to be paid in the near future.

Long position: The result of buying before selling, usually in expectation of a price increase. (See also **Short sale.**)

Maintenance margin: The margin required by a bank or other lender, below which a margin sale will occur.

Margin: (1) In a margin account, the amount of the investor's equity, sometimes expressed as a percentage of the current market value of the investment. (2) In a forward contract or a futures contract, the value of the investor's deposit, sometimes expressed as a percentage of the current market value of the investment.

Margin account: An investment account in which there is a call loan against the assets.

Margin call: A demand by the creditor of a margin account that the borrower reduce the loan—so that the loan amount will remain comfortably below the current market value of the assets.

Margin loan: A call loan for which an investment is used as collateral.

Margin sale: A sale of assets to satisfy the requirements of a margin call.

Market: (1) A group of transactions integrated by geography or items traded. (2) An opportunity to exchange.

Marketable: Saleable without large transaction costs.

Market-maker: A dealer who continually offers to buy and sell a given investment.

Maturity: The date on which a contractual obligation (such as repayment of a bond) falls due.

Metric ton: See **Gram.**

Monetarism: The economic school of thought based on the principle that changes in the **money supply** are a dominant factor in fluctuations in general economic activity and the level of prices.

Monetary inflation: An increase in the **money supply.**

Money: An instrument that is immediately acceptable as a medium of exchange.

Money market fund: A **mutual fund** that invests only in **money market instruments.**

Money market instrument or **paper:** An easily marketable short-term note or bill carrying little risk of **default.**

Money supply: Currency held outside of commercial banks, as well as bank deposits that can be withdrawn on demand.

Moratorium: A period during which a debtor (such as a bank, company, or individual) is legally permitted to delay payment of its obligations.

Municipal bond: A bond issued by a state or city government, or by an agency associated with a state or city government.

Mutual fund: A company that invests its stockholders' money in other investments (usually in **securities**) and has assumed the obligation to redeem its shares at **net asset value** upon request.

Negative interest tax: A special tax imposed from time to time by the Swiss government on new bank balances above a specified level (usually 100,000 francs or so) held by foreigners. The last such tax was removed on November 29, 1979.

Negotiable instrument: A certificate of ownership that can be transferred to a buyer without registration with the issuer.

Net asset value: The amount, per share, of total **assets** minus total **liabilities.**

On the money: The condition of a **warrant** or an **option** (put or call) when the price of the **underlying investment** is equal to the **striking price.**

509

Option: See Call option and Put option.

Ordinary income: For tax purposes, income from all sources other than capital gains. (See also Earned income and Unearned income.)

Out of the money: The condition of a call option or a warrant when the price of the underlying investment is lower than the striking price. The condition of a put option when the striking price is lower than the price of the underlying investment.

Paper claim or **paper investment:** An investment that relies on a promise.

Paper money: Money in the form of banknotes or bank deposits.

Par: (1) See Par value. (2) Equal in value.

Par value: The nominal or face value of a security or currency.

Permanent portfolio: An assortment of investments that is meant to go unchanged in character from year to year. (See also Variable portfolio.)

Personal holding company (domestic): Any corporation in which five or fewer persons own more than 50% of the value of the stock, and which receives more than 60% of its income from investments, rather than business activities. (See also Foreign personal holding company.)

Personal service income: Earned income.

Portfolio: An assortment of investments.

Power of attorney: Signature authority.

Premium: (1) The amount by which a security is priced above its face value, book value, or the value of its constituent parts. (2) The amount by which the forward price exceeds the spot price. (3) The amount by which the price of a coin exceeds the value of the coin's metallic content. (4) The amount by which the price of an option exceeds its exercise value. (5) The payment made to keep an insurance policy in force.

Price inflation: An increase in the general price level.

Prime rate: The interest rate quoted on loans by commercial banks to their best customers.

Public market: An investment market in which most relevant information is publicly available.

Publicly traded investment fund: A closed-end investment company.

Purchasing power: The value of a unit of money or other asset measured by the goods and services it can purchase.

Purchasing power parity: The exchange rate at which a country's price level is equivalent to the price level in another country.

Put option: The right to sell a specific investment at a fixed price or a specified date or, in some cases, any time prior to a specified date.

Ratio scale: A graphic scale in which any given percentage difference between prices will cover the same vertical distance, no matter at what level it occurs.

Recession: A period during which standards of living decline.

Redemption: (1) The repurchase of a security by its issuer. (2) The conversion of a currency into gold or silver by the currency's issuer.

Registered security: A security whose ownership is recorded with the issuer.

Regulation Q: A ceiling placed by the Federal Reserve on the interest rates that banks may pay.

Repo: Repurchase agreement.

Repurchase agreement: A contract under which an investment is sold by one party to another with the stipulation that it will be repurchased on a specified date at a specified price. It is, in effect, a loan of money using the investment as collateral, with the difference in the two prices representing the interest.

Reserve: (1) An allocation of capital for possible losses or to meet a statutory requirement. (2) For a bank, the money available to meet withdrawal requests.

Reserve Bank: One of 12 banks making up the Federal Reserve System.

Resource: Anything—natural, human, or fabricated—that has a value in use or exchange.

Restrike: A coin that was minted after the date marked, but which is genuine.

Revaluation: An increase in value or price. (If a currency is revalued, the event is the opposite of a devaluation; if the gold reserves backing a currency are revalued to a higher price, the event is a devaluation.)

Risk: The probability of loss and the extent of the potential loss.

Round lot. The minimum size of an investment transaction that does not incur special charges.

Runaway inflation: A rapid rise in prices aggravated by a widespread drop in the demand for money.

Safekeeping account: A custodial account.

Secured loan: A loan for which collateral is pledged.

Security: (1) A token, such as a stock or bond certificate, representing capital entrusted to another. (2) An asset pledged to secure a loan. (3) Safety.

Share capital: Capital provided by shareholders.

Short sale: (1) The sale of a borrowed security. (2) The sale of an asset for future delivery—whether or not the seller currently possesses the assets. (See also Long position.)

Signature authority: The authority given by the owner of an account to another person to transact business for the account.

Soft landing: An end to inflation not accompanied by either a depression or a runaway inflation.

Specialist market: An investment market in which most relevant information is avaliable only through dealers.

Speculation: Any investment made with the hope of profiting from a change in price.

Speculative: In normal usage, involving more than a minimum of risk.

Spot price: The price for immediate delivery of an asset. (See also Forward price.)

Spread: (1) The difference between the bid price and the ask price. (2) A form of hedge or arbitrage in which the purchase of an asset for delivery on one date is balanced by the sale of the asset for delivery on a different date.

Stop-loss order: An instruction given to a bank or broker to sell an investment if the price drops to a stated level.

Striking price: The price at which the holder of a warrant or a call option may buy an asset; also, the price at which the holder of a put option may enforce a sale. Also called the *exercise price*.

Supply of money: See Money supply.

Swap: (1) An arrangement by which a government borrows foreign currency from the government that issues it, to finance intervention in foreign exchange markets. (2) A repurchase agreement. (3) A spread (#2).

Tael: A unit of weight used in the Far East for precious metals, equal to 1.1972 troy ounces or 37.238 grams of .995 fineness.

Tax: Property, usually money, demanded from its owner by a government.

Tax credit: A dollar-for-dollar reduction in one's tax bill.

Tax deferral: The delaying of a tax liability.

Tax haven: A country whose government offers tax advantages to foreigners.

Tax shelter: An investment or arrangement that legally provides tax deferral or tax reduction.

T-bills: See Treasury securities.

Technical analysis: A system of investment analysis that considers factors relating to supply and demand only within the investment market without regard for fundamental values. (See also Fundamental analysis.)

Technology: Knowledge, skills, and tools that increase the productivity of human effort.

Time deposit: A bank deposit that is not withdrawable until a fixed date.

Tola: An Indian unit of weights, sometimes used for precious metals, equal to .375 troy ounces or 11.664 grams.

Ton, metric: See Gram.

Trade balance: A nation's exports of products less its imports of products. (See also Balance of Payments and Current Account #2.)

Transaction costs: Commissions, spreads, or other costs incurred in buying and selling investments.

Treasury securities: Direct-obligation debts of the U.S. government including bills (sold at a discount and redeemed at face value one year or less after issue), notes (maturing 10 years or less after issue), and bonds (maturing more than 10 years after issue).

Troy ounce: The unit of weight used to measure gold and silver. One troy ounce equals 1.097 avoirdupois ounces.

Trust: An entity created and financed by one person (the **grantor**) for the benefit, usually, of another person (the **beneficiary**), and controlled by a third person (the **trustee**).

Trust account: A discretionary account.

Trustee: The controlling party of a **trust**, often empowered to buy and sell investments for the trust.

Underlying investment: For an asset such as an **option, warrant,** or other **convertible security,** the investment for which the asset provides the right of purchase or sale.

Unearned income: For tax purposes, interest, dividends, royalties, capital gains, and other non-business income. Unearned income is taxed at rates up to 70%, while **earned income** (from salary or other occupational sources) is taxed at rates up to 50%.

Upvaluation (colloquial): A **revaluation;** the opposite of a **devaluation.**

Value date: The date on which payment is considered to have been made or is due.

Variable portfolio: An assortment of investments that is altered as investment prospects change. (See also **Permanent portfolio.**)

Walk-away mortgage: A mortgage for which the lender does not have the legal right, in a foreclosure, to demand from the borrower any deficiency between the loan balance and the price at which the property is sold.

Warrant: An option to purchase a share of stock at a fixed price until a specified date. (A warrant differs from a **call option** in that a warrant is issued by the company whose stock is involved.)

Wealth: Resources that can be used or sold.

Yield: The interest or dividend stated as a percentage of the current market value of the investment.

B

SUGGESTED READING

HERE ARE A NUMBER OF BOOKS THAT ONE OR BOTH OF THE authors have found useful, as well as three books by Harry Browne. When we wrote this, every book listed but one could be ordered from its publisher and, except where noted, all could be purchased from any bookstore. If a book has since gone out of print, you can order it from a used-book dealer.

INVESTMENTS

New Profits from the Monetary Crisis by Harry Browne. Although the book discusses the Permanent Portfolio and makes many suggestions regarding it, the primary emphasis is on the Variable Portfolio. (Hardcover: William Morrow & Co., 105 Madison Ave., New York, N.Y. 10016; $12.95. Paperback: Warner Books, 75 Rockefeller Plaza, New York, N.Y. 10019; $2.95.)

The Money Market: Myth, Reality, and Practice by Marcia Stigum provides a thorough survey of the markets for cash substitutes, explaining what the substitutes are, how they differ from one another, and how the markets function. There are detailed discussions of Treasury bills, commercial paper, Euro-CDs, and other cash substitutes we haven't discussed. The book leaves few questions unanswered. (Hardcover: Dow Jones Books, Box 300, Princeton, N.J. 08540; $22.50.)

The Complete Bond Book by David M. Darst. A thorough, well-written, easy-to-understand explanation of all types of bonds and other fixed-income securities. It will tell

515

you anything you've ever wanted to know about bonds. (Hardcover: McGraw-Hill Book Co., 1221 Avenue of the Americas, New York, N.Y. 10020; $25.95.)

Handbook of Investment Products and Services by Victor L. Harper. A basic introduction to many investment markets —stocks, bonds, real estate trusts, options, mutual funds, life insurance, commodities, annuities, tax shelters, and so on. (Hardcover: Prentice-Hall Inc., Englewood Cliffs, N.J. 07632; $17.95.)

The International Man by Douglas R. Casey. An overview of foreign investment markets—with special attention to the political and social factors that affect the stability of those markets. (Hardcover: Available only from Kephart Communications, 901 N. Washington St., Alexandria, Va. 22314; $14.95.)

Crisis Investing by Douglas R. Casey is a general introduction to the economic difficulties of today and their causes. The author offers an investment strategy for coping with the difficulties. (Hardcover: Stratford Press/Harper & Row, Publishers, Inc., 10 East 53rd Street, New York, N.Y. 10022; $12.50.)

SWISS BANKS

The Complete Guide to Swiss Banks by Harry Browne. A guide book for using a Swiss bank account—explanations of the types of accounts available, commission rates, fees, numbered accounts, sample instructions to give to the bank, privacy suggestions, and so forth. (Hardcover: Available only from Harry Browne Special Reports, Box 5586B, Austin, Tex. 78763; $14.95.)

The Swiss Banks, by T. R. Fehrenbach. Although now out of print (published in 1966, by McGraw-Hill Book Co.), this is probably still the best book available explaining why Switzerland is and will continue to be the money haven of the world.

U.S. BANKING SYSTEM

The Coming Credit Collapse by Alexander P. Paris. A

discussion of the illiquid state of American banks and corporations. The reading is a little difficult in places, but you won't miss the point. The author's investment suggestions are well worth considering. The book was originally published in 1974, but a new edition updates it to late 1979. (Hardcover: Arlington House, 333 Post Road West, Westport, Conn. 06880; $12.95.)

ECONOMICS

The soundest and most precise explanations of economics aren't going to be the easiest to read; there is simply too much ground to cover. For the person who wants a deep understanding of the economic events of today, we've listed the books that one or both of us has found especially useful. The readability varies, and so we've indicated the ease or difficulty you might encounter.

The Inflation Crisis and How to Resolve It by Henry Hazlitt. A sound, easy-to-read primer on inflation—covering many aspects of the subject we didn't have room for here. Henry Hazlitt has one of the best economic minds in the world today. (Hardcover: Arlington House, 333 Post Road West, Westport, Conn. 06880; $8.95.)

An Economist's Protest by Milton Friedman. A collection of his *Newsweek* columns. Many of the articles are on money and inflation; all of them are provocative and very easy reading. (Hardcover: Thomas Horton and Daughters, 22 Appleton Place, Glen Ridge, N.J. 07028; $4.95.)

University Economics by Armen A. Alchian and William R. Allen. This may be the most entertaining economics textbook ever written—meticulously complete but with an interesting and humorous style for most of the book. The first 31 chapters provide a valuable course in economics from the ground up. For some reason, the final chapters are not nearly so sound or readable. (Hardcover: Wadsworth Publishing Co., Inc., 10 Davis Drive, Belmont, Calif. 94002; $16.95.)

Human Action by Ludwig von Mises. This book explains in detail the theory of human action—which in turn explains the whole of economics. It isn't easy reading, but it's engrossing for anyone interested in economics. And with a copy of *Mises Made Easier* (see below), you won't have trouble with the terminology. Harry Browne's thinking has been influenced more by Ludwig von Mises than by any other economist. (Hardcover: Contemporary Books, Inc., 180 Michigan Ave., Chicago, Ill. 60601; $20.00.)

The Theory of Money and Credit by Ludwig von Mises. Everything said regarding *Human Action* applies to this book as well. However, this book is concerned solely with money and inflation. (Hardcover: Foundation for Economic Education, Irvington-on-Hudson, N.Y. 10533; $6.00.)

On the Manipulation of Money and Credit by Ludwig von Mises. Concentrating on money and inflation, this book is much easier reading than the two listed before. Although some of the essays were written in the early part of the century, the material is quite revelant to today's problems. (Hardcover: Available only from Free Market Books, Box 298, Dobbs Ferry, N.Y. 10522; $14.00.)

Mises Made Easier by Percy L. Greaves, Jr. A glossary of the scientific and possibly unfamiliar terms used in the books of Ludwig von Mises. It is virtually a necessity for studying von Mises' work, but it's also interesting reading on its own. (Hardcover: Available only from Free Market Books, Box 298, Dobbs Ferry, N.Y. 10522; $14.00.)

Man, Economy and State by Murray N. Rothbard. While easier reading than most of the von Mises works, this is still a scholarly work and will require effort in places. It is a complete course in economics, taking the reader from the foundations of human action to specific examples of government and free-market activity. (Hardcover: Green Hill Pubs., 236 Forest Park Place, Ottawa, Ill. 61350; $10.00.)

The Failure of the "New Economics" by Henry Hazlitt. A line-by-line critique of *The General Theory of Employment, Interest, and Money*—the book by John Maynard Keynes that is at the root of economic policy in nearly every country of the non-communist world. No one is likely to take the "new economics" seriously after reading Hazlitt's critique. (Hardcover: Arlington House, 333 Post Road West, Westport, Conn. 06880; $11.95.)

How I Found Freedom in an Unfree World by Harry Browne. The first half of the book explains the author's view of human action and forms the basis for his economic and investment philosophies. (Paperback: Avon Books, 959 Eighth Ave., New York, N.Y. 10019; $2.75.)

ECONOMIC HISTORY

A Monetary History of the United States by Milton Friedman and Anna Schwartz. A scholarly study, but an engrossing narrative of economic and monetary events and policies in the U.S. from 1867 to 1960. The authoritative work on the subject. (Paperback: Princeton University Press, Princeton, N.J. 08540; $8.95.)

The Economics of Inflation by Constantino Bresciani-Turroni. A dry, but informative, history of the famous German inflation of 1914–1923, useful more for the information than for the author's interpretation of the events. (Hardcover: Augustus M. Kelley, Publishers, 305 Allwood Rd., Clifton, N.J. 07012; $17.50.)

Exchange, Prices, and Production in Hyper-Inflation: Germany, 1920–1923 by Frank D. Graham. Like the above book, this is dry reading, but it provides a great deal of information about the German inflation—complementing Bresciani-Turroni's book. (Hardcover: Russell & Russell Publishers, 122 E. 42nd St., New York, N.Y. 10017; $11.00.)

C

TREASURY BILL
AUCTIONS

NEWLY ISSUED 13-WEEK AND 26-WEEK TREASURY BILLS ARE sold at auction once a week. The auction is normally held on Monday, and the bills are actually issued three days later. When Monday is a holiday, the auction is held the previous Friday.

An auction for 52-week bills is held every four weeks. Normally, the auction is held on a Thursday, and the bills are issued the following Wednesday.

Most of the T-bills sold at auction are bought by banks and brokers, who enter competitive bids. The competitive bidders state in writing the price they're willing to pay. The Treasury accepts enough bids to sell the quantity of bills it's offering, starting at the highest bid and working downward. So, depending on how much he offers, a competitive bidder either will get the T-bills at his bid price or he won't get them at all.

In addition to the competitive bids, the Treasury accepts non-competitive bids. Submitting a non-competitive bid simply means that you're willing to purchase T-bills at whatever average price prevails at the auction.

You can submit a non-competitive bid for any amount divisible by $5,000—with a minimum of $10,000 and a maximum of $500,000. You can count on the bid being accepted, and the price will be the average of all the prices paid by the successful competitive bidders.

To prepare a non-competitive bid, write or phone any

office of a Federal Reserve Bank (listed at the end of this appendix). Ask for a form titled "Tender for Treasury Bills." Fill out the form and return it with a cashier's or certified check (which you can buy at a local bank) for the face amount of the Treasury bill.

The check must be for the face amount, so it will be a dollar amount divisible by 5,000—$10,000, $15,000, $20,000, and so on.

Three days after the auction takes place, the Federal Reserve Bank will send you a check for the difference between the face value and the auction price. For example, if you ask for $10,000 worth of 52-week Treasury bills, and the auction price turns out to be $9,100, the Federal Reserve will send you a check for $900.

Unless you request otherwise, the Treasury will send you a second check, for the full face value, when the bills mature. In the above example, you'd receive a check for $10,000 after waiting 52 weeks.

However, you can ask for the Treasury bills to be "rolled over." This means the Treasury will automatically enter a non-competitive bid for you when your Treasury bills approach maturity. To obtain the roll-over service on your original purchase, write "I wish these bills to be rolled over upon maturity" on the tender form.

The roll-over request is good for only one reinvestment. The request must be repeated for each reinvestment and must reach the Treasury at least 10 business days before the old bills mature. A form requesting the roll-over can be obtained either from the Treasury or from a Federal Reserve Bank.

The need to repeat the roll-over request is one reason to use 52-week bills rather than shorter maturities.

FEDERAL RESERVE BANK OFFICES

The following list includes headquarters and branches of the twelve Federal Reserve Banks. You can obtain a "Tender for Treasury Bills" by writing to "Federal Reserve Bank" at any of the addresses shown, or by calling any of the telephone numbers.

Atlanta, Georgia 30303
(404) 231-8500

Baltimore, Maryland 21203
(301) 539-6552

Birmingham, Alabama 35202
(205) 252-3141

Boston, Massachusetts 02016
(617) 973-3000

Buffalo, New York 14240
(716) 849-5000

Charleston, West Virginia
  23511
(304) 345-8020

Charlotte, North Carolina
  28230
(704) 373-0592

Chicago, Illinois 60690
(312) 380-2320

Cincinnati, Ohio 45201
(513) 721-4787

Cleveland, Ohio 44101
(216) 293-9800

Columbia, South Carolina
  29210
(803) 772-1940

Columbus, Ohio 43216
(614) 846-7050

Cranford, New Jersey 07016
(201) 272-9000

Dallas, Texas 75222
(214) 651-6111

Denver, Colorado 80217
(303) 534-5500

Des Moines, Iowa 50306
(515) 284-8800

Detroit, Michigan 48231
(313) 961-6880

El Paso, Texas 79999
(915) 544-4730

Helena, Montana 59601
(406) 442-3860

Houston, Texas 77001
(713) 659-4433

Indianapolis, Indiana 46204
(317) 269-2800

Jericho, New York 11753
(516) 997-4500

Kansas City, Missouri 64198
(816) 881-2000

Lewiston, Maine 04240
(207) 784-2381

Little Rock, Arkansas 72203
(501) 372-5451

Los Angeles, California
90051
(213) 683-8563

Louisville, Kentucky 40232
(502) 587-7351

Memphis, Tennessee 38101
(901) 523-7171

Miami, Florida 33152
(305) 591-2065

Milwaukee, Wisconsin 53202
(414) 276-2323

Minneapolis, Minnesota
55480
(612) 783-2345

Nashville, Tennessee 37203
(615) 259-4006

New Orleans, Louisiana
70161
(504) 586-1505

New York, New York 10045
(212) 791-5000

Oklahoma City, Oklahoma
73125
(405) 235-1721

Omaha, Nebraska 68102
(402) 341-3610

Philadelphia, Pennsylvania
19105
(215) 574-6000

Pittsburgh, Pennsylvania
15230
(412) 261-7910

Portland, Oregon 97208
(503) 221-5931

Richmond, Virginia 23261
(804) 649-3611

St. Louis, Missouri 63166
(314) 421-1700

Salt Lake City, Utah 84125
(810) 355-3131

San Antonio, Texas 78295
(512) 224-2141

San Francisco, California
94120
(415) 450-2000

Seattle, Washington 98124
(206) 442-1650

Utica at Oriskany, New York
13424
(315) 736-8321

Washington, D.C. 20551
(202) 452-3000

Windsor Locks, Connecticut
06096
(203) 623-2561

D

MONEY MARKET CERTIFICATES OR T-BILL ACCOUNTS

U.S. BANKS AND SAVINGS AND LOAN ASSOCIATIONS OFFER SPEcial time deposits called T-bill Accounts or Money Market Certificates (MMCs). Superficially, these accounts appear to be a convenient way of holding U.S. Treasury bills. However, there are a number of ways in which MMCs fall short of offering the return and safety you can get with Treasury bills.

Effective Interest Rate

MMCs pay the interest rate currently quoted for 26-week Treasury bills (or in some cases, a fraction of a percent higher), and seem to offer investors the same yield. However, the actual yield on a Treasury bill is higher than the rate quoted, and therefore higher than what banks pay on MMCs.

A Treasury bill is quoted on a "discount basis"—which means that the dollar amount you earn is quoted as a percentage of the bill's face value. However, the amount you pay to buy a T-bill is less than its face value; you pay the face value minus the discount.

For example, if you purchase a 360-day Treasury bill with a quoted discount of 8%, you will pay $92 per $100 of face value. Since you're investing only $92, the interest on the investment is $8 ÷ 92 = 8.7%. In addition, it takes only 360 days to earn the $8, not a full year. So the true annual yield will work out to 8.8%.

For shorter maturities, the difference between the quoted

discount and the true yield is less, but it still can be substantial. On a 26-week bill quoted at 8%, the true yield is 8.6%.

The gap between quoted discounts and true yields widens as interest rates go higher.

The actual meaning of the quoted rate on Treasury bills is ignored in determining what banks may pay on MMCs; banks simply pay the quoted rate. Semi-annual compounding makes up for a small amount of the discrepancy, but not much.

The table on page 257 gives examples of the differences between true yields and quoted T-bill rates (which are the same as MMC rates).

Liquidity

A Treasury bill can be sold on a moment's notice. For the smallest Treasury bill ($10,000), the brokerage fee is about $25 plus dealer costs of perhaps $10, bringing the total liquidation cost to about $35. For sales of larger amounts, the costs would be proportionately smaller. And when you sell a T-bill prior to maturity, you receive all the interest earned through the date of sale.

It is far more expensive to close out an MMC early. If you close it during the first 60 days, you can actually lose part of the principal in penalties. If you withdraw after 90 days, you lose all interest for the first 90 days, and receive only passbook interest (5¼% in 1980) for the time after that. On an 8% account, the cost of an early withdrawal could run as high as $275.

A Treasury bill is much more liquid than a Money Market Certificate.

Backing

A T-bill Account or Money Market Certificate has no connection with the U.S. Treasury. It is an obligation of the bank that issues it, and is not in any way backed by Treasury bills.

Risk

An MMC is as safe or as risky as any other deposit in a bank or a savings and loan association. The certificates, like other deposits, are insured up to $100,000 by the FDIC or the FSLIC.

In our opinion, the risk is greater than with Treasury bills, for the reasons described on pages 235–246 and 254–255.

Taxes

Interest on Treasury bills is exempt from state and local income taxes, while interest on an MMC is taxed by all levels of government that levy an income tax.

The importance of this consideration will depend on your income and local tax rates. For high income earners living in tax disaster areas like New York City, it can mean a difference of 1% or more on the after-tax yield. In other areas, the difference may be less—or there may be no difference at all.

E

REFERENCE TABLES

THE TABLES ON THE FOLLOWING PAGES ALLOW YOU TO COM-pute answers to questions discussed at various points in the book.

LIFE EXPECTANCY

Present Age	Number of Years Expected to Live Male	Female	Present Age	Number of Years Expected to Live Male	Female
26	45	52	56	19	24
27	44	51	57	18	24
28	43	50	58	18	23
29	42	49	59	17	22
30	41	48	60	16	21
31	41	47	61	16	20
32	40	46	62	15	20
33	39	45	63	14	19
34	38	44	64	14	18
35	37	43	65	13	17
36	36	42	66	13	16
37	35	41	67	12	16
38	34	40	68	12	15
39	33	39	69	11	14
40	32	39	70	10	14
41	31	38	71	10	13
42	30	37	72	10	12
43	30	36	73	9	11
44	29	35	74	9	11
45	28	34	75	8	10
46	27	33	76	8	10
47	26	32	77	8	9
48	25	31	78	7	9
49	24	30	79	7	8
50	24	30	80	6	8
51	23	29	81	6	8
52	22	28	82	6	7
53	21	27	83	5	7
54	21	26	84	5	6
55	20	25	85	5	6

Source: *Statistical Abstract of the United States*, 1976.

PRESENT VALUE OF MORTGAGE
(per $1 of monthly mortgage payment)

Years	3%	4%	5%	6%	7%	8%	9%	10%	11%	12%	13%	15%	17%	20%
1	11.65	11.54	11.43	11.32	11.21	11.11	11.01	10.91	10.81	10.71	10.62	10.43	10.26	10.00
2	22.96	22.63	22.31	22.00	21.70	21.40	21.11	20.83	20.55	20.28	20.02	19.51	19.02	18.33
3	33.94	33.30	32.68	32.08	31.49	30.93	30.38	29.84	29.32	28.82	28.33	27.40	26.52	25.28
4	44.61	43.56	42.55	41.58	40.65	39.75	38.88	38.04	37.23	36.45	35.69	34.26	32.92	31.06
5	54.96	53.42	51.95	50.55	49.20	47.91	46.68	45.49	44.35	43.26	42.21	40.23	38.39	35.89
6	65.01	62.91	60.91	59.01	57.20	55.47	53.83	52.26	50.77	49.34	47.97	45.41	43.07	39.91
7	74.76	72.02	69.44	66.99	64.67	62.48	60.40	58.42	56.55	54.77	53.07	49.93	47.07	43.26
8	84.24	80.79	77.56	74.52	71.66	68.96	66.42	64.02	61.75	59.61	57.59	53.85	50.49	46.05
9	93.43	89.22	85.29	81.62	78.18	74.96	71.94	69.11	66.44	63.94	61.58	57.26	53.41	48.37
10	102.36	97.33	92.66	88.32	84.28	80.52	77.01	73.73	70.67	67.80	65.11	60.23	55.90	50.31
11	111.03	105.13	99.68	94.65	89.98	85.67	81.66	77.94	74.48	71.25	68.24	62.80	58.04	51.92
12	119.45	112.62	106.36	100.61	95.31	90.43	85.93	81.76	77.91	74.33	71.01	65.05	59.86	53.27
13	127.62	119.83	112.72	106.23	100.29	94.85	89.84	85.24	81.00	77.08	73.46	67.00	61.42	54.39
14	135.55	126.76	118.78	111.54	104.95	98.93	93.43	88.40	83.78	79.54	75.63	68.69	62.75	55.33
15	143.26	133.42	124.56	116.55	109.29	102.71	96.73	91.27	86.29	81.73	77.55	70.17	63.89	56.11

Years	3%	4%	5%	6%	7%	8%	9%	10%	11%	12%	13%	15%	17%	20%
16	150 73	139 83	130 05	121 27	113 36	106 22	99 75	93 88	88 55	83 69	79 25	71 45	64 86	56 75
17	157 99	145 99	135 29	125 73	117 16	109 46	102 52	96 26	90 59	85 44	80 75	72 57	65 70	57 30
18	165 04	151 91	140 28	129 93	120 71	112 46	105 07	98 42	92 42	87 00	82 08	73 54	66 41	57 75
19	171 89	157 61	145 02	133 90	124 03	115 24	107 40	100 38	94 07	88 39	83 26	74 38	67 01	58 12
20	178 53	163 08	149 55	137 64	127 13	117 82	109 54	102 16	95 56	89 63	84 30	75 11	67 53	58 43
21	184 98	168 35	153 85	141 17	130 03	120 20	111 51	103 78	96 90	90 74	85 22	75 75	67 98	58 70
22	191 24	173 41	157 96	144 50	132 73	122 41	113 31	105 26	98 11	91 74	86 03	76 30	68 36	58 91
23	197 32	178 28	161 86	147 64	135 27	124 45	114 96	106 60	99 20	92 62	86 76	76 79	68 68	59 09
24	203 23	182 96	165 58	150 60	137 63	126 35	116 48	107 82	100 18	93 41	87 39	77 21	68 96	59 25
25	208 96	187 46	169 13	153 40	139 84	128 10	117 87	108 92	101 06	94 12	87 96	77 57	69 19	59 37
26	214 52	191 79	172 50	156 04	141 91	129 72	119 15	109 93	101 86	94 75	88 46	77 89	69 40	59 48
27	219 92	195 96	175 72	158 53	143 84	131 22	120 32	110 85	102 57	95 31	88 90	78 16	69 57	59 56
28	225 17	199 96	178 78	160 87	145 65	132 61	121 39	111 68	103 22	95 81	89 29	78 40	69 72	59 64
29	230 26	203 80	181 69	163 09	147 33	133 90	122 38	112 44	103 80	96 26	89 64	78 61	69 84	59 70
30	235 21	207 50	184 47	165 18	148 91	135 09	123 28	113 12	104 33	96 66	89 95	78 79	69 95	59 75

To find the value of a fully amortized, fixed-interest mortgage (not the interest rate on your mortgage). Multiply the number you own or owe, find the row corresponding to the number of years remaining until the mortgage is paid off and the column corresponding to the *current* interest rate on new mortgages in that row and column by the monthly payment on the mortgage. The result will be the present capital value of the mortgage.

PRESENT VALUE OF FUTURE PAYMENT
(per $1 of payment)

Years	3%	4%	5%	6%	7%	8%	9%	10%	11%	12%	13%	15%	17%	20%
1	.9709	.9615	.9524	.9434	.9346	.9259	.9174	.9091	.9009	.8929	.8850	.8696	.8547	.8333
2	.9426	.9246	.9070	.8900	.8734	.8573	.8417	.8264	.8116	.7972	.7831	.7561	.7305	.6944
3	.9151	.8890	.8638	.8396	.8163	.7938	.7722	.7513	.7312	.7118	.6931	.6575	.6244	.5787
4	.8885	.8548	.8227	.7921	.7629	.7350	.7084	.6830	.6587	.6355	.6133	.5718	.5337	.4823
5	.8626	.8219	.7835	.7473	.7130	.6806	.6499	.6209	.5935	.5674	.5428	.4972	.4561	.4019
6	.8375	.7903	.7462	.7050	.6663	.6302	.5963	.5645	.5346	.5066	.4803	.4323	.3898	.3349
7	.8131	.7599	.7107	.6651	.6227	.5835	.5470	.5132	.4817	.4523	.4251	.3759	.3332	.2791
8	.7894	.7307	.6768	.6274	.5820	.5403	.5019	.4665	.4339	.4039	.3762	.3269	.2848	.2326
9	.7664	.7026	.6446	.5919	.5439	.5002	.4604	.4241	.3909	.3606	.3329	.2843	.2434	.1938
10	.7441	.6756	.6139	.5584	.5083	.4632	.4224	.3855	.3522	.3220	.2946	.2472	.2080	.1615
11	.7224	.6496	.5847	.5268	.4751	.4289	.3875	.3505	.3173	.2875	.2607	.2149	.1778	.1346
12	.7014	.6246	.5568	.4970	.4440	.3971	.3555	.3186	.2858	.2567	.2307	.1869	.1520	.1122
13	.6810	.6006	.5303	.4688	.4150	.3677	.3262	.2897	.2575	.2292	.2042	.1625	.1299	.0935
14	.6611	.5775	.5051	.4423	.3878	.3405	.2992	.2633	.2320	.2046	.1807	.1413	.1110	.0779
15	.6419	.5553	.4810	.4173	.3624	.3152	.2745	.2394	.2090	.1827	.1599	.1229	.0949	.0649
16	.6232	.5339	.4581	.3936	.3387	.2919	.2519	.2176	.1883	.1631	.1415	.1069	.0811	.0541
17	.6050	.5134	.4363	.3714	.3166	.2703	.2311	.1978	.1696	.1456	.1252	.0929	.0693	.0451
18	.5874	.4936	.4155	.3503	.2959	.2502	.2120	.1799	.1528	.1300	.1108	.0808	.0592	.0376
19	.5703	.4746	.3957	.3305	.2765	.2317	.1945	.1635	.1377	.1161	.0981	.0703	.0506	.0313
20	.5537	.4564	.3769	.3118	.2584	.2145	.1784	.1486	.1240	.1037	.0868	.0611	.0433	.0261

Years	3%	4%	5%	6%	7%	8%	9%	10%	11%	12%	13%	15%	17%	20%
21	.5375	.4388	.3589	.2942	.2415	.1987	.1637	.1351	.1117	.0926	.0768	.0531	.0370	.0217
22	.5219	.4220	.3418	.2775	.2257	.1839	.1502	.1228	.1007	.0826	.0680	.0462	.0316	.0181
23	.5067	.4057	.3256	.2618	.2109	.1703	.1378	.1117	.0907	.0738	.0601	.0402	.0270	.0151
24	.4919	.3901	.3101	.2470	.1971	.1577	.1264	.1015	.0817	.0659	.0532	.0349	.0231	.0126
25	.4776	.3751	.2953	.2330	.1842	.1460	.1160	.0923	.0736	.0588	.0471	.0304	.0197	.0105
26	.4637	.3607	.2812	.2198	.1722	.1352	.1064	.0839	.0663	.0525	.0417	.0264	.0169	.0087
27	.4502	.3468	.2678	.2074	.1609	.1252	.0976	.0763	.0597	.0469	.0369	.0230	.0144	.0073
28	.4371	.3335	.2551	.1956	.1504	.1159	.0895	.0693	.0538	.0419	.0326	.0200	.0123	.0061
29	.4243	.3207	.2429	.1846	.1406	.1073	.0822	.0630	.0485	.0374	.0289	.0174	.0105	.0051
30	.4120	.3083	.2314	.1741	.1314	.0994	.0754	.0573	.0437	.0334	.0256	.0151	.0090	.0042

Use this table to evaluate a single, lump-sum amount that will be paid in the future. Find the row corresponding to the number of years remaining until the payment will be made, and the column corresponding to the *current* interest rate prevailing for the type of obligation involved (not the interest rate that may be promised on the payment). Multiply the number in that row and column by the amount to be paid in the future. The result will be the present capital value of the payment.

TAX RULES GOVERNING CAPITAL GAINS

When you sell an investment, the result is a capital gain or capital loss. The transaction is "long term" if the investment was held for over one year, "short term" if it was held for one year or less. (For transactions on U.S. commodity futures exchanges, the dividing line is six months.)

To determine your tax liability:

1. Subtract short-term losses from short-term gains.

2. Subtract long-term losses from long-term gains.

3a. If you have a net short-term loss (after step #1) *and* a net long-term gain (after step #2), deduct the short-term loss from the long-term gain.

3b. If you have a net short-term gain (step #1) *and* a net long-term loss (#2), deduct the long-term loss from the short-term gain.

4. After making the deductions in steps #1 and #3b, if you have a net short-term gain remaining, add it to ordinary income. It will be taxed at the rates up to 70% that are applied to interest and other "unearned" income.

5. After making the deductions in steps #2 and #3a, if you have a net long-term gain remaining, multiply it by 40% and add the result to ordinary income. It will be taxed at the rates up to 70% that are applied to interest and other "unearned" income. Thus the effective maximum rate on net long-term gains is 28% (40% × 70% = 28%).

6. After making the deductions in steps #1 and #3a, if you have a net short-term loss remaining, deduct it from this year's ordinary income. However, the maximum deduction against ordinary income is $3,000 per year.

7. After making the deductions in steps #2 and #3b, if you have a net long-term loss remaining, multiply it by 50% and deduct it from this year's ordinary income. However, the maximum deduction against ordinary income for steps #6 and #7 *together* is $3,000 per year. (Note that long-term *gains* are multiplied by 40% while long-term *losses* are multiplied by 50% before being applied to income.)

8. If any losses remain (after steps #6 and #7), they will be included in next year's capital-gain calculations. A net short-term loss remaining from this year will be combined with next year's short-term transactions, and a net long-term loss remaining from this year will be combined with next year's long-term transactions.

TAX RATES ON PERSONAL INCOME

Single Taxpayers			Joint Returns		
Net taxable income	Tax + %	of amount over	Net taxable income	Tax + %	of amount over
up to $2,300	$ 0 + 0%		up to $3,400	$ 0 + 0%	
$ 2,300 - 3,400	0 + 14%	$ 2,300	3,400 - 5,500	0 + 14%	$ 3,400
3,400 - 4,400	154 + 16%	3,400	5,500 - 7,600	294 + 16%	5,500
4,400 - 6,500	314 + 18%	4,400	7,600 - 11,900	630 + 18%	7,600
6,500 - 8,500	692 + 19%	6,500	11,900 - 16,000	1,404 + 21%	11,900
8,500 - 10,800	1,072 + 21%	8,500	16,000 - 20,200	2,265 + 24%	16,000
10,800 - 12,900	1,555 + 24%	10,800	20,200 - 24,600	3,273 + 28%	20,200
12,900 - 15,000	2,059 + 26%	12,900	24,600 - 29,900	4,505 + 32%	24,600
15,000 - 18,200	2,605 + 30%	15,000	29,900 - 35,200	6,201 + 37%	29,900
18,200 - 23,500	3,565 + 34%	18,200	35,200 - 45,800	8,162 + 43%	35,200
23,500 - 28,800	5,367 + 39%	23,500	45,800 - 60,000	12,720 + 49%	45,800
28,800 - 34,100	7,434 + 44%	28,800	60,000 - 85,600	19,678 + 54%	60,000
34,100 - 41,500	9,766 + 49%	34,100	85,600 - 109,400	33,502 + 59%	85,600
41,500 - 55,300	13,392 + 55%	41,500	109,400 - 162,400	47,464 + 64%	109,400
55,300 - 81,800	20,982 + 63%	55,300	162,400 - 215,400	81,464 + 68%	162,400
81,800 - 108,300	37,677 + 68%	81,800	215,400 or more	117,504 + 70%	215,400
108,300 or more	55,697 + 70%	108,300			

The maximum tax rate on income from wages, salary, and self-employment is 50%—regardless of the amount. Marginal rates above 50% apply only to "unearned" income—such as interest, dividends, royalties, and capital gains.

F
ACKNOWLEDGMENTS

HARRY BROWNE IS GRATEFUL FOR WHAT HE HAS LEARNED from many people—but most particularly Ludwig von Mises, Murray Rothbard, Henry Hazlitt, Alvin Lowi, and Andrew Galambos—and is grateful to Jerome F. Smith for bringing him into the investment world in 1967.

Terry Coxon acknowledges his intellectual debts to Milton Friedman and Benjamin Klein, the guidance on tax matters provided by Kim Marois, Robert Gilmartin, and Leonard Radomile, and the assistance on government securities provided by Jim Benham.

The authors appreciate the interest shown by William Morrow & Company, and editor Howard Cady's patience in waiting for a long-overdue manuscript.

The text of the book was composed on a Hewlett Packard 9845T computer—which greatly facilitated the work. The graphs and tables were prepared and set in type by Data Resources, Inc., Lexington, Massachusetts, in many cases from data it provided.

THE AUTHORS

HARRY BROWNE WAS BORN IN NEW YORK CITY IN 1933 AND grew up in Los Angeles. He graduated from high school, but attended college for only two weeks.

Following high school graduation, he held a variety of jobs, mostly in sales and advertising. In 1962, with two partners, he established a newspaper feature service, which he managed for five years. The columns and editorials he wrote dealt primarily with economics. In 1964 he began giving courses in economics.

In 1967 he became associated with Economic Research Counselors, an investment service that helps customers arrange Swiss bank accounts and advises them on hard-money investments. He also began giving seminars to show how investors could profit from the coming devaluation of the dollar.

His first book was published in 1970. Since then, he has devoted his working time to writing books, speaking, and writing his newsletter, *Harry Browne's Special Reports,* which began publication in 1974.

Since 1977 he has lived in Zurich, Switzerland. Outside of economics and investments, his main interests are classical music, opera, sports, and fiction. He is working on a book entitled *Why People Hate Opera,* which is tentatively scheduled for publication in the year 2015.

Terry Coxon was born in Oakland, California, in 1944 and moved to Palo Alto eight years later. He is a graduate of Stanford University (philosophy) and holds an M.A. in economics from UCLA.

He has been, at various times, a Christmas card salesman, apricot picker, messenger, telephone company management trainee, and computer programmer. Between Stanford and UCLA he served as a disbursing officer in the U.S. Navy.

In 1974 he left UCLA to become a consultant to Harry Browne (then in Vancouver, B.C.). In 1976 he returned to California to open his practice as an investment advisor.

He has numerous interests outside of investments, all of which he claims have been sorely neglected during the writing of this book. He lives in Petaluma, California, with his wife, Betsy, and their two children.

INDEX

543

BEST OF BUSINESS
FROM WARNER BOOKS